Native Americans in Early North Carolina:

A Documentary History

The Colonial Records of North Carolina
Special Series
Jan-Michael Poff, Series Editor

Native Americans in Early North Carolina:

A Documentary History

Compiled and Edited by
Dennis L. Isenbarger

Office of Archives and History
North Carolina Department of Cultural Resources
Raleigh
2013

Printed by United Book Press, Inc.

www.ncpublications.com

Contents

Foreword vii

Introduction ix

Folkways 1

Religion. 53

Trade 85

Land 135

War 192

Colonial Interaction 249

Reservations. 275

Sources Cited 305

Index 313

Foreword

The first of ten volumes of *The Colonial Records of North Carolina*, edited by William L. Saunders, was produced in 1886. Since that time, the state of North Carolina has been publishing its early documents, first under the auspices of the North Carolina Historical Commission and later through the Department of Archives and History, which became the Office of Archives and History. To coincide with the 300th anniversary of the Carolina Charter of 1663, a second series of hard-bound, documentary volumes commenced in the 1960s. This complementary series contains transcripts and annotation for thousands of primary documents on the founding and development of the colony and have proved to be invaluable to researchers of North Carolina history.

In an effort to reach a wider audience, Robert J. Cain, former editor of *The Colonial Records of North Carolina [Second Series]*, envisioned a "Special Series" of soft-cover titles which would feature selected records about a specific topic. In his words: "It is intended to be of interest to a wide range of readers, suitable for the classroom and indeed anyone curious about the lives of North Carolinians as recorded by the colony's citizens and visitors during the earliest years of its history." Books in the series include *Society in Early North Carolina: A Documentary History*, edited by Alan D. Watson (2000); *North Carolina Headrights: A List of Names, 1663-1744*, compiled by Caroline B. Whitley (2001); and *African Americans in Early North Carolina: A Documentary History*, edited by Alan D. Watson (2005).

Dennis L. Isenbarger, former editor with the Historical Publications Section, compiled and edited this latest title in the series, *Native Americans in Early North Carolina: A Documentary History*. A variety of seventeenth- and eighteenth-century sources help tell the story of Indians in North Carolina, albeit primarily from the white man's perspective. They include British records, county records, court records, published documentaries, governors' papers, journals and private correspondence, land records, legislative documents, military records, and newspapers. The commentary introduces and ties together excerpts from the documents themselves and is set in bold type.

Spelling, capitalization, and use of italics, punctuation, and numbers appear as they did in the originals.

Mr. Isenbarger holds a master's degree in history from Western Carolina University. He would like to acknowledge his wife and daughter. Numerous other individuals helped make this publication possible: State Archives current staff members Kim Andersen, Vann Evans, and Gwen Mays and former staff members Ron Vestal and the late George Stevenson; State Library staff members Steve Case and Cynthia Jones; Office of State Archaeology staff members Steve Claggett, Dolores Hall, and Susan Myers; University of North Carolina at Chapel Hill staff members Bob Anthony of the North Carolina Collection and Dr. Brett Riggs and Dr. R. P. Stephen Davis Jr. of the Research Laboratories of Archaeology; Dr. Debra Jost deTreville, formerly of North Carolina State University; Dr. Charles R. Ewen of East Carolina University; Dr. Alan Craig Downs of Georgia Southern University; and Charles L. Heath Jr. who works for the Department of Defense.

Christopher Arris Oakley, associate professor of history at East Carolina University, wrote the introduction and Elizabeth Crowder, a freelance editor from Raleigh, completed the index. Jan Poff, former editor of *The Colonial Records of North Carolina [Second Series]* provided invaluable oversight of the project. Dennis Isenbarger and Susan Trimble designed the cover art and Mrs. Trimble typeset the work. Lisa D. Bailey and the section administrator proofread selected portions of the book.

The documents in *Native Americans in Early North Carolina* outline the clash of cultures between two groups of people and the back-and-forth struggle over land rights, trade, broken promises, sacrifice, and reconciliation. Funding to print this title was provided by the Carolina Charter Corporation to commemorate the 350th anniversary of the Carolina Charter.

Donna E. Kelly, Administrator
Historical Publications Section

Introduction

At the turn of the sixteenth century, there were at least 50,000 Native Americans, and perhaps many more, living in more than thirty tribal nations within the borders of what would eventually become North Carolina. These original Tar Heels could broadly be divided into three language groups. Algonquian speakers, including the Hatteras, Pamlicos, Weapemocs, and Pasquotanks, lived in the Albemarle region of coastal North Carolina. Siouan speakers, such as the Waccamaws, Saponis, Occaneechis, and Enos, resided in the Piedmont and Cape Fear River valley. The two largest nations—the Tuscaroras, who occupied land between the Siouans and Algonquians, and the Cherokees, who settled in the mountains—spoke Iroquoian languages.

Although politically distinct, these indigenous nations shared a common culture within a well-developed and interconnected society. Native Americans living in the North American Southeast in the sixteenth century were matrilineal, tracing their ancestry through their mother's clan. The men fished and hunted, while the women tended fields of corn, beans, and squash and gathered wild greens, nuts, and berries. Most lived in bark and thatch houses along waterways in small towns, which were typically autonomous and governed by councils, although residents often joined with others in defensive confederations. Council members sought to govern by consensus, and all tribal and village members could express opinions at meetings. There was an extensive trade network that connected Native Americans in North Carolina to others in North America, including those of Mesoamerica. Indigenous peoples in the region were animistic, pantheistic, and strove to maintain harmony in the middle world, which was precariously balanced between the upper world and the lower world. Competition for tribal hunting grounds and trade connections occasionally led to warfare and the acquisition of captives from rival nations and villages.

Throughout the sixteenth century, European explorers, traders, and settlers inserted themselves into this native society. In the 1520s, Italian sailor Giovanni da Verrazzano, sailing for France, explored the Outer Banks of North Carolina. From 1539 to 1542, Spaniard Hernando de Soto and six hundred soldiers scoured the Southeast for gold and other precious metals. And in the 1580s, Walter Raleigh financed several expeditions to "Virginia" for Queen Elizabeth and England before unsuccessfully attempting to establish a permanent settlement, the ill-fated Lost Colony of Roanoke. During these expeditions, John White, Thomas Hariot, and others described the local flora and fauna and recorded valuable information about the inhabitants. English colonists finally established a successful settlement on the Chesapeake Bay twenty years after the Lost Colonists mysteriously disappeared. During these initial expeditions, Spanish, French, and English explorers and settlers unwittingly and tragically introduced new diseases into a native population lacking immunities. Smallpox, measles, typhus, influenza, and other communicable diseases swept across the North American Southeast, often preceding actual contact and colonization. These virgin-soil epidemics devastated Native American populations, leading some demographers to contend that by 1600 the indigenous population of the entire continent had been reduced by 90 percent, thus opening the door to European conquest and colonization.

As the English settlement at Jamestown expanded outward from the Chesapeake in the mid-seventeenth century, settlers looking for new farmlands moved into the Albemarle region of present-day North Carolina. Although their numbers had been reduced by disease, the Algonquian-speaking peoples of the coastal region still inhabited the region. The Iroquoian-speaking Tuscaroras, the largest nation in the area, controlled lands to the west, occupying numerous towns in the Pamlico and Neuse river basins. In 1663, King Charles II issued a land grant for all English lands south of Virginia to eight loyal Lords Proprietors, who subsequently named the land Carolina, and eventually divided it into two colonies in the early 1700s.

English settlers and Native Americans initially coexisted peacefully in the Albemarle in the mid-seventeenth century. Both colonists and Indians benefited from the evolution of a thriving trade economy. Europeans exchanged guns, alcohol, metal tools, and clothing for deerskins, beaver pelts, and food. This trade, however, eventually altered the traditional Native American economic system in the region, as some Indians became dependent on European goods, though scholars continue to debate the degree of dependency. Moreover, an Indian slave trade developed as an offshoot of this exchange economy. Some Native Americans, such as the Westoes, who had migrated southward from the Great Lakes area, traded war captives to European traders who then sold them as slaves, many of whom were sent to the West Indies to work on sugar plantations. In the late 1600s and early 1700s, thousands of North Carolina Indians, mostly women and children, were sold into bondage.

As interaction between the English settlers and the local Native Americans increased, conflict became inevitable in the eighteenth century. Native societies, which were pantheistic, matrilineal, communal, and egalitarian, contrasted sharply with the patriarchal, monotheistic, individualistic culture of the newcomers. Ultimately, the expanding Indian slave trade, corrupt trading practices, and increasing land encroachment led to a major colonial war. The spark for this conflict was likely the founding of New Bern in 1710 at the confluence of the Trent and Neuse rivers on Tuscarora hunting land. In response to this encroachment, a Tuscarora leader known by the English as King Hancock recruited a pan-Indian group of warriors, including Tuscaroras, Machapungas, Corees, and others. Not all Tuscarora towns, however, supported Hancock. Northern Tuscaroras, led by King Blount, had closer trade ties to the colonists and remained neutral. In early 1711, Hancock and his men captured explorer and surveyor John Lawson and Christoph de Graffenreid, the founder of New Bern. The Indians tried, tortured, and executed Lawson but later released Graffenreid. In September of that year, Hancock led his army in a devastating attack on colonial settlements in eastern North Carolina. Unable to defend his colony, the governor of North Carolina requested aid from other colonies, and South Carolina eventually sent a force of militiamen and Yamasees to help its northern neighbor. The "Tuscarora War," as it somewhat inaccurately came to be known, ended in defeat for Hancock's army in 1713 at Fort Neoheroka. Hundreds of Tuscaroras and other coastal Native Americans died during the war, and colonial militiamen and their Indian allies captured and exported hundreds more as slaves.

The end of the Tuscarora War marked a turning point for Native Americans and European colonists in North Carolina. Most of the surviving Tuscaroras left the colony and migrated north to join their Iroquois brethren. Other indigenous peoples also left the colony. Those who stayed, even the ones who remained neutral or helped the colonists during the war, were forced onto reservations. Consequently, the indigenous peoples of eastern North Carolina lost their political autonomy; they became conquered, subjugated, and isolated. They did not, however, disappear. The survivors settled into isolated multi-tribal or pan-Indian communities.

With the Indian population of eastern North Carolina depleted and isolated, the rate of colonization and European settlement increased rapidly in the 1700s. As the line of settlement moved westward, colonists moved closer to the Cherokees, who successfully maintained their independence and autonomy because of their numbers and geographical advantages. The Cherokees also were more effective in politically and economically playing competing colonial powers off of one another in the eighteenth century, despite the devastating effects of disease. In the 1750s, however, the Cherokees were drawn into colonial wars, and after the American Revolution, they would face constant encroachment and pressure from a rapidly expanding and land-hungry nascent nation infected with the fever of Manifest Destiny.

This volume of selected primary sources, skillfully edited by Dennis Isenbarger, documents the history of Native Americans in North Carolina from contact with Europeans through the end of the eighteenth century. The book is divided into several thematic chapters: Folkways, Religion, Trade, Land, War, Colonial Interaction, and Reservations. Although some indigenous peoples had methods for recording important information, Indians in the North American Southeast lacked a written language. Consequently, most of the primary sources from the era are written by and from the perspective of Europeans. These include the firsthand accounts of explorers, traders, settlers, and government officials. Scholars who study early Native American history and culture often use written sources in conjunction with anthropological theories and archae- ological evidence to try to give voice to indigenous peoples who are often silent in the colonial records. The documents contained in this volume, like all primary sources, should be read critically, keeping in mind the ethnocentrism and cultural bias of the authors. Nevertheless, these documents are invaluable sources for learning about the culture and history of North Carolina's first inhabitants. Moreover, scholars have come to realize that it is impossible to understand colonial North Carolina history by excluding Native Americans. These sources illustrate that Indians were active participants, not simply passive victims, in the early history of

North Carolina. Furthermore, they show that Indians were remarkably adaptive and persistent. Although devastated by decades of disease, encroachment, and warfare, Native Americans did not simply disappear from North Carolina during the colonial era; they survived and persevered into the nineteenth, twentieth, and now twenty-first centuries. According to the 2010 census, North Carolina contained the largest Native American population of any state east of the Mississippi River. This collection of primary sources helps document the remarkable persistence of their ancestors.

Christopher Arris Oakley
East Carolina University

Folkways

The ancestors of the peoples now known as Native Americans migrated to North America from Asia, perhaps as long as 50,000 years ago, across a land bridge that had formed in the Bering Sea during the last Ice Age. As naturalist and surveyor John Lawson explored central and eastern Carolina colony at the turn of the eighteenth century, he encountered Indians who hinted at those origins. Trader James Adair recalled similar stories.

[. . .] it seems very probable, that these People might come from some Eastern Country; for when you ask them whence their Fore-Fathers came, that first inhabited the Country, they will point to the Westward and say, *Where the Sun sleeps, our Forefathers came thence*, which, at that distance, may be reckon'd amongst the Eastern Parts of the World.

> John Lawson, *A New Voyage to Carolina*, ed. by Hugh T. Lefler (Chapel Hill: University of North Carolina Press, 1967), 173.

Their own traditions record them to have come to their present lands by the way of the west, from a far distant country, and where there was no variegation of colour in human beings.

> James Adair, *A History of the North-American Indians, Particularly Those Nations Adjoining to the Missisippi* [sic] *East and West Florida, Georgia, South and North Carolina and Virginia* (1775; reprint, Ann Arbor, Michigan: UMI Books on Demand, 2002), 2.

Traditions were passed orally among tribal groups of Native Americans for thousands of years. As those peoples died out, their institutional memory perished with them. Lacking any written language during the colonial period (Sequoyah presented his Cherokee syllabary in 1821), Indians did possess a few alternative methods of recording history and conveying information, but even some of those apparently functioned as mnemonic devices. Eastern North Carolina Indians relied upon notched reeds to recount past events. Colonel John Herbert observed that some Cherokees used knots on a string to communicate.

They [the Waxhaw] had Musicians, who were two Old Men, one of whom beat a Drum, while the other rattled a Gourd, that had Corn in it, to make a Noise withal: To these Instruments they both sung a mournful Ditty; the Burthen of their Song was, in Remembrance of their former Greatness, and Members of their Nation, the famous Exploits of their Renowned Ancestors, and all Actions of Moment that had (in former Days) been perform'd by their Forefathers. At these Festivals it is, that they give a Traditional Relation of what hath pass'd amongst them to the younger Fry. These verbal Deliveries being always publish'd in their most Publick Assemblies, serve instead of our Traditional Notes, by the use of Letters.

Lawson, *New Voyage to Carolina*, 45. At the beginning of the eighteenth century, the Waxhaws were located in present-day Mecklenburg and Union counties, North Carolina, and Lancaster County, South Carolina.

To prove the times more exactly, he [the conjurer] produces the Records of the Country, which are a Parcel of Reeds, of different Lengths, with several distinct Marks, known to none but themselves; by which they seem to guess, very exactly, at Accidents that happen'd many Years ago; nay two or three Ages or more. The Reason I have to believe what they tell me, on this Account, is, because I have been at the Meetings of several *Indian* Nations; and they agreed, in relating the same Circumstances, as to Time, very exactly; as, for Example, they say, there was so hard a Winter in *Carolina*, 105 years ago, that the great Sound was frozen over, and the Wild Geese came into the Woods to eat Acorns, and that they were so tame, (I suppose, through Want) that they kill'd abundance in the Woods, by knocking them on the Head with Sticks.

Lawson, *New Voyage to Carolina*, 187.

A messenger was dispatched away from hence [Keowee] to Tomausey for the head Warriour of that Town who sent his brother & excused himselfe because he had promis'd to go out with some hunters & told his Brother to let me know that he would be at the meeting, The said Warriour's Brother was dispatched away with the foregoing Letter to Mr: Wiggan & had orders to tell the messenger (by whom he should send the sd: letter) that he was to acquaint the towns (he should go through) that they were to meet me with the rest of the head men at Nequisey at the time appointed wch: they would see by the String & knotts sent them by the said messenger, likewise the said Warriour promis'd to send away a messenger to Tuccaseegey parts with the same message.

Entry of November 11, 1727, in *Journal of Colonel John Herbert, Commissioner of Indian Affairs for the Province of South Carolina, October 17, 1727 to March 1727/8*, ed. by Alexander S. Salley (Columbia: Printed for the Historical Commission of South Carolina, 1936), 8-9. Keowee, principal town of the Cherokee Lower Towns, is now submerged under Lake Keowee in Oconee County, South Carolina. Tomassee ("Tomausey"), another Lower Town, stood approximately ten miles northwest of Keowee, near present-day Tamassee, South Carolina. The Lower Towns occupied land along the Keowee and Savannah rivers and their tributaries in present-day northwestern South Carolina and northeastern Georgia. A second Cherokee town named Tomassee stood at the junction of Burningtown Creek and the Little Tennessee River in present-day Macon County, North Carolina. Franklin, the Macon County seat, rests atop the Middle Cherokee town of Nikwasi ("Nequisey"). "Tuccaseegey parts" refers to the Cherokee Out Towns in the Tuckasegee River Valley.

Approximately thirty tribes, and at least as many differing dialects, existed in North Carolina as the eighteenth century dawned. Those dialects have been divided among three language families: Algonquian, spoken primarily by the native peoples of the coastal region; Siouan, prevalent in the Piedmont and foothills among the Catawba confederacy; and Iroquoian, the linguistic root of the western Cherokees and eastern Tuscaroras. Thomas Hariot noted the diversity of language among Tidewater Indians. Corroborating Hariot's observations, John Lawson's list of Tuscarora, Pamlico, and Woccon words illustrates the dissimilar vocabularies of three neighboring tribes. James Adair criticized European American attempts at representing Indian speech in print.

The language of every government is different from any other, and the further they are distant the greater is the difference.

Thomas Hariot, "A briefe and true report of the new found land of Virginia . . . ," February 1588, in David B. Quinn, ed., *The Roanoke Voyages, 1584-1590*, 2 vols. (London: For the Hakluyt Society, 1955), 1:370.

English.	Tuskeruro.	Pampticough.	Woccon.
One	*Unche*	*Weembot*	*Tonne*
Two	*Necte*	*Neshinnauh*	*Num-perre*
Three	*Ohs-sah*	*Nish-wonner*	*Nam-mee*
[. . .]			
White	*Ware-occa*	*Wopposhaumosh*	*Waurraupa*
Red	*Cotcoo-rea*	*Mish-cosk*	*Yauta*
Black or blue,	*Caw-hunshe*	*Mowcottowosh*	*Yah-testea*
[. . .]			
Englishmen	*Nickreruroh*	*Tosh shonte*	*Wintsohore*
Indians	*Unqua*	*Nuppin*	*Yauh-he*

Lawson, *New Voyage to Carolina*, 233, 234, 235.

About the year 1743, their nation [the Catawba] consisted of almost 400 warriors, of above twenty different dialects. I shall mention a few of the national names of those, who make up this mixed language;—the *Kátahba*, is the standard, or court-dialect—the *Wateree*, who make up a large town; *Eenó*, *Charàh*, now *Chowan, Canggaree, Nachee, Yamasee, Coosah*, &c.

Adair, *History of the North-American Indians*, 224-225. The Wateree town stood on the Wateree River near present-day Camden, South Carolina.

3

S is not a note of plurality with the Indians; when I mention therefore either their national, or proper names, that common error is avoided, which writers ignorant of their language constantly commit. [. . .] What Indian words we had, being exceedingly mangled, either by the fault of the press, or of torturing pens, heretofore induced skilful persons to conjecture them to be heiroglyphical characters, in imitation of the ancient Egyptian manner of writing their chronicles.

Adair, *History of the North-American Indians*, 2n, 63.

Indians expressed periods of time in terms of natural occurrences.

They name the Months very agreeably, as one is the Herring-Month, another the Strawberry-Month, another the Mulberry-Month. Others name them by the Trees that blossom; especially, the Dogwood-Tree; or they say, we will return when Turkey-Cocks gobble, that is in *March* and *April*. The Age of the Moon they understand, but know no different Name for Sun and Moon. They can guess well at the time of the Day, by the Sun's Height. Their Age they number by Winters, and say, such a Man or Woman is so many Winters old. They have no Sabbath, or Day of Rest.

Lawson, *New Voyage to Carolina*, 240.

The physical appearance of Native Americans fascinated European observers. Naturalist William Bartram portrayed the prince of Whatoga, a Cherokee chief, as the stereotypical noble savage. John Lawson wrote that Indians he met owed their distinctive physique to the custom of cradle-boarding, and described the process the Waxhaws ("flat Heads") employed to ensure that their offspring grew into adults who conformed to the tribe's standard of beauty. Long fingernails served a practical purpose.

He [the prince of Whatoga] was tall and perfectly formed; his countenance cheerful and lofty, and at the same time truly characteristic of the red men, that is, the brow ferocious, and the eye active, piercing or fiery, as an eagle. He appeared to be about sixty years of age, yet upright and muscular, and his limbs active as youth.

William Bartram, *Travels through North and South Carolina, Georgia, East and West Florida* (1791; reprint, Savannah: Beehive Press, 1973), 350. Whatoga was located approximately three miles north of Nikwasi, along Watauga Creek on the Little Tennessee River, in present-day Macon County, North Carolina.

The *Indians* of North-*Carolina* are a well-shap'd clean-made People, of different Staturies, as the *Europeans* are, yet chiefly inclin'd to be tall. They are a very streight People, and never bend forwards, or stoop in the Shoulders, unless much overpower'd by old Age. Their Limbs are exceeding well-shap'd. As for their Legs and Feet, they are generally the handsomest in the World. Their Bodies are a little flat, which is occasion'd, by being laced hard down to a Board, in their Infancy. [. . .] Their Eyes are black, or of a dark Hazle; The White is marbled with red Streaks, which is ever common to these People, unless when sprung from a white Father or Mother. Their Colour is of a tawny, which would not be so dark, did they not dawb themselves with Bears Oil, and a Colour like burnt Cork. This is begun in their Infancy, and continued for a long time, which fills the Pores, and enables them better to endure the Extremity of the Weather.

Lawson, *New Voyage to Carolina*, 174.

These *Indians* are of an extraordinary Stature, and call'd by their Neighbours flat Heads, which seems a very suitable Name for them. In their Infancy, their Nurses lay the Back-part of their Children's Heads on a Bag of Sand, (such as Engravers use to rest their Plates upon.) They use a Roll, which is placed upon the Babe's Forehead, it being laid with its Back on a flat Board, and swaddled hard down thereon, from one End of this Engine, to the other. This Method makes the Child's Body and Limbs as straight as an Arrow.

Lawson, *New Voyage to Carolina*, 39-40.

They let their Nails grow very long, which, they reckon, is the Use Nails are design'd for, and laugh at the *Europeans* for pairing theirs, which, they say, disarms them of that which Nature design'd them for.

Lawson, *New Voyage to Carolina*, 176.

At the time the first Europeans arrived in what is now North Carolina, Indians wore little. Clothing initially was made from animal skins and feathers. Both men and women wore match coats (mantles) and moccasins. As trade with whites became widespread, Native Americans adopted European fabrics and fashion. Although John Lawson stated that Indian men never wore European-style breeches, John Brickell recalled visiting chiefs who did. Lieutenant Henry Timberlake noted that some Cherokees, among whom he lived as an emissary of the British, missed their traditional modes of dress.

The old people still remember and praise the ancient days, before they were acquainted with the whites, when they had but little dress, except a bit of skin about their middles, mockasons, a mantle of buffalo skin for the winter, and a lighter one of feathers for the summer.

Henry Timberlake, *Lieutenant Henry Timberlake's Memoirs, 1756-1765*, ed. by Samuel Cole Williams (Johnson City, Tennessee: The Watauga Press, 1927), 77.

Their Feather Match-Coats are very pretty, especially some of them, which are made extraordinary charming, containing several pretty Figures wrought in Feathers, making them seem like a fine Flower Silk-Shag; and when new and fresh, they become a Bed very well, instead of a Quilt. Some of another sort are made of Hare, Raccoon, Bever, or Squirrel-Skins, which are very warm. Others again are made of the green Part of the Skin of a Mallard's Head, which they sew perfectly well together, their Thread being either the Sinews of a Deer divided very small, or Silk-Grass. When these are finish'd, they look very finely, though they must needs be very troublesome to make.

Lawson, *New Voyage to Carolina*, 200.

The Womens Dress is, in severe Weather, a hairy Match-coat in the Nature of a Plad, which keeps out the Cold, and (as I said before) defends their Children from the Prejudices of the Weather. At other times, they have only a sort of Flap or Apron containing two Yards in Length, and better than half a Yard deep. Sometimes, it is a Deer-Skin dress'd white, and pointed or slit at the bottom, like Fringe. When this is clean, it becomes them very well. Others wear blue or red Flaps made of Bays and Plains, which they buy of the *English*, of both which they tuck in the Corners, to fasten the Garment, and sometimes make it fast with a Belt. [. . .] Sometimes, they wear *Indian* Shooes, or Moggizons, which are made after the same manner, as the Mens are.

Lawson, *New Voyage to Carolina*, 197. A *plad*, or plaid, is a mantle of a style worn in the Scottish Highlands. *Bays* refers to baize fabric; *plain* is a type of flannel.

The women's dress consists only in a broad softened skin, or several small skins sewed together, which they wrap and tye round their waist, reaching a little below their knees: in cold weather, they wrap themselves in the softened skins of buffalo calves, with the wintery shagged wool inward, never forgetting to anoint, and tie up their hair, except in their time of mourning. [. . .] The women, since the time we first traded with them, wrap a fathom of the half breadth of Stroud cloth round their waist, and tie it with a leathern belt, which is commonly covered with brass runners or buckles: but this sort of loose petticoat, reaches only to their hams, in order to shew their exquisitely fine proportioned limbs.

Adair, *History of the North-American Indians*, 6-7, 8. *Stroud* is a fabric used to make blankets for trade or sale to the Indians.

The *Indian* Men have a Match-Coat of Hair, Furs, Feathers, or Cloth, as the Women have. [. . .] Betwixt their Legs comes a Piece of Cloth, that is tuck'd in by a Belt both before and behind. This is to hide their Nakedness, of which Decency they are very strict Observers, although never practised before the Christians came amongst them. They wear Shooes, of Bucks, and sometimes Bears Skin, which they tan in an Hour or two; with the Bark of Trees boil'd, wherein they put the Leather whilst hot, and let it remain a little while, whereby it becomes so qualify'd, as to endure Water and Dirt, without growing hard. These have no Heels, and are made as fit for the Feet, as a Glove is for the Hand, and are very easie to travel in, when one is a little us'd to them.

Lawson, *New Voyage to Carolina*, 197, 200.

They [men] formerly wore shirts, made of drest deer-skins, for their summer visiting dress: but their winter-hunting clothes were long and shaggy, made of the skins of panthers, bucks, bears, beavers, and otters; the fleshy sides outward, sometimes doubled, and always softened like velvet-cloth, though they retained their fur and hair. The needles and thread they used formerly (and now at times) were fish-bones, or the horns and bones of deer, rubbed sharp, and deer's sinews, and a sort of hemp, that grows among them spontaneously, in rich open lands. [. . .] The men wear, for ornament, and the conveniencies of hunting, thin deer-skin boots, well smoked, that reach so high up their thighs, as with their jackets to secure them from the brambles and braky thickets. They sew them about five inches from the edges, which are formed into tassels, to which they fasten fawns trotters, and small pieces of tinkling metal, or wild turkey cock-spurs.

Adair, *History of the North-American Indians*, 6, 7.

Some of their great Men, as Rulers and such, that have Plenty of Deer Skins by them, will often buy the *English*-made Coats, which they wear on Festivals and other Days of Visiting. Yet none ever buy any Breeches, saying, that they are too much confin'd in them, which prevents their Speed in running, *&c.*

Lawson, *New Voyage to Carolina*, 200.

[1729-1730.] King *Blunt* being the most powerful of these I have mentioned, had a Suit of *English* Broadcloth on, and a pair of Women's Stockings, of a blue Colour, with white Clocks, a tolerable good Shirt, Cravat, Shoes, Hat, *&c.*

King *Durant* had on an old Blue Livery, the Wastecoat having some remains of Silver Lace, with all other Necessaries fit for wearing Apparel such as Shirt, Stockings, Shoes, *&c.* made after the *English* manner.

King *Highter* had on a Soldiers red Coat, Wastecoat, and Breeches, with all other conveniences for wearing Apparel, like the former: And it is to be observed, that after their return home to their Towns, that they never wear these Cloaths till they make the next State Visit amongst the *Christians.*

John Brickell, *Natural History of North Carolina* (1737; reprint, Murfreesboro, North Carolina: Johnson Publishing Company, 1968), 283-284. Tom Blunt led the Tuscaroras; John Durant, the Yeopim Indians; and John Hoyter ("Highter"), the Chowans. *Clocks* are patterns, worked in silk thread, on the sides of stockings.

Native Americans adorned themselves with jewelry and feathers. Eastern (as Lawson described) and western Indians styled their hair differently. Timberlake mentioned the paint and tattoos worn by Cherokee men as well as the practice of ear-slitting.

The Hair of their [the women's] Heads is made into a long Roll like a Horses Tail, and bound round with *Roanoak* or *Porcelan*, which is a sort of Beads they make of the Conk-Shells. Others that have not this, make a Leather-String serve.

The Indian Men [. . .] Their Hair is roll'd up, on each Ear, as the Womens, only much shorter, and oftentimes a Roll on the Crown of the Head, or Temples, which is just as they fancy; [. . .]

Lawson, *New Voyage to Carolina*, 197, 200.

Some of the *Indians* wear great Bobs in their Ears, and sometimes in the Holes thereof they put Eagles and other Birds, Feathers, for a Trophy. When they kill any Fowl, they commonly pluck off the downy Feathers, and stick them all over their Heads. Some (both Men and Women) wear great Necklaces of their Money made of Shells. They often wear Bracelets made of Brass, and sometimes of Iron Wire.

Lawson, *New Voyage to Carolina*, 203.

The Cherokees are of a middle stature, of an olive colour, tho' generally painted, and their skins stained with gun powder, pricked into it in very pretty figures. The hair of their head is shaved, tho' many of the old people have it plucked out by the roots, except a patch on the hinder part of the head, about twice the bigness of a crown-piece, which is ornamented with beads, feathers, wampum, stained deers hair, and such like baubles. The ears are slit and stretched to an enormous size, putting the person who undergoes the operation to incredible pain, being unable to lie on either side for near forty days. To remedy this, they generally slit but one at a time; so soon as the patient can bear it, they are wound round with wire to expand them, and are adorned with silver pendants and rings, which they likewise wear at the nose. This custom does not belong originally to the Cherokees, but taken by them from the Shawnese, or other northern nations. [. . .]

The women wear the hair of their head, which is so long that it generally reaches to the middle of their legs, and sometimes to the ground, club'd, and ornamented with ribbons of various colours; but, except their eyebrows, pluck it from all the other parts of the body [. . .]

> Timberlake, *Memoirs, 1756-1765*, 75-76, 76-77. The Shawnees resided in the Ohio River and Cumberland River valleys in present-day Kentucky, Ohio, and Tennessee.

Many Native Americans preferred to live in towns, an arrangement that reinforced the sense of attachment among people of the same clan or nation, facilitated farming, and offered protection from enemies.

Their townes are but small, & neere the sea coast but fewe, some containing but 10. or 12. houses: some 20. the greatest that we have seene have bene but of 30. houses: if they be walled it is only done with barks of trees made fast to stakes, or els with poles onely fixed upright and close one by another.

> Hariot, "A briefe and true report," in Quinn, *Roanoke Voyages*, 1:369.

The 29th I marched hard all day and most of the night, that if possible I might surprise this great town [Torhunta], but to my great disappointment they discovered us, being continually upon their guard since the massacre. Tho' this be called a town, it is only a plantation here and there scattered about the Country, no where 5 houses together, and then ¼ a mile such another and so on for several miles, so it is impossible to surprize many before the alarm takes.

> Report of February 4, 1712, in John Barnwell, "Journal of John Barnwell," Part I, *Virginia Magazine of History and Biography* 5 (April 1898): 394. The Tuscarora town of Torhunta was located five miles northeast of modern-day Goldsboro, North Carolina, near Beaver Dam Run. Barnwell called the town "Narhantes."

[. . .] the Map of the Catawbaws is not worth sending, there being only seven Towns lying all within two or three miles of one another; [. . .]

> Governor James Glen of South Carolina to the Board of Trade, December 1757, in Colonial Office 5/373, British Records, State Archives, Office of Archives and History, Raleigh. The map dismissed by Glen might be one created by Catawba trader John Evans, in 1756, upon which he marked the towns of Nassaw, Weyapee, and Noostee along the east bank of the Catawba River; and Sucah, Weyane, and Charraw along Sugar Creek outside present-day Fort Mill, South Carolina. Evans noted that Weyane was also known as Kings Town, which could account for the seventh town cited by the governor.

Towns typically were located on or near a stream or river, which provided fresh drinking water, fertile soil along its banks, a thoroughfare, and a source of food. In rugged Cherokee country, wrote James Adair, bottomlands were the only places level enough to inhabit. Proximity to flowing water also had spiritual and hygienic benefits, as will be seen later.

[. . .] Sir Pray Enter for me in machapungo River on the Est Side from the first Creeke up the River to the Creeke whear the Indians now inhabits, [. . .]

Godfr Spruill (Seal)

Godfrey Spruill to William Glover, June 25, 1696, Land Papers and Wills, Colonial Court Records 187, State Archives, Office of Archives and History, Raleigh. The "machapungo River" is now known as the Pungo River.

Their towns [Cherokee] are still scattered wide of each other, because the land will not admit any other settlement: it is a rare thing to see a level tract of land of four hundred acres. They are also strongly attached to rivers,— all retaining the opinion of the ancients, that rivers are necessary to constitute a paradise. Nor is it only ornamental, but likewise beneficial to them, on account of purifying themselves, and also for the services of common life,— such as fishing, fowling, and killing of deer, which come in the warm season, to eat the saltish moss and grass, which grow on the rocks, and under the surface of the waters. Their rivers are generally very shallow, and pleasant to the eye; for the land being high, the waters have a quick descent; they seldom overflow their banks, unless when a heavy rain falls on a deep snow.—Then, it is frightful to see the huge pieces of ice, mixed with a prodigious torrent of water, rolling down the high mountains, and over the steep craggy rocks, so impetuous, that nothing can resist their force.

Adair, *History of the North-American Indians*, 227-228.

Cherokee dwellings were rectangular, constructed from logs, and chinked with clay. Eastern Indians built dome-like wigwams.

The Cherokees construct their habitations on a different plan from the Creeks; that is, but one oblong four square building, of one story high; the materials consisting of logs or trunks of trees, stripped of their bark, notched at their ends, fixed one upon another, and afterwards plaistered well, both inside and out, with clay well tempered with dry grass, and the whole covered or roofed with the bark of the chesnut tree or long broad shingles.

This building is however partitioned transversely, forming three apartments, which communicate with each other by inside doors; [. . .]

Bartram, *Travels through North and South Carolina*, 365. The Creeks, named for Ocheese Creek (now Ocmulgee River), were a confederacy of Indian nations that inhabited the river valleys of present-day Georgia and Alabama.

These Savages live in *Wigwams*, or Cabins built of Bark, which are made round like an Oven, to prevent any Damage by hard Gales of Wind. They make the Fire in the middle of the House, and have a Hole at the Top of the Roof right above the Fire, to let out the Smoke. These Dwellings are as hot as Stoves, where the *Indians* sleep and sweat all Night. The Floors thereof are never paved nor swept, so that they have always a loose Earth on them. They are often troubled with a multitude of Fleas, especially near the Places where they dress their Deer-Skins, because that Hair harbours them; yet I never felt any ill, unsavory Smell in their Cabins, whereas, should we live in our Houses, as they do, we should be poison'd with our own Nastiness; which confirms these *Indians* to be, as they really are, some of the sweetest People in the World.

The Bark they make their Cabins withal, is generally Cypress, or red or white Cedar; and sometimes, when they are a great way from any of these Woods, they make use of Pine-Bark, which is the worser sort. In building these Fabricks, they get very long Poles, of Pine, Cedar, Hiccory, or any Wood that will bend; these are the Thickness of the Small of a Man's Leg, at the thickest end, which they generally strip of the Bark, and warm them well in the Fire, which makes them tough and fit to bend; afterwards, they stick the thickest ends of them in the Ground, about two Yards asunder, in a Circular Form, the distance they design the Cabin to be, (which is not always round, but sometimes oval) then they bend the Tops and bring them together, and bind their ends with Bark of Trees, that is proper for that use, as Elm is, or sometimes the Moss that grows on the Trees, and is a Yard or two long, and never rots; then they brace them with other Poles, to make them strong; afterwards, cover them all over with Bark, so that they are very warm and tight, and will keep firm against all the Weathers that blow. They have other sorts of Cabins without Windows, which are for their Granaries, Skins, and Merchandizes; and others that are cover'd over head; the rest left open for the Air. These have Reed-Hurdles, like Tables, to lie and sit on, in Summer, and serve for pleasant Banqueting-Houses in the hot Season of the Year. The Cabins they dwell in have Benches all round, except where the Door stands; on these they lay Beasts-Skins, and Mats made of Rushes, whereon they sleep and loll. In one of these, several Families commonly live, though all related to one another.

Lawson, *New Voyage to Carolina*, 180, 182.

The council house, designed to accommodate all the inhabitants of a town, was a venue for dances, festivals, and conducting tribal affairs. Some seated hundreds of people. One such building stood atop "an ancient artificial mount of earth."

This Edifice resembles a large Hay-Rick; its Top being Pyramidal, and much bigger than their other Dwellings, and at the Building whereof, every one assists till it is finish'd. All their Dwelling-Houses are cover'd with Bark, but this differs very much; for, it is very artificially thatch'd with Sedge and Rushes: As soon as finish'd, they place some one of their chiefest Men to dwell therein, charging him with the diligent Preservation thereof, as a Prince commits the Charge and Government of a Fort or Castle, to some Subject he thinks worthy of that Trust. In these State-Houses is transacted all Publick and Private Business, relating to the Affairs of the Government, as the Audience of Foreign Ambassadors from other *Indian* Rulers, Consultation of waging and making War, Proposals of their Trade with neighbouring *Indians*, or the *English*, who happen to come amongst them. In this Theater, the most Aged and Wisest meet, determining what to Act, and what may be most convenient to Omit, Old Age being held in as great Veneration amongst these Heathens, as amongst any People you shall meet withal in any Part of the World.

Lawson, *New Voyage to Carolina*, 42-43.

The council or town-house is a large rotunda, capable of accommodating several hundred people: it stands on the top of an ancient artificial mount of earth, of about twenty feet perpendicular, and the rotunda on the top of it being above thirty feet more, gives the whole fabric an elevation of about sixty feet from the common surface of the ground. But it may be proper to observe, that this mount on which the rotunda stands, is of a much ancienter date than the building, and perhaps was raised for another purpose. The Cherokees themselves are as ignorant as we are, by what people or for what purpose these artificial hills were raised; they have various stories concerning them, the best of which amount to no more than mere conjecture, and leave us entirely in the dark; but they have a tradition common with the other nations of Indians, that they found them in much the same condition as they now appear, when their forefathers arrived from the West and possessed themselves of the country, after vanquishing the nations of red men who then inhabited it, who themselves found these mounts when they took possession of the country, the former possessors delivering the same story concerning them: perhaps they were designed and apropriated by the people who constructed them, to some religious purpose, as great altars and temples similar to the high places and sacred groves anciently amongst the Canaanites and other nations of Palestine and Judea.

The rotunda is constructed after the following manner: they first fix in the ground a circular range of posts or trunks of trees, about six feet high, at equal distances, which are notched at top, to receive into them from one to another, a range of beams or wall plates; within this is another circular order of every large and strong pillars, above twelve feet high, notched in like manner at top, to receive another range of wall plates; and within this is yet another or third range of stronger and higher pillars, but fewer in number, and standing at a greater distance from each other; and lastly, in the centre stands a very strong pillar, which forms the pinnacle of the building, and to which the rafters centre at top; these rafters are strengthened and bound together by cross beams and laths, which sustain the roof or covering, which is a layer of bark neatly placed, and tight enough to exclude the rain, and sometimes they cast a thin superficies of earth over all. There is but one large door, which serves at the same time to admit light from without and the smoak to escape when a fire is kindled; but as there is but a small fire kept, sufficient to give light at night, and that fed with dry small sound wood divested of its bark, there is but little smoak. All around the inside of the building, betwixt the second range of pillars and the wall, is a range of cabins or sophas, consisting of two or three steps, one above or behind the other, in theatrical order, where the assembly sit or lean down; these sophas are covered with mats or carpets, very curiously made of thin splints of Ash or Oak, woven or platted together; near the great pillar in the centre the fire is kindled for light, near which the musicians seat themselves, and round about this the performers exhibit their dances and other shows at public festivals, which happen almost every night throughout the year.

Bartram, *Travels through North and South Carolina*, 365-367.

The types of government among Indian nations varied. The Catawbas were a confederacy comprised of several smaller tribes. When Sir Walter Raleigh's colonists encamped on Roanoke Island, Thomas Hariot found that coastal Indians typically were dominated by strong chiefs. Conversely the Cherokees, according to John Stuart and James Adair, had civil and military leaders who lacked coercive powers but led because sufficient numbers of their towns' inhabitants chose to follow them.

In some places of the countrey one onely towne belongeth to the government of a *Wiròans* or chiefe Lorde; in other some two or three, in some six, eight, & more; the greatest *Wiròans* that yet we had dealing with had but eighteene townes in his government, and able to make not above seven or eight hundred fighting men at the most.

Hariot, "A briefe and true report," in Quinn, *Roanoke Voyages*, 1:370.

The whole Cherokee Nation is govern'd by seven Mother Towns, each of these Towns chuse a King to preside over them and their Dependants; he is elected out of certain Families, and they regard only the Descent by the Mother's Side.

The Towns which chuse Kings, are Tannassie, Kettooah, Ustenary, Telliquo, Estootowie, Keyowee, Noyohee; whereof four of the Kings are dead, and their Places are to be supply'd by new Elections.

The Kings now alive, are the Kings of Tannassie in the Upper Settlements, the King of Kettooah in the Middle Settlements, and the King of Ustenary in the Lower Settlements.

"Journal of Sir Alexander Cuming (1730)," in Samuel Cole Williams, ed., *Early Travels in the Tennessee Country, 1540-1800* (Johnson City, Tennessee: The Watauga Press, 1928), 122. The Overhill or Upper Cherokee town of Tanasi ("Tannassie") stood on the south side of the Little Tennessee River, east of present-day Vonore, Tennessee; the state and river draw their names from this town. The Overhill Cherokees inhabited land along the Little Tennessee and Hiwassee rivers in present-day eastern Tennessee. The Cherokee Out Town of Kituwah ("Kettooah") was situated near the Tuckasegee River, two miles west of present-day Ela, North Carolina. Ustenary stood on the Keowee River south of the Lower town of Keowee, previously identified in this volume. "Telliquo" may refer to Great Tellico, an Overhill town on the Upper Tellico River in eastern Tennessee; Little Tellico, a Valley Cherokee town on the Valley River in Cherokee County, North Carolina; or Little Tellico, a Middle town on Tellico Creek in Macon County, North Carolina. "Estootowie" may be one of three Lower Cherokee towns called Estatoe: one formerly located at the confluence of the Tugaloo and Chatooga rivers in Stephens County, Georgia; another near present-day Dillard, Rabun County, Georgia; and a third on Eastatoe Creek in Pickens County, South Carolina. Two possibilities exist for "Noyohee": Neowee, on the Valley River in present-day Cherokee County, North Carolina; and Noyowe, which had stood on the Tugaloo River in Oconee County, South Carolina.

Of Indian Principles of Government

Altho the Several Nations of Indians differ from each other in particular Customes, yet in their principles and their Mode of Government they are Similar. As I am best acquainted with the Cherokees, I begg leave to give your Lordships such a View of their polic[y] as I am capable of.

In the Cherokee Nation every Town is governed by a principal Warrior and a Beloved Man: and in Matters merely relating to itself has no manner of Dependence on the rest of the Nation. The head Warrior is Obeyed and followed in War. The Beloved man is Councellor and Judge in all matters relating to the internal Police of his Town. Neither of them have any coercive Power; yet they are tollerably well obeyed. [. . .]

No People behave with more Civility and decorum among themselves. I do not remember to have seen Two Indians, abuse or Scold each other, except when intoxicated with Rum, which is deemed a sufficient excuse for any excess, unless Death should ensue. But upon all other Occasions their behavior is grave Peaceable and inoffensive.

In Riches they are much upon an Equality. That Family in which there are the best hunters, are best cloathed and best provided with necessaries. But this Circumstance carries neither Influence nor respect with it. The head Warrior and Beloved man are often the poorest and worst provided of any in the community. [. . .]

The Indians are unacquainted with Luxury and Covet nothing more than what is necessary. Riches would give them no additional consequence in the Eyes of their Countrymen therefore they despise them. But Thirst of Power and Governing is their ruling Passion: Every Indian Aims at this and it is therefore his Study by every means to make himself popular and to gain that confidence and affection From His Country, upon which all Power and Influence among them is founded. Thus, My Lords, The fear of loosing the Good Will of His Countrymen Make every Indian Civil and honest: and a Principle of self defence produces Justice and personal Security.

John Stuart, superintendent of Indian Affairs for the southern district, to the Board of Trade, March 9, 1764, in Colonial Office 323/17, British Records, State Archives, Office of Archives and History, Raleigh.

In general, it consists in a foederal union of the whole society for mutual safety. As the law of nature appoints no frail mortal to be a king, or ruler, over his brethren; and humanity forbids the taking away at pleasure, the life or property of any who obey the good laws of their country, they consider that the transgressor ought to have his evil deeds retaliated upon himself in an equal manner. The Indians, therefore, have no such titles or persons, as emperors, or kings; nor an appellative for such, in any of their dialects. Their highest title, either in military or civil life, signifies only a *Chieftain*: they have no words to express despotic power, arbitrary kings, oppressed, or obedient subjects; neither can they form any other ideas of the former, than of "bad war chieftains of a numerous family, who inslaved the rest." The power of their chiefs, is an empty sound. They can only persuade or dissuade the people, either by the force of good-nature and clear reasoning, or colouring things, so as to suit their prevailing passions. It is reputed merit alone, that gives them any titles of distinction above the meanest of the people. If we connect with this their opinion of a theocracy, it does not promise well to the reputed establishment of extensive and puissant Indian American empires. When any national affair is in debate, you may hear every father of a family speaking in his house on the subject, with rapid, bold language, and the utmost freedom that a people can use. Their voices, to a man, have due weight in every public affair, as it concerns their welfare alike. Every town is independent of another.

Their own friendly compact continues the union. An obstinate war leader will sometimes commit acts of hostility, or make peace for his own town, contrary to the good liking of the rest of the nation. But a few individuals are very cautious of commencing war on small occasions, without the general consent of the head men: for should it prove unsuccessful, the greater part would be apt to punish them as enemies, because they abused their power, which they had only to do good to the society. They are very deliberate in their councils, and never give an immediate answer to any message sent them by strangers, but suffer some nights first to elapse. They reason in a very orderly manner, with much coolness and good-natured language, though they may differ widely in their opinions. Through respect to the silent audience, the speaker always addresses them in a standing posture. In this manner they proceed, till each of the head men hath given his opinion on the point in debate. Then they sit down together, and determine upon the affair. Not the least passionate expression is to be heard among them, and they behave with the greatest civility to each other. In all their stated orations they have a beautiful modest way of expressing their dislike of ill things. They only say, "it is not good, goodly, or commendable." And their whole behaviour, on public occasions, is highly worthy of imitation by some of our British senators and lawyers.

Adair, *History of the North-American Indians*, 427-429.

Indian nations were made up of clans, which dictated and controlled behavior and also were a source of mutual aid. Membership in a clan was matrilineal, eternal, and guaranteed full citizenship within the nation. Each one was distinguished by a totem.

They are very kind, and charitable to one another, but more especially to those of their own Nation; for if any one of them has suffer'd any Loss, by Fire or otherwise, they order the griev'd Person to make a Feast, and invite them all thereto, which, on the day appointed, they come to, and after every Man's Mess of Victuals is dealt to him, one of their Speakers, or grave old Men, makes an Harangue, and acquaints the Company, That that Man's House has been burnt, wherein all his Goods were destroy'd; That he, and his Family, very narrowly escaped; That he is every Man's Friend in that Company; and, That it is all their Duties to help him, as he would do to any of them, had the like Misfortune befallen them. After this Oration is over, every Man, according to his Quality, throws him down upon the Ground some Present, which is commonly Beads, *Ronoak, Peak*, Skins or Furs, and which very often amounts to treble the Loss he has suffer'd. The same Assistance they give to any Man that wants to build a Cabin, or make a Canoe. They say, it is our Duty thus to do; for there are several Works that one Man cannot effect, therefore we must give him our Help, otherwise our Society will fall, and we shall be depriv'd of those urgent Necessities which Life requires.

Lawson, *New Voyage to Carolina*, 184.

The Indians, however, bear no religious respect to the animals from which they derive the names of their tribes, but will kill any of the species, when opportunity serves. The *wolf* indeed, several of them do not care to meddle with, believing it unlucky to kill them; which is the sole reason that few of the Indians shoot at that creature, through a notion of spoiling their guns. [...]

When we consider the various revolutions these unlettered savages are likely to have undergone, among themselves, through a long-forgotten measure of time; and that, probably, they have been above twenty centuries, without the use of letters to convey down their traditions, it cannot be reasonably expected they should still retain the identical names of their primogenial tribes. [...] they are so hospitable, kind-hearted, and free, that they would share with those of their own tribe, the last part of their provisions, even to a single ear of corn; and to others, if they called when they were eating; for they have no stated meal-time. An open generous temper is a standing virtue among them; to be narrow-hearted, especially to those in want, or to any of their own family, is accounted a great crime, and to reflect scandal on the rest of the tribe. Such wretched misers they brand with bad characters, and wish them the fate of Prometheus, to have an eagle or vulture fastened to their liver: or of Tantalus, starving in the midst of plenty, without being able to use it. The Cheerake Indians have a pointed proverbial expression, to the same effect—*Sinnawàb nà wóra;* "The great hawk is at home." However, it is a very rare thing to find any of them of a narrow temper: and though they do not keep one promiscuous common stock, yet it is to the very same effect; for every one has his own family, or tribe: and, when one of them is speaking, either of the individuals, or habitations, of any of his tribe, he says, "He is of my house;" or, "It is my house." [...]

When the Indians are traveling in their own country, they enquire for a house of their own tribe; and if there be any, they go to it, and are kindly received, though they never saw the persons before—they eat, drink, and regale themselves, with as much freedom, as at their own tables; which is the solid ground covered with a bear-skin. [...] I have known some of the frolicksome young sparks to ask the name of the deceased person's tribe; and once, being told it was a *raccoon*, (the genealogical name of the family) one of them scoffingly replied, "then let us away to another town, and cheer ourselves with those who have no reason to weep; for why should we make our hearts weigh heavy for an ugly, dead raccoon?"

But notwithstanding they are commonly negligent of any other tribe but their own, they regard their own particular lineal descent, in as strict a manner as did the Hebrew nation.

Adair, *History of the North-American Indians,* 16-17, 18.

The clan determined whom one could marry. When a couple separated, the mother took the children.

[. . .] they will in noe wise marrie with a woman of thire own famely Counting them thire proper sisters when they teakes a wife itt must be of an other famely counting after they are marid that thire wives is noething akin to them.

Alexander Longe, "A Small Postcript on the Ways and Manners of the Indians called Cherokees," ed. by David H. Corkran, *Southern Indian Studies* 21 (October 1969), 33.

As for the *Indian* Marriages, I have read and heard of a great deal of Form and Ceremony used, which I never saw, nor yet could learn in the Time I have been amongst them, any otherwise than I shall give you an Account of; which is as follows.

When any young *Indian* has a Mind for such a Girl to his Wife, he, or some one for him, goes to the young Woman's Parents, if living; if not, to her nearest Relations; where they make Offers of the Match betwixt the Couple. The Relations reply, they will consider of it, which serves for a sufficient Answer, till there be a second Meeting about the Marriage, which is generally brought into Debate before all the Relations (that are old People) on both Sides; and sometimes the King, with all his great Men, give their Opinions therein. If it be agreed on, and the young Woman approve thereof, (for these Savages never give their Children in Marriage, without their own Consent) the Man pays so much for his Wife; and the handsomer she is, the greater Price she bears.

Lawson, *New Voyage to Carolina,* 192-193.

[. . .] for it is a certain Rule and Custom, amongst all the savages of *America,* that I was ever acquainted withal, to let the Children always fall to the Woman's Lot; for it often happens, that two *Indians* that have liv'd together, as Man and Wife, in which Time they have had several Children; if they part, and another Man possesses her, all the Children go along with the Mother, and none with the Father.

Lawson, *New Voyage to Carolina,* 192.

In addition to childbirth, clan populations increased through the adoption of war prisoners, as Frenchman Antoine Bonnefoy learned from his Cherokee captors.

At the beginning of January we were adopted by men of prominence in the party. I was adopted as brother by a savage who bought me of my master, which he did by promising him a quantity of merchandise, and giving me what at that time I needed, such as bed-coverings, shirts, and mittens, and from that time I had the same treatment as himself. My companions were adopted by other savages, either as nephews or as cousins, and treated in the same manner by their liberators and all their families. [. . .] The savage who had adopted me gave me, before setting out upon the march, a gun, some powder, and some bullets. The pirogues having been unloaded, each savage carried, as well as ourselves, his pack of booty [. . .] The next day, *February 8*, in the morning, the savages having *mataché* themselves according to their custom, *matachèrent* our whole bodies, having left us nothing but our breeches, made the entry into their village in the order of a troop of infantry, marching four in each rank, half of them in front of us, who were placed two and two after being tied together, and having our collars dragging. The rest of the savages made the rear guard in the order of the prisoners. They made us march in this order, singing, and having, as we had had the evening before, a white stick and a rattle in our hands, to the chief square of the village and march three or four times around a great tree which is in the middle of that place. Then they buried at the foot of the tree a parcel of hair from each one of us, which the savages had preserved for that purpose from the time when they cut our hair off. After this march was finished they brought us into the council-house, where we were each obliged to sing four songs. Then the savages who had adopted us came and took away our collars. I followed my adopted brother who, on entering into his cabin, washed me, then, after he had told me that the way was free before me, I ate with him, and there I remained two months, dressed and treated like himself, without other occupation than to go hunting twice with him. We were absent thirteen days the first time and nine days the last. [. . .] The savage who adopts a captive promises a quantity of merchandise to the one to whom he belongs at the moment when he buys him. This merchandise is collected from all the family of the one who makes the purchase, and is delivered in an assembly of all the relatives, each one of whom brings what he is to give and delivers it, piece by piece, to him who sold the slave, and at the receipt of each piece he makes the rounds of the assembly, constantly carrying what has been given to him, it being forbidden to lay down any piece on the ground, for then it would belong to whoever touched it first.

"Journal of Antoine Bonnefoy, 1741/42," in Newton D. Mereness, ed., *Travels in the American Colonies* (New York: Antiquarian Society, 1961), 244, 245-246, 247. The Cherokee warriors apparently stained themselves (*mataché*) and their adoptees with dye.

The clan meted out punishment whenever a member was wronged. In cases of murder, the immediate relatives of the victim sought and killed the offender; if the perpetrator were a foreign enemy, the death of anyone from his nation sufficed. Material compensation and sarcasm were also used to satisfy grievances.

When one Indian kill another, of a different Family, the Lux talionis is rigorously insisted upon by the Relations of the deceased, to whom Satisfaction must be given; for amongst Indians, revenging the Death of a Relation is esteemed the point of honor, (if I may use the Expression) The Sentence of the whole Nation for the most heinous Crime cannot be carried into execution but by a Near Relation only, and Drunkeness, accident, or self defence are not considered as any attenuation.

In such cases the Chiefs of the Deceased's Family, apply to the Relations of the person who killed him and demmand satisfaction A compensation of Leather usually 500 lb. or a Slave is generally offered: if refused, the offenders Family resolve on putting him to Death immediately before he can make his Escape: in which Event the Friends of the dead person, and they only, have a right to kill any of the aggressors family they first meet; without being called to any Account for it.

> John Stuart to the Board of Trade, March 9, 1764, in Colonial Office 323/17, British Records, State Archives. *Lex talionis* is the law of retaliation, commonly stated as "an eye for an eye; a tooth for a tooth."

To the Hon. Mr President, with the Honll Councill of State, ye Tuscaroroe Indians Complaine—
Virga fset.

That whereas, lately a murder was Committed upon an Indian Called parridge, yor petionrs not being willing to have any other Sattisfaction than what is Usual amongst themselves, Desire to have Six hundred Cubitts of Roanoke & one hundred and twenty Cubitts of Peake, two Gunns, Six White Stript Blanketts, tenn bottles of Powder, Six thousand Shott, Six Cloath Coats, & and twenty four yrds of plaines, (coarse blue woollen cloth.)

> Entry of April 19, 1707, in William P. Palmer, ed., *Calendar of Virginia State Papers and Other Manuscripts, 1652-1781*, 11 vols. (1875-1883; reprint, New York: Kraus Reprint Company, 1968), 1:113.

They have no penal Laws yet each Individual enjoys his property with tollerable security: and if wronged of it, makes reprisals with very little Ceremony, having first obtained the Approbation of the Beloved Man.

The shame and Odium incurred by being detected in a dishonest action, are generally sufficient to render such Things uncommon. Their Customs with respect to property are observed with [some] degree of strictness. About their Lands, no Doubts, consequently no Disputes can arise: and as their riches generally consist of Arms, Utensils for agriculture, their apparel and a few domestick Necessaries; their property in them is very easily ascertained. If one Man kills another's Horse, breaks his Gun, or destroys an thing, belonging to him, by Accident, intentionally; or when in Liquor; the Value in Deer Skins is ascertained before the Beloved man; and if the aggressor has not the quantity of Leather ready he either collects it amongst his Relations or goes into the woods to hunt for it.

> John Stuart to the Board of Trade, March 9, 1764, in Colonial Office 323/17, British Records, State Archives.

There are many petty crimes which their young people are guilty of—to which our laws annex severe punishment, but their's only an ironical way of jesting. They commend the criminal before a large audience, for practicing the virtue, opposite to the crime, that he is known to be guilty of. If it is for theft, they praise his honest principles; and they commend a warrior for having behaved valiantly against the enemy, when he acted cowardly; they introduce the minutest circumstances of the affair, with severe sarcasms which wound deeply. I have known them to strike their delinquents with those sweetened darts, so good naturedly and skilfully, that they would sooner die by torture, than renew their shame by repeating the actions.

> Adair, *History of the North-American Indians*, 429-430.

One method the Indians of eastern North Carolina employed to curb inappropriate youthful behavior was *huskanawing.* **Tribal elders believed the practice was beneficial in maintaining discipline among teenaged boys and girls, hardening them to the privations of adult life. Governor Arthur Dobbs referred to its use by the Tuscaroras as they readied their young men to fight in the French and Indian War.**

You must know, that most commonly, once a Year, or, at farthest, once in two Years, these People take up so many of their young Men, as they think are able to undergo it, and *husquenaugh* them, which is to make them obedient and respective to their Superiors, and (as they say) is the same to them, as it is to us to send our Children to School, to be taught good Breeding and Letters. This House of Correction is a large strong Cabin, made on purpose for the Reception of the young Men and Boys, that have not passed this Graduation already; and it is always at *Christmas* that they *husquenaugh* their Youth, which is by bringing them into this House, and keeping them dark all the time, where they more than half-starve them. Besides, they give them Pellitory-Bark, and several intoxicating Plants, that make them go raving mad as ever were any People in the World; and you may hear them make the most dismal and hellish Cries, and Howlings, that ever humane Creatures express'd; all which continues about five or six Weeks, and the little Meat they eat, is the nastiest, loathsome stuff, and mixt with all manner of Filth it's possible to get. After the Time is expired, they are brought out of the Cabin, which never is in the Town, but always a distance off, and guarded by a Jaylor or two, who watch by Turns. Now, when they first come out, they are as poor as ever any Creatures were; for you must know several die under this diabolical Purgation. Moreover, they either really are, or pretend to be dumb, and do not speak for several Days; I think, twenty or thirty; and look so gastly, and are so chang'd, that it's next to an Impossibility to know them again, although you was never so well acquainted with them before. I would fain have gone into the mad House, and have seen them in their time of Purgatory, but the King would not suffer it, because, he told me, they would do me, or any other white Man, an Injury, that ventured in amongst them; so I desisted. They play this Prank with Girls as well as Boys, and I believe it a miserable Life they endure, because I have known several of them run away, at that time, to avoid it. Now, the Savages say, if it was not for this, they could never keep their Youth in Subjection, besides that it hardens them ever after to the Fatigues of War, Hunting, and all manner of Hardship, which their way of living exposes them to. Besides, they add, that it carries off those infirm weak Bodies, that would have been only a Burden and Disgrace to their Nation, and saves the Victuals and Cloathing for better People, that would have been expended on such useless Creatures.

Lawson, *New Voyage to Carolina*, 241-242.

I Hear that the Tuskaruras, who have Joyned the Six Nations, have sent to the Tuskaruras here for 30 men to Joyn them next Spring, and that they are Susquehanning them to have them ready, [. . .]

Governor Arthur Dobbs of North Carolina to Governor Robert Hunter Morris of Pennsylvania, December 18, 1755, in Samuel Hazard et al., eds., *Pennsylvania Archives*, multiple series (Philadelphia: Joseph Severn, 1852–), 1st ser., 2:537. The Five Nations, or Iroquois Confederacy, became the Six Nations after the Tuscaroras joined in 1722. The original five were the Cayuga, Mohawk, Oneida, Onondaga, and Seneca Indians, which occupied present-day western New York.

Native Americans largely sustained themselves through farming, and every able-bodied person assisted in preparing the soil and planting crops. Fields often adjoined each town. Overworked farmlands were abandoned and new acreage would be cleared. The Cherokees subdivided a community's land into family plots. Cultivation was carefully planned: corn and beans were planted together because corn depleted the soil and beans replenished it. Despite the potential for bountiful harvests, famines sometimes occurred, as Captain Raymond Demere reported of the inhabitants of Keowee.

The ground they never fatten with mucke, dounge, or any other thing, neither plow nor digge it as we in England, but onely prepare it in sort as followeth. A few daies before they sowe or set, the men with wooden instruments, made almost in forme of mattockes or hoes with long handles; the women with short peckers or parers, because they use them sitting, of a foote long and about five inches in breadth: doe onely breake the upper part of the ground to rayse up the weedes, grasse, & olde stubbes of corne stalks with their rootes. The which after a day or twoes drying in the Sunne, being scrapte up into many small heapes, to save them labour for carrying them away; they burne into ashes. (And whereas some may thinke that they use the ashes for to better the ground, I say that then they would either disperse the ashes abroad, which wee observed they do not, except the heapes bee to great: or else would take speciall care to set their corne where the ashes lie, which also wee finde they are carelesse of.) And this is all the husbanding of their ground that they use.

Then their setting or sowing is after this maner. First for their corne, beginning in one corner of the plot, with a pecker they make a hole, wherein they put foure graines, with that care they touch not one another (about an inch asunder) and cover them with the moulde againe: and so through out the whole plot, making such holes and using them after such maner: but with this regard, that they bee made in rankes, every ranke differing from other halfe a fadome or a yarde, and the holes also in every ranke, as much. By this meanes there is a yard spare ground betwene every hole: where according to discretion here and there, they set as many Beanes and Peaze; in divers places also among the seedes of *Macóqwer, Melden* and Planta solis.

The ground being thus set according to the rate by us experimented, an English Acre conteining fourtie pearches in length, and foure in breadth, doeth there yeeld in croppe or ofcome of corne, beanes, and peaze, at the least two hundred London bushelles, besides the *Macóqwer, Melden,* and Planta solis:

When as in England fourtie bushelles of our wheate yeelded out of such an acre is thought to be much.

> Hariot, "A briefe and true report," in Quinn, *Roanoke Voyages*, 1:341-342. *Macóqwer* are "Pompions, Mellions, and Gourdes"; *pompions* are pumpkins. *Melden* are varieties of spinach or beets. *Planta solis* are sunflowers.

[. . .] they deadened the trees by cutting through the bark, and burned them, when they either fell by decay, or became thoroughly dry. [. . .] By the aforesaid difficult method of deadening the trees, and clearing the woods, the contented natives got convenient fields in process of time. [. . .] Now, in the first clearing of their plantations, they only bark the large timber, cut down the sapplings and underwood, and burn them in heaps; as the suckers shoot up, they chop them off close by the stump, of which they make fires to deaden the roots, till in time they decay. Though to a stranger, this may seem to be a lazy method of clearing the wood-lands; yet it is the most expeditious method they could have pitched upon, under their circumstances, as a common hoe and small hatchet are all their implements for clearing and planting.

> Adair, *History of the North-American Indians*, 405-406.

In their Lands near their Towns which they Cultivate for Provisions they have a sort of Distinct property. When the planting lands of any Town, become impoverished and worn out, the Inhabitants move with one consent to a fresh spot. The principal Warrior, and Beloved Man, measure a certain proportion of Land to each Family; in doing which regard is had to their Numbers, and the Exactest equality and Justice observed. The greatest Man amongst them, would, by the least partiality, for ever forfeit the good Opinion of His Towns men; upon which alone His influence and power depend. At the proper Season the Inhabitants of the Town, Join, in cultivating and planting the Lands belonging to it: from which Labor none but the Sick and disabled are exempt. A [Point] of Distinction is upon this occasion laid aside after which every Family depends upon the produce of the Land alloted it. When a Family removes to another Town, the Property of the Land they possessed reverts to the whole, and is in the same manner bestowed on the first New Settler. This Oeconomy is common to all the Indian Nations within this District.

> John Stuart to the Board of Trade, March 9, 1764, in Colonial Office 323/17, British Records, State Archives.

I passed through [Etchoe], and continued three miles farther to Nucasse, and three miles more brought me to Whatoga. Riding through this large town, the road carried me winding about through their little plantations of Corn, Beans, &c. up to the council-house, which was a very large dome or rotunda, situated on the top of an ancient artificial mount, and here my road terminated. All before me and on every side, appeared little plantations of young Corn, Beans, &c. divided from each other by narrow strips or borders of grass, which marked the bounds of each one's property, their habitation standing in the midst. Finding no common high road to lead me through the town, I was now at a stand how to proceed further; when observing an Indian man at the door of his habitation, three or four hundred yards distance from me, beckoning me to come to him, I ventured to ride through their lots, being careful to do no injury to the young plants, the rising hopes of their labour and industry; crossed a little grassy vale watered by a silver stream, which gently undulated through; then ascended a green hill to the house, where I was chearfully welcomed at the door, and led in by the chief, giving the care of my horse to two handsome youths, his sons.

> Bartram, *Travels through North and South Carolina*, 348. Etchoe stood south of Nikwasi ("Nucasse") along the Little Tennessee River near present-day Otto, Macon County, North Carolina.

The chief part of the Indians begin to plant their out-fields, when the wild fruit is so ripe, as to draw off the birds from picking up the grain. This is their general rule, which is in the beginning of May, [. . .]

> Adair, *History of the North-American Indians*, 406.

The People of Keowee Town and the whole Nation are almost starved for Want of Provisions. I have been obliged to assist the Keowee People with Rice and Beef several Times. I have had Accounts from the Middle Settlements of several People being starved to death the Famine has been so great among them.

> Captain Raymond Demere, commander of Fort Loudoun, to Governor William Henry Lyttelton of South Carolina, July 19, 1756, in William L. McDowell Jr., ed., *Documents Relating to Indian Affairs, 1754-1765*, in *The Colonial Records of South Carolina*, Series 2 (Columbia: South Carolina Archives Department, 1970), 145.

Although men might lend assistance during planting and harvest, agriculture primarily was the work of women—who, in the case of the Cherokees, also owned the land and controlled food distribution. Timberlake believed that the temperate climate and richness of the soil made it feasible for women to tend crops.

The country being situated between thirty-two and thirty-four degrees north latitude, and eighty-seven degrees thirty minutes west longitude from London, as near as can be calculated, is temperate, inclining to heat during the summer-season, and so remarkably fertile, that the women alone do all the laborious tasks of agriculture, [. . .]

Timberlake, *Memoirs, 1756-1765*, 68.

I have bought five Cannoe Loads of Corn since my last, and am going to send to buy more immediately, and in a few Days I propose to send to Tellico to buy some which may come here by Water. I hear there is a large Quantity there and the Women will be glad to dispose of some for Necessaries.

Captain Raymond Demere to Governor William Henry Lyttelton, January 6, 1756, in McDowell, *Documents Relating to Indian Affairs, 1754-1765*, 310.

The women plant also pompions, and different sorts of melons, in separate fields, at a considerable distance from the town, where each owner raises an high scaffold, to over-look this favourite part of their vegetable possessions: and though the enemy sometimes kills them in this their strict watch duty, yet it is a very rare thing to pass by those fields, without seeing them there at watch. This usually is the duty of the old women, who fret at the very shadow of a crow, when he chances to pass on his wide survey of the fields; but if pinching hunger should excite him to descend, they soon frighten him away with their screeches. When the pompions are ripe, they cut them into long circling slices, which they barbecue, or dry with a slow heat.

Adair, *History of the North-American Indians*, 408.

[. . .] they fasten stakes in the ground, and tie a couple of long split hiccory, or white oak-sapplings, at proper distances to keep off the horses: though they cannot leap fences, yet many of the old horses will creep through these enclosures, almost as readily as swine, to the great regret of the women, who scold and give them ill names, calling them ugly mad horses, and bidding them "go along, and be sure to keep away, otherwise their hearts will hang sharp within them, and set them on to spoil them, if envy and covetousness lead them back." Thus they argue with them, and they are usually as good as their word, by striking a tomohawk into the horse, if he does not observe the friendly caution they gave him at the last parting. [. . .] The women however tether the horses with tough young bark-ropes, and confine the swine in convenient penns, from the time the provisions are planted, till they are gathered in [. . .]

Adair, *History of the North-American Indians*, 406.

Corn was the principal crop grown by Indians in North Carolina and throughout the Americas. Its cultivation transformed them from a hunting and gathering society to an agricultural one.

Corn is their chief produce, and main dependence. Of this they have three sorts; one of which hath been already mentioned. The second sort is yellow and flinty, which they call "hommony-corn." The third is the largest, of a very white and soft grain, termed "bread-corn." In July, when the chesnutt and corn are green and full grown, they half boil the former, and take off the rind; and having sliced the milky, swelled, long rows of the latter, the women pound it in a large wooden mortar, which is wide at the mouth, and gradually narrows to the bottom: then they knead both together, wrap them up in green corn-blades of various sizes, about an inch-thick, and boil them well, as they do every kind of seethed food. This sort of bread is very tempting to the taste, and reckoned most delicious to their strong palates. They have another sort of boiled bread, which is mixed with beans, or potatoes; they put on the soft corn till it begins to boil, and pound it sufficiently fine; — their invention does not reach to the use of any kind of milk. When the flour is stirred, and dried by the heat of the sun or fire, they sift it with sieves of different sizes, curiously made of the coarser or finer cane-splinters. The thin cakes mixt with bear's oil, were formerly baked on thin broad stones placed over a fire, or on broad earthen bottoms fit for such a use: but now they use kettles. When they intend to bake great loaves, they make a strong blazing fire, with short dry split wood, on the hearth. When it is burnt down to coals, they carefully rake them off to each side, and sweep away the remaining ashes: then they put their well-kneeded broad loaf, first steeped in hot water, over the hearth, and an earthen bason above it, with the embers and coals a top. This method of baking is as clean and efficacious as could possibly be done in any oven; when they take it off, they wash the loaf with warm water, and it soon becomes firm, and very white. It is likewise very wholesome, and well-tasted to any except the vitiated palate of an Epicure.

Adair, *History of the North-American Indians*, 407-408. The first variety to which Adair alluded was a "smaller sort of Indian corn, which usually ripens in two months, from the time it is planted; though it is called by the English, the six weeks corn." *History of the North-American Indians*, 406.

Besides corn and other domestic crops, Native Americans ate wild foods, such as nuts and fruit.

Medlars a kinde of verie good fruit, so called by us chieflie for these respectes: first in that they are not good untill they be rotten: then in that they open at the head as our medlars, and are about the same bignesse: otherwise in taste and colour they are farre different: for they are as red as cheries and very sweet: but whereas the cherie is sharpe sweet, they are lushious sweet.

Metaquesúnnauk, a kinde of pleasaunt fruite almost of the shape & bignesse of English peares, but that they are of a perfect red colour as well within as without. They grow on a plant whose leaves are verie thicke and full of prickles as sharpe as needles. Some that have bin in the Indies, where they have seen that kind of red die of great price, which is called Cochinile, to grow, doe describe his plant right like unto this of *Metaquesúnnauk* but whether it be the true cochinile or a bastard or wilde kinde, it cannot yet be certified, seeing that also as I heard, Cochinile is not of the fruite but found on the leaves of the plant; which leaves for such matter we have not so specially observed.

Grapes there are of two sorts which I mentioned in the marchantable commodities.

Straberies there as good & as great as those which we have in our English gardens.

Mulberies, Applecrabs, Hurts or Hurtleberies, such as wee have in England.

Sacquenúmmener a kinde of berries almost like unto capres but somewhat greater which grow together in clusters upon a plant or herbe that is found in shalow waters: being boiled eight or nine houres according to their kind, are very good meat and holesome, otherwise if they be eaten they will make a man for the time franticke or extremely sicke.

There is a kinde of reed which beareth a seed almost like unto our rie or wheat, & being boiled is good meate.

In our travailes in some places wee found wilde peaze like unto ours in England but that they were lesse, which are also good meate.

Hariot, "A briefe and true report," in Quinn, *Roanoke Voyages*, 1:351-353, 354. The fruit of the European medlar tree (*Mespilus germanica*) is matte brown in color; although some scholars assume that Hariot was describing persimmons, in 1990 a small stand of medlars (*Mespilus canescens*) was discovered in Arkansas that bore bright red fruit. *Metaquesúnnauk* is the fruit of the prickly pear cactus. *Sacquenúmmener* might be the berries of arrow arum (*Peltandra virginica*) or golden club (*Orontium aquaticum*).

Chestnuts, there are in divers places great store: some they use to eate rawe, some they stampe and boile to make spoonemeate, and with some being sodden they make such a manner of dowe bread as they use of their beanes before mentioned.

Walnuts: There are two kindes of Walnuts, and of them infinit store: In many places where [are] very great woods for many miles together the third part of trees are walnut-trees. The one kind is of the same taste and forme or litle differing from ours of England, but that they are harder and thicker shelled: the other is greater, and hath a verye ragged and harde shell: but the kernell great, verie oylie and sweete. Besides their eating of them after our ordinarie maner, they breake them with stones and pound them in morters with water to make a milk which they use to put into some sorts of their spoonmeate; also among their sodde wheat, peaze, beanes and pompions which maketh them have a farre more pleasant taste. [. . .]

There is a kind of berrie or acorne, [. . .] that grow on several kinds of trees; the one is called *Sagatémener*, the second *Osámener*, the third Pummuckǔner. These kind of acorns they use to drie upon hurdles made of reeds with fire underneath almost after the maner as we dry malt in England. When they are to be used they first water them until they be soft & then being sod they make a good victual, either to eate so simply, or els being also pounded, to make loaves or lumpes of bread. These be also the three kinds of which, I said before, the inhabitants used to make sweet oyle.

Another sort is called *Sapúmmener*, which being boiled or parched doth eate and taste like unto chestnuts. They sometime also make bread of this sort.

Hariot, "A briefe and true report," in Quinn, *Roanoke Voyages*, 1:350-351, 354. *Sagatémener*, *Osámener*, *Pummuckóner*, and *Sapúmmener* refer to nuts from the oak, hazelnut, and chinquapin trees indigenous to the coast.

Indians also grew tobacco, the smoking of which welcomed strangers and punctuated council meetings. Tobacco pipes could be large and elaborate in design.

Their Teeth are yellow with Smoaking Tobacco, which both Men and Women are much addicted to. They tell us, that they had Tobacco amongst them, before the *Europeans* made any Discovery of that Continent. It differs in the Leaf from the sweet-scented, and *Oroonoko*, which are the Plants we raise and cultivate in *America*. Theirs differs likewise much in the Smell, when green, from our Tobacco, before cured. They do not use the same way to cure it as we do; and therefore, the Difference must be very considerable in Taste; for all Men (that know Tobacco) must allow, that it is the Ordering thereof which gives a Hogoo [relish] to that Weed, rather than any Natural Relish it possesses, when green. Although they are great Smokers, yet they never are seen to take it in Snuff, or chew it.

Lawson, *New Voyage to Carolina*, 175-176.

The harrangue being finished, several pipes were presented me by the headsmen, to take a whiff. This ceremony I could have waved, as smoking was always very disagreeable to me; but as it was a token of their amity, and they might be offended if I did not comply, I put on the best face I was able, though I dared not even wipe the end of the pipe that came out of their mouths; which, considering their paint and dirtiness, are not of the most ragoutant, as the French term it.

Timberlake, *Memoirs, 1756-1765*, 60-61. *Ragoutant* means "appetizing" in French.

They make beautiful stone pipes; and the Cheerake the best of any of the Indians: for their mountainous country contains many different sorts and colours of soils proper for such uses. They easily form them with their tomohawks, and afterward finish them in any desired form with their knives; the pipes being of a very soft quality till they are smoked with, and used to the fire, when they become quite hard. They are often a full span long, and the bowls are about half as large again as those of our English pipes. The fore part of each commonly runs out with a sharp peak, two or three fingers broad, and a quarter of an inch thick—on both sides of the bowl, lengthwise, they cut several pictures with a great deal of skill and labour; such as a buffalo and a panther on the opposite sides of the bowl; a rabbit and a fox; and, very often, a man and a woman [. . .]. The savages work so slow, that one of their artists is two months at a pipe with his knife, before he finishes it: indeed, as before observed, they are great enemies to profuse sweating, and are never in a hurry about a good thing. The stems are commonly made of soft wood about two feet long, and an inch thick, cut into four squares, each scooped till they join very near the hollow of the stem: the beaus always hollow the squares, except a little at each corner to hold them together, to which they fasten a parcel of bell-buttons, different sorts of fine feathers, and several small battered pieces of copper kettles hammered, round deer-skin thongs, and a red painted scalp; this is a boasting, valuable, and superlative ornament. According to their standard, such a pipe constitutes the possessor, a grand beau. They so accurately carve, or paint hieroglyphic characters on the stem, that all the war-actions, and the tribe of the owner, with a great many circumstances of things, are fully delineated.

Adair, *History of the North-American Indians*, 423-424.

In late fall, after the crops were harvested and animals had developed their dense winter coats, Indians typically commenced hunting. The Tuscaroras, observed John Lawson, set out in groups of several hundred, established camps far from their towns, and then lit the surrounding forests ablaze, hemming game into vast killing zones. All able-bodied men were expected to hunt; those who could not were assigned to other tasks.

When these Savages go a hunting, they commonly go out in great Numbers, and oftentimes a great many Days Journey from home, beginning at the coming in of the Winter; that is, when the Leaves are fallen from the Trees, and are become dry. 'Tis then they burn the Woods, by setting Fire to the Leaves, and wither'd Bent and Grass, which they do with a Match made of the black Moss that hangs on the Trees in *Carolina*, and is sometimes above six Foot long. [. . .] Thus they go and fire the Woods for many Miles, and drive the Deer and other Game into small Necks of Land and Isthmus's, where they kill and destroy what they please. In these Hunting-Quarters, they have their Wives and Ladies of the Camp, where they eat all the Fruits and Dainties of that Country, and live in all the Mirth and Jollity, which it is possible for such People to entertain themselves withal. Here it is, that they get their Complement of Deer-Skins and Furs to trade with the *English*, (the Deer-Skins being in Season in Winter, which is contrary to *England*.) All small Game, as Turkeys, Ducks, and small Vermine, they commonly kill with Bow and Arrow, thinking it not worth throwing Powder and Shot after them. [. . .] I have been often in their Hunting-Quarters, where a roasted or barbakued Turkey, eaten with Bears Fat, is held a good Dish; and indeed, I approve of it very well; [. . .] The Savage Men never beat their Corn to make Bread; but that is the Womens Work, especially the Girls, of whom you shall see four beating with long great Pestils in a narrow wooden Mortar; and every one keeps her Stroke so exactly, that 'tis worthy of Admiration. Their Cookery continues from Morning till Night. The Hunting makes them hungry; and the *Indians* are a People that always eat very often, not seldom getting up at Midnight, to eat. [. . .] At their setting out, they have *Indians* to attend their Hunting-Camp, that are not good and expert Hunters; therefore are employ'd to carry Burdens, to get Bark for the Cabins, and other Servile Work; also to go backward and forward, to their Towns, to carry News to the old People, whom they leave behind them. The Women are forced to carry their Loads of Grain and other Provisions, and get Fire-Wood; for a good Hunter, or Warriour in these Expeditions, is employ'd in no other Business, than the Affairs of Game and Battle.

Lawson, *New Voyage to Carolina*, 215-217.

[. . .] on October 3, 1567, the captain, being in the place called Cauchi, saw an Indian walking among the Indian women with an apron before him as [the women] wear it and he did what they did. The captain, having seen this, summoned Guillermo Rufín, interpreter, and the other interpreters and when they were thus called, the captain, before many soldiers of his company, told them to ask why that Indian went among the Indian women, wearing an apron as they did. The interpreters asked the above mentioned of the cacique of the place and the cacique replied through the interpreters that the Indian was his brother and that because he was not a man for war nor carrying on the business of a man, {*Look*} he went about in that manner like a woman and he did all that is given to a woman to do.

> Charles M. Hudson, *The Juan Pardo Expeditions: Exploration of the Carolinas and Tennessee, 1566-1568*, trans. Paul E. Hoffman (Washington: Smithsonian Institution Press, 1990), 267. Evidence suggests that Cauchi stood at the junction of Garden Creek and Pigeon River near present-day Canton, North Carolina.

Indian men used the same weapons for both hunting and warfare. Before contact with whites, they fashioned bows, arrows, axes, and clubs from wood and stone. Afterward, their arsenals included European-made arms.

Maple, and also Wich-hazle, whereof the inhabitants use to make their bowes. [. . .] having no edge tooles or weapons of yron or steele to offend us withall, neither knowe they how to make any: those weapons that they have, are onlie bowes made of Witch hazle, & arrowes of reeds, flat edged truncheons also of wood about a yard long, neither have they any thing to defend themselves but targets made of barks, and some armours made of stickes wickered together with thread.

> Hariot, "A breife and true report," in Quinn, *Roanoke Voyages*, 1:364, 369.

The Indians formerly had stone axes, which in form commonly resembled a smith's chisel. Each weighed from one to two, or three pounds weight— They were made of a flinty kind of stone: I have seen several, which chanced to escape being buried with their owners, and were carefully preserved by the old people, as respectable remains of antiquity. They twisted two or three tough hiccory slips, of about two feet long, round the notched head of the axe; [. . .]

> Adair, *History of the North-American Indians*, 405.

The warlike arms used by the Cherokees are guns, bows and arrows, darts, scalpping knives, and tommahawkes, which are hatchets; the hammer-part of which being made hollow, and a small hole running from thence along the shank, terminated by a small brass-tube for the mouth, makes a compleat pipe. There are various ways of making these, according to the country or fancy of the purchaser, being all made by the Europeans; some have a long spear at top, and some different conveniencies on each side. This is one of their most useful pieces of field-furniture, serving all the offices of hatchet, pipe, and sword; neither are the Indians less expert at throwing it than using it near, but will kill at a considerable distance.

> Timberlake, *Memoirs, 1756-1765*, 77-78.

Game such as deer, bears, rabbits, and the rare buffalo, was killed for its meat and hide. However, not all animals were fit for consumption: predators and other creatures were unclean and not to be eaten.

Deare, in some places there are great store: neere unto the Sea coast they are of the ordinarie bignes as ours in England, & some lesse: but further up into the countrey where there is better feed they are greater: they differ from ours onely in this, their tailes are longer and the snags of their hornes looke backward.

Conies, Those that we have seen & al that we can heare of are of a grey colour like unto hares: in some places there are such plentie that all the people of some townes make them mantles of the furre or flue of the skinnes of those they usually take.

Saquénuckot & *Maquüwoc*, two kinds of small beastes greater then conies which are very good meat. We never tooke any of them our selves but sometimes eate of such as the inhabitants had taken & brought unto us.

Squirels, which are of a grey colour, we have taken and eaten. Beares which are all of blacke colour. The beares of this countrey are good meat; the inhabitants in time of winter do use to tke & eate manie, so also sometime did wee. They are taken commonlie in this sort. In some Ilands or places where they are, being hunted for, as soone as they have spiall of a man they presently run awaie, & then being chased they clime and get up the next tree they can, from whence with arrowes they are shot down starke dead, or with those wounds that they may after easily be killed; we sometime shotte them downe with our callevers. [. . .] The inhabitants sometime kill the Lyon, and eat him: [. . .]

> Hariot, "A briefe and true report," in Quinn, *Roanoke Voyages*, 1:355-356, 357. Quinn believed that *Saquénuckot* and *Maquüwoc* might have been muskrat, mink, raccoon, beaver, or opossum. *Conies* are rabbits; a *caliver* ("callever") is a harquebus or light musket of the sixteenth century.

They reckon all birds of prey, and birds of night, to be unclean, and unlawful to be eaten. [. . .] Eagles of every kind they esteem unclean food; likewise ravens (though the name of a tribe with them) crows, buzzards, swallows, bats, and every species of owls: and they believe that swallowing flies, muskeetoes, or gnats, always breeds sickness, or worms. [. . .]

None of them will eat of any animal whatsoever, if they either know, or suspect that it died of itself. [. . .]

They reckon all those animals to be unclean, that are either carnivorous, or live on nasty food; as hogs, wolves, panthers, foxes, cats, mice, rats. And if we except the bear, they deem all beasts of prey unhallowed, and polluted food; all amphibious quadrupeds they rank in the same class.

Adair, *History of the North-American Indians*, 130, 131, 132.

The *Buffelo* is a wild Beast of *America*, which has a Bunch on his Back, as the Cattle of St. *Laurence* are said to have. He seldom appears amongst the *English* Inhabitants, his chief Haunt being in the Land of *Messiasippi*, which is, for the most part, a plain Country; yet I have known some kill'd on the Hilly Part of *Cape-Fair*-River, they passing the Ledges of vast Mountains from the said *Messiasippi*, before they can come near us. I have eaten of their Meat, but do not think it so good as our Beef; yet the younger Calves are cry'd up for excellent Food, as very likely they may be. It is conjectured, that these Buffelos, mixt in Breed withour tame Cattle, would much better the Breed for Largeness and Milk, which seems very probable. Of the wild Bull's Skin, Buff is made. The *Indians* cut the Skins into Quarters for the Ease of their Transportation, and make Beds to lie on. They spin the Hair into Garters, Girdles, Sashes, and the like, it being long and curled, and often of a chesnut or red Colour.

Lawson, *New Voyage to Carolina*, 120-121.

Women, the slaves of Indians, and males who proved ineffective at hunting, dressed and cured or tanned the raw animal skins.

Their Way of dressing their Skins is by soaking them in Water, so they get the Hair off, with an Instrument made of the Bone of a Deer's Foot; yet some use a sort of Iron Drawing-Knife, which they purchase of the *English*, and after the Hair is off, they dissolve Deers Brains, (which beforehand are made in a Cake and baked in the Embers) in a Bowl of Water, so soak the Skins therein, till the Brains have suck'd up the Water; then they dry it gently, and keep working it with an Oyster-Shell, or some such thing, to scrape withal, till it is dry; whereby it becomes soft and pliable. Yet these so dress'd will not endure wet, but become hard thereby; which to prevent, they either cure them in the Smoke, or tan them with Bark, as before observ'd; not but that the young *Indian* Corn, beaten to a Pulp, will effect the same as the Brains.

Lawson, *New Voyage to Carolina*, 217.

[. . .] for dressing the deer Skins is the work of their Women in their Towns after returning from Hunting.

John Stuart to Lieutenant Governor William Bull of South Carolina, December 2, 1769, in Colonial Office 5/71, British Records, State Archives, Office of Archives of History, Raleigh.

Whether in camp or in town, women also fashioned elaborate baskets and mats from reeds and rushes that they had gathered and dyed. They made earthenware pots, as well.

The Mats the *Indian* Women make, are of Rushes, and about five Foot high, and two Fathom long, and sew'd double, that is, two together; whereby they become very commodious to lay under our Beds, or to sleep on in the Summer Season in the Day-time, and for our Slaves in the Night.

There are other Mats made of Flags, which the *Tuskeruro Indians* make, and sell to the Inhabitants.

The Baskets our Neighbouring *Indians* make, are all made of a very fine sort of Bulrushes, and sometimes of Silk-grass, which they work with Figures of Beasts, Birds, Fishes, &c.

Lawson, *New Voyage to Carolina*, 195-196.

They make the handsomest clothes baskets, I ever saw, considering their materials. They divide large swamp canes, into long, thin, narrow splinters, which they dye of several colours, and manage the workmanship so well, that both the inside and outside are covered with a beautiful variety of pleasing figures; and, though for the space of two inches below the upper edge of each basket, it is worked into one, through the other parts they are worked asunder, as if they were two joined a-top by some strong cement. A large nest consists of eight or ten baskets, contained within each other. Their dimensions are different, but they usually make the outside basket about a foot deep, a foot and an half broad, and almost a yard long.

The Indians, by reason of our supplying them so cheap with every sort of goods, have forgotten the chief part of their ancient mechanical skill, so as not to be well able now, at least for some years, to live independent of us. Formerly, those baskets which the Cheerake made, were so highly esteemed even in South Carolina, the politest of our colonies, for domestic usefulness, beauty, and skilful variety, that a large nest of them cost upwards of a moidore.

Adair, *History of the North-American Indians*, 424. A *moidore* was a Portuguese gold coin, worth approximately 27 shillings, accepted as legal tender in eighteenth-century England.

They make earthen pots of very different sizes, so as to contain from two to ten gallons; large pitchers to carry water; bowls, dishes, platters, basons, and a prodigious number of other vessels of such antiquated forms, as would be tedious to describe, and impossible to name. Their method of glazing them, is, they place them over a large fire of smoky pitch pine, which makes them smooth, black, and firm. Their lands abound with proper clay, for that use; and even with porcelain, as has been proved by experiment.

Adair, *History of the North-American Indians*, 424-425.

Writers like Lawson, Hariot, and Timberlake agreed that Indians were adept at fishing as well as hunting. Weirs, snares, spears, lines, and bows and arrows were used to take fresh and saltwater fish. Shellfishing required baited reeds and lines.

They are not only good Hunters of the wild Beasts and Game of the Forest, but very expert in taking the Fish of the Rivers and Waters near which they inhabit, and are acquainted withal. Thus they that live a great way up the Rivers practise Striking Sturgeon and Rock-fish, or Bass, when they come up the Rivers to spawn; besides the vast Shoals of Sturgeon which they kill and take with Snares, as we do Pike in *Europe*. The Herrings in *March* and *April* run a great way up the Rivers and fresh Streams to spawn, where the Savages make great Wares, with Hedges that hinder their Passage only in the Middle, where an artificial Pound is made to take them in; so that they cannot return. This Method is in use all over the fresh Streams, to catch Trout and the other Species of Fish which those Parts afford. Their taking of Craw-fish is so pleasant, that I cannot pass it by without mention; When they have a mind to get these Shell-fish, they take a Piece of Venison, and half-barbakue or roast it; then they cut it into thin Slices, which Slices they stick through with Reeds about six Inches asunder, betwixt Piece and Piece; then the Reeds are made sharp at one end; and so they stick a great many of them down in the bottom of the Water (thus baited) in the small Brooks and Runs, which the Craw-fish frequent. Thus the *Indians* sit by, and tend those baited Sticks, every now and then taking them up, to see how many are at the Bait; where they generally find abundance; so take them off, and put them in a Basket for the purpose, and stick the Reeds down again. By this Method, they will, in a little time, catch several Bushels, which are as good, as any I ever eat.

Lawson, *New Voyage to Carolina*, 217-218.

[. . .] having as yet no nets, the Indians catch the fish with lines, spears, or dams; which last, as it seems particular to the natives of America, I shall trouble the reader with a description of. Building two walls obliquely down the river from either shore, just as they are near joining, a passage is left to a deep well or reservoir; the Indians then scaring the fish down the river, close the mouth of the reservoir with a large bush, or bundle made on purpose, and it is no difficult matter to take them with baskets, when inclosed within so small a compass.

Timberlake, *Memoirs, 1756-1765*, 69.

For foure monethes of the yeere, February, March, Aprill and May, there are plentie of Sturgeons. And also in the same monethes of Herrings, some of the ordinary bignesse as ours in England, but the most part farre greater, of eighteene, twentie inches, and some two foote in length and better; both these kindes of fishe in those monethes are most plentifull, and in best season, which wee found to bee most delicate and pleasaunt meate.

There are also Troutes: Porpoises: Rayes: Oldwives: Mullets: Plaice: and very many other sortes of excellent good fish, which we have taken & eaten, whose names I know not but in the countrey language; we have of twelve sorts more the pictures as they were drawn in the countrey with their names.

The inhabitants use to take them two maner of wayes, the one is by a kinde of wear made of reedes which in that countrey are very strong. The other way, which is more strange, is with poles made sharpe at one ende, by shooting them into the fish after the maner as Irishmen cast dartes; either as they are rowing in their boats or els as they are wading in the shallowes for the purpose.

There are also in many places plentie of these kindes which follow.

Sea crabbes, such as we have in England.

Oysters, some very great, and some small; some rounde and some of a long shape: They are founde both in salt water and brackish, and those that we had out of salt water are far better than the other, as in our owne countrey.

Also Muscles: Scalopes: Periwinkles: and Creuises.

Seékanauk, a kinde of crustie shel fishe which is good meate about a foote in breadth, having a crustie tayle, many legges like a crab; and her eyes in her backe. They are found in shallowes of salt waters, and sometime on the shoare.

There are many Tortoyses both of lande and sea kinde, their backes & bellies are shelled very thicke; their head, feete, and taile, which are in appearance, seeme ougly as though they were members of a serpent or venemous: but notwithstanding they are very good meate, as also their egges. Some have bene founde of a yard in bredth and better.

Hariot, "A briefe and true report," in Quinn, *Roanoke Voyages*, 1:359-362. Although Quinn asserts that the *Seékanauk* was the king crab, Hariot seems to be describing the horseshoe crab.

Those *Indians* that frequent the Salt-Waters, take abundance of Fish, some very large, and of several sorts, which to preserve, they first barbakue, then pull the Fish to Pieces, so dry it in the Sun, whereby it keeps for Transportation; as for Scate, Oysters, Cockles, and several sorts of Shell-fish, they open and dry them upon Hurdles, having a constant Fire under them. The Hurdles are made of Reeds or Canes in the shape of a Gridiron. Thus they dry several Bushels of these Fish, and keep them for their Necessities. At the time when they are on the Salts, and Sea Coasts, they have another Fishery, that is for a little Shell-fish, which those in *England* call Blackmoors Teeth. These they catch by tying Bits of Oysters to a long String, which they lay in such places, as, they know, those Shell-Fish haunt. These Fish get hold of the Oysters, and suck them in, so that they pull up those long Strings, and take great Quantities of them, which they carry a great way into the main Land, to trade with the remote *Indians*, where they are of great Value; but never near the Sea, by reason they are common, therefore not esteem'd. Besides, the Youth and *Indian* Boys go in the Night, and one holding a Lightwood Torch, the other has a Bow and Arrows, and the Fire directing him to see the Fish, he shoots them with the Arrows; and thus they kill a great many of the smaller Fry, and sometimes pretty large ones.

Lawson, *New Voyage to Carolina*, 218-219.

Light-draft dugout canoes, hewn from the trunk of a single tree, were ideal for navigating miles of streams, rivers, and coastline.

Rakiock, a kinde of trees so called that are sweet wood of which the inhabitants that were neere unto us doe commonly make their boats or Canoes of the forme of trowes; onely with the helpe of fire, hatchets of stones, and shels; we have knowen some so great being made in that sort of one tree that they have carried well xx. men at once, besides much baggage: the timber being great, tal, streight, soft, light, & yet tough enough I thinke (besides other uses) to be fit also for masts of ships.

Hariot, "A briefe and true report," in Quinn, *Roanoke Voyages*, 1:363-364. *Rakiock* are softwoods such as the tulip tree (*Liriodendrum tulipifera*), bald cypress (*Taxodium distichum*), or Atlantic white cypress (*Chamaecyparis thyoides*).

Their canoes are the next work of any consequence; they are generally made of a large pine or poplar, from thirty to forty feet long, and about two broad, with flat bottoms and sides, and both ends alike; the Indians hollow them now with the tools they get from the Europeans, but formerly did it by fire: they are capable of carrying about fifteen or twenty men, are very light, and can by the Indians, so great is their skill in managing them, be forced up a very strong current, particularly the bark canoes; but these are seldom used but by the northern Indians.

Timberlake, *Memoirs, 1756-1765*, 84-85.

Games provided entertainment; some, like ball and chunkey, honed the skills and endurance required for survival. A precursor to modern-day lacrosse, ball was popular among Indians across the Southeast. It also was a very physical sport, which the Cherokees nicknamed "little brother of war." (Bartram recounts the ball-play dance, below.) Chunkey was played on an outdoor court: one participant threw a discoidal stone along the ground while another hurled a spear at it. The person whose weapon fell closest to the stone won. Eastern Carolina Indians favored a pastime that Lawson referred to as "Arithmetick." Bets on games were sometimes large.

The Indians are much addicted to gaming, and will often stake every thing they possess. Ball-playing is their chief and most favourite game: and is such severe exercise, as to shew it was originally calculated for a hardy and expert race of people, like themselves, and the ancient Spartans. The ball is made of a piece of scraped deer-skin, moistened, and stuffed hard with deer's hair, and strongly sewed with deer's sinews.—The ball-sticks are about two feet long, the lower end somewhat resembling the palm of a hand, and which are worked with deer-skin thongs. Between these, they catch the ball, and throw it a great distance, when not prevented by some of the opposite party, who fly to intercept them. The goal is about five hundred yards in length: at each end of it, they fix two long bending poles into the ground, three yards apart below, but slanting a considerable way outwards. The party that happens to throw the ball over these, counts one; but, if it be thrown underneath, it is cast back, and played for as usual. The gamesters are equal in number on each side; and, at the beginning of every course of the ball, they throw it up high in the center of the ground, and in a direct line between the two goals. When the crowd of players prevents the one who catched the ball, from throwing it off with a long direction, he commonly sends it the right course, by an artful sharp twirl. They are so exceedingly expert in this manly exercise, that, between the goals, the ball is mostly flying the different ways, by the force of the playing sticks, without falling to the ground, for they are not allowed to catch it with their hands. It is surprising to see how swiftly they fly, when closely chased by a nimble footed pursuer; when they are intercepted by one of the opposite party, his fear of being cut by the ball sticks, commonly gives them an opportunity of throwing it perhaps a hundred yards; but the antagonist sometimes runs up behind, and by a sudden stroke dashes down the ball.

It is a very unusual thing to see them act spitefully in any sort of game, not even in this severe and tempting exercise. [. . .]

The warriors have another favourite game, called *Chungke*; which, with propriety of language, may be called "Running hard labour." They have near their state house, a square piece of ground well cleaned, and fine sand is carefully strewed over it, when requisite, to promote a swifter motion to what they throw along the surface. Only one, or two on a side, play at this ancient game. They have a stone about two fingers broad at the edge, and two spans round: each party has a pole of about eight feet long, smooth, and tapering at each end, the points flat. They set off a-breast of each other at six yards from the end of the play ground; then one of them hurls the stone on its edge, in as direct a line as he can, a considerable distance toward the middle of the other end of the square: when they have ran a few yards, each darts his pole anointed with bear's oil, with a proper force, as near as he can guess in proportion to the motion of the stone, that the end may lie close to the stone—when this is the case, the person counts two of the game, and, in proportion to the nearness of the poles to the mark, one is counted, unless by measuring, both are found to be at an equal distance from the stone. In this manner, the players will keep running most part of the day, at half speed, under the violent heat of the sun, staking their silver ornaments, their nose, finger, and ear rings; their breast, arm, and wrist plates, and even all their wearing apparel, except that which barely covers their middle. All the American Indians are much addicted to this game, which to us appears to be a task of stupid drudgery: it seems however to be of early origin, when their fore-fathers used diversions as simple as their manners. The hurling stones they use at present, were time immemorial rubbed smooth on the rocks, and with prodigious labour; they are kept with the strictest religious care, from one generation to another, and are exempted from being buried with the dead. They belong to the town where they are used, and are carefully preserved.

Adair, *History of the North-American Indians*, 399-400, 401-402.

Their chiefest Game is a sort of Arithmetick, which is managed by a Parcel of small split Reeds, the Thickness of a small Bent; these are made very nicely, so that they part, and are tractable in their Hands. They are fifty one in Number, their Length about seven Inches; when they play, they throw part of them to their Antagonist; the Art is, to discover, upon sight, how many you have, and what you throw to him that plays with you. Some are so expert at their Numbers, that they will tell ten times together, what they throw out of their Hands. Although the whole Play is carried on with the quickest Motion it's possible to use, yet some are so expert at this Game, as to win great *Indian*

Estates by this Play. A good Sett of these Reeds, fit to play withal, are valued and sold for a dress'd Doe-Skin.

Lawson, *New Voyage to Carolina*, 178, 180.

Dances and feasts were elaborate affairs. They could commemorate wartime exploits, the harvesting of the annual corn crop, spirited competition with a neighboring town, or friendship with another Indian nation.

Their Dances are of different Natures; and for every sort of Dance, they have a Tune, which is allotted for that Dance; as, if it be a War-Dance, they have a warlike Song, wherein they express, with all the Passion and Vehemance imaginable, what they intend to do with their Enemies; how they will kill, roast, sculp, beat, and make Captive, such and such Numbers of them; and how many they have destroy'd before. All these Songs are made new for every Feast; nor is one and the same Song sung at two several Festivals. Some one of the Nation (which has the best Gift of expressing their Designs) is appointed by their King, and War-Captains, to make these Songs.

Others are made for Feasts of another Nature; as, when several Towns, or sometimes, different Nations have made Peace with one another; then the Song suits both Nations, and relates, how the bad Spirit made them go to War, and destroy one another; but it shall never be so again; but that their Sons and Daughters shall marry together, and the two Nations love one another, and become as one People.

They have a third sort of Feasts and Dances, which are always when the Harvest of Corn is ended, and in the Spring. The one, to return Thanks to the good Spirit, for the Fruits of the Earth; the other, to beg the same Blessings for the succeeding Year. [. . .]

At these Feasts, which are set out with all the Magnificence their Fare allows of, the Masquerades begin at Night, and not before.

Lawson, *New Voyage to Carolina*, 177, 178.

This Feast was held in Commemoration of the plentiful Harvest of Corn they [the Waxhaw] had reap'd the Summer before, with an united Supplication for the like plentiful Produce the Year ensuing. [. . .]

Now, to return to our State-House, whither we were invited by the Grandees: As soon as we came into it, they plac'd our *Englishmen* near the King; it being my Fortune to sit next him, having his great General, or War-Captain, on my other Hand. The House is as dark as a Dungeon, and as hot as one of the *Dutch*-Stoves in *Holland*. They had made a circular Fire of split Canes in the middle of the House. It was one Man's Employment to add more split Reeds to the one end as it consum'd at the other, there being a small Vacancy left to supply it with Fewel. They brought in great store of Loblolly, and other Medleys, made of *Indian* Grain, stewed Peaches, Bear-Venison, &c. every one bringing some Offering to enlarge the Banquet, according to his Degree and Quality. When all the *Viands* were brought in, the first Figure began with kicking out the Dogs, [. . .]

After the Dogs had fled the Room, the Company was summon'd by Beat of Drum; the Musick being made of a dress'd Deer's Skin, tied hard upon an Earthen Porridge-Pot. Presently in came fine Men dress'd up with Feathers, their Faces being covered with Vizards made of Gourds; round their Ancles and Knees, were hung Bells of several sorts, having Wooden Falchions in their Hands, (such as Stage-Fencers commonly use;) in this Dress they danced about an Hour, shewing many strange Gestures, and brandishing their Wooden Weapons, as if they were going to fight each other; oftentimes walking very nimbly round the Room, without making the least Noise with their Bells, (a thing I much admired at;) again, turning their Bodies, Arms and Legs, into such frightful Postures, that you would have guess'd they had been quite raving mad: At last, they cut two or three high Capers, and left the Room. In their stead, came in a parcel of Women and Girls, to the Number of Thirty odd; every one taking place according to her Degree of Stature, the tallest leading the Dance, and the least of all being plac'd last; with these they made a circular Dance, like a Ring, representing the Shape of the Fire they danced about: Many of these had great Horse-Bells about their Legs, and small Hawk's Bells about their Necks. [. . .]

Their way of Dancing, is nothing but a sort of stamping Motion, much like the treading upon Founders Bellows. This Female-Gang held their Dance for above six Hours, being all of them of a white Lather, like a Running Horse that has just come in from his Race. My Landady was the Ringleader of the *Amazons*, who, when in her own House, behav'd herself very discreetly, and warily, in her Domestick Affairs; yet, Custom had so infatuated her, as to almost break her Heart with Dancing amongst such a confused Rabble. During this Dancing, the Spectators do not neglect their Business, in working the Loblolly-Pots, and the other Meat that was brought thither; more or less of them being continually Eating, whilst the others were Dancing.

Lawson, *New Voyage to Carolina*, 42, 43-45. *Loblolly* was a thick gruel made of Indian corn.

About the close of the evening I accompanied Mr. Galahan and other white traders to the rotunda, where was a grand festival, music and dancing. This assembly was held principally to rehearse the ball-play dance, this town [Cowee] being challenged to play against another the next day.

The people being assembled and seated in order, and the musicians having taken their station, the ball opens, first with a long harangue or oration, spoken by an aged chief, in commendation of the manly exercise of the ball-play, recounting the many and brilliant victories which the town of Cowe had gained over the other towns in the nation, not forgetting or neglecting to recite his own exploits, together with those of other aged men now present, coadjutors in the performance of these athletic games in their youthful days.

This oration was delivered with great spirit and eloquence, and was meant to influence the passions of the young men present, excite them to emulation, and inspire them with ambition.

This prologue being at an end, the musicians began, both vocal and instrumental; when presently a company of girls, hand in hand, dressed in clean white robes and ornamented with beads, bracelets and a profusion of gay ribbands, entering the door, immediately began to sing their responses in a gentle, low, and sweet voice, and formed themselves in a semicircular file or line, in two ranks, back to back, facing the spectators and musicians, moving slowly round and round. This continued about a quarter of an hour, when we were surprised by a sudden very loud and shrill whoop, uttered at once by a company of young fellows, who came in briskly after one another, with rackets or hurls in one hand. These champions likewise were well dressed, painted, and ornamented with silver bracelets, gorgets and wampum, neatly ornamented with moccasins and high waving plumes in their diadems: they immediately formed themselves in a semicircular rank also, in front of the girls, when these changed their order, and formed a single rank parallel to the men, raising their voices in responses to the tunes of the young champions, the semicircles continually moving round. There was something singular and diverting in their step and motions, and I imagine not to be learned to exactness but with great attention and perseverance. The step, if it can be so termed, was performed after the following manner; first, the motion began at one end of the semicircle, gently rising up and down upon their toes and heels alternately, when the first was up on tip-toe, the next began to raise the heel, and by the time the first rested again on the heel, the second was on tip toe, thus from one end of the rank to the other, so that some were always up and some down, alternately and regularly, without the least baulk or confusion; and they at the same time, and in the same motion, moved on obliquely or sideways, so that the circle performed a double or complex motion in its progression, and at stated times exhibited a grand or universal movement, instantly and unexpectedly to the spectators, by each rank turning to right and left, taking each others places: the movements were managed with inconceivable alertness and address, and accompanied with an instantaneous and universal elevation of the voice, and shrill short whoop.

The Cherokees, besides the ball play dance, have a variety of others equally entertaining. The men especially exercise themselves with a variety of gesticulations and capers, some of which are ludicrous and diverting enough; and they have others which are of the martial order, and others of the chace; these seem to be somewhat of a tragical nature, wherein they exhibit astonishing feats of military prowess, masculine strength and activity. Indeed all their dances and musical entertainments seem to be theatrical exhibitions or plays, [. . .]

Bartram, *Travels through North and South Carolina*, 367-369. Cowee ("Cowe") stood at the mouth of Cowee Creek on the Little Tennessee River, approximately three miles north of Whatoga, in present-day Wests Mill, Macon County, North Carolina.

I cannot however conclude [. . .], without a few remarks concerning the Indian methods of *making peace*, and of renewing their old friendship. They first smoke out of the friend-pipe, and eat together; then they drink of the *Cassena*, using such invocations as have been mentioned, and proceed to wave their large fans of eagles-tails,—concluding with a dance. The persons visited, appoint half a dozen of their most active and expert young warriors to perform this religious duty, who have had their own temples adorned with the swan-feather-cap. They paint their bodies with white clay, and cover their heads with swan-down; then approaching the chief representative of the strangers, who by way of honour, and strong assurance of friendship, is seated on the central white or holy seat, "the beloved cabin" (which is about nine feet long and seven feet abroad), they wave the eagles tails backward and forward over his head. Immediately they begin the solemn song with an awful air, and presently they dance in a bowing posture; then they raise themselves so erect, that their faces look partly upwards, waving the eagles tails with their right hand toward heaven, sometimes with a flow, at others with a quick motion; at the same time they touch their breast with their small callabash and pebbles fastened to a stick of about a foot long, which they hold in their left hand, keeping time with the motion of the eagles tails: during the dance, they repeat the usual divine notes, YO, &c. and wave the eagles tails now and then over the stranger's head, not moving above two yards backward or forward before him. They are so surprisingly expert in their supposed religious office, and observe time so exactly, with their particular gestures and notes, that there is not the least discernable discord. [. . .] they had very sweating work, for every joint, artery, and nerve, is stretched to the highest pitch of exertion; [. . .]

Adair, *History of the North-American Indians*, 167-168.

In addition to the friendship ceremony described above, Indians observed other diplomatic rituals. The dignified proceedings of Captain Arthur Barlowe's 1584 audience with Granganimeo on the North Carolina coast rivaled European practice. Wishes and promises were solemnized with offerings of wampum, belts consisting of bits of shells painstakingly rendered into beads. Cherokee and Catawba chiefs exchanged clothing to signify their peaceful intentions. To avoid misunderstandings, Indians of one nation would appoint an ambassador to represent their interests in another.

The next day there came unto us divers boates, and in one of them the Kings brother, accompanied with fortie or fiftie men, very handsome, and goodly people, and in their behaviour as mannerly, and civill, as any of Europe. His name was Granganimeo, and the King is called Wingina, the countrey Wingandacoa, (and nowe by her Majestie, Virginia,) the manner of his comming was in this sorte: hee left his boates altogether, as the first man did a little from the shippes by the shoare, and came along to the place over against the shippes, followed with fortie men. When hee came to the place, his servants spread a long matte uppon the grounde, on which he sate downe, and at the other ende of the matte, foure others of his companie did the like: the rest of his men stoode round about him, somewhat a farre off: when wee came to the shoare to him with our weapons, he never mooved from his place, nor any of the other foure, nor never mistrusted any harme to be offered from us, but sitting still, he beckoned us to come and sitte by him, which we perfourmed: and being sette, hee makes all signes of joy, and welcome, striking on his head, and his breast, and afterwardes on ours, to shewe we were all one, smiling, and making shewe the best hee could, of all love, and familiaritie. After hee had made a long speech unto us, wee presented him with divers thinges, which hee receaved very joyfully, and thankefully. None of his companye durst to speake one worde all the tyme: onely the foure which were at the other ende, spake one in the others eare very softly.

> Arthur Barlowe, "Discourse of the First Voyage" [1584-1585], in Quinn, *Roanoke Voyages*, 1:98-100. Sir Walter Raleigh claimed that *Wingandacoa* did not denote the surrounding area but that "the English wore good clothes"; the Indians themselves referred to the region as *Ossomocomuck*.

Their Money is of different sorts, but all made of Shells, which are found on the Coast of *Carolina*, which are very large and hard, so that they are very difficult to cut. Some *English* Smiths have try'd to drill this sort of Shell-Money, and thereby thought to get an Advantage; but it prov'd so hard, that nothing could be gain'd. They often times make, of this Shell, a sort of Gorge, which they wear about their Neck in a string; so it hangs on their Collar, whereon sometimes is engraven a Cross, or some odd sort of Figure, which comes next in their Fancy. There are other sorts valued at a Doe Skin, yet the Gorges will sometimes sell for three or four Buck-Skins ready drest. There be others, that eight of them go readily for a Doe Skin; but the general and current Species of all the *Indians* in *Carolina*, and, I believe, all over the Continent, as far as the Bay of *Mexico*, is that which we call *Peak*, and *Ronoak*; but *Peak* more especially. This is that which at *New-York*, they call *Wampum*, and have used it as current Money amongst the Inhabitants for a great many Years. This is what many Writers call *Porcelan*, and is made at *New-York* in great Quantities, and with us in some measure. Five Cubits of this purchase a dress'd Doe-Skin, and seven or eight purchase a dress'd Buck Skin. An *English*-man could not afford to make so much of this *Wampum* for five or ten times the Value; for it is made out of a vast great Shell, of which that Country affords Plenty; where it is ground smaller than the small End of a Tobacco-Pipe, or a large Wheat-Straw. Four or five of these make an Inch, and every one is to be drill'd through, and made as smooth as Glass, and so strung, as Beds are, and a Cubit of the *Indian* Measure contains as much in Length, as will reach from the Elbow to the End of the little Finger. They never stand to question, whether it is a tall Man, or a short one, that measures it; but if this *Wampum Peak* be black or purple, as some Part of that Shell is, then it is twice the Value. This the *Indians* grind on Stones and other things, till they make it current, but the Drilling is the most difficult to the *English*-men, which the *Indians* manage with a Nail stuck in a Cane or Reed. Thus they roll it continually on their Thighs, with their Right-hand, holding the Bit of Shell with their Left, so in time they drill a Hole quite through it, which is a very tedious Work; but especially in making their *Ronoak*, four of which will scarce make one Length of *Wampum*. The *Indians* are a People that never value their time, so that they can afford to make them, and never need to fear the *English* will take the Trade out of their Hands. This is the Money with which you may buy Skins, Furs, Slaves, or any thing the *Indians* have; it being the Mammon (as our Money is to us) that entices and persuades them to do any thing, and part with every thing they possess, except their Children for Slaves.

Lawson, *New Voyage to Carolina*, 203-204.

Whereas John Auston A saponia Indian and Harry a susquhanah Indian and Thos A Cattaba Aplied for a pass to the Cattaba Nation being now on their Journey to Conclude a Genl. Peace with the Cattabas in be half of the said Nations and Also presented 3 Belts of Wampum to said Court by which the said Treaty is to be Concluded.

Minutes of the Rowan County Court of Pleas and Quarter Sessions, April 19, 1755, State Archives, Office of Archives and History, Raleigh. The Saponi Indians had settled in

North Carolina at separate times on the Yadkin and Roanoke rivers during the early eighteenth century. By 1755 they and the Susquehanna (Conestoga) Indians lived in the Susquehanna River valley, in present-day Pennsylvania, as tributaries to the Six Nations.

Proceedings of a General Congress of the Six Nations &ca The Chiefs of Coghnawagey and of the Seven Confederate Nations of Canada and the Deputys sent from the Cherokee Nation to treat of Peace with the former before Sir William Johnson Baronet at Johnson Hall in March 1768 [. . .]

Brothers

We now present a Belt from our Women to yours, and we know that they will hear us for it is they who undergo the pains of Childbirth and produce Men, Surely therefore they must feel Mothers pains for those killed in War, and be desirous to prevent it. A Belt

Brothers

Here is a Belt from our Boys to you, who are now but small and therefore their Speech must be Childish, untill they arrive at Manhood, all they desire is that they may be once more enabled to venture out to hunt Birds and Rabbits without the risk of being carried away or killed, and therefore all they beg is peace A Small Belt

> Excerpt, Address from Cherokee Delegation, Proceedings of Sir William Johnson, superintendent of Indian Affairs for the northern department, March 6, 1768, in E. B. O'Callaghan and Berthold Fernow, eds., *Documents Relative to the Colonial History of the State of New York*, 15 vols. (Albany, New York: Weed, Parsons and Company, 1853-1887), 8:38, 43. The Kahnawake or Caughnawaga ("Coghnawagey") Indians were tribesmen of the Iroquois Confederacy who had been converted to Catholicism by French Jesuit priests and relocated to Quebec in the late seventeenth century. The Kahnawakes were later instrumental in the creation of a confederacy centered on seven villages or nations along the St. Lawrence River that included elements of the Abenaki, Algonquian, Nippissing, and Huron Indians. Many Kahnawakes departed Quebec for present-day western Ohio after France's defeat by the British in the French and Indian War in 1763.

Extract of a Letter from Charlestown, S. Carolina, *dated* Sept. 13.

"The Country is at present very sickly, owing to some great Rains which had occasioned Floods in several Places. Three Bodies of Indians, being the Chiefs of three different Nations (*Cherokees, Catawbaes*, and *Creeks*) lately arrived in Town, and made Peace with each other, at the same Time renewing their Alliance with us. Friday and Saturday they were shewn the Armory, the Church, where the Organs play'd, the Forts, where some Shot were fir'd of 24 Pound weight, and whatever else was thought curious to them; and they are now returning to their respective Countries. The Manner of their Meeting to make Peace with each other was somewhat singular, which I shall therefore relate. The Cherokees were arriv'd within a Mile of Town, and the Catawbaes about four Miles, when Messages were sent on both Sides, to signify their Desire of living in Friendship, and renewing their Peace. Their Messengers being returned to their respective Chiefs, both Bodies march'd with the greatest Solemnity, and so slow, that they were three Hours going a Mile and a half each. When they were approached pretty near each other, the principal Man of each Body, stript himself as naked as he was born, went forward, and embraced the other, and after a serious Discourse, standing hand-in-hand each put on the other's Clothes, which was followed by a great Shout from both Nations. Then both Bodies join'd, and march'd in great Order, the Chiefs at their Head, down to the Camp of the Cherokees, where they all din'd; the next Day the Cherokees din'd with the Catawbaes at their Camp."

New-York Gazette, or Weekly Post-Boy, October 16, 1749.

I must not omit Mentioning another custom common to all the Indians, of which, the French availed themselves to great advantage, in Governing the Nations in their Interest. In every Town in the Cherokee Nation, are Beloved men appointed, by the Creeks, Chickasaws, Catawbas, and other Nations with whom they are at Peace. A Deputation sent from any of these Tribes for this purpose, installs some Cherokee of Influence with much Ceremony, and the Appointment is approved of by the Inhabitants. The person so appointed ever after and on all occasions interests himself in the affairs of his constituents; and is looked upon by them as conservator of their rights and protector of their persons.

John Stuart to the Board of Trade, March 9, 1764, in Colonial Office 323/17, British Records, State Archives. The Chickasaws had inhabited present-day northern Mississippi and western Tennessee.

No people in the World understand and pursue their true National Interest, better than the Indians. How sanguinary soever they are towards their Enemies, from a misguided Passion of Heroism, and a love of their country; yet they are otherways truly humane, hospitable, and equitable. And how fraudulent soever they have been reputed, from the Appearance of their military Actions, in which according to their method of War, Glory cannot be accquired without Cunning & Strategem; Yet in their publick Treaties no People on earth are more open, explicit, and Direct. Nor are they excelled by any in the observance of them.

Wilbur R. Jacobs, ed., *Indians of the Southern Colonial Frontier: the Edmond Atkin Report and Plan of 1755* (Columbia: University of South Carolina Press, 1954), 40.

An integral part of diplomacy among Native Americans was the exchange of presents, a gesture which symbolized friendship and equality. They continued the practice when dealing with European visitors—as Arthur Barlowe, one of Walter Raleigh's advance men for the First Colony, discovered. In time, whites adopted a more cynical attitude toward the process, giving presents of better quality to headmen than to warriors in order to curry favor and gain influence. The differentiation was a shock to an egalitarian people; to whites it was tantamount to paying a bribe.

On those Occasions heretofore, according to the practice of the Eastern Nations of the World, there was an Exchange of Presents, (however small on the part of the Indians on Account of their Poverty yet) as expressive of the true footing upon which they met, a mutual Friendship.

Jacobs, *Edmond Atkin Report and Plan of 1755*, 28.

We remained by the side of this Island [Hatteras] two whole daies, before we sawe any people of the Countrey: the third daye we espied one small boate rowing towards us, having in it three persons: this boate came to the landes side, foure harquebushot from our shippes, and there two of the people remaining, the thirde came along the shoare side towards us, and we being then all within boord, he walked up and downe uppon the point of the lande next unto us: then the Master, and the Pilot of the Admirall, Simon Ferdinando, and the Captaine Philip Amadas, my selfe, and others, rowed to the lande, whose comming this fellowe attended, never making any shewe of feare, or doubt. And after he had spoken of many things not under- stoode by us, we brought him with his own good liking, aboord the shippes, and gave him a shirt, a hatte, and some other things, and made him taste of our wine, and our meate, which he liked very well: and after having viewed both barkes, he departed, and went to his owne boate againe, which hee had left in a little Cove, or Creek adioyning: assoone as hee was two bowe shoote into the water, hee fell to fishing, and in lesse then halfe an howre, he had laden his boate as deepe, as it could swimme, with which he came againe to the point of the lande, and there he devided his fishe into two partes, pointing one part to the shippe, and the other to the Pinnesse: which after he had (as much as he might,) requited the former benefits receaved, he departed out of our sight.

Barlowe, "Discourse of the First Voyage," in Quinn, *Roanoke Voyages*, 1:97-98.

Meeting of the King and head men of all the Upper Settlements and of 24 Towns of the Lower Settlemts at Elejoy.

[. . .]

After they gave me the foregoing Answer I returned them thanks for their presents of Skines and Informed them that I did not come among them to receive any presents but to give them the English talk for their good, and to keep the Traders among them in good Order. They answered That it was their thougts that I should take the Skines because that when any of their head men go down to the English they always have presents made them and that now they have a beloved Man of the English among them, its good to make presents to him and to treat him as well as they can. [. . .] As for the Skines which the Indians were pleased to make me a present of (and which I could not refuse without Affronting them) I know not how to gett them down without I have horses sent for them, Your Honour being well Acquainted with the bulk of an Indians Present of Skines.

> "Journal of Colonel George Chicken," August 21, 1725, in Mereness, *Travels in the American Colonies*, 126, 130, 139. Colonel Chicken and the Cherokee headmen met in the town of Ellijay ("Elejoy") on Ellijay Creek in present-day Macon County, North Carolina.

The Friendship of this Nation [Cherokee] is so very advantageous to the French that they will spare no Cost whatever to carry their Point, and I think that [it's] equally as advantageous to us. Indians are a Comodity that are to be bought and sold, and the French will bid very high for them. And on this particular Occasion if we don't bid as high we shall [absolutely] lose them, for Indians are but Indians and are but very little to be depended on; the highest Bidder carries them off.

> Captain Raymond Demere to Governor William Henry Lyttelton of South Carolina, November 18, 1756, in McDowell, *Documents Relating to Indian Affairs, 1754-1765*, 248, 249.

Gift-giving became a financial burden that the colonies attempted to limit. To use those funds more effectively, they began issuing commissions that entitled certain headmen to largess and a level of access to colonial officials not enjoyed by others. The process imposed an artificial hierarchy and forced the members of a nation to send delegates designated by whites, instead of people having been chosen by themselves, to treat with government representatives.

I received last month a visit from King Pow of the Catawba Nation who came with three of his Chiefs under the usual pretext of respect and amity to furnish themselves with conveniences and luxuries, which they beg with no very scrupulous delicacy.

> Governor Josiah Martin of North Carolina to earl of Hillsborough, December 12, 1771, in William L. Saunders ed., *The Colonial Records of North Carolina*, 10 vols. (Raleigh: State of North Carolina, 1886-1890), 9:66, 69.

The making Medal Chiefs will introduce subordination among the Indians. The great Chiefs will depend on us for their power and influence, while Commissions of any inferior nature to which certain degrees of preeminence and profit should be annexed are to be hence forward given According to the recommendation of the great Medal Chiefs whose power and Consequence must thereby be increased and the people from Motives of interest become dependant on them which cannot fail of Rendering the Government of Indians more practicable.

John Stuart to Lieutenant Governor William Bull, August 10, 1765, in Colonial Office 323/23, British Records, State Archives, Office of Archives and History, Raleigh.

23 November, 1751
In the Council Chamber

Present: His Excellency &c.

The following Articles were then advised to be given by his Excellency to the Cherokee Nation:

Eufassee

For the Raven a scarlet Coat, Wastcoat and Breches, ruffled Shirt, gold-laced Hat, Shoes, Buckles, Buttons, Stockins and Gartring, Saddle, one of the best Guns, Cutlass, a Blanket and Knife, a Peice of Stroud, 5 Yards of Callico, ten Yards of Em[bossed] Serge.

For the Raven's Son, Moitoy, one of the best Coats out of the Publick Store, a white Shirt, a Gun, Flag, Shoes and Stockins, Buckles and Garters, a laced Hat and 5 Yards of em[bossed] Serge and a Commission.

For Tossetee, a Notchee of the said Town, the same as the Raven's Son except the Serge.

[. . .]

Tukaseegee

For Chucheechee, the same as the Raven's Son, with a Commission

Stekoe

For Tosetee the same as the Raven's Son except Serge and Commission

[. . .]

For the remaining 19 Chiefs of an inferior Rank, a Coat, Gun, Shirt, Flax, Hat, Boots each.

Sixty-four Guns and sixty-four Hatchets be distributed by the Head Men of the Cherokees think proper and a Shirt, Hat and Boots to each of the 128 Men.

For each of the Women now in Town 5 Yards of embossed Serge, some Beads, Needles, Thread, Ear Bobs, Cadiz, Gartering, Ribons, Scisors, Pea Buttons, Ivory Combs and Trunks.

To each of the Indians a Blanket and Knife, and some Pipes and Tobaco to be divided, 12 brass and 12 fine Kettles, 24 Pots, 24 looking Glasses, 5 Pounds Wire, 48 Steels.

To be sent up to the Nation 400 Weight Powder, 800 Bullets, 2,000 Flints, 10 Pounds Vermilion, one gross Brass Nailes.

Memorandum: Tassetee of Stekoe desires a new Saddle, what he has being broken and unfit for use.

Minutes of the South Carolina Council, November 23, 1751, in William L. McDowell Jr., ed., *Documents Relating to Indian Affairs, 1750-1754*, in *The Colonial Records of South Carolina, Series 2* (Columbia: South Carolina Archives Department, 1958), 161-162. "Eufassee" was Hiwassee. The Cherokees had two towns named Hiwassee: Little Hiwassee, at the confluence of Peachtree Creek and Hiwassee River in present-day Cherokee County, North Carolina; and Great Hiwassee, located further downstream on the Hiwassee River, approximately two miles south of present-day Delano, Polk County, Tennessee. Raven, Moitoy, and Tossetee lived in Little Hiwassee. Tossetee was a Natchez ("Notchee") Indian: a portion of the Natchez tribe, from what is now Natchez, Mississippi, had settled among the Cherokees after their defeat by the French and Choctaws in 1730. Tuckasegee stood on the Tuckasegee River near present-day Webster, Jackson County, North Carolina. "Stekoe" refers to one of three Cherokee towns called Stecoe: one on Stekoa Creek, near present-day Clayton, Rabun County, Georgia; a second on the Tuckasegee River near present-day Whittier, Jackson County, North Carolina; and a third on Stecoah Creek at present-day Stecoah, Graham County, North Carolina.

James Bullen, a half Breed, showed me a Commission sent to him by the Governor of North Carolina of which I have a Copy.

Entry of October 20, 1755, "Journal of John Evans," in McDowell, *Documents Relating to Indian Affairs, 1754-1765*, 86.

I would be glad that you would renew the Indian Commissions which I conveyed to you, and send them, with the Medals, by the first opportunity, as they are at present much wanted to be given, as a Memorial of our Friendship towards the Cherokees, which the Creeks endeavour to depreciate, as much as possible. One dozen Medals is the least that is necessary for them, and if you think proper to be distributed as follows, to *Ouonnastotah*, *Kittagusta*, *Attacullahcullah*, *Willinnawah*, *Otassatch*, of the Overhills: *Moitoy* of the Valley, the *Mankiller* of Nuccassie, who now lives in little Choteh, to the Southward of the Valley: *Tiftoe*, *Ecuy*, Saluy, and the Wolf lower Towns, and Tooguloo.

Alexander Cameron, commissary to the Cherokees, to John Stuart, May 10, 1766, in Colonial Office 5/66, British Records, State Archives, Office of Archives and History, Raleigh. Little Chota stood in the Nacoochee Valley in present-day White County, Georgia. Tugaloo was located approximately six miles east of present-day Toccoa, Georgia: today it lies underneath the waters of Hartwell Lake.

Religion

It is difficult to give a precise portrayal of Native American religion in early North Carolina. As with their other traditions, Indians rarely codified their religious beliefs and practices and were not always forthcoming when asked by curious whites. It is clear, however, that they thought the spirit and temporal worlds were intricately intertwined. Several Indian priests informed Thomas Hariot that they believed that God had created numerous minor deities to facilitate the creation and maintenance of the world; their gods took human form; woman was made before man; and there was an afterlife. According to John Lawson, the Indians of eastern North Carolina were ruled by a good spirit and an evil spirit. The Cherokees, wrote trader Alexander Longe in 1725, were governed by a supreme being whose will was carried out by messengers controlling the four winds—all of which had to be appeased for life on Earth to remain in balance.

They beleeve that there are many Gods which they call *Montóac*, but of different sortes and degrees; one onely chiefe and great God, which hath bene from all eternitie. Who as they affirme when hee purposed to make the worlde, made first other goddes of a principall order to bee as meanes and instruments to be used in the creation and government to follow; and after the Sunne, Moone, and Starres as pettie gods, and the instruments of the other order more principall. First they say were made waters, out of which by the gods was made all diversitie of creatures that are visible or invisible.

For mankinde they say a woman was made first, which by the working of one of the goddes, conceived and brought foorth children: And in such sort they say they had their beginning. But how many yeeres or ages have passed since, they say they can make no relation, having no letters nor other such meanes as we to keepe recordes of the particularities of times past, but onely tradition from father to sonne.

They thinke that all the gods are of humane shape, & therefore they represent them by images in the formes of men, which they call *Kewasówak* one alone is called *Kewás*; them they place in houses appropriate or temples, which they call *Machicómuck*; Where they worship, praie, sing, and make manie times offerings unto them. In some *Machicómuck*, we have seene but on *Kewás*, in some two, and in other some three; The common sort thinke them to be also gods.

They beleeve also the immortalitie of the soule, that after this life as soone as the soule is departed from the bodie, according to the workes it hath done, it is eyther carried to heaven the habitacle of gods, there to enjoy perpetuall blisse and happinesse, or els to a great pitte or hole, which they thinke to bee in the furthest partes of their part of the worlde toward the sunne set, there to burne continually: the place they call *Popogusso*.

For the confirmation of this opinion, they tolde mee two stories of two men that had been lately dead and revived againe, the one happened but few yeres before our comming into the countrey of a wicked man which having beene dead and buried, the next day the earth of the grave being seene to move, was taken up againe; Who made declaration where his soule had beene, that is to saie, very neere entring into *Popogusso*, had not one of the gods saved him and gave him leave to returne againe, and teach his friends what they should doe to avoid that terrible place or torment.

The other happened in the same yeere wee were there, but in a towne that was three score miles from us, and it was tolde mee for straunge newes that one beeing dead, buried and taken up againe as the first, shewed that although his bodie had lien dead in the grave, yet his soule was alive, & had travailed farre in a long broade waie, on both sides whereof grewe most delicate and pleasaunt trees, bearing more rare and excellent fruites, then ever hee had seene before or was able to expresse, and at length came to most brave and faire houses, neere which hee met his father, that had beene dead before, who gave him great charge to goe backe againe and shew his friendes what good they were to doe to enjoy the pleasures of that place, which when he had done he should after come againe.

What subtilty soever be in the *Wiroances* and Priestes, this opinion worketh so much in manie of the common and simple sort of people that it maketh them have great respect to their Governours, and also great care what they do, to avoid torment after death, and to enjoy blisse; although notwithstanding there is punishment ordained for malefactours, as stealers, whoremongers, and other sortes of wicked doers; some punished with death, some with forfeitures, some with beating, according to the greatnes of the factes.

And this is the summe of their religion, which I learned by having special familiarity with some of their priestes. Wherein they were not so sure grounded, nor gave such credite to their traditions and stories, but through conversing with us they were brought into great doubts of their owne, and no small admiration of ours, with earnest desire in many, to learne more then we had meanes for want of perfect utterance in their language to expresse.

Thomas Hariot, "A briefe and true report of the new found land of Virginia . . . ," February 1588, in David B. Quinn, ed., *The Roanoke Voyages, 1584-1590*, 2 vols. (London: For the Hakluyt Society, 1955), 1:372-375.

Many other Customs they have, for which they will render no Reason or Account; and to pretend to give a true Description of their Religion; it is impossible; for there are a great many of their Absurdities, which, for some

Reason, they reserve as a Secret amongst themselves; or otherwise, they are jealous of their Weakness in the practising them; so that they never acquaint any Christian with the Knowledge thereof, let Writers pretend what they will; for I have known them amongst their Idols and dead Kings in their *Quiogozon* for several Days, where I could never get Admittance, to see what they were doing, though I was at great Friendship with the King and great Men; but all my Persuasions avail'd me nothing. Neither were any but the King, with the Conjurer, and some few old Men, in that House; as for the young Men, and chiefest Numbers of the *Indians*, they were kept as ignorant of what the Elders were doing, as myself.

They all believe, that this World is round, and that there are two Spirits; the one good, the other bad: The good one they reckon to be the Author and Maker of every thing, and say, that it is he, that gives them the Fruits of the Earth, and has taught them to hunt, fish, and be wise enough to overpower the Beasts of the Wilderness, and all other Creatures, that they may be assistant, and beneficial to Man; to which they add, that the *Quera*, or good Spirit, has been very kind to the *English* Men, to teach them to make Guns, and Ammunition, besides a great many other Necessaries, that are helpful to Man, all which, they say, will be deliver'd to them, when that good Spirit sees fit. They do not believe, that God punishes any Man either in this Life, or that to come; but that he delights in doing good, and in giving the Fruits of the Earth, and instructing us in making several useful and ornamental things. They say, it is a bad Spirit (who lives separate from the good one) that torments us with Sicknesses, Disappointments, Losses, Hunger, Travel, and all the Misfortunes, that Humane Life is incident to.

John Lawson, *A New Voyage to Carolina*, ed. by Hugh T. Lefler (Chapel Hill: University of North Carolina Press, 1967), 219-220. The *Quiogozon* was the "Royal Tomb or Burial-Place of their Kings and War-Captains" (see below).

Thire opoinon of the devine poure, they owne on sopreame power that is above the fermement and that poure they say was he that mead the heavens and the Erth and all things that is therein and Governs all acourding to his will and pleshers. this grate king as the[y] Call him has 4 meshengers that he has placed in the 4 winds Est west north and south these 4 meshengers are alwise there to atend the 4 Seasons of the yeare which we call the 4 quarters of the yeare and to mind the mouving of the sone and mone and stares moreover they are obleged to keep strick wach over the winds that they shall nott pas such and such bounds as they apoynte them leastt they should meate all foure together one the Erth and strive for victorie and blow down and overthrow the Erth and blow all the Inhabitants thereof away they are continialy in action day and night and Every seson they have the grate talks given them from the grate Empoerrore what they shall doe and acte for that Seson likewise with the

Rest I myselfe have seen them. When there has aney deare killed for the town that meate is killed by orders of the pristt and brought up to the high place where thire temple is bulded quire Round with and is suported with grate pilers of wood and a Round harth in the middle of the house the fire never goes out. this deare flesh is never Eate by aney body till the priste Cutts a peace of itt and throws itt in the midst of the fire and when Soe done he cuts 4 other peacess and throws one north the other South the other Est and the other west when soe done they teakes all the Rest of the meate and meakes itt pass thrue the fleme of the fire and then gives itt to the woemen to dress for the pristt and all others that pleases to Eate of itt [.]

All this I see acted before me in their temple and by the prest which mead mee sensible of thire douctrin of which Ile give a verrie feaire and plaine account. I aksed the prest whie or forfore he burned that peace of meate in the fire he tould me that itt was to the grate king above and that itt was burnt in honor and obbidionce to him being supreme lord and Emperore of all things veseble and oneveseble. I asked him againe for what Reson Doe yow throw meate towards the 4 winds he tould me that he never ofered them aney ofering mead by fire but onely geave itt to them Raw. I asked him againe whie he gave them aney att all. because said he they have the charge of the 4 winds. and he that is In the north was give him meate because he Should nott lett the north wind Rine to longe to distroy us with could. he is a black god colered like the negro and he is verrie cross and we are forst to give him meate to keep foure squaer with him that he should nott sterve us all with Could. that in the Est is the couler of us Indians and hee is something beter then the other we give him meate because he should nott send strong Est winds and over sett all our Coren when a toseling or in the Eare. and he that is in the south is a verrie good one and white as yow Inglish are, and soe mild that we love him out of meshor and gives him meate and Wise as much as all the others he sends us good wether and soe mild that itt Causes all things to grow apase Apeace he is good all over and is verrie much Respected by the Grate king above [. . .] but yow have forgott to tell me about that in the west true said he but Ile Explain that meshenger to yow, he is of the Colour of the spanards and is prite good and assistent to the meshenger of the south and sometimes they mix winds Together and Causes Raine to come and water our Cropes but itt is by the ordenation of that god in the south that has The Rule over him [. . .]

Alexander Longe, "A Small Postscript on the Ways and Manners of the Indians called Cherokees," ed. by David H. Corkran, *Southern Indian Studies* 21 (October 1969): 11, 13.

Baron Christopher De Graffenried, who founded New Bern in 1710, described an altar and its use. When one of its wooden totems was defaced by a settler, the baron attempted to placate a distraught headman.

I also noticed among the Indians who dwell at the place where I settled and started the building of New-Bern, another kind of rites which come nearer to the christian divine worship. They had there a kind of altar, cunningly interwoven with small sticks, and vaulted like a dome. In one place was an opening, like a small door or wicket, through which they put their offerings. In the midst of this heathenish chapel was a concavity where they sacrificed beans, corals, and also Wampons. Facing the rising sun, was planted in the ground a wooden post, with a carved head, painted half red and half white. In front of it stood a big stick with a small crown at its end, wrapped up in red and white; on the other side, which looks towards the setting sun, was another image, with a horrid face painted in black and red. By the first, they mean some god, and by the other the Demon, which they know far better.

I cannot but relate here, to amuse the reader, what happened to one of my tenants, a tall, strong, well-built fellow: passing near by these idols, he examined them, and knew at once the difference between the good god, and the one which represented the devil. The latter being painted in *red* and *black*, which happen precisely to be the colours of the Bernese flag and arms, he became so angry about it, that he split in two, with his axe, the Devil's statue. When he came home, he boasted about it, as if it had been an heroic feat, saying that he had split the devil in two with one stroke. Though I could not help smiling, I could not approve his action. Soon after, the Indian King came, exasperated at this sacrilege, and complained loudly. I first told him, in a jocose way, that it was only the wicked Idol, that there was not much harm done, but that if he had cut the good Idol to pieces, I should have rigorously chastised him, and that, in the future, orders would be given in order that no such thing could happen any more.

Although the Indian King saw well that I spoke of the all thing as a joke, he did not like it much, but looked very serious. I accordingly told him, quite as seriously, that that man's action did not please me at all, —and that, if he could show me the one who had committed such a scandalous offence, he should be rigorously punished. To appease a little those Indians, I treated the King and his retinue to some *rum*, a liquor distillated from sugar-dregs, and a very healthy beverage, when taken moderately. My courtesy put them in a more serene mood, and they left my home quite satisfied.

"De Graffenried's Manuscript," in William L. Saunders, ed., *The Colonial Records of North Carolina*, 10 vols. (Raleigh: State of North Carolina, 1886-1890), 1:981-982.

Most Native Americans were animists, believing that everything—soil, rocks, vegetation, insects, animals, the weather, and people—possessed a spirit; and that the universal energy they shared enabled them to communicate with each other in the spirit as well as temporal worlds. The universe consisted of three planes: the Upper World, the Terrestrial World, and the Lower World. The Upper World embodied order and purity; the Lower World was characterized by disorder and chaos; the Terrestrial World represented a balance between the two. When they remained distinct, harmony ensued. But whenever those planes mixed in conflicting combinations, chaos—in the form of disease, famine, death, and the like—erupted. Indians often became fearful whenever those worlds collided. For example, fire, a close ally of the sun, represented the Upper World. The Cherokees corrected Alexander Longe when he lit his pipe with the sacred fire, tended by priests inside the council house, and then attempted to leave the building. Trader James Adair's hosts were aghast when he extinguished a cooking fire (Upper World) with water (Lower World), instead of using dirt (Terrestrial World).

They will neaver sufer aney fire to be karid out of the Temple by noe means. I have light my pipe at the fire As I have been goeing home the prist has given orders To teake the pipe out of my mouth and bett out the fire And delivered me the pipe againe and prayed me nott to be Angray for they dreaded letting the fire that belonged to the temple [. . .] to be karid abrod like common fire And that the Grat god did nott permite to karrie aney thing That was sett aparte for him abrod and to be mixed with Comon fire. they are so Exact in thire laws that they Will nott sufer the ashes thats teaken of the alter to be karid out of the Temple onely once a yeare and then the prest ofers meate oferings mead by fire and those that is apoynted to karrie out the Ashes must fastt [. . .] and Drink fisicke Two dayes and there is a place apoynted Close by the Temple to put these ashes. the place is called Skeona being Interpreted the Spirite or place of sparits There will noebody young or ould aproch that place but them that are apoynted to goe there if the Childrin Goes there as they doe sometimes the prist sends for Them and has them Scratcht al over thire bodys there is noe such thing as Remeshon for them the law must be fulfilled there is noe goeing back. itt is to noe purpose to strive to seave them from the ponishment that the prist has perposed to give them. [. . .]

Longe, "Ways and Manners of the Indians called Cherokees," 37.

[. . .] and they reckon it unlawful, and productive of many temporal evils, to extinguish even the culinary fire with water. In the time of a storm, when I have done it, the kindly women were in pain for me, through fear of the ill consequences attending so criminal an act.

James Adair, *A History of the North-American Indians, Particularly Those Nations Adjoining to the Missisippi* [sic] *East and West Florida, Georgia, South and North Carolina and Virginia* (1775; reprint, Ann Arbor, Michigan: UMI Books on Demand, 2002), 405.

Creatures that possessed features from multiple worlds held great power. One of them was the *uktena*, a mythical snake (Lower World) with a crystal (Upper World) in its forehead.

Between the heads of the northern branch of the lower Cheerake river, and the heads of that of Tuckasehchee, winding round in a long course by the late Fort-Loudon, and afterwards into the Missisippi, there is, both in the nature and circumstances, a great phenomenon—Between two high mountains, nearly covered with old mossy rocks, lofty cedars, and pines, in the valleys of which the beams of the sun reflect a powerful heat, there are, as the natives affirm, some bright old inhabitants, or rattle snakes, of a more enormous size than is mentioned in history. They are so large and unwieldy, that they take a circle, almost as wide as their length, to crawl round in their shortest orbit: but bountiful nature compensates the heavy motion of their bodies, for as they say, no living creature moves within the reach of their sight, but they can draw it to them; which is agreeable to what we observe, through the whole system of animated beings. Nature endues them with proper capacities to sustain life;— as they cannot support themselves, by their speed, or cunning to spring from an ambuscade, it is needful they should have the bewitching craft of their eyes and forked tongues.

The description the Indians give us of their colour, is as various as what we are told of the camelion, that seems to the spectator to change its colour, by every different position he may view it in; which proceeds from the piercing rays of light that blaze from their foreheads, so as to dazzle the eyes, from whatever quarter they post themselves – for in each of their heads, there is a large carbuncle, which not only repels, but they affirm, sullies the meridian beams of the sun. They reckon it so dangerous to disturb those creatures, that no temptation can induce them to betray their secret recess to the prophane. They call them and all of the rattle-snake kind, kings, or chieftains of the snakes; and they allow one such to every different species of the brute creation. An old trader at Cheeowhee told me, that for the reward of two pieces of stroud-cloth, he engaged a couple of young warriors to shew him the place of their resort; but the head-men would not by any means allow it, on account of a superstitious tradition—for they fancy the killing of them would expose them to the danger of being bit by the other inferior species of that serpentine tribe, who love their chieftains, and know by instinct those who maliciously killed them, as they fight only in their own defence, and that of their young ones, never biting those who do not disturb them. Although they esteem those rattle snakes as chieftains of that species, yet they do not deify them [. . .]

> Adair, *History of the North-American Indians*, 237-238. A *carbuncle* was a ruby, garnet, or other precious red stone. The "Cheerake river" was the Tennessee River. Fort Loudoun stood on the south bank of the Little Tennessee River adjacent to the Overhill Cherokee town of Tuskegee, approximately three miles east of present-day Vonore, Tennessee. Constructed in 1757 by the colony of South Carolina, the fort was seized by the Cherokees during the Cherokee War in 1760 and later burned. Tellico Lake now covers the site of Tuskegee. Cheoah ("Cheeowhee") was located near Sweetwater Creek at Cheoah, Graham County, North Carolina.

Indian mothers reared their children on the skins of certain animals so they would absorb the characteristics of those animals. Blood was never ingested.

[. . .] Their male children they chuse to raise on the skins of panthers, on account of the communicative principle, which they reckon all nature is possest of, in conveying qualities according to the regimen that is followed: and, as the panther is endued with many qualities, beyond any of his fellow animals in the American woods, as smelling, strength, cunning, and a prodigious spring, they reckon such a bed is the first rudiments of war. But it is worthy of notice, they change the regimen in nurturing their young females; these they lay on the skins of fawns, or buffalo calves, because they are shy and timorous [. . . .]

> Adair, *History of the North-American Indians*, 420-421.

The Indians through a strong principle of religion, abstain in the strictest manner, from eating the Blood of any animal; as it contains the life, and spirit of the beast, [. . .]

> Adair, *History of the North-American Indians*, 134.

The green corn ceremony was an important annual festival observed by many Eastern tribes. The late-summer celebration marked the harvesting of the corn crop by giving, as Lawson observed, "Thanks to the good Spirit, for the Fruits of the Earth." It also was a time for Indians to purify themselves, forgive others, and clean their dwellings and the town house. New fires were lit and any old food left in storage was discarded. Longe described the conjuror's ("priest's") role in the Cherokee version of the ceremony.

They are so strick and Exact in that feast that from the time that the coren is in the Eare they are alwise a preching To the people about itt and telling them that they must nott polute themselves by Eateing of the first fruts before they have brought the first partt of itt to the high place and give itt to the prest that he may ofer itt to the most high god and Return him thanks for giveing itt.

[Quoting the priest: "] [. . .] yow women Restraine yor Chilldrin from sucking the green Coren stalks or form eateing aneything of the frute if they by Chance or yow hapen to see them tuch itt yow shall bring them up to the high place and have them scrached all over thire bodies with garefish teeth and if one of yor sucking Chilldrin Chance to Chaw thereof yow Shall bring them allsoe that they may Receive punishment Alsoe teak Care that yow doe nott polute the feast nor yr Selves. [. . .] I command yow that 4 dayes before the buske that yow keep yrselves from wemen and all that 4 dayes yow shall prepare and purge yr selves with fisick and by often washing yr selves in the water yr fisick shall be quall Eaque which is ye grate snake Roote and one the fift day yow shall Eate of the feast when permited Soe to Doe by the prist but teake care that yow Remember this[."]

Thisnow to give you furder insight in this feast of the first fruts the prist fasts 4 dayes without Eateing any thing seave drinking Rutes fisiks. and Every day after sone Down he drinks a letell of the thin grate homonie. and the Last day of his fasting he teakes noethin at all. all the ould senatturs dus the same. I asked him what was the Reson whie they did soe the ould pristould me that They fasted for the grate king of haven. and to purge out the ould Coren before that they Eate the new. [. . .] when the 4 dayes of fasting is ended the women that night they Are all hands prepareing the feast dressing vitols of all sorts of the first frutess. beaked boyled and Rosted the had warers goeing All night from house to house. and telling the woemen to teake Speashell Care that they doe nott Eate nor sofer thire Chilldrin to tuch thereof . before itt is blessed by the prest in the morning by sone Rising the women comes up to the high place with the vitolls that they have dressed and setts itt down before the preste The ould priste sitts as modest and lokes as serrious as a Judge till all is Come into the house. then he Rises up with a white wing in his hand and Comands silence which is emediatly obayed. then he goes to Every sorte of vitells and teakes a letell out of Every sorte and puts it in a new Erthen pan pinted all over Reed. when soe don he goes toward the fire with the pan in his hand and the white wing in his Right hand and there stands and talks in a lingoe or gibrige that none Can onderstand but himselfe for the space of one oure till the swett Rones down of him like water and now and then houlding up his hand towards heaven and when Ended he throws the vitells unto the fire and stands there till itt is all brned to a cole and ends Ends.

Longe, "Ways and Manners of the Indians called Cherokees," 15, 17, 21, 23.

Because of their ability to communicate with the spirits, conjurers, or medicine men, held great sway. They were responsible for the good health of their people and officiated over religious ceremonies. Preventing disaster was another specialty, as Alexander Cameron attests.

Their Priests are the Conjurors and Doctors of the Nation.

Lawson, *New Voyage to Carolina*, 220.

[. . .] I Sett out for highwassie on the 28 Ult. and Arrived at Tellico, The warriors of that Town told me the path was very Dangerous, for the Enemy; but if I was Determined to go, that they would Order the Conjurer to Work; I thanked them, and told them (for fear of giving offence) that it was very good; The Conjurer was at it all night, and Next Morning My Landlord came in, and very Chearfully told me, that the wise Man had Conjured very strong and that I should go and Come without being Troubled.

Alexander Cameron, commissary to the Cherokees, to John Stuart, superintendent of Indian Affairs for the southern district, June 6, 1765, in Colonial Office 323/23, British Records, State Archives, Office of Archives and History, Raleigh.

Native American medicine was holistic. Treatment included specific remedies for the physical manifestation of an illness or injury and its spiritual causes. John Lawson described several healing methods that he witnessed among coastal tribes. James Adair held Indian medicine men in such high esteem that he preferred their therapeutic techniques over any other.

I will therefore begin with their Physick and Surgery, which is next: You must know, that the Doctors or Conjurers, to gain a greater Credit amongst these People, tell them, that all Distempers are the Effects of evil Spirits, or the bad Spirit, which has struck them with this or that Malady; therefore, none of these Physicians undertakes any Distemper, but that he comes to an Exorcism, to effect the Cure, and acquaints the sick Party's Friends, that he must converse with the good Spirit, to know whether the Patient will recover or not; if so, then he will drive out the bad Spirit, and the Patient will become well. Now, the general way of their Behaviour in curing the Sick, (a great deal of which I have seen, and shall give some Account thereof, in as brief a manner as possible) is, when an *Indian* is sick, if they think there is much Danger of Life, and that he is a great Man or hath good Friends, the Doctor is sent for. As soon as the Doctor comes into the Cabin, the sick Person is sat on a Mat or Skin, stark-naked, lying on his Back, [. . .] In this manner, the Patient lies, when the Conjurer appears; and the King of that Nation comes to attend him with a Rattle made of a Gourd with Pease in it. This the King delivers into the Doctor's Hand, whilst another brings a Bowl of Water, and sets it down: Then the Doctor begins, and utters some few Words very softly; afterwards he smells of the Patient's Navel and Belly, and sometimes scarifies him a little with a Flint, or an Instrument made of Rattle-Snakes Teeth for that purpose; then he sucks the Patient, and gets out a Mouthful of Blood and *Serum*, but *Serum* chiefly; which, perhaps, may be a better Method in many Cases, than to take away great Quantities of Blood, as is commonly practis'd; which he spits in the Bowl of Water. Then he begins to mutter, and talk apace, and, at last, to cut Capers, and clap his Hands on his Breech and Sides, till he gets into a Sweat, so that a Stranger would think he was running mad; now and then sucking the Patient, and so, at times, keeps sucking till he has got a great Quantity of very ill-coloured Matter out of the Belly, Arms, Breast, Forehead, Temples, Neck, and most Parts, still continuing his Grimaces, and antick Postures, which are not to be match'd in *Bedlam*. At last, you will see the Doctor all over of a dropping Sweat, and scarce able to utter one Word, having quite spent himself; then he will cease for a while, and so begin again, till he comes in the same Pitch or Raving and seeming Madness, as before, (all this time the sick Body never so much as moves, although, doubtless, the Lancing and Sucking must be a great Punishment to them; but they, certainly, are the patientest and most steady People under any Burden, that I ever saw in my Life.) At last, the Conjurer makes an end, and tells the Patient's Friends, whether the Person will live or die; and then one that waits at this Ceremony, takes the Blood away, (which remains in a Lump, in the middle of the Water) and buries it in the Ground, in a Place unknown to any one, but he that inters it. Now, I believe a great deal of Imposture in these Fellows; yet I never knew their Judgment fail, though I have seen them give their Opinion after this Manner, several times: Some affirm, that there is a smell of Brimstone in the Cabins, when they are Conjuring, which I cannot contradict. Which way it may come, I will not argue, but proceed to a Relation or two, which I have from a great many Persons, and some of them worthy of Credit.

Lawson, *New Voyage to Carolina*, 222-223.

The Bark of the Root of the Sassafras-Tree, I have observ'd, is much used by them. They generally torrefy it in the Embers, so strip off the Bark from the Root, beating it to a Consistence fit to spread, so lay it on the griev'd Part; which both cleanses a fowl Ulcer; and after Scarrification, being apply'd to a Contusion, or Swelling, draws forth the Pain, and reduces the Part to its pristine State of Health, as I have often seen effected.

Lawson, *New Voyage to Carolina*, 230.

[. . .] the Cheerake [. . .] as well as the other Indian nations, have a great knowledge of specific virtues in simples; applying herbs and plants, on the most dangerous occasions, and seldom if ever, fail to effect a thorough cure, from the natural bush. In the order of nature, every country and climate is blest with specific remedies for the maladies that are connatural to it—Naturalists tell us they have observed, that when the wild goat's sight begins to decay, he rubs his head against a thorn, and by some effluvia, or virtue in the vegetable, the sight is renewed. Thus the snake recovers after biting any creature, by his knowledge of the proper antidote; and many of our arts and forms of living, are imitated by lower ranks of the animal creation: the Indians, instigated by nature, and quickened by experience, have discovered the peculiar properties of vegetables, as far as needful in their situation of life. For my own part, I would prefer an old Indian before any chirugeon whatsoever, in curing green wounds by bullets, arrows, &c. both for the certainty, ease, and speediness of cure; for if those parts of the body are not hurt, which are essential to the preservation of life, they cure the wounded in a trice. They bring the patient into a good temperament of body, by a decoction of proper herbs and roots, and always enjoin a most abstemious life: they forbid them women, salt, and every kind of flesh-meat, applying mountain allum, as the chief ingredient. [. . .]

I do not remember to have seen or heard of an Indian dying by the bite of a snake, when out at war, or a hunting; although they are then often bitten by the most dangerous snakes—every one carries in his shot-pouch, a piece of the best snake-root, such as the *Seneeka*, or fern-snake-root,—or the wild hore-hound, wild plantain, St. Andrew's cross, and a variety of other herbs and roots, which are plenty, and well known to those who range the American woods, and are exposed to such dangers, and will effect a thorough and speedy cure if timely applied. When an Indian perceives he is struck by a snake, he immediately chews some of the root, and having swallowed a sufficient quantity of it, he applies some to the wound; which he repeats as occasion requires, and in proportion to the poison the snake has infused into the wound. For a short space of time, there is a terrible conflict through all the body, by the jarring qualities of the burning poison, and the strong antidote; but the poison is soon repelled through the same channels it entered, and the patient is cured.

Adair, *History of the North-American Indians*, 234, 235-236.

A clean body ensured spiritual purity. Spiritual purity led to good health, prevented adversity, and allowed humans to draw upon other-worldly powers. Methods of internal and external purification included sequestration, bathing, sweating, and the use of purgatives.

Cherokee warriors returning from hunts or military campaigns, and a Cherokee female who came into contact with an enemy, were required to temporarily isolate themselves. An Indian could be punished with dry-scratching if he or she abstained from bathing.

But when they have prospered at war and has: killed aney of thire enemies. They that has killed or tuched aney bodie or dead Corps of the Enemies they reckon Themselves polluted and all thire war Instruments and Close they come to the place apoynted hard by the town and there they stay 4 dayes to purefie themselves the ware king stayes with them and sees that they doe what is ordred in thire law [. . .] the maner that they purefie themselves is one this wayes they sit them down by the war fire and Drinks fisike for 4 days the 4th day at night after the sone down they wash thire Close and bodies in the water and Causes all thire arems to pass threw the flame of the faire if they have aney slaves they purrifie Them as they doe themselves [. . .]

Longe, "Ways and Manners of the Indians called Cherokees," 45, 47.

[. . .] here I Likewise Visited my old Consort the Queen, who acording to the Indian Custom, was obliged to undergoe Eight days Confinement in the Town house, after Returning from, or being a Prisoner to any Enimy whatsoever, and after that to be strip'd, dip'd, well wash'd, and so Conducted home to their Husband, wife, or friends.

William L. Anderson, ed., "Cherokee Clay, from Duché to Wedgwood: The Journal of Thomas Griffiths, 1767-1768," *North Carolina Historical Review* 63 (October 1986): 504.

The first and principal Exercise of the Indians is bathing and swiming, in which they are very dextrous. Every Morning, immediately after rising, both in Summer and N.B. in Winter, coming out of their hot Houses, they take their Babes under their Arms, and lead their Children to the Rivers, in which they enter be it ever so cold. The Mothers learn their Babes swiming before they can walk, which greatly encreases their Strength, and of Course their Growth.

Louis De Vorsey Jr., ed., *De Brahm's Report of the General Survey in the Southern District of North America* (Columbia: University of South Carolina Press, 1971), 107-108.

Their frequent bathing, or dipping themselves and their children in rivers, even in the severest weather, [. . .] they practise it as a religious duty, unless in very hot weather, which they find by experience to be prejudicial to their health, when they observe the law of mercy, rather than that of sacrifice. In the coldest weather, and when the ground is covered with snow, against their bodily ease and pleasure, men and children turn out of their warm houses or stoves, reeking with sweat, singing their usual sacred notes, [. . .] at the dawn of day, [. . .] at the gladsome sight of the morn; and thus they skip along, echoing praises, till they get to the river, when they instantaneously plunge into it. If the water is frozen, they break the ice with a religious impatience: After bathing, they return home, rejoicing as they run for having so well performed their religious duty, and thus purged away the impurities of the preceding day by ablution. The neglect of this hath been deemed so heinous a crime, that they have raked the legs and arms of the delinquent with snake's teeth, not allowing warm water to relax the stiffened skin.

Adair, *History of the North-American Indians*, 120.

Native Americans sweated away impurities in "hot houses," small conical structures that functioned like saunas. While Lawson stressed their therapeutic benefits, Adair stated that the Cherokees utilized them strictly for warmth during the cold winter months in the Appalachians.

The *Indians* of these Parts use Sweating very much. If any Pain seize their Limbs, or Body, immediately they take Reeds, or small Wands, and bend them Umbrella-Fashion, covering them with Skins and Matchcoats: They have a large Fire not far off, wherein they heat Stones, or (where they are wanting) Bark, putting it into this Stove, which casts an extraordinary Heat: There is a Pot of Water in the *Bagnio*, in which is put a Bunch of an Herb, bearing a Silver Tassel, not much unlike the *Aurea Virga*. With this Vegetable they rub the Head, Temples, and other Parts, which is reckon'd a Preserver of the Sight and Strengthener of the Brain.

Lawson, *New Voyage to Carolina*, 48. A *bagnio* is a bath or bathing house equipped to sweat its users. *Aurea Virga*, or goldenrod (*Solidago virgurea*), was used in Lawson's time as a topical medicine to heal wounds.

The clothing of the Indians being very light, they provide themselves for the winter with hot-houses, whose properties are to retain, and reflect the heat, after the manner of the Dutch stoves. To raise these, they fix deep in the ground, a sufficient number of strong forked posts, at a proportional distance, in a circular form, all of an equal height, about five or six feet above the surface of the ground: above these, they tie very securely large pieces of the heart of white oak, which are of a tough flexible nature, interweaving this orbit, from top to bottom, with pieces of the same, or the like timber. Then, in the middle of the fabric they fix very deep in the ground, four large pine posts, in a quadrangular form, notched a-top, on which they lay a number of heavy logs, let into each other, and rounding gradually to the top. Above this huge pile, to the very top, they lay a number of long dry poles, all properly notched, to keep strong hold of the under posts and wall-plate. Then they weave them thick with their split sapplings, and daub them all over about six or seven inches thick with tough clay, well mixt with withered grass: when this cement is half dried, they thatch the house with the longest sort of dry grass, that their land produces. They first lay on one round tier; placing a split sappling a-top, well tied to different parts of the under pieces of timber, about fifteen inches below the eave: and, in this manner, they proceed circularly to the very spire, where commonly a pole is fixed, that displays on the top the figure of a large carved eagle. At a small distance below which, four heavy logs are strongly tied together across, in a quadrangular form, in order to secure the roof from the power of envious blasts. The door of this winter palace, is commonly about four feet high, and so narrow as not to admit two to enter it abreast, with a winding passage for the space of six or seven feet, to secure themselves both from the power of the bleak winds, and of an invading enemy. As they usually build on rising ground, the floor is often a yard lower than the earth, which serves them as a breast work against an enemy: and a small peeping window is level with the surface of the outside ground, to enable them to rake any lurking invaders in case of an attack. As they have no metal to reflect the heat; in the fall of the year, as soon as the sun begins to lose his warming power, some of the women make a large fire of dry wood, with which they chiefly provide themselves, but only from day to day, through their thoughtlessness of to-morrow. When the fire is a little more than half burnt down, they cover it over with ashes, and, as the heat declines, they strike off some of the top embers, with a long cane, wherewith each of the couches, or broad seats, is constantly provided; and this method they pursue from time to time as need requires, till the fire is expended, which is commonly about day-light. While the new fire is burning down, the house, for want of windows and air, is full of hot smoky darkness; and all this time, a number of them lie on their broad bed places, with their heads wrapped up.

Adair, *History of the North-American Indians*, 419-420.

Indians believed that smoking tobacco cleansed their bodies and that its ritual sprinkling in powdered form could "pacifie their gods."

There is an herbe which is sowed apart by it selfe & is called by the inhabitants *uppówoc*. In the West Indies it hath divers names, according to the severall places & countreys where it groweth and is used: The Spaniardes generally call it Tobacco. The leaves thereof being dried and brought into pouder, they use to take the fume or smoke thereof by sucking it thorough pipes made of claie, into their stomacke and heade; from whence it purgeth superfluous fleame & other grosse humors, openeth all the pores & passages of the body: by which meanes the use thereof, not only preserveth the body from obstructions; but also if any be, so that they have not beene of too long continuance, in short time breaketh them: whereby their bodies are notably preserved in health, & know not many greevous diseases wherewithall wee in England are oftentimes afflicted.

This *Uppówoc* is of so precious estimation amongest them, that they thinke their gods are marvelously delighted therwith: Wherupon sometime they make hallowed fires & cast some of the pouder therein for a sacrifice: being in a storme uppon the waters, to pacifie their gods, they cast some up into the aire and into the water: so a weare for fish being newly set up, they cast some therein and into the aire: also after an escape of danger, they cast some into the aire likewise: but all done with strange gestures, stamping, sometime dauncing, clapping of hands, holding up of hands, & staring up into the heavens, uttering therewithal and chattering strange words & noises.

We our selves during the time we were there used to suck it after their maner, as also since our returne, & have found manie rare and wonderfull experiments of the vertues threof; of which the relation woulde require a volume by it selfe: the use of it by so manie of late men & women of great calling as else and some learned Phisitions also, is sufficient witnes.

Hariot, "A briefe and true report," in Quinn, *Roanoke Voyages*, 1:344-346.

A drink brewed from the leaves of the yaupon bush (*Ilex cassena*) was widely used as a purgative among Native Americans. Conjurers stewed the ingredients in large cauldrons before dispensing an elixir that many eyewitnesses dubbed "the black drink." Lawson noted that Indians in the coastal section of North Carolina enjoyed an abundance of this plant and exported it to tribes to the westward. Henry Timberlake described the consumption of yaupon tea when he visited the Cherokees, a practice eventually acquired by North Carolina colonists.

Last of Bushes, [. . .] is the famous *Yaupon*, of which I find two sorts, if not three. I shall speak first of the Nature of this Plant, and afterwards account for the different Sorts. This *Yaupon*, call'd by the South-*Carolina Indians, Cassena*, is a Bush, that grows chiefly on the Sand-Banks and Islands, bordering on the Sea of *Carolina*; on this Coast it is plentifully found, and in no other Place that I know of. It grows the most like Box, of any Vegetable that I know, being very like it in Leaf, only dented exactly like Tea, but the Leaf somewhat fatter. I cannot say, whether it bears any Flower, but a Berry it does, about the Bigness of a Grain of Pepper, being first red, then brown when ripe, which is in *December*; Some of these Bushes grow to be twelve Foot high, others are three or four. The Wood thereof is brittle as Myrtle, and affords a light ash-colour'd Bark. There is sometimes found of it in Swamps and rich low Grounds, which has the same figured Leaf, only it is larger, and of a deeper Green; This may be occasion'd by the Richness that attends the low Grounds thus situated. The third Sort has the same kind of Leaf, but never grows a Foot high, and is found both in rich, low Land, and on the Sand-Hills. I don't know that ever I found any Seed, or Berries on the dwarfish Sort, yet I find no Difference in Taste, when Infusion is made: Cattle and Sheep delight in this Plant very much, and so do the Deer, all which crop it very short, and browse thereon, wheresoever they meet with it. I have transplanted the Sand-Bank and dwarfish *Yaupon*, and find that the first Year, the Shrubs stood at a stand; but the second Year they throve as well as in their native Soil. This Plant is the *Indian* Tea, us'd and approv'd by all the Savages on the Coast of *Carolina*, and from them sent to the Westward *Indians*, and sold at a considerable Price. All which they cure after the same way, as they do for themselves; which is thus: They take this Plant (not only the Leaves, but the smaller Twigs along with them) and bruise it in a Mortar, till it becomes blackish, the Leaf being wholly defaced: Then they take it out, put it into one of their earthen Pots which is over the Fire, till it smoaks; stirring it all the time, till it is cur'd. Others take it, after it is bruis'd, and put it into a Bowl, to which they put live Coals, and cover them with the *Yaupon*, till they have done smoaking, often turning them over. After all, they spread it upon their Mats, and dry it in the Sun. to keep for Use.

Lawson, *New Voyage to Carolina*, 97-98.

As I was informed there was to be a physic-dance at night, curiosity led me to the townhouse, to see the preparation. A vessel of their own make, that might contain twenty gallons (there being a great many to take the medicine) was set on the fire, round which stood several goards filled with river-water, which was poured into the pot; this done, there arose one of the beloved women, who, opening a deer-skin filled with various roots and herbs, took out a small handful of something like fine salt; part of which she threw on the headman's seat, and part into the fire close to the pot; she then took out the wing of a swan, and after flourishing it over the pot, stood fixed for near a minute, muttering something to herself; then taking a shrub-like laurel (which I supposed was the physic) she threw it into the pot, and returned to her former seat. As no more ceremony seemed to be going forward, I took a walk till the Indians assembled to take it. At my return, I found the house quite full: they danced near an hour round the pot, till one of them, with a small goard that might hold about a gill, took some of the physic, and drank it, after which all the rest took in turn. One of their headmen presented me with some, and in a manner compelled me to drink, though I would have willingly declined. It was however much more palatable then I expected, having a strong taste of sassafras: the Indian who presented it, told me it was taken to wash away their sins; so that this is a spiritual medicine, and might be ranked among their religious ceremonies. They are very solicitous about its success; the conjurer, for several mornings before it is drank, makes a dreadful howling, yelling, and hallowing, from the top of the town-house, to frighten away apparitions and evil spirits. According to our ideas of evil spirits, such hideous noises would by sympathy call up such horrible beings; but I am apt to think with the Indians, that such noises are sufficient to frighten any being away but themselves.

Henry Timberlake, *Lieutenant Henry Timberlake's Memoirs, 1756-1765*, ed. by Samuel Cole Williams (Johnson City, Tennessee: The Watauga Press, 1927), 100-102.

Mr. Jams. Snowden		£	[s]	d
<1731 Novr.> […]				
<8>	To Yeopan		3	
	To Ditto		3	
	To Diet		3	
	To Diet and punch		4	
<9th>	To Yeopan		3	
	To Diet		3	
	To Yeopan		3	
	Ditto		1	6
<10th>	Ditto		1	6
<11th>	[…]			
	To Yeopan		3	
<12th>	To Ditto at Cards		6	
	To Yeopan and Cake		2	

Bar tab of James Snowden, 1733, Civil Papers—General Court, Colonial Court Records 156, State Archives, Office of Archives and History, Raleigh.

Native Americans lacked the medical knowledge and biological immunity to counteract diseases introduced by the Europeans. Thomas Hariot wrote that indigenous peoples succumbed to foreign illnesses as colonists visited one Indian town after another; the belief that whites could summon divine retribution upon their enemies also spread. Governor John Archdale saw "the Hand of God" in the removal of Indians, particularly the Pamlicos of Bath County, from lands that settlers coveted.

One other rare and strange accident, leaving others, will I mention before I ende, which moved the whole countrey that either knew or hearde of us, to have us in wonderfull admiration.

There was no towne where wee had any subtile devise practised against us, we leaving it unpunished or not revenged (because we sought by all meanes possible to win them by gentlenesse) but that within a few dayes after our departure from everie such towne, the people began to die very fast, and many in short space; in some townes about twentie, in some fourtie, in some sixtie, & in one six score, which in trueth was very manie in respect of their numbers. This happened in no place that wee coulde learne but where we had bene where they used some practice against us, and after such time; The disease also was so strange, that they neither knew what it was, nor how to cure it; the like by report of the oldest men in the countrey never happened before, time out of minde. A thing specially observed by us, as also by the naturall inhabitants themselves.

Insomuch that when some of the inhabitantes which were our friends & especially the *Wiroans Wingina* had observed such effects in foure or five towns to follow their wicked practises, they were perswaded that it was the worke of our God through our meanes, and that wee by him might kil and slaie whom wee would without weapons and not come neere them.

And thereupon when it had happened that they had understanding that any of their enemies had abused us in our journeyes, hearing that wee had wrought no revenge with our weapons, & fearing upon some cause the matter should so rest: did come and intreate us that we woulde bee a meanes to our God that they as others that had dealt ill with us might in like sort die; alleaging how much it would be for our credite and profite, as also theirs; and hoping furthermore that we would do so much at their requests in respect of the friendship we professe them.

Whose entreaties although wee shewed that they were ungodlie, affirming that our God would not subject himself to any such praiers and requestes of men: that in deede all thinges have beene and were to be done according to his good pleasure as he had ordained: and that we to shew our selves his true servants ought rather to make petition for the contrarie, that they with them might live together with us, bee made partakers of his trueth & serve him in righteousnes; but notwithstanding in such sort, that wee referre that as all other things, to bee done according to his divine will & pleasure, and as by his wisedome he had ordained to be best.

Yet because the effect fell out so suddenly and shortly after according to their desires, they thought neverthelesse it came to passe by our meanes, and that we in using such speeches unto them did but dissemble the matter, and therefore came unto us to give us thankes in their manner that although wee satisfied them not in promise, yet in deedes and effect we had fulfilled their desires.

This marvelous accident in all the countrie wrought so strange opinions of us, that some people could not tel whether to think us gods or men, and the rather because that all the space of their sicknesse, there was no man of ours knowne to die, or that was specially sicke: they noted also that we had no women amongst us, neither that we did care for any of theirs.

Some therefore were of opinion that wee were not borne of women, and therefore not mortall, but that wee were men of an old generation many yeeres past then risen againe to immortalitie.

Some woulde likewise seeme to prophesie that there were more of our generation yet to come, to kill theirs and take their places, as some thought the purpose was by that which was already done.

Those that were immediatly to come after us they imagined to be in the aire, yet invisible & without bodies, & that they by our intreaty & for the love of us did make the people to die in that sort as they did by shooting invisible bullets into them.

To confirme this opinion, their phisitions to excuse their ignorance in curing the disease, would not be ashamed to say, but earnestly make the simple people beleeve, that the strings of blood that they sucked out of the sicke bodies, were the strings wherewithall the invisible bullets were tied and cast.

Some also thought that we shot them our selves out of our pieces from the place were we dwelt, and killed the people in any such towne that had offended us as we listed, how farre distant from us soever it were.

And other some saide that it was the speciall woorke of God for our sakes, as wee our selves have cause in some sorte to thinke no lesse, whatsoever some doe or may imagine to the contrarie, specially some Astrologers knowing of the Eclipse of the Sunne which wee saw the same yeere before in our voyage thytherward, which unto them appeared very terrible. And also of a Comet which beganne to appeare but a fewe daies before the beginning of the said sicknesse. But to conclude them from being the speciall causes of so speciall an accident, there are farther reasons then I thinke fit at this present to be alleadged.

Hariot, "A briefe and true report," in Quinn, *Roanoke Voyages*, 1: 378-381.

I shall give you some farther Eminent Remark hereupon, and especially in the first Settlement of *Carolina*, where the Hand of God was eminently seen in thining the *Indians*, to make room for the *English*. [. . .] it at other times pleased Almighty God to send unusual Sicknesses amongst them, as the Smallpox, *&c.* to lessen their Numbers; so that the *English*, in Comparison to the *Spaniard*, have but little *Indian* Blood to answer for. Now the *English* at first settling in small Numbers, there seemed a Necessity of thining the barbarous *Indian* Nations; and therefore since our Cruelty is not the Instrument thereof, it pleases God to send, as I may say, an *Assyrian* Angel to do it himself. Yet will

I not totally excuse the *English*, as being wholly clear of the Blood of the *Indians* in some Respects, which I at present pass over. But surely we are all much to blame, in being so negligent of executing the proper Means for their Soul's Salvation, which being a gradual Work, the introducing a Civilized State would be a good and stable Preparatory for the Gospel State; even as the Divine Hand of Providence prepared us by the *Romans*, as all Historians mention that relate to us. I shall farther add one late more immediate Example of God's more immediate hand, in making a Consumption upon some *Indian* Nations in *North Carolina*, and that was in my time at the River *Pemlicoe*, and some Nations adjoining: This is a late Settlement, began about eight Years since. When I was in the *North* about eleven Years since, I was told then of a great Mortality that fell upon the *Pemlicoe Indians*; as also, that a Nation of *Indians* called the *Coranine*, a bloody and barbarous People, were most of them cut off by a Neighbouring Nation: Upon which I said, that it seemed to me as if God had an Intention speedily to plant an *English* Settlement thereabouts; which accordingly fell out in two or three Years, although at that time not one Family was there.

John Archdale, *A new description of that fertile and pleasant province of Carolina: with a brief account of its discovery, settling, and the government thereof to this time with several remarkable passages of divine providence during my time* (London: printed for John Wyat, 1707), 2-4. The Core Indians ("Coranine") lived along the Neuse River in present-day Craven and Carteret counties.

One of the European diseases that ravaged Native Americans was smallpox. Lawson states that within fifty years of the founding of Carolina, five-sixths of the local Indian population had died. Estimates suggest that the Cherokees suffered a 50 percent mortality rate during the epidemic of 1738-1739, which swept the Southeast. A smallpox outbreak in 1759 eradicated half the Catawba nation.

The Small-Pox has been fatal to them; they do not often escape, when they are seiz'd with that Distemper, which is a contrary Fever to what they ever knew. Most certain, it had never visited *America*, before the Discovery thereof by the Christians. Their running into the Water, in the Extremity of this Disease, strikes it in, and kills all that use it. Now they are become a little wiser; but formerly it destroy'd whole Towns, without leaving one *Indian* alive in the Village. The Plague was never known amongst them, that I could learn by what Enquiry I have made: [. . .] The Small-Pox and Rum have made such a Destruction amongst them, that, on good grounds, I do believe, there is not the sixth Savage living within two hundred Miles of all our Settlements, as there were fifty Years ago. These poor Creatures have so many Enemies to destroy them, that it's a wonder one of them is left alive near us.

Lawson, *New Voyage to Carolina*, 231-232.

The Cherokee Indians, as will appear by the Affidavits sent over to England by Colonel Stephens, which I hope are arrived, were destroyed by Rum and the Small Pox, carried up by Traders from Carolina, some of whom had been licenced at Charles Town, and some without any Licences but encouraged from thence. Above 1000 of the Indians died and the sickness raged so that they could not attend their Corn fields, They demanded Justice from all the English, threatned Revenge and sent to the French for Assistance. Their Deputies met me at Fort Augusta, I asked them if they were Georgia Traders that had sold the Rum, they said No, and I prevailed with them not only to be pacified with the English, but also to promise me the Assistance of a body of Men against the Spaniards. When they told me of the starving Condition they would be in by their having lost their Corn harvest by the Sickness, I ordered as far as 15000 bushells of Corn to be bought at Augusta, & to be given to the Cherokee Nation if they came down to fetch the Same, to be divided amongst all the Towns where the Dearth of Corn was. Upon my acquainting the Chiefs of my having done this before they asked it, they said, that the Trustees treated them as Fathers do their Children, they did not give them Toys nor unwholsome liquor, but gave them Wisdom & Justice, and supplied their Wants when Misfortunes came upon them. They called them the Preservers of their Nation, as they did the Carolina Traders, the Destroyers of it.

General James Oglethorpe to Harman Verelst, October 19, 1739, in Allen D. Candler, ed., *Colonial Records of the State of Georgia* (Atlanta, Georgia: The Franklin Printing and Publishing Company, 1904–), 22, part 2:247-248.

About the year 1738, the Cheerake received a most depopulating shock, by the small pox, which reduced them almost one half, in about a year's time: it was conveyed into Charles-town by the Guinea-men, and soon after among them, by the infected goods. At first it made slow advances, and as it was a foreign, and to them a strange disease, they were so deficient in proper skill, that they alternately applied a regimen of hot and cold things, to those who were infected. The old magi and religious physicians who were consulted on so alarming a crisis, reported the sickness had been sent among them, on account of the adulterous intercourses of their young married people, who the past year, had in a most notorious manner, violated their ancient laws of marriage in every thicket, and broke down and polluted many of the honest neighbours bean-plots, by their heinous crimes, which would cost a great deal of trouble to purify again. To those flagitious crimes they ascribed the present disease, as a necessary effect of the divine anger; and indeed the religious men chanced to suffer the most in their small fields, as being contigious to the town-house, where they usually met at night to dance, when their corn was out of the stalks; upon this pique, they shewed their priest-craft. However, it was thought needful on this occasion, to endeavour to put a stop to the progress of such a dangerous disease: and as it was believed to be brought on them by their unlawful copulation in the night dews, it was thought most practicable to try to effect the cure, under the same cool element. Immediately, they ordered the reputed sinners to lie out of doors, day and night, with their breast frequently open to the night dews, to cool the fever: they were likewise afraid, that the diseased would otherwise pollute the house, and by that means, procure all their deaths. Instead of applying warm remedies, they at last in every visit poured cold water on their naked breasts, sung their religious mystical song, *Yo Yo*, &c. with a doleful tune, and shaked a calabash with the pebble-stones, over the sick, using a great many frantic gestures, by way of incantantion. [. . .]

When they found their theological regimen had not the desired effect, but that the infection gained upon them, they held a second consultation, and deemed it the best method to sweat their patients, and plunge them into the river,—which was accordingly done. Their rivers being very cold in summer, by reason of the numberless springs, which pour from the hills and mountains— and the pores of their bodies being open to receive the cold, it rushing in through the whole frame, they immediately expired: upon which, all the magi and prophetic tribe broke their old consecrated physic-pots, and threw away all the other pretended holy things they had for physical use, imagining they had lost their divine power by being polluted; and shared the common fate of their country. A great many killed themselves; for being naturally proud, they are always peeping into their looking glasses, and are never genteelly drest, according to their mode, without carrying one hung over their shoulders: by which means, seeing themselves disfigured, without hope of regaining their former beauty, some shot themselves, others cut their throats, some stabbed themselves with knives, and others with sharp-pointed canes; many threw themselves with sullen madness into the fire, and there slowly expired, as if they had been utterly divested of the native power of feeling pain.

Adair, *History of the North-American Indians*, 232-233.

Charles Town (South Carolina) December 1.

[. . .]

It is pretty certain, that the Small Pox has lately raged with great Violence among the Catawba Indians, and that it has carried off near one Half of that Nation, by throwing themselves into the River as soon as they found themselves ill. This Distemper has since appeared amongst the Inhabitants at the Charraws and Waterees, where many Families are down; so that unless especial Care is taken, it must soon spread through the whole Country, the Consequences of which are much to be feared.

Pennsylvania Gazette, January 24, 1760.

I have nothing to add but that I hear there are about 100 Catawba Warriors, who have returned to their Town, out of 250 they had when they dispersed upon acct of the Small Pox.

Governor Arthur Dobbs to [Philip Bearcroft], secretary, Society for the Propagation of the Gospel, April 15, 1760, in Saunders, *Colonial Records*, 6:235.

As more of their people succumbed to pathogens transmitted by whites, Native Americans developed an aversion to colonial towns. Charleston, South Carolina, seat of the government that controlled much of the trade and diplomacy with North Carolina Indians, earned a notorious reputation. Indians who traveled to the city for talks in 1749, and did not die from disease, were killed by rival tribesmen.

Another Inconvenience attending the Indian Meetings in Charles Town, is the Sickness contracted there by them from the great change of Air, but chiefly of the Water. The latter never fails after a Short stay to produce a remarkable Alteration in their Health; to which a freer Diet also Contributes; which renders them very impatient to be gone again. Fevers and Fluxes attack them soon after, and frequently carry off some in their return homeward. When long delayed in Town, which hath been too often the Case, many have shared the fate together.

Wilbur R. Jacobs, ed., *Indians of the Southern Colonial Frontier: the Edmond Atkin Report and Plan of 1755* (Columbia: University of South Carolina Press, 1954), 30.

I shall next mention to your Lordships what has lately happened to the Indians invited to Charles Town to receive the present Sent from his Majesty, and that Peace might be made between the Creeks and Cherokees; when I had defeated all the French Efforts to perpetuate the War, and had Sent for them down, the Captain of the Albama Fort and the Governor of Moville spread Reports that they were Sent for to Charles Town to be Sacrificed, They also hired a Gang of Three Score Indians to fall upon Some of the Out Towns of the Cherokees, which they Accordingly did immediately after their Headmen Set out for this place, these Reports so industriously propogated made the Indians extremely unwilling to Come down, Accordingly they Sent me Several pressing Letters earnestly praying that I would meet them at Fort Moore, a Fort belonging to this Province, at about one hundred and Fifty Miles distance from Charles Town, in this request both the Creeks and Cherokees joined, and the Council and Assembly who were then Sitting intended to have addressed me for that purpose, but I acquainted them that your Lordships were of opinion that Charles Town was the properest place to transact matters of this kind, and therefore that I would meet the Indians no where else; Such of the Indian Traders as were then in Town were Consulted as to the most proper time of their Coming, and they all Agreed that the end of August or the begining of September was the fittest Season, great Care was also taken to hire Convenient houses for them at a Mile or two's distance from Town, where they might have the benefite of fresh Air and wholsome Water and plenty of Food of the best kind was provided for them, notwithstanding of all which as they came with the greatest reluctance and unwillingness, they Stayed with great uneasiness, and many of them very Soon fell Sick, and tho they were Attended by the best Physicians here, yet they began to drop off, in particular, the Wife of a great Warriour Called the Yellow Bird, died, a noted friend to the English, upon which he prayed for a Couple of Waggons to have him and Some other of their Sick People carried Some part of their way home, but he himself died that night, and the Prince of Tannessie's Son next morning, the rest Continued their Journey, but Continued also to die dayly, and upon the Road they received Accounts that the French Indians (not the Gang of Sixty that I before mentioned) had fallen upon their Overhills Towns and had killed Several of their People, and also that they had killed and Scalped one of our Traders, Robert Kelley, a most usefull person to this Government, as he had lived long amongst the Indians and kn[ew] their manners and Language very well; many of their People wh[o] lived to get home, died of the distemper they had Catched here, soon After, particularly the greatest Warriour in the Cherokee Nation called halfbreed Johnie, and no life was expected for the Emperor by the last Accounts from thence; The Creeks were also very Sickly while here, and buried many of their People and Some of their Headmen upon their way homewards, and they all gave out that what wa[s] told them by the French was too true; The Catabaws who were als[o] present at this Meeting Suffered more than the rest, they were wa[y]laid in their way home by their Enemies, who Attacked them even in our Settlements, and killed nine of them, but the Sickness which they Carried with them from hence, proved their greatest Enemie, and Carried of their King, whom every person that knew, must Acknowledge to be the finest Indian that ever was Seen, and as he was a very great Warriour, and a remarkable friend to the English, his loss is irrepareable, besides him the whole Headmen died, towit Captain Taylor, Captain Harris, Captain Jamie, Captain Peter etc. to the number of fifteen and upwards and I am Affraid it must End in the Total destruction of that poor Nation, they having now few or none left to be Leaders, I have some thoughts of proposing to them to go and live amongst the Cherokees and Creeks for their protection, but then this Country will be quite open and exposed on that quarter where these People have hitherto proved a good Barrier to us.

Governor James Glen to the Board of Trade, December 23, 1749, in Colonial Office 5/389, British Records, State Archives, Office of Archives and History, Raleigh. The "Albama Fort" was Fort Toulouse, which the French constructed in 1717 at the convergence of the Coosa and Tallapoosa rivers, south of present-day Wetumpka, Alabama, in territory controlled by the Alabama Indians of the Upper Creek Confederacy. Two captains had commanded the post in 1749: Captain Jean Paul Le Sueur and Captain Louis de Bonnille. Moville was present-day Mobile, Alabama; the governor of Louisiana was Pierre François de Rigaud, Marquis de Vaudreuil-Cavagnal. Fort Moore stood on the east bank of the Savannah River, in Aiken County, South Carolina, opposite present-day Augusta, Georgia. Nopkehe, known later as King Hagler, assumed the mantle of leadership of the Catawbas: the lone headman to survive the epidemic, he had gone hunting when his nation's contingent departed for Charleston.

The effects of disease among Native Americans temporarily stifled trade with South Carolina; forced the Catawbas to postpone peace negotiations with the Iroquois Confederacy in Albany, New York; and caused the Cherokees to delay setting a boundary line with North Carolina.

Saturday, April 12, 1718

[. . .]

Forasmuch as it is found, that for some Time past, the Trade in Charles Town with our neighbouring Indians hath abated in a very great Measure, supposed to be chiefly occasioned by the Smallpox, it's being in the same;

Resolved therefore to appoint and settle some certain Place of Trade, for the Indians to resort unto and be supplied with such Goods as they may want, in the Country;

Ordered that Letters be sent to such Persons as are conveniently seated in the Country for trading with the neighbouring Indians, to propose the same to them, and also to know of each respective Person on what Terms he will undertake to trade and deal with the said Indians, on Account of the Publick.

Entry of April 12, 1718, in William L. McDowell Jr., ed., *Journals of the Commissioners of the Indian Trade, September 20, 1710-August 29, 1718*, in *The Colonial Records of South Carolina, Series 2* (Columbia: South Carolina Archives Department, 1955), 266.

Annonida, November 23, 1751

Brothers of the Catawba Nation, We the Head Men of the Annonida, Tuskarorah, and Mohawk Nations being met together to consider your Talk on Paper which was delivered to us Yesterday by our Brother Aaron Stevens, Interpreter. [. . .]

Brothers, we are very sorry to learn by your Paper that Sickness has taken hold of your Nation which you say has prevented your seeing us at Albany this Fall. We hope God will take the Sickness from amongst you that you may be able as you desire to meet us there next Spring so soon as the Leaves shall begin to adorn the Trees and bring with you what People you shall have of ours. We thank you for the Regard you Express to preserve the Pledge of Peace we gave you at Albany.

Message from the Oneida, Tuscarora, and Mohawk Nations, November 23, 1751, in William L. McDowell Jr., ed., *Documents Relating to Indian Affairs, 1750-1754*, in *The Colonial Records of South Carolina, Series 2* (Columbia: South Carolina Archives Department, 1958), 202. The "Annonida" were the Oneida Indians of the Iroquois Confederacy.

A talk from the Cherokee Chiefs and Headmen of the Nation to their Father in Charles Town 22th September 1766.

Yesterday we received your talk for which we return you our thanks; but the times is so much Altered with us since we spoke to you last, that we could not attend at the fixing of the Boundary Line before the Spring. We shall be at Reedy River with our Brother Mr. Cameron by the 10th of the 7th Moon (April) before which time, We hope the Governor and beloved Men of Virginia will agree to settle the Line on the back of their Country, so as to make a final Conclusion of the whole at once. We request that you wou'd thank the Governor of North Carolina for his readiness in agreeing with you to have the Line run this Winter; and altho' it is now so late in the Season, nothing but the Mortality that has seized our People wou'd have prevented us from settling that important piece of business. But altho' we came yesterday to a resolution to set out with our Brother here on the 10th of next Moon for that Service, the dismal Scenes about us this Morning Weakened our resolutions; and we make no doubt but you will Admit of the following reasons as a sufficient Apoligie for our putting it off for this fall.

When I got up this Morning I cou'd hear nothing but the Cries of Women and Children for the loss of their Relations; in the Evenings there are nothing to be seen but smoak and houses on fire, the dwellings of the deceased; I never remember to see any Sickness like the present, except the small Pox; and if we shou'd attempt to go to run the Line, We might have been taken sick in the Woods, and die, as several of our people have already been served, who Attempted to escape this Devil of a Disorder.

Colonial Office 5/67, British Records, State Archives, Office of Archives and History, Raleigh.

Some colonists showed compassion toward ailing Native Americans. The vestry of St. John's Parish, Carteret County, looked after Indian Ned and ultimately paid for his burial.

St. Johns Parish Carteret County ss. At a Vestry held at the Chappel on the South side of Newport River on the 23rd day of March being Easter Monday 1761 and Quallified according to Law.

[. . .]

Agreed with Col. Joseph Bell to Take Indian Ned Parisher at Nine Shillings per month and if he Should fall Sick to be Allowd more; the Parrish finding Cloths.

[. . .]

St. Johns Parish Carteret County. At A Vestry begun [and Held] on Newport River on Saterday the 15th Day of October 176[ ].

[. . .]

Cart. County St. Johns parish on acount of Indain Ned.

	£	s.	d.
Dr.			
<1762 June 30th.> To 6 yds. of ozenbrigs @ 2s.4d. per yd.		.14.	—
To making 1 Shirt and trowsers and thread @		. 3.	—
<Der. 9th.> To 1 pear Shoose @		. 6.	—
To 3yds. of Cloath 4s. per yd. and making 1 Jacket and thred		.16.	—
<1763 March 4th.> To 6 yds. of Coten and wool Cloath at 3s.4d. per yd.	1.	—.	—
To making 1 Shirt and trowsers and thread.			
[. . .]			
<1764 Jary. 24th.> To 3 3/4 yds. of Cloath @ 4s. per yd.		.15.	—
To making 1 jacket and threed @		. 4.	8
To 14 mounths at 9s. per mounth	6.	6.	—
To 5 Do. as he was Sick and Sum times very Sick and by agreement I was to be allowed	3.	0.	0.
<April 7th.> he Departed this Life	12.22.	0.	
To 39 ten peney nails	0.	2.	—
To plank	0.	4.	—
To making the Coffen	0.	4.	—
To 1 old Sheet	0.	7.	—
To a bought a quart of Rum	0.	1.	6.
	£15.	19.	6.

<1763 May 24.> By Credit in parts of the above acount

By the hands   £ 7. 8s.—d.

Mr. Robert Read

Errors Excepted per Jos. Bell this 6th of August 1764.

Robert J. Cain and Jan-Michael Poff, eds., *The Church of England in North Carolina: Documents, 1742-1763*, Volume 11 of *The Colonial Records of North Carolina [Second Series]*, eds. Mattie Erma Edwards Parker, William S. Price Jr., Robert J. Cain, and Jan-Michael Poff (Raleigh: Division of Archives and History, Department of Cultural Resources [projected multivolume series, 1963–], 2007), 495, 497, 500-501.

Because he had become a ward of the parish, Indian Ned might have been given a Christian burial. John Lawson vividly describes how Native Americans in eastern Carolina observed the passing of one of their own. Indians generally were not an acquisitive people, and consequently interred the valuables of the deceased along with them; but James Adair writes that, by the mid eighteenth century, the influence of whites had caused the Cherokees to change that custom.

The Burial of their Dead is perform'd with a great deal of Ceremony, in which one Nation differs, in some few Circumstances, from another, yet not so much but we may, by a general Relation, pretty nearly account for them all.

When an *Indian* is dead, the greater Person he was, the more expensive is his Funeral. The first thing which is done, is, to place the nearest Relations near the Corps, who mourn and weep very much, having their Hair hanging down their Shoulders, in a very forlorn manner. After the dead Person has laid a Day and a Night, in one of their Hurdles of Canes, commonly in some Out-House made for that purpose, those that officiate about the Funeral, go into the Town, and the first young Men they meet withal, that have Blankets or Match Coats on, whom they think fit for their Turn, they strip them from their Backs, who suffer them so to do, without any Resistance. In these they wrap the dead Bodies, and cover them with two or three Mats, which the *Indians* make of Rushes or Cane; and last of all, they have a long Web of woven Reeds, or hollow Canes, which is the Coffin of the *Indians*, and is brought round several times, and tied fast at both ends, which indeed, looks very decent and well. Then the Corps is brought out of the House, into the Orchard of Peach-Trees, where another Hurdle is made to receive it, about which comes all the Relations and Nation that the dead Person belong'd to, besides several from other Nations in Alliance with them; all which sit down on the Ground, upon Mats spread there, for that purpose; where the Doctor or Conjurer appears; and, after some time, makes a Sort of *O-yes*, at which all are very silent; then he begins to give an Account, who the dead Person was, and how stout a Man he approv'd himself; how many enemies and Captives he had kill'd and taken; how strong, tall, and nimble he was; that he was a great Hunter, a Lover of his Country, and possess'd of a great many beautiful Wives and Children, esteem'd the greatest of Blessings among these Savages, in which they have a true Notion. Thus this Orator runs on, highly extolling the dead Man, for his Valour, Conduct, Strength, Riches, and Good-Humour; and enumerating his Guns, Slaves and almost every thing he was possess'd of, when living. After which, he addresses himself to the People of that Town or Nation, and bids them supply the dead Man's Place, by following his steps, who, he assures them, is gone into the Country of Souls, (which they think lies a great way off, in this World, which the Sun visits, in his ordinary Course) and that he will have the Enjoyment of handsome young Women, great Store of Deer to hunt, never meet with Hunger, Cold or Fatigue, but every thing to answer his Expectation and Desire. This is the Heaven they propose to themselves; but, on the contrary, for those *Indians* that are lazy, thievish amongst themselves, bad Hunters, and no Warriours, nor of much Use to the Nation, to such they allot, in the next World, Hunger, Cold, Troubles, old ugly Women for their Companions, with Snakes, and all sorts of nasty Victuals to feed on. Thus is mark'd out their Heaven and Hell. After all this Harangue, he diverts the People with some of their Traditions, as when there was a violent hot Summer, or very hard Winter; when any notable Distempers rag'd amongst them; when they were at War with such and such Nations; how victorious they were; and what were the Names of their War-Captains. [. . .] When this long Tale is ended, by him that spoke first; perhaps, a second begins another long Story; so a third, and fourth, if there be so many Doctors present; which all tell one and the same thing. At last, the Corps is brought away from that Hurdle to the Grave, by four young Men, attended by the Relations, the King, old Men, and all the Nation. When they come to the Sepulcre, which is about six Foot deep, and eight Foot long, having at each end (that is, at the Head and Foot) a Light-Wood, or Pitch-Pine Fork driven close down the sides of the Grave, firmly unto the Ground; (these two Forks are to contain a Ridge-Pole, as you shall understand presently) before they lay the Corps into the Grave, they cover the bottom two or three times over with Bark of Trees, then they let down the Corps (with two Belts, that the *Indians* carry their Burdens withal) very leisurely, upon the said Barks; then they lay over a Pole of the same Wood, in the two Forks, and having a great many Pieces of Pitch-Pine Logs, about two Foot and half long, they stick them in the sides of the Grave down each End, and near the Top thereof, where the other Ends lie on the Ridge-Pole, so that they are declining like the Roof of a House. These being very thick plac'd, they cover them (many times double) with Bark; then they throw the Earth thereon, that came out of the Grave, and beat it down very firm; by this Means, the dead Body lies in a Vault, nothing touching him; so that when I saw this way of Burial, I was mightily pleas'd with it, esteeming it very decent and pretty, as having seen a great many Christians buried without the tenth Part of that Ceremony and Decency. Now, when the Flesh is rotted and moulder'd from the Bone, they take up the Carcass, and clean the Bones, and joint them together; afterwards, they dress them up in pure white dress'd Deer-Skins, and lay them amongst their Grandees and Kings in the *Quiogozon*, which is their Royal Tomb or Burial-Place of their Kings and War-Captains. This is a very large magnificent Cabin, (according to their Building) which is rais'd at the Publick Charge of the Nation, and maintain'd in a great deal of Form and Neatness. About seven foot high, is a Floor or Loft made, on which lie all their Princes, and Great Men, that have died for several hundred Years, all attir'd in the Dress I before told you of. No Person is to have his Bones lie here, and to be thus dress'd, unless he gives a round Sum of their Money to the Rulers, for Admittance. If they remove never so far, to live in a Foreign Country, they never fail to take all these dead Bones along with them, though the Tediousness of their short daily Marches keeps them never so long on their Journey. They reverence and adore this *Quiogozon*, with all the Veneration and Respect that is possible for such a People to discharge, and had rather lose all, than have any Violence or Injury offer'd thereto. These Savages differ some small matter in their Burials; some burying right upwards, and otherwise, as you are acquainted withal in my Journal from South to North *Carolina*; Yet they all agree in their Mourning, which is, to appear every Night, at the Sepulcre, and howl and weep in a very dismal manner, having their Faces dawb'd over with Light-wood Soot, (which is the same as Lamp-black) and Bears Oil. This renders them as black as it is possible to make themselves, so that theirs very much resemble the Faces of Executed men boil'd in Tar. If the dead Person was a Grandee, to carry on the Funeral Ceremonies, they hire People to cry and lament over the dead Man. Of this sort there are several, that practice it for a Livelihood, and are very expert at Shedding abundance of Tears, and howling like Wolves, and so discharging their Office with abundance of Hypocrisy and Art. The Women are never accompanied with these Ceremonies after Death; and to what World they allot that Sex, I never understood, unless, to wait on their dead Husbands; but they have more Wit, than some of the Eastern Nations, who sacrifice themselves to accompany their Husbands into the next World. It is the dead Man's Relations, by Blood, as his Uncles, Brothers, Sisters, Cousins, Sons, and Daughters, that mourn in good earnest, the Wives thinking their Duty is discharg'd, and that they are become free, when their Husband is dead; so, as fast as they can, look out for another, to supply his Place.

Lawson, *New Voyage to Carolina*, 185, 187-189.

The buriell of the dead and thire way of morning for them all the while that the person or persones are laying one thire death bed the fathers mothers brothers or nearest Relations are Alwise them. and they will never shoe aney wayes Cast down before the sick person for feare of discoraging them till thire brath are out of thire bodyes and then all thire Relashons comes both fare and neare and setts up the dismalesstt Cray that would pitie The harte of stone. the father Craying out my sone or doughter the mother the same. and the brothers and Sisters my brother and all the other Relashons thire cuson.

they mourne 24 owrs and then The priste of the town is sent for to burrie the Corpes they are Burred as they white people dus. if itt be a king all the nashon morns for him and all that is of Royall asent burries a good Quantity of goods with him. likewise all the other Common people has vast quantities of all sorts of goods buried with them which is a grateadvantage to the merchats of South Carolina and Espeshaly to the Indian traidors that uses amonghst them. this goods that is burid with these corps is given part to them. to serve them in their voiges, and partt To present thire friends and Relations in the other world. speaking to the desesed telling them to give such and such things to such and such Relations. all the goods that belongs to the Dead they borne as loth to keep aney thing that belongs to To them least itt should be occation of thire nott goeing To that good place that is prepared for them. for they are of opinion That the soule will stay with the Richess till itt is conshumed etc.

Longe, "Ways and Manners of the Indians called Cherokees," 27.

The Cheerake of late years, by the reiterated persuasion of the traders, have entirely left off the custom of burying effects with the dead body; the nearest of blood inherits them. They, and several other of our Indian nations, used formerly to shoot all the live stock that belonged to the deceased, soon after the interment of the corpse; not according to the Pagan custom of the funeral piles, on which they burned several of the living, that they might accompany and wait on the dead, but from a narrow-hearted avaricious principle, [. . .]

As the Hebrews carefully buried their dead, so on any accident, they gathered their bones and laid them in the tombs of their fore-fathers: Thus, all the numerous nations of Indians perform the like friendly office to every deceased person of their respective tribe; insomuch, that those who lose their people at war, if they have not corrupted their primitive customs, are so observant of this kindred-duty, as to appropriate some time to collect the bones of their relations; which they call *bone gathering*, [. . .] The Cheerake, by reason of their great intercourse with foreigners, have dropped that friendly office: and as they seem to be more intelligent than the rest of our English-American Indians in their religious rites, and ceremonial observations, so I believe, the fear of pollution has likewise contributed to obliterate that ancient kindred duty. However, they separate those of their people who die at home, from others of a different nation; and every particular tribe indeed of each nation bears an intense love to itself, and divides every one of its people from the rest, both while living, and after they are dead.

Adair, *History of the North-American Indians*, 178, 179-180.

Trade

Native Americans had engaged in a thriving inter-tribal trade, which enabled them to acquire goods and materials normally unavailable in their area, centuries before the first Englishmen landed on Roanoke Island. The paths the Indians used to transact such business, and upon which they ventured out to hunt or to attack their enemies, crisscrossed North Carolina. The main roads of their time, those same trails facilitated white exploration, settlement, and trade.

Albemarle County No Carolina sst

His Excellency William Lord Craven Palatine & The Rest of the true and Absolute Lords Proprietors of Carolina Greeting in our Lord God Everlasting Know thee that we the said Lords and Absolute proprietors according to our great Deed of Grant bearing date the first day of May Anno Domini 1668 given to our County of Albemarle under our hands and great Seal of oure Province doe hereby give and grant unto Captain Fredrick Jones a tract of Land Containing Six hundred and fourty Acres Lying in Chowan Precinct at the Forke of Deep Creek, beginning at a Pine on the Northermost Side of the Creek Just by the Indian path going over the Creek running thence North West [. . .]

> Land Grant to Captain Frederick Jones, April 5, 1712, Proprietary Grants, Proprietary and Royal Land Grants, 1712-1775, Land Office (Colonial), Secretary of State Records, State Archives, Office of Archives and History, Raleigh.

Judith Coborn 400 [acres] [Anson], On the So. side of the Catawba River above Samuel Coborns land on the Tukesege Path or near [sd.] path.

> Entry of Judith Coborn, September 14, 1751, Entries for Warrants, 1742/43-1774, Court of Claims, Land Office (Colonial), Secretary of State Records, State Archives, Office of Archives and History, Raleigh.

One of the paths established by the Indians and later used by whites who traded with them was the Occaneechi Trail, which cut a south-westerly course across the Piedmont from current-day Petersburg, Virginia, toward upstate South Carolina. After fording the Haw River near what is now Swepsonville, North Carolina, John Lawson met a pack train on the Occaneechi in early 1701. Lawson's encounter hints at a relationship that continued throughout the colonial era: Native Americans in North Carolina dealt primarily with traders from other colonies, particularly Virginia and South Carolina. North Carolina never vigorously pursued commerce with inland tribes such as the Catawbas and Cherokees, even though they occupied considerable territory within its boundaries. **Content to let its northern and southern neighbors assume the risks and rewards of managing trade with those nations, North Carolina focused its more modest efforts on the Indians of the Coastal Plain.**

As soon as it was day, we set out for the *Achonechy*-Town, it being, by Estimation, 20 Miles off, which, I believe, is pretty exact. We were got about half way, (meeting great Gangs of Turkies) when we saw, at a Distance, 30 loaded Horses, coming on the Road, with four or five Men, on other Jades, driving them. We charg'd our Piece, and went up to them: Enquiring, whence they came from? They told us, from *Virginia*. The leading Man's Name was *Massey,* who was born about *Leeds* in *Yorkshire.*

> John Lawson, *A New Voyage to Carolina*, ed. by Hugh T. Lefler (Chapel Hill: University of North Carolina Press, 1967), 59n, 60-61. The "Achonechy" were the Occaneechi Indians. Achonechy Town was located on the Eno River near modern-day Hillsborough.

Some tribes functioned as intermediaries in the burgeoning trade with whites. Situated between the coastal settlements and the Indian nations farther inland, the Tuscaroras established themselves in such a role and used that status to their advantage, as Enoe Will, an Indian chief and Lawson's guide, explained—and as the Nottoways learned firsthand.

The next Day, early, came two *Tuskeruro Indians* to the other side of the River, but could not get over. They talk'd much to us, but we understood them not. In the Afternoon, *Will* came with the Mare, and had some Discourse with them; they told him, The *English*, to whom he was going, were very wicked People; and, That they threated the *Indians* for Hunting near their Plantations. These Two Fellows were going among the *Schoccores* and *Achonechy Indians*, to sell their Wooden Bowls and Ladles for Raw-Skins, which they make great Advantage of, hating that any of these Westward *Indians* should have any Commerce with the *English*, which would prove a Hinderance to their Gains. Their Stories deterr'd an Old *Indian* and his Son, from going any farther; but *Will* told us, Nothing they had said should frighten him, he believing them to be a couple of Hog-stealers; and that the *English* only sought Restitution of their Losses, by them; and that this was the only ground for their Report.

> Lawson, *New Voyage to Carolina*, 64. The "Schoccores" were the Shakoris. Lawson's depiction of Tuscarora Indians plying their goods among the Occaneechis is ironic. The Occaneechis had been dominant middlemen in the Indian trade until their defeat by the Iroquois and the colony of Virginia toward the end of the seventeenth century. They then abandoned their territory near present-day Clarksville, Virginia, and resettled in North Carolina.

The Nottoway Indians represent to His Excellency that the Tuskaruroe Indians (being incouraged thereto) do often come into the upper partes of the Countrey, about Appamattox, amongst the English, who furnish them with Gunns and Powder & shott, which enables them to hunt upon and burn up all their grounds, whereby their game is Destroyed and their hunting spoyled. That the English trust the Tuskaruroes in trade with Rum & other goods which they bring out amongst the Nottowayes, and sometimes set into Play, and lose all or great parte of those goods, and not being able to make satisfaccon to the English, they tell them the Nottoways take their goods from them, which occasions Differences and dissatisfaccons between the English and the Nottoways. They pray that His Excellency will be pleased to consider of these things and give such direccon therein as he shall thinke fit, [. . .]

Entry of May 2, 1699, in William Pitt Palmer et al., eds., *Calendar of Virginia State Papers and other manuscripts, 1652-1883*, 11 vols. (1875-1883; reprint, New York: Kraus Reprint Company, 1968), 1:65.

Trade between the Indians and whites developed into an economic system based upon credit. Factors in Britain shipped goods on credit to merchants in its American colonies who then either sold them directly to the Indians or contracted with traders to travel into their nations. That merchandise was offered to the Indians in exchange for the animal skins acquired from their next hunt. According to James Adair, traders evaluated the creditworthiness of Indian hunters by the effects they possessed. Matthew Toole, trader to the Catawbas, paid a large bond for trade goods to merchant John McCord.

[November 15, 1728.] The Common Method of carrying on this Indian Commerce is as follows: Gentlemen send for Goods proper for such a Trade from England, and then either Venture them out at their own risk to the Indian Towns, or else credit some Traders with them of Substance and Reputation, to be paid in Skins at a certain Price agreed betwixt them.

William Byrd, *History of the Dividing Line Betwixt Virginia and North Carolina* (Raleigh: North Carolina Historical Commission, 1929), 298.

It is a common trading rule with us, to judge of the value of an Indian's effects, by the weight of his fingers, wrists, ears, crown of his head, boots, and maccaseenes—by the quantity of red paint daubed on his face, and by the shirt about the collar, shoulders, and back, should he have one.

James Adair, *A History of the North-American Indians, Particularly Those Nations Adjoining to the Missisippi* [sic] *East and West Florida, Georgia, South and North Carolina and Virginia* (1775; reprint, Ann Arbor, Michigan: UMI Books on Demand, 2002), 170-172.

<South Carolina Berkly County> Know all men By These Presents That I Matthew Toole Indain Trader to the Cuttabas am held and firmly Bound unto John McCord of the said Province and County Merchant. In the Just and full Sum of Three Thousand Eight Hundred fourty four Pound So. Carolina Currency To the which Payment well and Truly to Be made and Done I Bind my Self Heirs Executors administrators firmly By these Presents Sealed with my Seal and Dated this Twenty Seventh Day of April anno Domini 1753 and In the 26th Year of his Majesties Reign.

The Condition of the above obligation is Such that If the above Bounden Matthew Toole he or Either of his heirs Executors Administrators or Either of them Doe well and Truly pay or Cause to be Paid to the abovesaid John McCord he or Either of his Ceartain Attorney heirs Executors Administrators or Assigns the Just and full Sum of one Thousand Nine Hundred and Twenty two Pound[s] Current money of the Province aforesaid with Lawfull Intrest at or Before the first Day of April Next without fraud Coven or further Delay Then the above obligation to Be Void and of noe Effect otherwise to Stand and Remain In full force and Virtue.

Matthew Toole

Signed Sealed and Deliver'd In the Presence off
Charles Russell
[*torn*]
Recd. 27th April 1753. 284 Raw Deer Skins In part pay of the within Bond after the Reducting the Charges out and what they sell for in Town to Give Credit for the weight of the above 284 Skins in Charles Town was 675 Wt. Sold to Mc. Corker at 6/ per Pound the Charges Reducting out at 35/ per hundred wt. the Credits on the within Bond is

<£202.10
11.16.3
£190.13.9>

Recd. March 2th 1754 in the Cottabwes Six hundread wt. of Raw Dear Skins in part of the within Bond at 7/6 per Pound. the Charges of the Above.

<£225
12
£213>

<South Carolina Berkly County> Memorandum that I the Subscriber Do Promise and oblidge my Self to make over my Right Title and Intrest of two Surveys of Land one of Six hundred and fourty acres and one of five hundred on the waters of fishing Creek to Mr. John McCord In the final Sum of five hundred Pound Current money of the province aforesaid to the which

payment well and Truly to Be made and Done I Bind my Self my heirs etc. and the abovesaid John McCord Doe promise and oblidge himself what ever the abovesaid Land Sells for to Give said matthew Toole Credibt for on his Bond In wittness whereof Both parties doth Sett their hands and Seals this 27th April 1753. [. . .]

Matthew Toole's promise to transfer title of land to John McCord, and Toole's bond, 1753, Ejectments, Miscellaneous Land Records, Salisbury District Superior Court, State Archives, Office of Archives and History, Raleigh.

Although deerskins were the main currency of the Indian trade, the hides of other animals were also in demand. Artisans in Britain and the colonies turned beaver pelts into hats.

Little River, North Carolina, October the 20th 1703

Acct. of goods on board the Sloop Speedwell Tho. Raymond master bound by gods grace to Philadelphia in pensilvania

To Lay on hunred forty three bushels of wheat	143
Buck skins two hundred seventy five	275
Doe skins forwer hundred ninty five	495
Fox and cat forty seven	047
Muskrat five minks eighteen raccoon thirty five	
Of beaver fiefty nine pounds	
Two fishins of redd Lead	
Prukets[?] and fawnes forty fower	
Bear skins six	

Being a full acct. of all on board, So witness my hand

Tho. Raymond

Octobr 21 mon Anopolis

Port Roanoke, Customs House Papers, Office of State Comptroller, Office of State Treasurer, State Archives, Office of Archives and History, Raleigh.

Imported in the Brig William directly from Bristol

[. . .] gentlemens superfine beaver hats and an assortment of felt hats, ladies riding hats, [. . .]

Advertisement submitted by John Burgwin, *Cape Fear Mercury* (Wilmington), December 29, 1773, in Colonial Office 5/302, Part II, British Records, State Archives, Office of Archives and History, Raleigh.

In exchange for animal skins, Native Americans obtained European goods from traders like John Vann, who conducted business among the Valley settlements of the Cherokees. John Lederer offered advice to would-be entrepreneurs. As Superintendent John Stuart observed, the luxuries once sought by Indians had become necessities.

	£ [s] [d]
Dr. Jno. Vann To George Parks.	
To	
4 pies. bristol strouds at 37£ eah.	148:
To 1 pie Duffd. Blankets	33. 15.
To 3 pies princes Linnen 89 Ells at 7/6	33. 11. 3
To 1 pie Gardia No 4	10 5.
To 1 pie Do No. 2	9 10
To 1 gross Cadice	2. 15.
To ½ gross fine Gartering at 4£/6	2. 7. 6
To ½ gross Course [illegible] 3£/9	1. 18. 4
To 3 doz. Mens shirts at 15£10 per doz	49. 10
To 1 doz Large Catterus at 5£/6	1. 12. 6
To 2 doz. small Do at 25/	2. 10.
To 2 pis broud Ribbon at 60/	6.
To 2 pies narrow Do at 40/	5.
To 1 pie Oznaburg Con. 127 yds [illegible]	9. 2.
To 1 small guilt Trunk	10
To 64 yds blue and wt Flannel at 12/	38. 8
To 10lb Vermillion at 50/	25.
To 31½ yds red and wt Flannel at 10/	15. 15
To 1lb Oznabrigs Thread	12. 6
To 16lb Paint at 22/6	1. 5.
To 32½ yds Stripd Holland at 18/4	29. 15.
To 35 [illegible] Holland at 8/	14.
[...]	
Brougt Over	£609. 5
To 1 brass Kettle 3 ¼. at 13/4	2. 7. 4
To 40lb Sugar at 3/9	7. 10
To 2 pr. Scissors at 10/	4.
To 2lb. Tea at 35/	3. 10
	£623. 3. 9.
The Advance at 20 pr. Cent.	124. 12. 2
	747. 15.11
To Rum 18½ Gallons at 35/	32. 7. 6
To 6 Hoggs	3. 8.
A bond given for the above	
Errors Exempted	784. 11. 5

Signed pr Geo. Parks

True Copy taken from
the Original the 11th July
1764 before

Edwd Wilkinson
J. Pritchard

Colonial Office 323/23, British Records, State Archives, Office of Archives and History, Raleigh.

If you barely designe a home-trade with neighbour-Indians, for skins of deer, beaver, otter, wild-cat, fox, raccoon, etc. your best truck is a sort of course trading cloth, of which yard and a half makes a matchcoat or mantle fit for their wear; as also axes, hoes, knives, sizars, and all sorts of edg'd tools. Guns, powder and shot, etc. are commodities they will greedily barter for: but to supply the Indians with arms and ammunition, is prohibited in all English governments.

[. . .]

To the remoter Indians, you must carry other kinde of truck, as small looking-glasses, pictures, beads and bracelets of glass, knives, sizars, and all manner of gaudy toys and knacks for children, which are light and portable. For they are apt to admire such trinkets, and will purchase them at any rate, either with their currant coyn of small shells, which they call roanoack or peack, or perhaps with pearl, vermilion, pieces of christal; and towards Ushery, with some odde pieces of plate or buillon, which they sometimes receive in truck from the Oestacks.

"The Discoveries of John Lederer, 1670," in Clarence Walworth Alvord and Lee Bidgood, eds., *First Explorations of the trans-Allegheny region by the Virginians, 1650-1674* (Cleveland: Arthur H. Clark Company, 1912), 169-170. The "Oestacks" were the Westos, an inland Indian nation that had migrated into Virginia and then South Carolina. They became one of the first tribes in the American southeast to be given European firearms, which they used to great effect during their many Indian slave raids. The Westos also served as middlemen in the trade with whites, a position they enjoyed until their destruction in 1680 at the hands of the Savannah Indians and South Carolina.

The Original great tye between the Indians and Europeans was Mutual conveniency. This alone could at first have induced the Indians to receive White people differing so much from themselves into their Country. Before they were acquainted with Europeans they supplyed their few wants with great labor for want of Instruments. Love of ease is natural, and they envied the facility with which they saw Europeans Satisfy much greater wants. An ax, a knife, a Gun, were then deemed inestimable acquisitions, and they could not too much caress or admire people, who contributed to their ease and happiness by furnishing them with such instruments. But their wants tho still moderate are greatly encreased by the facility with which they satisfy them. A Modern Indian cannot subsist without Europeans; And would handle a Flint Ax or any other rude utensil used by his Ancestors very awkwardly; So that what was only Conveniency at first is now become Necessity and the Original tye Strengthned.

> John Stuart, superintendent of Indian Affairs for the southern department, to the Board of Trade, March 9, 1764, in Colonial Office 323/17, British Records, State Archives, Office of Archives and History, Raleigh.

Indians could be tough customers, despite their insatiable appetite for European goods. Whether buying or selling, John Lederer recommended that traders be on their guard. The aggressive behavior of visitors to Cornelius Dougherty's trading establishment in Hiwassee, near present-day Murphy, might have resulted from motives other than mere hard bargaining: Britain and France were at war with each other by 1757 and used trade in an effort to build and maintain alliances with Indian nations.

In dealing with the Indians, you must be positive and at a word: for if they perswade you to fall any thing in your price, they will spend time in higgling for further abatements, and seldome conclude any bargain. Sometimes you may with brandy or strong liquor dispose them to an humour of giving you ten times the value of your commodity; and at other times they are so hidebound, that they will not offer half the market-price, especially if they be aware that you have a designe to circumvent them with drink, or that they think you have a desire to their goods, which you must seem to slight and disparage.

> Alvord and Bidgood, "Discoveries of John Lederer, 1670," 170.

The Examination of James Frazier taken the 4th Day of February, 1757.

In the Absence of Cornelius Doharty, Indian Trader of Highwassie, when the said Doharty was at Fort Loudoun, there came to the said Doharty's four Indian Fellows, two Women and a Boy of the Stinking Linguo's. One of the Fellows came to one McCloud which was at the said Doharty's, and said give me your Shirt for I am a King. Don't you know, says the Fellow, I am a King. If you don't gave me your Shirt, as you go along the Road I will kill you, and take your Shirt from you. What is the English like? for they come very slow. Oh! The French are very good, for they come very fast. What is it like for the English loves their Goods? The French are not so. They threw down a Parcel of Skins to Isaac Atwood that was in charge of the said Goods, and the said Atwood lays by so many Skins for a Matchcoat, a Blankett, a pair Boots, a Flap, which the said Atwood let them have for their Skins. Further the said Frazier says that two of the Fellows spoke in proper English and said, what are the English like Dam, D, D, the English, oh! The French are very good, striking themselves on there Breast at the same Time. They struck the said Doharty's Negroe Fellow, and pushed the said Atwood about and so went off. This is all I can declare on Oath.

Mark
James ——— Frazier's

He further said that Mr. Doharty thinks they are the right down French Indians, and are come as Spies, and they give an Account that there is ten more out, and they were to come to Highwassey, as the others went out. One of our Indians called the Pigeon, Brother to Moytoy, Son to the Mankiller of the abovesaid Town, was with them when all this happened, and was much inclined for joyning with them to any Mischief and was at the Head of them. His Brother, who was here then in the Fort with Mr. Doharty, at his Return Home gave him a good Whipping. On such an Affair as this Mr. Doharty has sent a Summons to all the seven Towns in the Valley to have a Meeting this very Day, and he is to acquaint me immediately with what shall be agreed upon by a Runner. I think it was the best Thing I could have done to give Presents to Moytoy of Highwassey, and to the other Indian called the Black Dog of the Town of Notoly which came both with Lieut. Howarth, and went away highly pleased as I mentioned the same to your Excellency in my Letter.

Rayd. Demere

This Day, the 11th, I heard the above Indians were gone off. There has been a Meeting of the seven Towns on the Valley; they are well affected to us. Mr. Doharty acquainted them with the Talk I gave at Chottee, and they are willing to go to War. I am to hear further in a very few Days.

William L. McDowell Jr., ed., *Documents Relating to Indian Affairs, 1754-1765*, in *The Colonial Records of South Carolina*, Series 2 (Columbia: South Carolina Archives Department, 1970), 330-331. Nottely ("Notoly") stood on the Valley River approximately two miles northeast of present-day Murphy, Cherokee County, North Carolina. Several maps made prior to 1760 place the town of Connostee at this location. Captain Christopher French, who served under Colonial James Grant during the Cherokee War in 1761, asserted that Nottely and Connostee were the same. Demere gave his talk in the Overhill town of Chota ("Chottee"), situated on the south bank of the Little Tennessee River approximately six miles east of present-day Vonore, Tennessee. A portion of Chota now sits beneath Tellico Lake.

Traders frequently married Indian women, who became essential to their husbands' physical and economic survival. In addition to their traditional roles, such as tending crops and preparing food, wives acted as interpreters, cultural instructors, and shopkeepers. The union also melded him into her nation's kinship network.

The *Indian* Traders are those which travel and abide amongst the *Indians* for a long space of time; sometimes for a Year, two, or three. These Men have commonly their *Indian* Wives, whereby they soon learn the *Indian* Tongue, keep a Friendship with the Savages; [. . .] they find these *Indian* Girls very serviceable to them, on Account of dressing their Victuals, and instructing 'em in the Affairs and Customs of the Country.

Lawson, *New Voyage to Carolina*, 190, 192.

Profits from commerce with the Indians could be substantial, an idea that successful trader and future North Carolina chief justice Christopher Gale tried to impress upon his father and brother. Admitting that his outing would have been even more rewarding if he had taken a larger inventory, John Lederer also recognized that goods offered or collected via trade required protection.

I cood wish Bro. Miles were w'th me Just now, for Tomorrow's light I sett out upon an Indian Voiage, in ord'r to followe a shallop's load off Indian goods, w'ch I sent away about 2 Months agoe for Cape Fare River, w'ch Voiage wood make him an expert Carolina Coaster, & Insure him soe far to ye Customes & language off ye Heathen, as to make him a well qualify'd Ind. Trader, by w'ch Imploym't (si adest fortune, & fortune Comes Indubitatus Fortitudo) he may secure for himselfe a Comfortable being in ye world. Iff he comes, he shall not want Imploym't, [. . .]

What Rarity's [thi]s Country affords I shall be M[aste]r off att my returne, being bound a foure Months' voyage or Travell (w'n we can goe noe furth'r by Water), as far to ye W[es]tw[ar]d as ye Appelachin Mountains, to settle an Indian Trade, for w'ch I engag'd in partnership in 100ll. bond.

[Christopher] Gale to Rev. Miles Gale Sr., August 5, 1703, in Walter Clark, ed., *The State Records of North Carolina*, 16 vols. (11-16) (Raleigh: State of North Carolina, 1895-1906), 22:732, 733. A *shallop* is a sloop. Christopher Gale mixed Latin and English in the phrase "si adest fortune, & fortune Comes Indubitatus Fortitudo": if good fortune is present and fortune comes, fortitude is certain.

Could I have foreseen when I set out, the advantages to be made by a trade with those remote Indians, I had gone better provided; though perhaps I might have run a great hazard of my life, had I purchased considerably amongst them, by carrying wealth unguarded through so many different nations of barbarous people: therefore it is vain for any man to propose to himself, or undertake a trade at that distance, unless he goes with strength to defend, as well as an adventure to purchase such commodities: for in such a design many ought to joyn and go in company.

Alvord and Bidgood, "Discoveries of John Lederer, 1670," 170-171.

Gale's rosy outlook aside, traders did experience financial problems. A poor hunt or short-sighted merchant adversely affected income, as Mr. Butler, who operated in the Valley section of the Cherokee nation, could attest. Ludovick Grant, in debt and escorting Cherokee headmen to talks in Charleston, asked South Carolina governor James Glen for protection. A creditor's call upon Cornelius Dougherty at Hiwassee started a chain of events that led to the death of a Cherokee from the town of Nottely.

I cannot help mentioning poor Butler whom I believe your Excellency has a regard for, and not undeservedly, for to my Knowledge there is not a Trader in this Nation, who trades with more Caution, and of whom the Indians complain least; which makes others envy him; he trades by a Yard and Measure he had of me, the Yard I made by a three-foot Rule, but his Indians with many other Towns in this Valley made but very poor Hunts this Winter past, so that a considerable Part of his Goods remain on his Hand. Expecting a summer Hunt, and as far as I can learn he [deals] with one who is not able to trust long, and is much unacquainted with the precarious Nature of this Trade, which chiefly and solely consists in the Indians making good Hunts, which every Winter they do not.

Docharty who was expected by others and did himself expect 13 or 14 thousand Weight of Leather this Winter, had the Indians made but tollerable Hunts will not reach to five thousand, Mr. Butler has taken more than any Man expected, though not in his own Town only; for the Indians knowing he deals honestly by came from other Towns and traded with him. The Town where he lives is hardly capable to maintain a Trader, and I hear his Merchant is neither able nor willing to supply him with Goods to maintain the Trade of a better.

Ludovick Grant to Governor James Glen of South Carolina, March 27, 1755, in McDowell, *Documents Relating to Indian Affairs, 1754-1765*, 44-45.

May it please your Excellency as at this Juncture I am come down with the Indians, and want much to have the Honour to talk to your Excellency before they have the first Hearing; I humbly pray that I may be included in one of your Excellency's Protections, without which I cannot safely appear, and although my Creditors can recover nothing of one in my Circumstances, being utterly incapable to pay the least Mite, yet a Prison might cost me my Life, though but a short one; [. . .]

Ludovick Grant to Governor James Glen, April 29, 1755, in McDowell, *Documents Relating to Indian Affairs, 1754-1765*, 55.

SIR, The other Day happened an Affair at Cornelius Daugherty's House near Highwassee, which I am afraid will be of great Consequence. On the 30th November last Mr. Goudy of Ninety Six, came in the Night at Daugherty's House accompanied with two Constables, and six Men, seized four Negroes and some Goods that were in the House, and carried them away and would have carried Daugherty himself had he not Time to make his Escape, and hide himself. It happened that there were in that Time, some Indians about the House, who seeing white Men carrying away the Negroes and taking the Goods, were frighted, run to Highwassee, and Natalee Towns, alarmed the Women and those that were not gone a hunting, and said that the white People were coming to carry them away, and told them what they had seen. In a little Time, the Women with their Children, and Men were seen crossing the River and taking the Woods to hide themselves, and it seems that some Time after they were told how it was and they came back again because Corporal Bacon whom I had sent to Charles Town to learn the new Exercise happened to come to Daugherty's House the same Morning that that Affair happened and passing through their Towns saw some Indians and Women who seemed to be not well pleased. Bacon has brought from Keowee, the Gun and Pipe Hatchett that your Excellency has sent for the Little Carpenter. The said Bacon has heard some Words when he was at Daugherty's House which he has told me, on which I have taken his Oath and his Deposition which I send to your Excellency. It appears to me that Daugherty was afraid that what he had said to Bacon should be reported to me. Therefore wrote to me four Days after in another Stile which Letter I send enclosed.

On the 4th Instant as Mr. Samll. Benn of Tannissee Town was coming from Ninety Six with a Cargo of Goods that he had been buying there, against the Time that the Indians should come back from Hunting he met Mr. Goudy with his Party, carrying away the Negroes and other Things. They had some Talk together and parted and as Samll. Benn was going away, a Negro Wench said to him, I am afraid, said she, that this Affair will be the Occasion that some Blood will be spilled between Highwassee and Natalee.

On the 8th Instant Benn came to Daugherty's House. He passed there that Night, and next Morning went away, having with him but his Son about eleven Years old, and a Negro Fellow. He passed through Highwassee very quiet and when he came near Natalee he crossed the River, and was surprised to see a great many Women on the Top of their Houses, and a little while after, as he was going up the Mountains, he perceived four Indians running after him, with [Hatchets] and Knives. He, having 17 Horses loaded with Goods, ordered his Son to go before, his Negro in the middle, and he behind. The Indians soon came to him. He asked them what they wanted. They said Rum. He said he had none. Well, said they, we want Goods. He told them they should have none, and the Goods that I have, said he, are for the Upper Towns. They attempted several Times to hold fast of some Horses and cut off the Wanters, but he hindered them as much as he could. He argued a long while with them, saying I have been nineteen Years among you and we were always Friends and have passed hundred and hundred Times through your Towns and you never said any Thing to me in Anger. What is the Matter with you now? They answered, The white People have begun to be Rogues, it is high Time for us to be so now. They endeavoured several Times to seize some Horses, but he hindered them. Then they said, He won't give us Goods, let us beat him. On which they took Sticks and Stones and threw at him. He begged and prayed several Times to let him alone, but all in vain, and finding that he could hold no longer, and ready to fall down from his Horse, he took one of his Pistols and as one of the most desperate was going to knock him with a large Stone, he shot at him and killed him. Then the others immediately left the Field and ran as fast as they could towards the Town.

The Negro Fellow seeing his Master half dead, told him to go away as fast as he could towards Tellico, saying, The Indians hearing that you have killed one of them will be here soon with their Arms, and will kill you. Perhaps finding you are gone, they won't kill us, upon which he pushed on his Horse as well as he could towards the Mountain. He had not been a great Way of that he saw the Indians coming with their Guns black painted. They soon joined the Negro Fellow and finding that Benn was gone away, they took a Horse along with them, that was loaded with Strouds and other Things, and carried away the dead Corps. In the same Time told the Fellow to go and encamp at a Place called Tuotee, and if he went further, he should be killed.

Saturday Night the 10th Instant, Samll. Benn came to his House at Tanissee and next Day he came to the Fort in a Canoe, not being able to sit on Horseback. The Doctor examined him, and in my Days I never saw a Man so much bruised from his Shoulders down to the Waste of his Back. He was as black as Ink; not able to go away that Night he staid in the Fort and was dressed. Next Morning I advised him to go with the Linguist and the Doctor to Chotee, and tell Old Hop how he had been used and relate to him the whole Story. Accordingly he did; and the Old Man saw him, and heard the Whole. He was very sorry for it and said if Chotee People, and Tanissee were come back from hunting, they would go immediately and ask Satisfaction for using their Traders in that Manner. He said further, I am sure that some white Man was the Occasion of this Usage, and has told the Indians some Story, for otherwise they would never have done it, but said he, it will be soon known for Indians will not keep it long secret. He told Samll. Benn to not be afraid of the Consequences, for it was the Indians' Fault, and their own Seeking, and it was in his own Defence, that he did kill him. [. . .]

On the 24th Instant Judge's Friend came from Hunting. He stopped at the Fort to know if any Thing had happened in his Absence. I related to him the whole Story of Samll. Benn, and how he had killed the Indian. He answered that the Indian had no Business to ask for Goods, as he knew that they were coming to the Towns and that he was seeking his Death, and that Samll. Benn did right. I told him likewise that the Lame Arm, Head Man of Tellico, had been with me, and that he was gone to Natalee, to fetch Benn's Goods and had promised me to come back immediately and that I intended to send an Express to your Excellency, to acquaint you with the Particulars, [. . .]

On the 28th Old Hop sent me Word that the Head Man of Tellico was come to Tanassee with Samll. Benn's Goods, and that as soon as he had examined what was wanting, he would send him to me. Accordingly the next Day he came to the Fort with all Tellico People and said Brother, according to my Promise, I have been to Natalee, and as you thought, as well me, that Cornelius Daugherty was the Occasion of this Mischief, I have been to his House, and have enquired into every Particular and I have found that he is innocent of this and has been with me to every Town, and all the Indians have cleared him. When I came back to Natalee said he and enquired after Samll. Benn's Goods, the Cock Eye Warriour told me, that the Goods were in the Camp, and said that he was sorry such a Thing had happened, that he never saw any such Thing before, that he was always very glad to see the English pass by his Town and wished it might continue so and desired him to tell me, that I would not think any more about it. That he himself was the Head Man of the Family of the young Man that was killed, the most numerous in all the Cherokees, that he was quite forgotten, as he knew very well, that it was his own Seeking. I have, said the Headman, brought all Samll. Benn's Horses and Goods, but if any Thing is missing, I am most sure, that the white Men have stole them. For my Part, I am very glad to find that the Indians think that they are so much in the wrong, for I am very well informed, that if Samll. Benn had paid them a Bagg of Salt, as he had promised them, and if he had not been so very hasty in pulling out his Pistol, Nothing of this would have happened.

Captain Paul Demere, commander of Fort Loudoun, to Governor William Henry Lyttelton of South Carolina, December 30, 1757, in McDowell, *Documents Relating to Indian Affairs, 1754-1765*, 426-428, 429, 430. Tuotee cannot be identified.

The Indian trade was rife with debt. Many Native Americans purchased goods on credit, promising payment with skins from a future hunt. A succession of poor hunts would push them deeper and deeper into trouble. Late-paying customers could expect visits from men like John Sharp and Bernard Hughs, who traded among the Cherokees, to settle overdue accounts. Indians caught in the credit trap struck back: Catuchee killed Hughs's assistant, and Atkin warned that large-scale reprisals were possible. To remove indebtedness as a flashpoint for violence, colonies attempted to restrict the amount of credit that traders could extend, but those efforts largely failed.

[August 21, 1725.] I must informe You that I have an Accot that Mr. Sharp one of Our Indian Traders amongst you came to one of the Towns of yr Nation in the Night time and took away what Skines was in the Town (and as I am informed) gave the Indians what he pleased for them. Now as your head men are altogether I Expect you [to] lett me know the truth of this Matter, that I may right the Persons that are injured being sent among you, to see that you have all Justice done you in Order that there may be a good Understanding betwixt you and us, who have always Esteemed you as our Brothers. [. . .]
To the foregoing talk they returned the following Answer:
I[n] Answer to the Parragraph in relation to Sharp, the head Warriour of Tuegelo Spoak as follows: That he knew the whole Matter and that Sharp did not take away any Skines from any Indians but was gathering in his Debts from them.

Entry of August 21, 1725, in "Journal of Colonel George Chicken," in Newton D. Mereness, ed., *Travels in the American Colonies* (New York: Antiquarian Society, 1961), 129, 130.

The 5th of this Instant I had Occasion to be at Mr. Butler's, where an Indian, Brother to the Warriour Usteneue, and a Messenger sent by the Headmen of Kettewa River to him, passed the Town Chewee, giving an Account that a Fellow of that Town Kettewa had killed a white Man, (Bernard Hughs's Man). It is said that Hugs with his Man [went throw] the Towns that Day a Debt Hunting, and in their Return homewards mett near to his House an Indian (Catuchee by Name, English, the Tail) who owed him 4 Weight of Leather, and asked him for his Debt. The Man told him he refused to trust him Ammunition in the Fall to kill his Debt, and having but little Powder he had killed but few Deer, and laid them out to cloath himself, but that he would pay him in the Summer, or the first he killed should be his, upon which the white Man abused the Fellow calling him Names, and seized his Gun for the Debt, the Indian being unwilling to part from it, they both fell upon him with their Horse Whips, and with the Lash, and butt Ends thereof cutt and bruised the Fellow very much and broke his Gun, with which he intended to go to War the next Day, the Enemy having killed a Woman 2 Days before belonging to Kettewa. The Indian seeing himself bloody and bruised run into the adjacent House and snatching up a Gun run at Hughs and the Man who was killed, who being next to him he shot dead on the Spot. He was one of, if not the strongest Man in the Province. There has been since several Councils held throughout the Nation concerning the Affair; what the Result will be, God knows. The Indians stick close to the Article of the late Ordinance, wherein it is ordered that no Trader shall plunder or beat any Indian for a Debt, and to speak the Truth it is all together wrong so to do. The Man killed was North Carolina by Birth, and being of a mild, obliging, affable Temper, believe he was sett on to abuse the Indian.

> Ludovick Grant to Governor James Glen, February 8, 1754, in William L. McDowell Jr., ed., *Documents Relating to Indian Affairs, 1750-1754*, in *The Colonial Records of South Carolina, Series 2* (Columbia: South Carolina Archives Department, 1958), 475-476. The "Kettewa River" was the Tuckasegee.

<*Indians not to be trusted with Goods.*> Order'd That for the future the Indian Traders do not presume to Trust or give any Credit to the Indians; and that the aforesaid Commissioners take Care to see this Order observed.

> North Carolina Executive Council Minutes, October 14, 1736, in Robert J. Cain, ed., *Records of the Executive Council, 1735-1754*, Volume 8 of *The Colonial Records of North Carolina* [*Second Series*], eds. Mattie Erma Edwards Parker, William S. Price Jr., Robert J. Cain, and Jan-Michael Poff (Raleigh: Division of Archives and History, Department of Cultural Resources, [projected multivolume series, 1963–], 1988), 62.

The pernicious Consequences of which larger Credit, are no less than these. It gives the Traders an undue Influence over such Indians in matters of Public Concern; It discourages the Indians from Hunting for Deer Skins and other Furrs, and renders them indolent, seeing in such Case the Product of their Labour is to go to pay only for what is past; If they are tempted with the same, instead of paying their Debts; to purchase supplies for their present or Future Wants, it thence produces Quarrels between them and the Traders; by which the Provincial Peace and Safety is Hazarded, seeing according to the Nature of Indian Governmt. the Nation is often involved in the Consequences of the Act of any Single Man. It also inclines the Young Fellows to mischief, and is an inducement with them in certain Conjunctures to break out War with us, or to Desert us, as being the surest and easiest method of Cancelling their Debts, when too heavy for them.

> Wilbur R. Jacobs, ed., *Indians of the Southern Colonial Frontier: The Edmond Atkin Report and Plan of 1755* (Columbia: University of South Carolina Press, 1954), 22-23.

Some traders treated their customers well: Mr. Butler, mentioned above, attracted business from a wide area because he was deemed to be fair, and a reputation for honesty protected Patrick Galahan of Cowee from attack. But others were cheats and could be abusive. John Sharp berated and assaulted his Indian customers. Indians complained repeatedly about false weights and measures, but traders believed that shorting them helped ensure profitability that in turn protected their credit. Ludovick Grant wrote that "iron yards" intended to assist the Indians in their transactions were never delivered. Colonial officials feared that rancor caused by traders' dishonest dealing, insulting behavior, and physical maltreatment would lead to retaliation by aggrieved tribes: it had been a major factor in the outbreak of the Tuscarora and Yamasee wars in 1711 and 1715, respectively.

I took my residence with Mr. Galahan the chief trader here, an ancient respectable man, who had been many years a trader in this country, and is esteemed and beloved by the Indians for his humanity, probity and equitable dealings with them; which, to be just and candid I am obliged to observe (and blush for my countrymen at the recital) is somewhat of a prodigy; as it is a fact, I am afraid too true, that the white traders in their commerce with the Indians, get great and frequent occasions of complaint of their dishonesty and violence: but yet there are few exceptions, as in the conduct of this gentleman, who furnishes a living instance of the truth of the old proverb, that "Honesty is the best policy;" for this old honest Hibernian has often been protected by the Indians, when all others round about him have been ruined, their property seized and themselves driven out of the country or slain by the injured, provoked natives.

William Bartram, *Travels through North and South Carolina, Georgia, East and West Florida* (1791; reprint, Savannah: Beehive Press, 1973), 351-352.

[. . .] we had one Mr. John Sharp a Factor that used them very roughly by beating and abuseing them Cutting severall of them with his Cutlash, and would scarce suffer them to come into his House, but turn'd them out by force, scarce suffering them to come within his doors to Trade, but as the Indians have often told me would make them take the goods out at the Doore or window, and continualy calling them ill names, such as Rogues and old Women, which there cannot be a greater affront given to an Indian then to call him an old Woman; [. . .] The Indians have offten made their complaint to me of his ill usage to 'em, I as offten exhibited the same to the Governor and Commissioners they went down severall on them with their great Conjurour at the Head of [*illegible*] purpose [*illegible*] complain of him themselves, and with all to desire that he might not come any more amongst them, but they found they could not be address'd till at last they told me that since he was sent up again that if he still continued his ways in abuseing them they would make no more Complaints but would take their own Satisfaction [...]

> Some Short Remarks on the Indian Trade in the Charikees and the Management thereoff since the year 1717, in The Society for the Propagation of the Gospel in Foreign Parts, Letterbooks, Series C, 7, British Records, State Archives, Office of Archives and History, Raleigh.

A Talk of the Warriors and beloved Men of the Valley of Highwassee and Tommothy ordered to be sent down to his Excellency by such of the Warriours as [were] present, and by the Warrior of Tommothy's Desire in the behalf of others who could not conveniently attend the Meeting, but gave their unanimous Consent to what he should say is as follows

THE WARRIOR OF TOMMOTHY, SPEAKER. He says he remembers still since the Warrior of Tecethece, Suttallitchee by Name, was in England and that when he returned he told them, before he saw the King, being surprized he was as it were in a Dream, not thinking there could be so great a Man, but after he had seen him, he was perswaded in himself that it was he, and that all the Talk they had between them was good. [...] that he had been before the Lords of Trade which he said were beloved Men appointed by the King, to see that all his Subjects traded honestly, who among several other Things they talkt of, told them, that if they at any Time should have any Complaint or Grievance, they had no doubt Men in their Nation who could write, and should inform the Governor thereof, and that the Governor would write to them, and what they complained of should be redressed, and that those head beloved Men further told Suttellitchee that if they wanted a Supply of Arms and Ammunition to assist them against their Enemies it should be sent them, and that they should be always well supplyed with a Trade from the English there Brothers.

He says further Suttelletchee told him, that he said to the King that the Path was now made streight between him and his People over the great Water where the King and his People lived, and that the Chain of Friendship which now was fastned to each of their Hearts, though it was at a great Distance, should never be broke, and that now as the Governor had lately made the Path between their Nation, and himself, and his People broad and streight, it should no more be spoiled while he lived. He says he only mentions these Things to the Governor to lett him know that though the Man he spoke of is dead, he was while alive always well affected to the white People and told him still to be the same. He says he still does and will remember his Talk and that he thinks thereon daily from the rising of the Sun to his going down and even when he is in Bed. And that as he is now an old Man and cannot expect to live long, he daily talks to his young Men, to be good and always to love the white

People, for what can they do without the English, and he hopes they will continue to love the English as long as any of them lives.

[. . .]

He says that where they have been supplyed from formerly they have had both short Measure of Cloath and Powder although the Governor and his beloved Men ordered good Measure of both. That most of the Traders had thrown the Governor's Talk away, and neither regarded him nor his beloved Men, when they were out of their Sight which he believes the Governor does not know. He says that he knows they have been in Times past much cheated by [false] Stilliards and short Yards, and desires that each Trader may bring up a Pair of true Stilliards, and yard and Powder measure, such as the Governor shall approve of.

> Warriors of Hiwassee and Tomotla to Governor James Glen of South Carolina, April 15, 1754, in McDowell, *Documents Relating to Indian Affairs, 1750-1754*, 504-506. "Tommothy" refers to Tomotla. Tomotla and Tasetche ("Tecethece") stood in the Valley River Valley. A *stilliard*, or steelyard, is a type of scale: "a balance consisting of a lever with unequal arms, which moves on a fulcrum; the article to be weighed is suspended from the shorter arm, and a counterpoise is caused to slide upon the longer arm until equilibrium is produced, its place on this arm (which is notched or graduated) showing the weight." *OED*.

Mr. Elliot begun well, and I believe would have continued, but finding himself to be the only Man, and a Stranger, soon found he must either follow the Multitude, endanger his own Safety, or find some other Way of living, which at that Time he could not safely do, in respect of his Credit from his Merchants, without hurting both himself and them; I don't pretend to say Mr. Elliot is without Faults, but this far I dare affirm, that he would be cautious not to hurt his Creditors or endanger the Peace of the Province, were he among Men who had Regard to the Laws, and their own and the Province's Safety.

I am confident there will be many and greivous Complaints made to your Excellency concerning the Trade, in cheating the Indians in the Prices of Goods, especially of light Goods, such as Linnings, Flannels, &c. &c., of fals Stilliards, short Yards, and little Measures, which I am conscious are not groundless in that respect on severals in this Nation, and although the Trade at Present is at such a low Ebb and the Price of Skins so smal, that it cannot be afforded cheaper especially Strouds, and Duffles, yet they may and ought to have the Yard and Measure your Excellency appointed; the Iron Yards which were made, and appointed to be left at the respective Towns in the Nation, were never brought up, but left at McGregor's House, where they are stil if not lost; and few or none of the Powder Measures were brought up, the Traders pretending they had no Punctual Orders to carry them; [. . .]

> Ludovick Grant to Governor James Glen of South Carolina, March 27, 1755, in McDowell, *Documents Relating to Indian Affairs, 1754-1765*, 41-42.

Determined to prevent the armed conflict that could arise from unethical behavior, colonial governments mandated that traders be licensed. Licensing would enable them to limit the number of traders who traveled into the Indian nations; restrict the towns in which the bearer was permitted to operate; and reduce competition among traders, thus creating stable markets and happy customers. Each trader submitted a bond to ensure his good conduct and was required to adhere to the appropriate regulations of the issuing colony. Licenses were obtained from the commissioners for the Indian trade, who were to enforce the rules of commerce.

> Resolved that a Commission Issue directed to Colonel Robert West Mr. Francis Pugh Mr. Thomas Bryant Mr. John Speir and Mr. Thomas Kearney constituting and appointing them Comissioners for the Indian Trade for and within this Province.

> Resolution of January 22, 1731/32, Cain, *Records of the Executive Council, 1735-1754*, 8:238.

I come back now to the Province of South Carolina. The place of Interviews and Treaties with Indian Chiefs is at Charles Town, from whence a Trade is carried on among several Numerous and Independent Nations, by Horse Carriage only, Eight Hundred Miles. To wit, the Catawbas, Cherokees, Creeks, Chicasaws; and not long since the Chactaws also. That Government hath appointed a Commissioner for regulating the Trade with the Indians in Friendship therewith, conformable to the particular directions of An Act made for Preserving Peace, and continuing a good Correspondence and for regulating the Trade with them. Which hath been revived, and alter'd from time to time; the last Act in force being passed in April 1739 and the present Act in May 1752. Since the fatal experience of the Indian War in 1715 which was occasioned by the Dealings of an Agent, the said Commissioner, and every Agent at any time to be sent among the Indians, hath been and is strictly prohibited to sell any Indian Trading Goods to any Indian or other Trading Person whatsoever; or to receive any Presents from any Indians, or Traders without the Leave of the Legislature, other than Provisions for his Subsistence while among them. No Person is allowed to Trade with any of them without a Licence from the Commissioner; who is required to give one to every Person applying, of honest Repute, and Sober Conversation; having publish'd their Names ten days at his office, and no just Cause appearing to the Contrary, and giving Bond for £200 Proclama. Money with Suerity that he, and the Men (of like Character) employed to go with him, whose Names are to be inserted in his Licence, will demean themselves well towards the Indians; and that he will Obey and Observe all Orders and Instructions given him from time to time by the Commissioner; who is to give him at first going

Instructions annex'd to his Licence, agreeable to the Law, under his hand and Seal of Office. And he is to insert in the Licence the Nation, and if it be among the Cherokees, or Creeks, the particular Town or Towns wherein such Trader intends and is permitted to Trade; but is not to transgress those Limits; allotting to each Trader two or more Towns, if one be too small; so that the whole be equally divided among the several Traders. Those Licences are to be in force only one Year (except the Chicasaw or Chactaw Nation, 18 Months) and to expire in March, April, May, or June; in one of which months every Trader is to come annually to Charles Town and take out a new Licence in Person as before; During which absence he may leave any one of the Men employed by him and named in his Licence, to take Care of his Storehouse & Goods; and empower him the mean while to Trade with the Goods so left in his Custody. But neither of them is at any other time to traffick with any Indian by any ways whatsoever. The Commissioner, or any Agent at any time sent by the Government, is empower'd and required to hear & determine all Complaints between any Indians and Traders; And to award to any Indian damages not exceeding £5 Proclama Money; And to agree with and employ Interpreters, and to swear them to Interpret faithfully the Talks and Discourses between the said Commissioner or Agent and any Indians; to the end that the Indian Trade may be the better Order'd and Settled, and that the Complaints of the Indians may be fully heard or understood, and their Grievances if any happen may be effectually redressed; And also to hire Messengers and Horses upon Emergencies, to send Express to the Commander in Chief, or to give Notice to the Inhabitants in case of Danger; the charge of which Interpreters and Messengers is to be paid out of the publick Treasury. And the said Commissioner is to do in all cases relating to the Indian Trade, as the Law directs, and is most conducive to the Good of that Province; And is also to observe such directions as from time to time he shall receive from the Governor and Council, or the General Assembly, and not otherways [except] in cases of an extraordinary [nature] wherein the immediate safety of that Province is Concern'd, and not directed and provided in that Act.

Jacobs, *Edmond Atkin Report and Plan of 1755*, 17-19.

[Sou]th Carolina

By Virtue of a Licence Granted to me by the Honorable Wm. Bull Esqr. Lieut. Governor etc., in and over Said province Bearing date June the 4th. Instant 1764.

Permitts John Vann to Trade with the Cherokee Indians in the Following Towns Videlicet Econourste, Higwassa Little Tellico, or any other Town in the Valley he being in my Employ and has given Bond with Sufficient Security as the Law Directs.

This permit Continu[es During Pleasure]

Given under my hand and Seal, this 4th. Day of June 1764.

(Signed) George Parks (Seal)

Copy taken from the
Original 11th July 1764
(Signed) Edward Wilkinson
       J Robinson Serjeant

It appears by the Inclosed acct. of Goods Sold to John Vann by George Parks that said Vann was to Trade by and for himself by virtue of the above permit at large and that he was not a substitute or agent for George Parks [*illegible*] General Licence from Lieutenant Governor Bull.

Colonial Office 323/23, British Records, State Archives.

Colonial officials relied on licensed traders to act on their behalf and to provide information on the tribes they visited. Their skills as interpreters were highly valued, although royal councilor and merchant Edmond Atkin believed they sometimes spoke too freely. Colonel George Chicken, trade commissioner for South Carolina, authorized Samuel Brown to travel to the Catawba nation and inspect the licenses of traders. James May was given the difficult assignment of serving an arrest warrant on another trader in the Cherokee Middle Settlements.

The Publick of No. Carolina to John Slocumb Dr.
To three day's attendance as interpreter for the Indians the first assembly held at Newbern per order of the Governor.

May 22, 1746, Box 1, Indian Affairs and Lands, Office of State Treasurer, State Archives, Office of Archives and History, Raleigh.

[. . .] None [the French] dare to talk with the Indians about State Affairs but standing Sworn Interpreters, and they only what is given in Charge; who occasionally throw out what is suitable for their Purposes. Whereas our Traders uncontrouled tell them every man what Story he pleases[.]

Jacobs, *Edmond Atkin Report and Plan of 1755*, 12.

Thursday the 26th day of August 1725:
[. . .]

Gave the following Authority to Mr. Saml. Brown Indian Trader:

You are hereby Authorized and required as soon as you Arrive in the Catabaw Nation to Inspect into the Lycences of all persons trading there and an Accot thereof to take and return to me on Oath as soon as possible as also an Accot of all persons Trading or residing in those parts without my leave or Lycence and all persons in the said Nation are hereby required to pay due Obedience to these my Orders as they will Answer the Contrary at their Peril.

Given under my hand and the Seal of Office for Regulating Indian Affairs this 26th day of August Anno Domo. 1725.

"Journal of Colonel George Chicken," August 25, 1725, in Mereness, *Travels in the American Colonies*, 132-133.

Cowee, Sept. 27th, 1755

MAY IT PLEASE YOUR EXCELLENCY, Yours I received by Troy and according to your Orders shewed your Letter to Mr. Dannoll. It was of no Use to give him a Copy as he could not read it. And the Day after Troy came home went in Pursuit of Branham, but meeting Mr. Crawford in the Path informed me, he was gone in the Horse Range, and there to stay 3 or 4 Nights on which I returned Home and he with me as there was a Green Corn Dance in the Town. In the first Place I pressed him to aid and assist in the taking of Branham for at the Juncture of Time as he told me he would be at Home I would be there. Next I commanded Ambrose Davis Alias Collier, but his Reply was I might be damned and my Orders too, [. . .] If I thought I could have answered it I would [have] tyed him that Moment and seized him with an Intent to do it.

To make short the Day prefixed, no Way disputing Mr. Dannoll he went in the Horse Range, which Troy asked him if he would not go. His Answer was he was in the Range, but, however to obey just Commands and your Excellency's Orders I went getting no one with me but Troy and one Thomas Norris, a Taylor here, who went very willingly, for I imagined as Mr. Crawford lived in the Town where Branham was thought I was sure of him and his Man, but they told me he was gone in the Horse Range. This so provoked me that I vowed, let what would befall me, I would have him, but meeting Chucheche he asked me my Errand which I told him and that it was his Request from your Excellency and asked him to go with me but his Answer was Branham had paid a great deal, never suspecting it was to save him, but soon found it after. I asked him where he was which he told me at such a House on which I went with a Gun in my Hand and there appeared Branham, his son, and one Aaron Price who I commanded directly to assist but he swore he would not. Branham had a Gun in his Hand, his Son another Pipe Hatchet and Knife. Branham swore if I did not stand of he would shoot me. I told him if I saw him offer to lift the Gun as far as his Knee, by all that was sacred I would shoot him down for neither he nor his Son should scare me. Price standing by told me I had better leave of or the Man Killer would kill me if I tyed him so directly found out how the Storey was and then know what Chucheche meant. Though did not take him at first, but I served his Majesty's Warrant on him notwithstanding his Fire Arms, [. . .]

Now I hope your Excellency sees how Indians will first desire a Favour and make Complaints and after how readily byast. And this Price by outward Appearance and his Behaviour seems he had a Notion of assisting Branham if Occasion served. He is one of the runnagade Aligena Traders who unfortunately fell in with Mr. Lambton which I am sorry for and supplies this Branham, that now its to be imagined it will take Half a Cargoe to pay for screening this Villain. I asked Checheche and Tossitee the Reason why they should give your Excellency all this unnecessary Trouble, first desire a Favour and now to hinder Branham to be carried which was their Desire, on which Chucheche spoke as follows (Viz.)

"He thanked you, his Brother, and found you were no Wayes neglectfull of your Promise, but he talked to Branham and he has promised to be good and there should be no more bad Talks of him."

Tossittee further said that those Accusations against Branham he believes was not all true though allows he both complained against him and wanted him from here.

Further any Whiteman or Indian that misses or has missed their Horses he'l take care to see, if in Branham's Range, they shall be delivered.

But had the White People come as I summoned we would have carried him away in spite of his Help or their should be better Men than we. Your Excellency may plainly see what little Regard they have to either his Majesty or you, who represents him, notwithstanding they are all sensible of the Fatigue, Cost and Trouble you have been at endeavouring to keep this Nation in Order but daily circumvented by a Parcel of idle People here telling the Indians every lying Report they hear which creates great Confusion and I am sensible no Place so pestered with them as the Middle Settlements, which to my great Loss as well as the Gentlemen who supplies me. [. . .] John Burns was run away out of the Nation before Troy came up, therefore if you see Cause to carry Branham down I'll take an Opportunity and stay at Home when they are gone a hunting, but shall proceed no further until I have your Excellency's Orders, [. . .] but I heartily wish you may find all his Majesty's Subjects in this Nation to hold their Integrity if Occasion serves and to be as willing and ready as I on any Call to serve the Country wherein I now belong.

James May to Governor James Glen of South Carolina, September 27, 1755, in McDowell, *Documents Relating to Indian Affairs, 1754-1765*, 80-81.

Traders supported their clients whenever possible. Moravian bishop August Gottlieb Spangenberg referred positively to Thomas Whitmell's relationship with the Tuscaroras. But advocacy sometimes ran afoul of official goals and policies. Edmond Atkin asserted that some traders actually disrupted the leadership hierarchy in a tribe when they eagerly tried to elevate the status of a particular Indian. Dead warriors could not buy goods or repay debts, traders reasoned, and James May did all he could to keep the Cherokees from joining the British forces against the French.

[September 19, 1752.] Their Interpreter, Mr. Thomas Whitemeal, was kind to us, took us to them [the Tuscarora], showed us their land, and introduced us to them. He was at one time a Trader among them, understands their language fairly well, and speaks it with ease. Now he is one of the richest men in the neighborhood, and is respected by everybody.

[. . .]

Mr. Whitemeal is their Agent and Advocate, and stands well with them.

Diary of Bishop August Gottlieb Spangenberg, in Adelaide L. Fries et al., eds., *Records of the Moravians in North Carolina*, 13 vols. (Raleigh: Office of Archives and History, Department of Cultural Resources, 1922-2006), 1:41.

As the Government in the situation before related, is under a Necessity of taking its information and Intelligence of the Indian Affairs almost intirely from the Indian Traders, whereby as I said before, its Acts or Measures are affected (being sometimes either kept in the Dark, or hurried into needless Expence just as it happens, there being nothing found so Difficult often times as to distinguish the Truth or Falsehood of their Intelligence); so when Indians come to Charles Town, Traders who write Letters by them, or come as Interpreters with them, by their recommendations impose their own Favourites or Friends upon the Government as Leading Men, for the sake of Presents; by which means many Indians receive valuable Presents, who have really very little Influence in their Nation. Nay sometimes such receive by the same means Commissions also, which cannot but displease the Men of Superior Sway in their own Towns.

Jacobs, *Edmond Atkin Report and Plan of 1755*, 28-29.

A Memorandum, April 20th, 1758. That as I, James Beamer, was a going to Jore with Colonel Byrd and Colonel Howarth, we mett an Indian Fellow at the Clay Pitts nigh Stecowee Old Town. Colonel Howarth and I stopt. Colonel Howarth desired me to ask the Indian if those in the Middle Settlements were ready to go according to their Promise (to him) to Virginia with Colonel Byrd. He said he could not tell, they were almost all out a Hunting and that the White Man of Cowee (James May) told them not to mind the Talks of the Warriors that came from Virginia and Carolina, but to remember how many of your People has dyed going to Carolina and to the Assistance of the White People at different Times, and that there Bones lay white upon the Road, and if you go with these Warriours to Virginia, it's so far that you will dye or be killed for not a Man of you will ever return.

> McDowell, *Documents Relating to Indian Affairs, 1754-1765*, 451-452. "Jore" is Ioree, which stood on Iotla Creek between Whatoga and Cowee. Clay pits had existed outside Stecoe on Stekoa Creek near present-day Clayton, Rabun County, Georgia.

Licensing held great promise as a concept, but in practice it did not stop scofflaws from cheating or abusing Indians. A Catawba headman was badly beaten after challenging two traders over a license. Nor did licensing make competition any less-cutthroat: rival traders continued underselling each other and bribing customers; Cornelius Dougherty seemed willing to bankrupt his business partner, John Elliott. Edmond Atkin observed that commissioners had been lax in their enforcement duties, because funds for journeys to Indian nations to check up on traders had not been forthcoming.

Catabaw Nation, 13th January, 1751/52

MAY IT PLEASE YOUR EXCELLENCY, When I was last in Charles Town Mr. Steel fitted a Negro Fellow out with Goods to come up to the Nation to trade. When he and the white Men that was with him came in, the King and another Head Man went to see them and he asked the Negro if he had a Paper from your Excellency that was Licence for to come here and trade, and told him that without that he should not stay here and was very angry about it. And they observing he was not willing that they should stay the Negro Fellow and one John Dudgeon made the King and the other Head Man drunk and amongst them beat and abused the King in a very gross Manner that he could not see out of his Eyes for five or six Days and was obliged to keep his Bed for a considerable Time. And when he recovered he was going to carry the white Man and the Negro down to your Excellency but I over persuaded him not to do it untill your Excellency would hear of it and your Answer concerning it. The King and what Head Men there is in the Nation at Present is very angry that a Negro should trade here and has told him to be gone with his Goods and carry them to Mr. Steel but he will not which gives them a great Deal of Uneasiness.

May it please your Excellency for to send how the Presents is to be divided amongst the Indians for I will be down as soon as they all come in with them to the Congerees whether the Indians is to divide them or not.

Matthew Toole to Governor James Glen, January 13, 1751/52, in McDowell, *Documents Relating to Indian Affairs, 1750-1754*, 201.

Besides their Neglect or Breach of their particular Instructions, in every which Case the public is consequently more or less affected, they cheat the Indians most abominably both in Weight and Measure; as well as otherways abuse them (against which things indeed tis remarkable their is no Instruction, nor—Penalty by Law) And no check being put upon their avarice, they exact what [Rates] they please for Goods. The principal Offences of the Traders against the Act of 1739 by breach of their Instructions, whereby the publick was most Affected, were, Vizt—1st. Their not [only] Transgressing themselves the Limits prescribed by their Licences, but permitting and employing their Servants, even Pack horse Men, whom they have sent to and left in Towns alone, to trade with the Indians; whose Behaviour, being for the most part the most worthless of Men, is more easy to be conceived than described.

Jacobs, *Edmond Atkin Report and Plan of 1755*, 22.

[. . .] it was impracticable to get the Traders to observe their Instructions while some did undersell the other, some used light other heavy Weights, some bribed the Indians to lay out their Skins with them, others told the Indians that their Neighbouring Traders had heavy Weights and stole their Skins from them, but that they themselves had light Weights and that their Goods were better; finding, I say, these Things must tend at last to distract and confound the Indians, and that while the Traders acted separately it was impracticable to prevent such Practices, I judged it must needs tend more to their own Benefit, as well as to the Security of the Friendship that ought to subsist always between the Indians and us, [. . .]

Captain Patrick McKey to Lieutenant Governor Thomas Broughton of South Carolina, July 12, 1735, in J. H. Easterby, ed., *The Journal of the Commons House of Assembly, November 10, 1736-June 7, 1739*, in *The Colonial Records of South Carolina, Series 1* (Columbia: The Historical Commission of South Carolina, 1951), 121-122.

Tomatly, April 30th, 1752

MAY IT PLEASE YOUR EXCELLENCY, Next Day after Mr. Elliot came Home, I went at his Request to Mr. Docharty's with him and read your Letter to him, and asking what Answer he would send, he swore by God he never said any Thing (what said he) I promise Elliott a Gang of my Horses for five and twenty Pound, no by God. I desired him take care what he said, and asked him did he think his Excellency would assert a Lie; that I myself heard him say so, both before he went to the Governour and again in the Governour's Presence confirm the same. He said again that if he ever said so he was drunk. I told him he was right in his Senses at the Time and himself proposed going to his Excellency's Lodging that Morning. I supposed to inform him what he had determined to do with Relation to the Partnership between him and Mr. Elliott, and that if I had thought him in the least drunk I should have been loth to have accompanied him thither for my own Creditt's Sake. I then repeated the Form of his Promise which was as follows, I told him that (if he would) he might remember one Morning he desired me to accompany him to the Governor, and that on the Street he said freely without any Suggestion of either Elliott or myself, Grant, I'll let the little Scotchman have forty Pack Horses for 25 Pounds a Head and that you would let him have them so cheap because being in Company with him you should have an equal Share of the Profitts of their Work to which I answered that you did right, and that I was sure it would turn out more to your Advantage than the whole Value of the Horses, and when you came before the Governor you told him, please, your Excellency, I have before Mr. Grant, let Mr. Elliott, as he is to be my Partner in Trade, have forty Pack Horses for 25 Pound per Head. This you said without the Governour's speaking one Word relating to the Affair at that Time and all this I told him he said of himself without the least Proposal or Argument to extort the same. His Answer was what? He let him have a Gang of his Horses. No, what had he running up and down like a Vagabond? No, by God, he would sooner go to Prison and there eat and drink them before any such whistling Monky Fellow should have it to say that he had bitt old Docharty. All this was in an unreasonable Passion so that I thought it needless to say any Thing further to a mad Man which he most resembled at that Time.

The Raven of Tunesee desired Mr. Elliott would please to come there after he had been over the Hills, which he did and I accompanied him thither the 2nd Time after the Indians. Thanks to your Excellency and the honourable Council, was delivered Mr. Elliott, and I called Mr. Docharty out by himself in order to talk to him privately. Mr. Elliott desired to know what Answer he had proposed to send your Excellency, and as he seemed inflexible, neither was determined to hear either Law or Reason, he intended to sett off for Carolina. He told him he might go, that when Kelly returned with the Answer to his Letters he would send then his Answer. That he had no Business with whither he went or stayed. Mr. Elliott desired that [what?] Skins there was might be sent down to the Merchant. He told him he had no Business with the Skins he had, that he would send them down by one that he could trust better, using opprobious Language which Mr. Elliott at that Time, as he said, was resolved to give a deaf Ear to till he could get him where he might have Justice. Mr. Docharty said he would not be long behind him, go when he would. Mr. Elliott told him he wished he could have the Honour of seeing him there. Docharty, in a boisterous Manner, made Answer, what, do you threaten. I value you not, nor no such Puppie, which last Word I believe Mr. Elliott did not hear or believe it would have tryed his Patience, for if a Man is old he ought to behave as such.

It is certain Mr. Elliott hath Regard to the Laws and Trades accordingly, so that it is no Wonder the Indians has no Regard to him when another hard by Trades at the old Random Rate, without Regard either to Law or Government, which must certainly end in Ruin either of the Trader or Merchant or both. What Esteem can these Infidels have of a Law (those solemnly injoyned before their Faces and so often read) when they see it disregarded by the Traders, trampled upon and not in the least minded. If a Government will be so imposed upon out of regard to any private Man's Interest, so as to let the whole suffer thereby, there is no more can be said. However, I beg Pardon for this Presumption in delivering my Thoughts so freely.

This Morning the Warriour of this Town came to my House and I speaking to him in Relation to Mr. Elliott, he told me that when Docharty came up, he told him that all the Valy belonged to him and that they must come to him for what they wanted, that the Goods were all his and that by and by he would send the little Man to Cheowee [because] they lay at some greater Distance and he should trade there. By which Means they still thought the Goods were Docharty's and finding Mr. Elliott did not trade as he did, but acted like one that would pay his Merchant and according to that Law which was wisely calculated to enable all and every One to do the same, no Wonder the Indians had but a mean Opinion of him, and that he was obliged to let them know as he traded accordingly as he was obliged by the Law. They had heard in Carolina he would not be imposed upon. However, all his Endeavours or any other honest Man's will be of no Effect so long as all are not brought under the same Law. He is a carefull and industrious, honest Man as far as can be seen of him and ought to be supported and countenanced by such. But I must say he has met with an infamous Partner of whom I never knew so much before, as I now do. The acting by Law would be more Advantage to Docharty and his Merchant, I am sure, than the Methods he takes. And although it is not my Business, yet I cannot help speaking my Mind when I see a Man so imposed upon as Mr. Elliott is for setting aside his Breach of Promises concerning the Horses. I can see Nothing but that Docharty intended to support his Trade, and Grandeur, and Villainy on Mr. Elliott's Creditt during the Co-partnership, and to leave him a bankrupt Beggar at last to look for a Parcell of Indian Debts for his Share, and those mostly trusted out contrary to Law, and so by that Law irrecoverable.

Ludovick Grant to Governor James Glen of South Carolina, in McDowell, *Documents Relating to Indian Affairs, 1750-1754*, 236-237.

From this Sketch, as by Implication it must be understood, that it is a part of the Business of the said Commissioner of Indian Affairs in So. Carolina, to visit some if not all the Nations from time to time, to Inquire into the Conduct of the Traders, to hear any complaints of the Indians, and to redress Grievances, it ought to be concluded that the managemt of the Indian Trade and Traders among the Southern Nations is well regulated and secured. But the case in Fact is just the Reverse. The Commissioner not being obliged by express Words in the Act to visit those Nations, nor any allowance having been established for that Service, altho it hath been one of his standing Instructions given to the Traders with their Licences, "That they are to take Notice, that he intended to visit the several Garrisons as often as occasion should require, in order to hear and redress any Complaints that should be made to him," yet no Commissioner hath gone to either Nation, or to any Place convenient for the Purpose, ever since the Year 1735; when the then Commissioner was sent by the Government to the Creek Nation in Quality of an Agent, upon a particular Occasion. And since that time, Agents have been sent only twice to the same Nation, and twice to the Cherokee Nation, on sudden and extraordinary Occasion. Tis True, by a Clause in the Act passed in 1752, setting forth "that since the Commissioner had not been obliged by law to go into the Indian Nations, many Irregularities had been committed by the Traders and other Persons, from whence great Terror and Disturbance had been brought upon his Majesty's Subjects, and the expenses for Indians greatly augmented;" He is therefore required under pain of forfeiting his office to go to any of the Nations (the Chicasaws and Chactaws by reason of their Distance excepted) But then it is at the same time limited thus, "whenever he should be ordered so to do by the Governor with the advice of the Council." And an allowance for that Service is indeed also specified payae. out of the Publick Treasury to him (fifty six Shilling Proclamation Money pr Diem for himself and two servants) or if he shall refuse or be unable to perform it to any other Person appointed by the Governor with advice of the Generall Assembly if sitting; and if not, with advice of the Council. But then there is no provision of a Fund for the payment of that money, or of any other Expence attending his Journey; which therefore still depends upon the Assembly; whose Spirit the Council is too well accquainted with, to advise the Governor to send the Commissioner, without first consulting them, when it can possibly be done. The Assembly if they differ in opinion or Disposition with the Council, in order to excuse themselves from providing the payment on any particular Occasion, will it may be presumed according to Custom if they have an Opportunity to do it in time, declare themselves against the Necessity of sending him; or afterwards, soon after his Arrival in any Nation, and the least favourable account of his Reception & Negotiation or Posture of Affairs, address the Governor to recall him immediately, merely to put a stop as soon as possible to the Expence. On so precarious a footing, no fit person can see it worth their while to turn their Backs suddenly upon their private Affairs to engage in such Service.

Without saying how far the Commissioners themselves have strictly observed the directions of the Law, with respect to the Traders, out of about twenty useful and Necessary Instructions given within their Licences, respecting their Behaviour towards the Indians, the Government, and to each other, which are fram'd agreeable to the express directions of that Law, and to long Experience, and which they give Bond to observe, I verily believe that not one hath been, or is duly observd by them all. And no Inspection or Inquiry being made into their Behaviour by the Commissioner on the Spot in any one of the Nations, information can come only from among the Traders themselves; who being all more or less Culpable, altho the one half of the several Penalties inflicted by the Law are given to him that shall Sue for the same, it cannot be imagined that any of them will in many Cases either give information or Offences, or support the Commissioner in the proof thereof. Accordingly I have never known any Penalty for a particular Offence sued for, nor any Bond Sued to a Recovery of the Penalty. So that the Law for regulating the Indian Trade is almost a dead Letter; and the Commissioner of little more use than going thro' the mere form of giving Licences to Traders, and taking Bonds for the Observance of Instructions, which not being duly enforced are so little Regarded, that the present Commissioner declared once to a Committee, That in the Space of a full Year then pass'd, he had received from all the Traders in all the Nations, conformable to those Instructions, only three Letters of Intelligence and no Journal at all of their Proceedings.

Jacobs, *Edmond Atkin Report and Plan of 1755*, 19-22.

In addition to licensing and credit control, other measures were adopted to regulate commerce and minimize the chance of conflict. The Albemarle assembly banned strangers from trading with Indians, Governor John Archdale recommended the creation of a joint-stock company, and in 1716 a law was enacted to create a public monopoly. John Stuart argued for a mechanism for the redress of Indians' trade grievances.

AN ACT PROHIBITING STRANGERS TRADING WITH THE INDIANS

For as much as there is often recourse of Strangers from other parts into this County to truck and trade with the Indians which is conceived may prove very prejudiciall Wherefore be it enacted by the Pallatine and Lords Proprietors by and with the advice and consent of the Grand Assembly and the authority thereof that if any person or persons of what quallity or

Condition soever they be shall presume to come into this County to truck or trade with any of our neighbouring Indians belonging to the County or that shall be found to have any Indian trade purchased from them or being found or appearing that they come to trade with any Indians as aforesaid Whether in their Townes or elsewhere within the County which is hereby left for the Magistrate to judge it shall bee lawfull for any person or persons to apprehend any such persons or Forreigners that shall be found amongst the Indians or elsewhere within the limitts of the County and him or them bring before the Governor or any one of the Councell who shall hereby have power to comitt them to prison there to abide till they have paid tenn thousand pounds of tobacco and caske otherwise to stand to the censure of the Vice Pallatine and Councell And it is further declared that whatsoever Trade is found with the person apprehended One halfe thereof and one halfe of the fine shall belong to the Apprehendor and the other halfe to the Lords Proprietors.

Acts of the Assembly of Albemarle, 1669/1670, in William L. Saunders, ed., *The Colonial Records of North Carolina*, 10 vols. (Raleigh: State of North Carolina, 1886-1890), 1:187.

Carolina

The first stepp, towards the advancement of this Collonie as I conceive, (and submit to better Judges) is the improvement of the Indian Trade wch might produce, many Comodities for Exportation, and consequently bring many more inhabitants to it, But that trade is now Confined within the Compass of very few hands, who lead the Natives at will, witness formerly Major [Maurice] Mathews and two or three more, and still remaines in the hands of as few as then it did, the Indians not discovering any thing, or selling any thing But to them.

Whereas that country affoards Variety of skins and Furrs, Besids herbs, plants, roots, Gumms, Turpentine, Burgamy pitch, and many more Medicinal secrets, all wch when the proper methods are Taken the Indians will Easily Discover.

But not until then The Question then consequently is what is or what are those methods, I answer,

According to my small Judgement, let all Traffick with Indians be forbidden with any privat or Publick person what soever and this done By Act of Assembly there.

At the same time, appoint a Certaine Number of persons inhabiting in severall parts in the Collonie to trade with the Indians; such persons to give in accounts Either monthly or Quarterly to the Company in whose hands the joynt stock of all Inhabitants, who puting in to the saide stock according to theire capacities, shall receive their proportion of all Devidents made of proffet.

It is not my Buissnis to Direct the Proprietors, in the Constiting such a Company but I am sure that they would vastly advance their Proprietor-ships, advance the interests of all inhabitants, and gaine the Intier Love and friendships of the Indians, and make Carolina flourish thereby.

[1706], Governor John Archdale, Colonial Governors' Papers, State Archives, Office of Archives and History, Raleigh.

AN ACT FOR THE BETTER REGULATION OF THE INDIAN TRADE, BY IMPOWERING THE COMMISSIONERS THEREIN NAMED TO MANAGE THE SAME FOR THE SOLE USE, BENEFIT AND BEHOOF OF THE PUBLICK.

S:I. Whereas, it has been found by Experience that the Indian Trade as formerly carried on by private Traders, has been prejudicial, and tended [very] much to the great Damage and Detriment of this Province, to prevent which Inconveniencies for the Future,

Be it enacted by his Excellency John Lord Carteret, Palatine, and [the] Rest of the true and absolute Lords and Proprietors of Carolina, [by] and with the Advice and Consent of the Rest of the Members of the General Assembly, now met at Charles Town for that Part of the said Province that lieth South and West of Cape Fear, and by the Authority of the same, that Col. George Logan, Col. James Moore, Ralph Izard, Esq., Col. John Barnwell, and Mr. Charles Hill, be, and they are hereby nominated Commissioners to order, direct and manage the Trade with the Indians, in Amity with this Government, for the sole Use, Benefit and Behoof of the Publick of this Province, [. . .]

Act of June 13, 1716, in William L. McDowell Jr., ed., *Journals of the Commissioners of the Indian Trade, September 20, 1710-August 29, 1718,* in *The Colonial Records of South Carolina, Series 2* (Columbia: South Carolina Archives Department, 1955).

But Laws only enforced by the principles on which they are founded, would have very little Efficacy in restraining English Traders and Pack horse men, whose few, Negative good Qualities are rather the fruit of coercive power than Moral Sentiments. The Necessities of the Indians; their incapacity of subsisting without European Commodities; as well as the fear of involving their Country with us; renders them so passive to the Enormities of the Traders.

I begg your Lordships leave to observe that some uniform Rules of decision, between us and the Indians, seems to be wanting. If an Indian wrongs a Trader, the Latter has recourse to the Beloved man, and his own Evidence with that of other Indians commonly procure him Justice. But if an Indian is cheated or robbed by a Trader the Latter seldom pays any regard to the decision of the Beloved man; and the Indian remains without Redress: as His own or Countrymen's Evidence cannot be admitted in any American court of Justice.

John Stuart to the Board of Trade, March 9, 1764, in Colonial Office 323/17, British Records, State Archives.

Traders sold a product to which too many Native Americans quickly became addicted: alcohol. The use of rum in particular was widespread, as noted by Lawson in eastern North Carolina; Toole, who traded among the Catawbas in the Piedmont; and Atkin, of the Cherokees in the west. Inebriated Indians engaged in behavior that was detrimental to themselves, their families, and their trade, and threatened their relations with other tribes as well as whites.

Most of the Savages are much addicted to Drunkenness, a Vice they never were acquainted with, till the Christians came amongst them. Some of them refrain from drinking strong Liquors, but very few of that sort are found amongst them. Their chief Liquor is Rum, without any Mixture. This the *English* bring amongst them, and buy Skins, Furs, Slaves and other of their Commodities therewith. They never are contented with a little, but when once begun, they must make themselves quite drunk; otherwise they will never rest, but sell all they have in the World, rather than not have their full Dose. In these drunken Frolicks, (which are always carried on in the Night) they sometimes murder one another, fall into the Fire, fall down Precipices, and break their Necks, with several other Misfortunes which this drinking of Rum brings upon them; and tho' they are sensible of it, yet they have no Power to refrain this Enemy.

Lawson, *New Voyage to Carolina*, 211.

There is one Moses Kirkland lives about fourty-odd Miles from the Nation below it on Wateree Creek that keeps Tavern and Goods. Invites the Indians down their to buy Rum of him. The Indians is continually going down to him, and fetching Rum up, and drinking that they drives us all out of our Houses, and breaking open our Doors that we run the greatest Resque of our Lives as can be imagined, and several others besides him on Peedee, and all over the Country. If there is any Liquor brought in here, wee may expect the Norrard and them will knock one another in the Head, if your Excellency does not put a Stop to it in Time. As for my part, I durst not sell a Drop of Liquor to no

Indian this two Years past. The Indians waits your Excellency's Answer which they expect in a short Time.

Matthew Toole to Governor James Glen of South Carolina, October 28, 1752, in McDowell, *Documents Relating to Indian Affairs, 1750-1754*, 359.

But the greatest Disorders, and the most pernicious Consquences of all, have been introduced by the many Traders licenced and unlicenced, who have made a constant Practice of [carrying] very little Goods, but chiefly, and for the most part intirely *Rum* from Augusta; from whence as soon as the Indian Hunters are expected in from their Hunts, they set out with small or large Quantities of that bewitching Liquor according to their Ability, for the Creeks and Cherokees, but chiefly the latter Nation, to which they get in four Days. Then some of those Rum Traders place themselves near the Towns, in the way of the Hunters returning home with their deer Skins. The poor Indians in a manner fascinated, are unable to resist the Bait; and when Drunk are easily cheated. After parting with the fruit of three or four Months Toil, they find themselves at home, without the means of buying the necessary Clothing for themselves or their Families. Their Domestick and inward Quiet being broke, Reflection sours them, and disposes them for Mischief. To the same cause is owing, that the Quality of their Leather is Debased. For those Rum Traders take any Skins, badly dressed, and untrimmed; which require one Horse the more in 5 or 6 to carry them, and harbour Worms that daily destroy them. And the Indians require the other Traders in their Towns to take them in the same Condition.

Jacobs, *Edmond Atkin Report and Plan of 1755*, 35-36.

The People inhabiting the Frontiers of this Province Carry on a Trade with the Indians by bartering Rum for Horses. The Chiefs complained of this as the Source of many disorders, their Young Men being thereby encouraged to Steal Horses from the neighboring Provinces; besides the Danger of committing Outrages, when intoxicated which may involve their Nation in Trouble. [. . .] The Indians Detest the back Inhabitants of these provinces, which will Account for the Reluctancy with which they give up any part of their Lands being anxious to keep such Neighbors at a Distance.

John Stuart to the earl of Hillsborough, secretary of state for the colonial department, January 3, 1769, in Colonial Office 5/70, British Records, State Archives, Office of Archives and History, Raleigh.

Although the Indians of eastern Carolina apparently did not punish drunken behavior, the Cherokees did. Chuetheake held perpetrators accountable for attacking a trader in Tuckasegee. Tribesmen "scratched" Little Carpenter for his rum-induced actions toward Captain Raymond Demere.

They never call any Man to account for what he did, when he was drunk; but say, it was the Drink that caused his Misbehaviour, therefore he ought to be forgiven.

Lawson, *New Voyage to Carolina*, 210.

The Indians, so far as I am come to as yet, are both thankfull to your Excellency and quiet with the Traders, and I hear Nothing to the Contrary of the Upper Party of the Nation only at Tuckasegee where the Indians being drunk, besett Crawford's House, and draging him out, and cut him in many Places in the Head, and afterwards (he having made his Escape) seized upon his Goods and devided them amongst them. But I hear Chuetheake, the Warriour, made them pay all, or the most of them.

Ludovick Grant to Governor James Glen of South Carolina, February 8, 1753, in McDowell, *Documents Relating to Indian Affairs, 1750-1754*, 367.

Sir, After having complyed with the Little Carpenter's Requests, by getting him a Cagg of Rum to drink with his Friends, he went to Keowee with all his People and was as good as his Word for neither he nor any of them came near the Fort till the next Morning about 8 o'Clock at which Time the Little Carpenter came into the Fort very drunk supported by 2 young Fellows belonging to Keowee, of the worst Sort, for none of his People would come with him because they know him to be a very troublesome Fellow when drunk. I happened to be seen by him when he came into the Fort and was obliged to sit with him. He soon became so troublesome that I could not stay any longer with him. Then he made a Motion to strike me in the Face with a Bottle that he had brought with him into the Fort. I immediately got up and desired several of the Indians from Keowee to carry him away which they did and I heard no more of him till the next Morning. As soon as he came in he began to make all the Apologies he possibly could for what he had been guilty of the Day before and told me that Rum was the Occasion of it and begged that nothing might be remembered. I told him that he had used me twice very ill after all my Civilities shown him and that the English had never used him in the like Manner. That if he had struck me with the Bottle that the Consequence might have proved very bad but that I was come for Peace and not for War; in short I thought it the best Way to put up with him at this present Time. Once more he replied that I would say no more but forget the whole of it for says he there was 3 of us together when the Thing happened, that I was the first, himself was the second, and the Rum was the third. That the People of Keowee had scratched him that Morning enough to make him remember it and to make his Blood good. After his expressing himself in this Manner to me I promised him that I would never more think of it. [. . .] All his Men as well as the Keowee People behaved themselves very well and were concerned at the Carpenter's Behaviour to me. They say that he would use his Father King George or his Brother the Governor in the like Manner when in drink.

> Captain Raymond Demere to Governor William Henry Lyttelton of South Carolina, July 25, 1756, in McDowell, *Documents Relating to Indian Affairs, 1754-1765*, 147-148. Little Carpenter's altercation with Raymond Demere transpired at Fort Prince George. Built adjacent to Keowee by the colony of South Carolina in 1753, it, like the Lower Cherokee town, is now underneath the waters of Lake Keowee.

Native American headmen made their wishes clear to colonial officials that no rum would be sold among their people, but the combination of willing sellers and eager buyers made prohibition impossible. Governor William Bull indicated that his hands were tied.

About five years ago, when *Landgrave Daniel* was Governour, he summon'd in all the *Indian* Kings and Rulers to meet, and in a full Meeting of the Government and Council, with those *Indians*, they agreed upon a firm Peace, and the *Indian* Rulers desired no Rum might be sold to them, which was granted, and a Law made, that inflicted a Penalty on those that sold Rum to the Heathens; but it was never strictly observ'd, and besides, the young *Indians* were so disgusted at that Article, that they threatened to kill the *Indians* that made it, unless it was laid aside, and they might have Rum sold them, when they went to the *Englishmens* Houses to buy it.

> Lawson, *New Voyage to Carolina*, 211-212. Robert Daniel was awarded the rank of landgrave in 1691 and served as deputy governor of North Carolina, 1703-1705.

Copy of a Conference held with the King and Warriors of the Cataubas by Mr. Chief Justice Henley at Salisbury in North Carolina in May 1756. [. . .]

[King Hagler:] I desire a stop may be put to the selling strong Liquors by the White people to my people especially near the Indian Nation. If the White people make strong drink let them sell it to one another or drink it in their own Families. This will avoid a great deal of mischief which otherwise will happen from my people getting drunk and quarrelling with the White people. Should any of my people do any mischief to the White people I have no strong prisons like you to confine them for it, Our only way is to put them under ground and all these men (pointing to his Warriors again) will be ready to do that to those who shall deserve it.

[. . .]

[Chief Justice Peter Henley:] Your Observation in respect to the White peoples selling Liquor to the Indians is very just as there is no Law at present to prevent it I will mention to the Governour the necessity of making one to restrain these pernicious practices for the future.

Saunders, *Colonial Records of North Carolina*, 5:579, 581, 583.

I am very sensible and have been so for many years that the disturbances among Indians either accidental or premiditated are always Occasioned or promoted and artfully inflamed by means of Rum. and I have always been of Opinion that it ought as much as Possible to be a contriband Article and in this their old Men agree. but as to the unlimited Introduction of it being only from this Province I believe I may say with great Truth Iliacos intra Muros peccatur & Extra. For I have heard that from Augusta in Georgia where you Say it is prohibited Supplies of that Civil and political person are carried to Toogoloo and other Cherokee Towns whether by licenced Traders or not I do not Know. Those Indians Receive some from the Western Settlers of North Carolina and fear some from Virginia also as well as from this Province. Latterly I have urged the Merchants who furnish the Cargo to the actual Trader the expediency of sending no rum which they consent to and this I think is all I can do under the present Circumstances.

Lieutenant Governor William Bull of South Carolina to John Stuart, August 18, 1765, in Colonial Office 323/23, British Records, State Archives. *Iliacos intra Muros peccatur & Extra*: It was a mistake within the walls of Iliam (Troy) and beyond.

Colonial governments, knowing that Indians had become dependent upon European goods, enacted trade embargoes against tribes as punishment. Virginia halted commerce with the Tuscaroras in 1708 for the killing of a white; before the ban was lifted in 1709, it had been extended to include North Carolinians. South Carolina imposed an embargo upon the Cherokees in 1751 after the inhabitants of the towns of Kituwah, Connutra, and Stecoe ransacked the stores of trader Bernard Hughs.

At a Council held at the Capitol the 4th of June 1708

[. . .]

Whereas the persons appointed to go to the Tuscarura Indians to demand the delivery of three of that nation suspected of the murder of Jeremiah Pate have reported their proceedings therein And that they had given the said Tuscaruros the space of twenty days time to comply with the said Demand or offer their Reason for their not complyance. Which time being now near expired and no answer come from the said Indians, It is the opinion of the Council that Mr President write to the Sheriffs of the Countys of Henrico Prince George, Surry, Isle of Wight & Nansemond requireing them forthwith to signify to every one of the Indian Traders within their respective Countys that it is the desire of the Council that they do not furnish or sell to the said Tuscaruro Indians or any other for their use any Arms powder or Shott untill further order, Which they may expect as soon as Satisfaction is made to this Governmt concerning ye three Indians suspected of the aforesaid Murder.

Council Minutes of June 4, 1708, in H.R. McIlwaine et al., eds., *Executive Journals of the Council of Colonial Virginia*, 6 vols. (Richmond, Virginia: D. Bottom, superintendant of public printing, 1925-1966), 3:181, 182.

Whereas this Board are informed that certain Inhabitants of North Carolina have been indeavouring to purchase ammunition and other goods in this Country with a designe to sell the same again to the Tuscaruro Indians and it being very apparent that supplys the said Indians have hitherto had from thence has been the Cause of their delaying to deliver up to justice those Criminals who committed the late murder in this Colony. The Council do therefore strictly prohibite all persons from within this Colony to furnish or sell any powder Shott or other Indian tradeing goods whatsoever to any of the Inhabitants of Carolina [. . .]

Council Minutes of March 1708, in McIlwaine, *Executive Journals of the Council of Colonial Virginia*, 3:211.

GENTLEMEN, As this Government has thought proper to send to the Cherokees to demand Satisfaction for the insolent and outdacious Behavior of some of their People, and as it will very much conduce to the Security and Welf[ar]e of this Province, as well as to the Safety of his Majesty's Subjects, the Traders in that Nation, that all trade and commerce with them be stoped till such Time as they come to a better Way of thinking. And to comply with the Terms that we have required of them, I therefore by the Advice of his Majesty's honorable Council, and in his Majesty's Name and Authority, order you and each of you forthwith to leave the Cherokee Nation with all your Effects as you will answer the Contrary at your Peril.

Governor James Glen of South Carolina to the traders within the Cherokee nation, [May-June 1751], in McDowell, *Documents Relating to Indian Affairs, 1750-1754*, 66-67.

Euphersee, May 14th, 1751

MAY IT PLEASE YOUR EXCELLENCY, By Orders of the Emperor to the Raven of Hiwasee, together with his Head Men and Warriors of his Towns to have a Meeting, the Raven as Spokesman for them all gives his Talks as follows. He says he is partly sorrow that the People of his Nation should have any bad Thoughts in their Hearts, but the Warriours that was at the Southward at Warr that killed the white People reported that Wm. Carr should tell them, the People of Keowee and Esternorie, that your Excellency should say that you would send up an Army of Men to kill the Norwards wherever they were to be found, in any of our Towns. So when they got this in their Heads, they could not believe it was the Norwards you intended to kill, but they themselves. So upon the same the People of Keowee and Echoe had a Meeting, at this Echoe, being a Mother Town by themselves they not acquainting no other Town of the same. So when their Meeting was over they sent Messuages to Kittawa being another Mother Town, to acquaint them of what Carr should say, and they believed it. So upon the same Sticoe, Keneeteroy and Kittawa joined in Arms, and took the white Man's Goods.

The Raven being gon to Timotly meets a Messenger with a Letter from Mr. Maxwell to Mr. Doharty, but for the Raven at the same Time, to acquaint him that Bernard Hughs and his Men was killed. But when the Letter came to be read it was Daniel Murphey, which his Heart was sorrow to hear of the white Man being killed. But afterwards found to his great Satisfaction, that it was a false Report.

Mr. Bunyont sent by the Town of Tucherechee at the same Time to acquaint the Raven that the white Man's Goods was stole, so directly the Raven sent of a Messenger to the seven Towns over the Hills to be at Timothly in 5 Nights to have a Meeting. That if it had been that the white Men was killed, they would seek for Revenge for the white Men and the Goods. So directly the Raven sent his Son, Skienah, and 5 Warriours with Mr. Bunyon to those Towns to search and get what they could belonging to the white People, but when they heard these People was coming from the Raven, those that was Rogues, took the Goods with their Women and Children and was afraid to see them. [. . .]

Soe in their Return when they staid at Joree for an Answer from those rogue Towns. And they sent a Messenger to tell the Warriours that was sent by the Raven, to tell them their Doggs, and their Hoggs, and themselves, run mad, and it was all by a lying Talk from Keowee, that they did what they did do, but they was sorrow for it, and they would return the Goods, and if any should be wanting, they would pay for them. The Slave Ketcher of Kenntory, who was the Man was supposed to a'killed Murphy, was obstinate and would not return the Goods that he had stole from Bernard Hughs, so to favour him Danl. Murphy paid the said Hughs for this Rogue 20 Lb. Leather. So the

Raven heard it, and was vext at Murphy for doing so, does not think him a proper Man to trade in their Nation for sideing with the Rogue, and he thinks they are both Rogues alike.

And the Raven desires that those Towns who done this Mischief should have no Traders amongst them, that is, Kenotoroy, Sticoe and Kittawa, nor yet no Indian nor Half-breed should be Factor from any white Man among them, till they acknowledge their Faults, and see the Want of a white Man, and that they themselves, and their Women and Children should have weary Leggs to walk to Traders in other Towns to buy what they want.

The Raven sais that he and his head Men and Warriours has not forgot all the good Talks that they have heard from Time to Time, nor never shall be forgot, as long as Grass grows and Water runs, and we will hand it down to our young People comeing up, and graft it in their Hearts, as your Excellency has done in theirs, for they do not want to know any other People but the English, and they hope your Excellency will not let them suffer for those that has been the Rogues, as he and his Parts has put a Stop to it all, but that you will let their Traders come up as usual, for the Good of both, for we are in great Want of Ammunition, and as we are outside Towns, the French are daily upon us, and for the Want of Ammunition, we don't know how soon we may be cutt off.

[. . .]

The Raven and the Emperor is both in one Heart for the English, and they hope your Excellency is the same for them, and that the bad Talks that has been, that Mr. Maxwell has heard and carried down to you is forgot, for we have rectified among ourselves and [h]opes that you and your beloved Men will beleive the same, and that there [is] no white Man killed, and the Goods that is stole shall be returned again or paid for.

[. . .]

The Warriour of Nottally says that the white People and them lives upon one Earth, and hopes our Hearts is as one to each other. And that he never was at the English, but has heard all good Talks that come from his Father and beloved Men, by the old Emperor.

The Raven desires that the Talk you send to the Emperor may be by itself, and his Talk by themselves, and as for the Lower Parts, their Talk by themselves, and Mr. Beamer to be Interpreter for them, and Mr. Bunning for us. And that I am glad the Warriour of Keowee and all the Lower Towns has sent down a good Talk, which I am pleased with. And now I think my Heart is at Ease, and yours the same when you see the Messenger, and I have allotted him 31 Days till I have an Answer.

THE RAVEN his Mark for All of Highwassee

The Raven to Governor James Glen of South Carolina, May 14, 1751, in McDowell, *Documents Relating to Indian Affairs, 1750-1754*, 74-76. "Esternorie" was Estatoe. "Timothly"

125

was Tomotla. Connutra ("Kenotoroy") had been located on the Tuckasegee River. Tuckaleechee ("Tucherechee") stood at the junction of Deep Creek and Tuckasegee River at present-day Bryson City, North Carolina.

Colonies and nations competed for trade dominance. South Carolina and Virginia vied for control of commerce with the Catawbas and Cherokees, apparently resorting to whatever means necessary to gain the advantage: on one occasion, Virginia traders were robbed by their South Carolina adversaries. With shorter overland routes to the back country and a thriving port at Charleston, South Carolina ultimately triumphed over its rival. After Georgia started making inroads among the Cherokees, three South Carolinians encouraged Indians to rob and assault a trader from that colony. As noted earlier, North Carolina never posed a challenge to its neighbors. Atkin stated that the English ignored the elderly headmen who held considerable sway within the town house, an oversight the French readily exploited.

A Trader from this or any Province, did not look upon himself as Subject to the Regulations made in any of the other three, and was Responsible for his behaviour to that Government only where he had his License, or Traded from. Hence a Competition between the Provinces sometimes arose; Parties were allways formed by the different Traders among the Indians; and Confusion and disorder were the consequences.

John Stuart to the Board of Trade, March 9, 1764, in Colonial Office 323/17, British Records, State Archives.

The Deposition of Robert Hix aged fourty-five years or thereabouts being sworne saith

That in or about October 1707 this Deponent with his Partner David Crawly being a trading with the Western Indians about four hundred miles from Virginia and about two hundred miles from Charlestown in South Carolina this Deponent left fifteen hundred buck and Doe skins at a Town of Indians called the Shutterees and went further into the Country a trading, while we were gone one James Moor by order of Sr Nathaniel Johnson Governor of South Carolina seized all our Skins and other goods to about the value of 140 £ Sterling and carried all to the house of one George Starling about one hundred and twenty miles from the Indian town where they were left which obliged this Deponent to go to the Governor and after much time and trouble and Charges, with severall presents this Deponent [*illegible*] an order for his Skins which he had accordingly but they were pick'd and Charged that the Skins this Deponent received were not of above half the value of the Skins taken from him, and the other things taken from him were utterly lost [. . .]

Deposition of Robert Hix, February 19, 1708/9, in Colonial Office 5/1316, British Records, State Archives, Office of Archives and History, Raleigh. The "Shutterees" were the Sugarees, which had inhabited present-day Mecklenburg County, North Carolina, and York County, South Carolina.

The next Morning the White Men were all called to the Town House and the Letters read and interpreted, and I found the chief Contents of the Governor of Virginia's Letters to be as before related, and further he had appointed them a Place of their first Rendeavous where they were to be met at a Place called Red Creek by one Colonel Buckannan and there to be supplied with Necessaries, Arms, and Ammunition for their farther Journey and Presents promised them, which last Article, together with a great and constant Trade, which was promised them only by Guest, the Messenger, took much with them all; so that to me they, in general, seemed willing to go to Virginia, though I verily believe more for the sake of the Presents and Trade from that Colony than for Honour, and by Reason of an almost hatred that [they] have contracted for most of the Traders from Carolina occasioned by their Mismanagement which I have hinted at in many of my former Letters; and if they were yet extant might be seen.

Ludovick Grant to Governor James Glen of South Carolina, March 27, 1755, in McDowell, *Documents Relating to Indian Affairs, 1754-1765*, 41.

[. . .] And this Depon[ent] further saith that in the Begining of February last (to the Best of this Deponent's Remembrance as to the Time) that one Ambrose Davies, otherwise called the Collier, David McDonald, and one James May all formerly fitted out by Mr. Maxwell, and since by Messrs. Wrags and Lambton, by Mr. Maxwell's Recommendation, as this Deponent is informed, encour[aged] the Indians to plunder this Deponent of two Caggs of Rum of which [t]hey partook in the Town House as the Indians when sober declared to this Deponent by a Linguister. On being ask't how they could use this Deponent in such a Manner, alledging that the aforesaid three Persons set them on. And this Deponent further saith that he hath often heard several Complaints against the said three Persons as to their Behaviour to the Indians themselves, in killing their Fowls and otherwise plundering them, and particularly that the said Ambrose Davies, otherwise Collier, burnt one of their Houses, and to this Deponent certain Knowledge he is a general Disturber both to the white and to the Indians in the Nation.

Deposition of John Williams, Augusta, Ga., May 21, 1751, in McDowell, *Documents Relating to Indian Affairs, 1750-1754*, 19-20.

The Traders from Georgia, if they cannot be perswaded or obliged to trade as those of Carolina are obliged to do, must certainly ruin the Carolina Traders, for I do not find by their Licence that they are restrained any other Ways save only to trade in their own Towns therein specified, and that they may trade promiscuously with any Indian of any other Town if they bring their Skins to him where he resides. What View the Magistracy of Georgia has in not consulting the Interest of Carolina conjunctly with their own I cannot conceive. The Company of Augusta intends as I hear to Licence from Georgia several Men of this Nation, and fitt them out with Goods against Winter through the Towns licenced from Carolina and particularly against poor Mr. Elliott because he is none of them. A monstrous Sett of Rogues for the major Part of whom the Gallows groans.

Ludovick Grant to Governor James Glen of South Carolina, May 3, 1752, in McDowell, *Documents Relating to Indian Affairs, 1750-1754*, 263.

North Carolina, having not hitherto carried on any Commerce with the Cherokees behind it, consequently hath left the regulation thereof intirely to South Carolina posessed of their whole Trade.

Jacobs, *Edmond Atkin Report and Plan of 1755*, 13.

[. . .] Even trifles are put on the footing of things of Value at the French Forts, by bestowing them chiefly on the old Head Men of Note, who being past the fatigue of War and constant Hunting for their Livelyhood, but on Account of their Age held in great Veneration for their Wisdom and Experience, spend the remainder of their days almost intirely in the Town Round Houses, where the Youth and others daily report; relating to them the History of their Nation, discoursing of Occurrences, and delivering precepts and Instructions for their Conduct and Welfare. Which is all the Indian Education. To these old men who are unable to purchase Necessaries, or to perform long Journeys, when they visit those Forts the French give from time to time a Load or two of Powder and Ball, a Flint, a Knife, a little Paint, a flap or shirt, and the like. The Old Men repay the French largely for these Trifles, in their Harrangues at the round Houses, by great Encomiums on their kindness, and recommendations of them to favour; which often inculcated, make impressions on the Youth, that grow up with them into a confirm'd prejudice.

Jacobs, *Edmond Atkin Report and Plan of 1755*, 10.

Each of Britain's American colonies had its own approach to trade and diplomacy with the Indians, and none of them had proven capable of promoting fair treatment, preventing conflict with whites, or protecting

British interests. By the 1750's increasing numbers of officials on both sides of the Atlantic had concluded that royal oversight was crucial to counteract the growing favor that France, with its centrally controlled trade and diplomatic strategy, was enjoying among the Indian nations. Direct supervision by Britain began with the creation of the "Indian superintendency": two superintendents for Indian affairs served as diplomatic and political agents, as well as commerce monitors. Appointed by the crown in February 1756, the first superintendents were Sir William Johnson in the northern district and Edmond Atkin in the southern. The Royal Proclamation of 1763, the primary purpose of which was to reserve all lands west of the ridge line of the Appalachians for the Indians, reinforced the superintendents' trade authority. After consulting with the region's governors, John Stuart, Atkin's successor, published instructions for Indian traders in the southern colonies in 1767.

[. . .] And we do, by the advice of our Privy Council, declare and enjoin, that the trade with the said Indians shall be free and open to all our subjects whatever; provided that every person, who may incline to trade with the said Indians, do take out a licence for carrying on such trade, from the Governor or Commander in Chief of any of our colonies, respectively, where such person shall reside, and also give security to observe such regulations as we shall at any time think fit, by ourselves or by our Commissaries, to be appointed for this purpose, to direct and appoint for the benefit of the said trade. And we do hereby authorize, enjoin, and require the Governors and Commanders in Chief of all our colonies respectively, as well those under our immediate Government, as those under the government and direction of Proprietaries, to grant such licence without fee or reward, taking especial care to infer therein a condition, that such licence shall be void and the security forfeited, in case the person to whom the same is granted, shall refuse or neglect to observe such regulations as we shall think proper to prescribe as aforesaid. [. . .]

Given at Our Court at St. James's, the 7th of October, 1763 in the third year of Our Reign

GOD save the KING

"Royal Proclamation of 1763," *Boston Gazette*, December 19, 1763.

REGULATIONS For the better carrying on the TRADE With the INDIAN Tribes in the SOUTHERN District.

<REGULATION I.> NO Trader shall employ any Person as Clerk, Pack-Horseman, or Factor, in his Service, before an Agreement be first entered

into between them, in Writing, specifying the Time and Conditions of Service, and having his or their Names inserted or indorsed on the Back of the Licence, so that the principal Trader shall be rendered responsible for, and subjected to, the Penalties which may be incurred by his or their bad Conduct.

II. No Trader, while in any *Indian* Nation, shall employ in his Service, any Clerk, Pack-Horseman, or Factor, who may have formerly been engaged with any other Trader, until the Time of Service stipulated by his said Agreement be expired, or a regular Discharge from such former Master shall first have been had and produced to the Person hiring such Servant, shewing that the former Contract had been dissolved by mutual Consent, or else till said Servant shall have produced a Certificate from the Commissary shewing that the former Contract had been dissolved for good and sufficient Reasons, shewn before him the said Commissary.

III. Every Trader on employing any Clerk, Pack-Horseman, or Factor, while residing in any *Indian* Nation, shall give Notice within three Weeks thereafter to the Commissary residing in said Nation, whose Permission for employing such Clerk, Pack-Horseman, or Factor must be obtained, within the Space of six weeks, at farthest, after giving Notice as above, and the said Employer must give Security for his Behaviour.

IV. No Trader shall employ any Negro, *Indian*, or Half-breed professing himself an *Indian* or under *Indian* Government, as a Factor or Deputy, to trade in any Town, or Village, on Account of said Trader.

V. No *Indian* Trader shall harbour in his House, any White Person, for a Time exceeding Fourteen Days, unless under the foregoing Regulations, or by Virtue of a particular Permission from the Commissary.

VI. All Factors, Clerks, Pack-Horsemen and Traders, shall, when regularly and legally called upon, be aiding and assisting to the Commissary in apprehending any Offender.

VII. No Trader shall by himself, Servant, or Substitutes, sell, deliver, or give, on any Pretence whatever, to the *Indians*, Swan-shot or Riffle barreled Guns.

VIII. All Goods shall be sold to the *Indians*, according to a certain Tariff hereunto annexed, and no Trader by himself, Servants, or Substitutes, shall sell Goods to *Indians* at any other Prices or Rates, than what are contained in the said Tariff, unless in Consequence of any Alteration hereafter made and agreed to at a general Meeting.

IX. No Trader shall credit any *Indian* for more than Thirty Pounds Weight of *Indian* dressed Deer Skins, and all Debts due by *Indians*, above that Sum, shall be considered as not recoverable, neither shall any Trader credit an *Indian* for more than five Pounds of Gunpowder, and twelve Pounds of Bullets, in one hunting Season.

X. The Weights and Measures of every Trader in the *Indian* Nations, shall conform exactly to the Standard Weight and Measure lodged with the Commissaries residing in the respective Nations.

XI. No Trader shall by himself, Servants, or Substitutes, propagate any false Report or Reports among *Indians*; nor shall convene any Meeting with them, or deliver any Message or Talk to them, without the Concurrence and Consent of the Commissary first obtained in Writing, except such as shall be sent under the Hand and Seal of the Governour of a Province, or the Superintendant of the District.

XII. All Traders, their Pack-Horsemen, Clerks, Deputies and Servants, shall communicate all Intelligence, any way relating to Peace or War, or by which his Majesty's Service can be in any Degree affected, to the Commissaries in the respective Nations where such Traders shall reside.

XIII. No Trader shall refuse or neglect to appear at any Congress, or general Meeting of the *Indians* with the Commissary, when duly summoned by the Commissary, except in case of Sickness, or for other lawful, unforeseen, or unavoidable Cause.

XIV. No Trader shall himself, or permit any of his Servants to, hunt Deer or Bear, or set Traps for Beaver, in any of the *Indian* Hunting-Grounds, or shall by himself, Servants, or Substitutes, purchase Deer-Skins, Furs, or Peltry of any Sort, from any White Person hunting or laying Traps as aforesaid, nor shall he or they in any way deal for such Goods, by Barter with, or receive the same from, or dispose of, or carry the same to Market for, such Hunters.

XV. No Trader shall by himself, Servants, Deputies, or Substitutes, sell to, or barter Rum or other spirituous Liquors, with, any *Indian* or *Indians*, for half dressed or raw Deer-Skins, Bear-Skins, Furs, or Peltry of any Sort.

XVI. No Trader shall by himself, Substitute, or Servant, carry more than fifteen Gallons of Rum, at any one Time, into any Nation of *Indians*, or have any more than fifteen Gallons of Rum, in his or their Possession, at any one Time. Such Importation of fifteen Gallons of Rum as aforesaid, shall not be repeated till after an Interval of three Months.

XVII. No Trader, Clerk, Factor, or Pack-Horseman, shall beat or abuse any *Indian*, but shall, on the contrary, pay a proper Respect to the Medal-Chiefs and Captains bearing Commissions.

XVIII. No Trader by himself, Servants, or Substitutes, or any of them, shall trade with any of the *Indians*, in the Woods, or before their Return to their respective Towns from Hunting, under any Pretence whatsoever.

XIX. No Trader shall himself, or by his Servants and Substitutes, buy, or take in Barter for Goods, any Hides or Deer-Skins in the Hair, or before they are dressed by the *Indians*, except in the proportion of four undressed Skins in the Hair to one hundred and fifty Pounds Weight of *Indian* dressed Deer Skins.

XX. All Traders immediately upon their Arrival in the Nations, Towns, or Tribes, for which Licences have been granted them, before any Goods are sold or bartered with the *Indians*, shall produce such Licences to the Commissaries appointed for Direction or Inspection of the Trade at such Posts or Truck-Houses, or in such Tribes, Towns, or Nations, to whom they shall give an exact List of their Servants, Clerks and Pack-Horsemen.

XXI. All Traders employing Negroes, or Mulattoes, in any Capacity whatsoever, shall give a List of their Names and Employments to the Commissary in the Nation to which they trade, and become bound in a sufficient Sum for their good Behaviour, within one Month at furthest after their Arrival in said Nation.

Regulations of 1767, in Colonial Office 5/68, British Records, State Archives, Office of Archives and History, Raleigh. The commissary was the superintendent's representative.

Superintendent for the southern district from 1762 until 1779, Stuart early in his career suggested to his superiors a number of policy changes that were intended to curtail the practices of traders that so antagonized Native Americans. Many of his recommendations were incorporated into the "Plan for the Future Management of Indian Affairs," prepared by the Board of Trade. The "Plan of 1764," as it was also known, broadened the superintendents' powers at the expense of colonial governments: they were granted political and regulatory jurisdiction over the Indians, and received the power to supervise trade and traders, although licensing authority remained with the colonial governors. The entire plan never received official approval, but both Stuart and Johnson executed its provisions to the extent to which they believed they were allowed; Stuart's regulations of 1767, above, were based on them. Ultimately the board concluded that Britain alone could not afford the cost to administer the plan. Waging the French and Indian War left the country mired in debt. Parliament lacked the political will to raise taxes further at home, and there was growing hostility in the American colonies toward direct taxation from London. Control of the Indian trade was returned to the colonies in 1768. Despite the reversal, the board acknowledged that the regulations imposed by the superintendents had accomplished considerable good, and the king relied upon the colonies to adopt them "as far as local Circumstances, and peculiar Situations, will admit." Stuart later complained that southern lawmakers seemed slow to embrace trade legislation.

Whitehall, April 15th. 1768

I have the Satisfaction to acquaint You, that in consequence of a Report made to His Majesty by the Lords of Trade, the Plan for the Management of Indian Affairs adopted by the Superintendents has been fully laid before His Majesty.

Upon mature Consideration of the present Regulations, the great Expence of the variety of Establishments far exceeding the Value of the Object; and the Difficulties which have attended the Execution of the Plan in general, for want of a due Authority in the Superintendents, His Majesty has thought fit that it shall be laid aside; That the Regulation of the Trade shall be left to the Colonies, whose Legislatures must be the best Judges of what their several Situations and Circumstances may require; That the Office of Superintendents shall however be continued, for such Matters as are of immediate Negociation between His Majesty and the Savages, and cannot therefore be regulated by Provincial Authority; and that the Boundary Line between the Indians, and the Settlements of His Majesty's Subjects, (every where Negociated upon, and, in many parts settled and ascertained) shall be finally ratified and confirmed.

[...]

It is unnecessary for me to use any Arguments to shew how greatly both the Interests and Safety of the Colonies depend upon a close Attention to these Objects; and as many of the Regulations of the present Plan of Superintendency have evidently operated to the Benefit of the Trade, and to the giving that Satisfaction and content to the Savages, by which alone the Colonies can hope to derive either immediate Profit, or lasting Peace, His Majesty trusts, that they will be adopted, as far as local Circumstances, and peculiar Situations will admit, always having regard to that freedom of Trade with the Indians, which His Majesty has graciously granted to all His Subjects by His Proclamation of 1763.

> Circular letter, earl of Hillsborough, secretary of state for the colonial department, to ten North American colonial governors, including William Tryon of North Carolina, April 15, 1768, in Colonial Office 5/69, British Records, State Archives, Office of Archives and History, Raleigh.

[...] I take this opportunity of acquainting you that it has pleased his Majesty, to put the Trade to Indian Nations under the Management of the respective Provinces, and that the Traders are not now under my direction as formerly, You will notwithstanding be supplyed with Goods, and the Governors have received His Majesty's orders to get Laws passed in their several Provinces for regulating the Trade, from them, and there is no doubt but Provision will be made by them for Governing and restraining the abuses of the Traders.

Mr. Cameron will continue to act as my Deputy. He will be frequently in your Nation and will hear your Complaints, and you may be assured that I shall upon all occasions use my utmost Endeavours to procure you Justice and redress of your greivances, with which I desire you will always make me acquainted.

a String of White Beads.

John Stuart, Treaty Conference at Hard Labour, South Carolina, October 17, 1768, in Colonial Office 323/28, British Records, State Archives, Office of Archives and History, Raleigh.

[. . .] I am very glad of having an opportunity of endeavouring to put a Stop, to the disorders of some outlawed Creeks, who have lately committed great Depredations on the back Settlers in Georgia, and driven off a great Number of their Horses and Sold them to Our Traders in the Cherokee Nation, and in the back Settlements of this Province and North Carolina, no Regulations for preventing such Disorders, and for the Management of the Indian Trade, have as yet been agreed upon by any Assembly within this District, the want of which is daily and loudly complained of by every Nation.

John Stuart to the earl of Hillsborough, July 25, 1769, Colonial Office 5/227, British Records, State Archives.

Land

The earliest recorded voyage to the North Carolina coast was made in 1524 by Florentine navigator Giovanni da Verrazzano, hired by Francis I of France to find a western trade route to Asia. Initially believing the "new land" to be unoccupied, Verrazzano quickly discovered otherwise. Native Americans were there to greet him.

We continued on our westerly course, keeping rather to the north. In another xxv days we sailed more than four hundred leagues, where there appeared a new land which had never been seen before by any man, either ancient or modern. At first it appeared to be rather low-lying; having approached to within a quarter of a league, we realized that it was inhabited, for huge fires had been built on the seashore. We saw that the land stretched southward, and coasted along it in search of some port where we might anchor the ship and investigate the nature of the land, but in fifty leagues we found no harbor or place where we could stop with the ship. Seeing that the land continued to the south, we decided to turn and skirt it toward the north, where we found the land we had sighted earlier. So we anchored off the coast and sent the small boat in to land. We had seen many people coming to the seashore, but they fled when they saw us approaching; several times they stopped and turned around to look at us in great wonderment. We reassured them with various signs, and some of them came up, showing great delight at seeing us and marveling at our clothes, appearance, and our whiteness; they showed us by various signs where we could most easily secure the boat, and offered us some of their food. [. . .] This land lies at 34 degrees.

Lawrence C. Wroth, *The Voyages of Giovanni da Verrazzano, 1524-1528*, (New Haven: Published for the Pierpont Morgan Library by the Yale University Press, 1970), 133-134.

Before the arrival of European colonizers and African slaves, Native Americans had been the sole human inhabitants of the land encompassing current-day North Carolina. The territory which each Indian nation held included town sites and farmland as well as extensive tracts of hunting ground. English explorers who set out from Roanoke in the mid 1580s learned of some of the many tribal villages of the Coastal Plain. Farther west the Catawbas, centered upon the river basin from which they derived their name, occupied the Carolina Piedmont; greatly diminished by disease and warfare by the time John Stuart described it in 1764, the nation had a population of more than 5,000 in the early seventeenth century. The Cherokees lived in what is now eastern Tennessee, southwestern North Carolina, and upstate South Carolina; they also claimed hunting grounds as far north as the Ohio River and south to central Georgia.

The uttermost place to the Southward of any discoverie was Secotan, being by estimation foure score miles distant from Roanoak. The passage from thence was thorowe a broad sound within the mayne, the same being without kenning of land, and yet full of flats and shoales: [. . .]

To the Northwarde our furthest discoverie was to the Chesepians, distant from Roanoak about 130. miles, the passage to it was very shalow and most dangerous, by reason of the breadth of the sound, and the little succour that upon any flawe was there to be had. [. . .]

To the Northwest the farthest place of our discoverie was to Choanoke distant from Roanoak about 130. miles. Our passage thither lyeth through a broad sound, but all fresh water, and the chanell of a great depth, navigable for good shipping, but out of the chanell full of shoales.

The Townes about the waters side situated by the way, are these following: Pysshokonnok, The womans Towne, Chipanum, Weopomiok, Muscamunge, and Mattaquen: all these being under the jurisdiction of the king of Weopomiok, called Okisco: from Muscamunge we enter into the River, and jurisdiction of Choanoke: There the River beginneth to straighten untill it come to Choanoke, and then groweth to be as narrowe as the Thames betweene Westminster, and Lambeth.

Between Muscamunge and Choanoke upon the left hand as we passe thither, is a goodly high land, and there is a Towne which we called the blinde Towne, but the Savages called it Ooanoke, and hath a very goodly corne field belonging unto it: it is subiect to Choanoke.

Choanoke it selfe is the greatest Province and Seigniorie lying upon that River, and the very Towne it selfe is able to put 700. fighting men into the fielde, besides the forces of the Province it selfe.

Ralph Lane, "Discourse on the First Colony," August 17, 1585 -June 18, 1586, in David B. Quinn, ed., *The Roanoke Voyages, 1584-1590*, 2 vols. (London: For the Hakluyt Society, 1955), 1:256, 257, 258-259. The village of Secotan, named for the tribe that built it, stood on the south bank of the Pamlico River in present-day Beaufort County, North Carolina. The Chesepians formerly inhabited land currently surrounding Norfolk, Virginia. The Chowanoc, or Chowan Indians, occupied the Chowan River valley; their town of Chowanoc ("Choanoke") was located on the west bank of the Chowan River near present-day Harrellsville, North Carolina. The Weapemeoc Indians controlled what is now northeastern North Carolina north of Albemarle Sound and east of the Chowan River. "Pysshokonnok" is probably Pasquenoc, which stood on present-day Camden Point, Camden County, North Carolina; although the location of the "womans Towne" remains unknown, English scholar Richard Hakluyt believed that it and Pysshokonnok were the same. Chipanum had been located near the mouth of the Perquimans River. The site of the town of Weapemeoc ("Weopomiok") is unknown. Muscamunge stood near present-day Edenton, North Carolina, and Mattaquen occupied the west bank of the mouth of the Chowan River. The "blind Towne" was situated on the west bank of the Chowan River, south of Chowanoc.

Of the Cherokee Indians.

The Country inhabited by the Cherokees lyes between 35 and 36 degrees North Latitude; and extends about 160 Miles from East to West by the Calculation of Travellers. This Nation consists of about 13500 Souls, having 2700 men able to bear arms. As the Country they possess is extremely Mountainous, they live greatly dispersed. They are divided into four Districts distinguished by the Names of the Overhills, the Valley, the Middle, and Lower Settlements. The Overhill, Valley, and Middle Settlements are upon different Branches of the Cherokee River which falls into the Ohio, about 60 Miles above its Confluence with the Mississippi. The Lower Settlements are upon the most Northern Branch of Savannah River. [. . .]

The Country claimed by the Cherokees, as their hunting Ground, is very extensive, to the No. West and N. of them are no Inhabitants of any sort nearer than 600 Miles. Their Claim to the West extends about 120 Miles to the confines of the Chickasaw Land. South W. South and So. East they are bounded by the Creek Lands within 60 or 70 miles of their Towns. So that the Boundaries of both Nations are determined by Cherokeehatchee or Broad River, which falls into Savannah River, and a Line drawn by the Sources of the Coosa, Chatahootchie, and Cherokeehatchee Rivers. To the Eastward their Claim was limited to forty miles from Keewee by the Treaty of Peace concluded with them in 1761, and the back settlements of this Province are advanced within less than 60 Miles of their Towns. To the N. East Their claim extends to Holsteins River and to its most Northern Source; one of its principal Branches takes rise in Augusta County in Virginia; the other in the Mountains that run behind North Carolina which gives them an Extent that way of 220 Miles. [. . .]

Of the Catawbas

The Catawbas now reduced to about 60 Men bearing Arms, are Situated N W from hence about 200 Miles upon a branch of Santee River. Their Village is within the Boundary Line of North Carolina, Yet they look upon themselves as dependant upon this Province.

John Stuart, superintendent of Indian Affairs for the southern department, to the Board of Trade, March 9, 1764, in Colonial Office 323/17, British Records, State Archives, Office of Archives and History, Raleigh. The "Cherokee River" was the Tennessee; "this Province" refers to South Carolina.

Contemporary writers penned effusive depictions of the bountiful land occupied by Native Americans—and which awaited potential colonists. Virginian John Pory, traveling along the Chowan ("South") River, and William Hilton, a New Englander who led expeditions up

the Cape Fear ("Charles"), appear to suggest that the indigenous peoples offered no great obstacle to white settlement or enterprise.

In February last he likewise discovered to the South River, some 60 miles over land from us, a very fruitfull and pleasant Countrey, full of Rivers, wherein are two harvests in one yeere (the great King giving him friendly entertainment, and desirous to make a league with us) hee found also there in great quantity of the same *Silk-grasse*, (as appeareth by the samples sent us) wherof Master *Heriott* in his booke 1587 makes relation, who then brought home some of it, with which a piece of Grogeran was made, and given to Queene *Elizabeth*, and some heere who have lived in the *East Indies* affirme, that they make all their *Cambaya* Stuffes of this, and Cotten-wooll.

Also in his passage by land, Master *Porey* discovered a Countrey, full of Pine trees, above twenty miles long, whereby a great abundance of *Pitch* and *Tarre* may be made: and other sorts of woods there were, fit for *Pot-ashes* and *Soe-ashes*.

"Journal of John Pory," 1622, in Susan Myra Kingsbury, ed., *Records of the Virginia Company of London*, 4 vols. (Washington, D.C.: Government Printing Office, 1906-1935), 3:641-642. *Grogeran* is grosgrain, a kind of silk ribbon or cloth; *Cambaya* is Cambay, a cotton fabric made in India and named for a port city in that country. *Pot-ashes* were alkaline substances used as fertilizers, "obtained originally by lixiviating or leaching the ashes of terrestrial vegetables and evaporating the solution in large iron pans or pots (whence the name.)" *OED*. A *soe* is "a large tub"; *Soe-ashes* might refer to soap-ashes, derived from the "ashes of certain kinds of wood used in forming a lye in soap-making" as well as fertilizer. *OED*.

[. . .] we found many faire and deep rivers, all ye way running into this Charles River: which abounds with sturgeon, and variety of other well tasted fish, [. . .] All ye way up ye river there are abundance of vast meddows, besides upland fields, that renders ye country fit to be called a Land for Catle, whereby they that dwell here, may enjoy ye freedom from that toyle in other plantations, where they are necessitated to provide hay. And there are besides greatt swamps laden with varieties of great oakes, and other trees of all sortes, and some very great Ciprus-trees, tall Cedars, Ash, Maple, poplar, great bay-trees, willows, Large grape-vines in abundance, and other fruites. [. . .] We found also some barren land, and other exceeding good land, most of it very easy to plow up. There is scarce a stone to be seene, only in 2. or 3. places by ye side of ye river we spied some rocks in a very sandy ground. We have seen india Corn Stalks as big as a mans wrist, 11. or 12. foot long; and ye weeds thick: Amongst it there is very good clay. We saw severall mulberry trees grow up and down in ye wood, and some baggs of silk worms; some of us sawe bees swarming, though ye latter end of October. Few of us saw any mosquitos, and they that did, saw but few. Some of us supposed we heard a kennel off wolves, one night in our travell. There appeared to us no kind off rattle-snakes: some other snakes there be which the natives boyle with their victuals: ye indians here are very poor and silly Creatures, divers of them are very aged; but they are not numerous: for in all our various travells for 3. weeks and more, we saw not 100 in all. They were very courteous to us, and affraid of us, but they are very theevish; By our best observation we cannot conceive this climat and place admits of any considerable winter, if any at all, besides ye Consideration of ye many Palmettos growing naturally there, which renders it a summer country. We found ye trees some flourishing some blossoming, and some falling. There are abundance of Deer, as appeare by ye many tracks, which we cannot avoyd almost, if we goe ashoare: We saw two run by us: There are store of Otters; and of fowles there is abundance, [. . .] We know no fruit or grain that grows in New England, but will grow there very well. Besides potatoes, Oranges, Lemons, Plantines, Olives, Cotton-trees; and we know not, why ye Pine apple will not grow there, and also ye Sugar-cane, for there are excellent tall and strong wilde canes in abundance: Tobacco must needs excell. [. . .] We conceive many of ye premises may be brought in a few years to a very considerable trade by ye Employment if prudently managed. We may find present room enough, and very good land for severall towns, besides for multitudes of farms [. . .]

J. Leitch Wright Jr., ed., "William Hilton's Voyage to Carolina in 1662," *Essex Institute Historical Collections* 105 (April 1969): 100-101.

From Juan Pardo in the sixteenth century to Thomas Griffiths in the eighteenth, Europeans and colonists sought precious metals, jewels, and china clay in Indian lands. Native Americans learned to distrust strangers "peeping in amongst the rocks, or digging up their earth."

[. . .] the captain, Juan Pardo, continuing his return on November 24, 1567, departed with his company from the city of Cuenca, which, in the Indian language is called Joara. On this day he made a halt in a certain unpopulated place and slept that night. On the following day he reached a small place (*lugarejo*) five leagues beyond there which belongs to a mandador of Yssa, who is called Dudca. There he made a halt and slept that night. The following day, which was the twenty-sixth day of the month, marching with his company directly to Yssa, a distance of a quarter of a league further on, he passed along a left-hand bend of the road and another [bend] to the right a little further on, as he was guided by Hernando Moyano de Morales, sergeant of his company, and Andrés Suarez, silversmith, who by command of the *captain, on the seventh day of the said month had come by that road to examine a crystal mine which was on it. In the presence of me, the notary, they showed* the captain the beginning of the mine which I, the notary, saw, [and] how it had begun to be dug, which I attest. [. . .] Juan Pardo, who, as he has said, on the seventh day of this month being lodged in the city of Cuenca with his company, commanded him to come to the place of Dudca to examine the mine and on the eighth day of the month he returned to the city of Cuenca with some rocks of the crystal which he had obtained with the point of a mattock from the said mine and he showed and gave them to the captain, [. . .]

> Charles M. Hudson, *The Juan Pardo Expeditions: Exploration of the Carolinas and Tennessee, 1566-1568*, trans. Paul E. Hoffman (Washington: Smithsonian Institution Press, 1990), 279-280. Joara was located northwest of current-day Morganton, Burke County. Juan Pardo renamed the town Cuenca after his native city in Spain. Yssa was probably located near Lincolnton; it is believed the Catawbas or their possible ancestors inhabited the town. Uncertainty remains as to the location of Dudca.

[. . .] the interpreter with overtravelling himself fell sick; yet the Tuskarorawe proffered him, if he would go, he would in three days journey bring him to a great salt sea, and to places where they had copper out of the ground, the art of refining which they have perfectly; for our people saw much amongst them, and some plates of a foot square. There was one Indian had two beads of gold in his ears, big as rounceval peas; and they said, there was much of that not far off. These allurements had drawn them thither, [. . .]

> "Journal of Francis Yeardley," 1654, in Alexander S. Salley, ed., *Narratives of Early Carolina* (New York: Scribner, 1911), 27.

The humble Petition of James Maxwell and Cornelius Doharty of South Carolina Indian Traders on behalf of themselves and others Inhabitants of the said Province.
[. . .]
That this favourable Conjuncture and disposition of the Indians seemed to Your Majestys Petitioners a proper opportunity of tying the bond of Friendship more fast and of preventing the design long entertained by the French of getting footing amongst the Cherokees and therefore Your Majestys Petitioners proposed to purchase the property of a tract of Land containing in length about eight Miles and in breadth about Six Miles in the Cherokee Nation for a valuable Consideration which the Indians readily agreed to and accordingly in their method of transferring the Property of Lands conveyed to Your Majestys Petitioners their Heirs and Assigns for ever All those Lands and Territorys lying in the Cherokee Nation within a Line beginning at a Creek called Aqua-ne-wa-rotee down the River Yw-facee to Custowee and up the River Tellicoe by Connostee and little Tellicoe to the beginning of the long Savannah called Co-a-tee Con-na-hetta and from thence to the Tuskequa Mount Mountain with all the Priveleges Rights Members appurtenances and hereditaments whatsoever to the said Lands and

Towns and each and every of them respectively belonging or in any wise appertaining And also all the Woods Timber and timber Trees therein or thereon growing or being And all the Mountains Hills Wastes Waters Water Courses and all Mines Minerals and Metals whatsoever in or upon the same, and whether the same be or contain Gold or Silver Copper Lead Tin Iron or any other sort of mineral Metal or Precious Stones and whether the same be now opened Digged up or Discovered or which shall or may hereafter be digged up opened or discovered within the Lands Territorys or Premises aforesaid or any of them respectively [. . .]

> Petition of James Maxwell and Cornelius Dougherty, 1744, in Colonial Office 5/370, British Records, State Archives, Office of Archives and History, Raleigh. The tract the two men wished to buy from the Cherokees would have been in modern-day North Carolina. "Aqua-ne-wa-rotee" may have referred to the town of Aquonatuste, which stood less than one mile east of Hiwassee, on Hiwassee River; "Aqua-ne-wa-rotee Creek" may have been Brasstown Creek, which flows northwest into the Hiwassee River in what is now Cherokee County. The boundary line west of Aquonatuste followed the "Yw-facee" or Hiwassee River to Custowee, which presumably had been located near present-day Murphy, at the junction of the Hiwassee and Valley rivers. The line then stretched along the Valley River northeast or upstream, past the towns of Connostee and Little Tellico, to a plain near the town of Konahete ("Con-na-hetta") which lay west of present-day Andrews. From Konahete the line turned southeast into the Tusquitee Mountains, possibly ending at Tusquitee Bald ("Tuskequa Mount") in present-day Clay County.

[. . .] the Cherokees extremely jealous of white people travelling about their mountains, especially if they should be seen peeping in amongst the rocks, or digging up their earth.

> William Bartram, *Travels through North and South Carolina, Georgia, East and West Florida* (1791; reprint, Savannah: Beehive Press, 1973), 329.

[1767] [. . .] at this Fort I deliver,d up my Squaw (woman) and Letter to Ensign McKeough, the commanding officer of that place, who Rece,d me with much politeness: here I allso met with Capt. Cameron our deputy Commissary for Indian Affairs; and Likewise the great Prince of Chotee, the old woolf of Keowee and Kinettita, the gutt of Toquah, the old and young Wariers, and attaw kullcullah or ockulla Stotastotah, the Little Carpenter, besides the great Bear and the Riseing faun, being most of the Cheifs of the Cherokee Nation; all then, met at this Fort to call a Counsell and hold a grand Talk concerning a peace with the Norward Enemies; and to apoint proper persons to proceed to New York and the Mohawk Nation for that purpose, after I had Eat, drank, smoak,d and began to be famileer with these Strainge Copper Collour,d Gentry, I thought it a fair opportunity to Request Leave to Travill through their Nation, in search of anything that curiosity might Lead me to; and in particular to speculate on their ayoree white Earth; and accordingly the Commanding Officer made the Motion, and the Linguist was desired to be very particular on the subject: This they granted, after a long hesitation, and severall debates among themselves; the Young Warier & one more seem,d to consent with Some Reluctance; saying they had been Trubled with some young Men long before, who made great holes in their Land, took away their fine White Clay, and gave ,em only Promises for it: however as I came from their father and had behaved like a True Brother, in taking care to conduct their Squaw safe home. they did not care to disappoint me for that time; but if I sho,d want more for the future, they must have some satisfaction for they did not know what use that Mountain might be to them, or their Children; and if it would make fine punch Bowls, as they had been told, they hop,d I wo,d let ,em drink out of one; and thus we shook hands and settled the matter.

> William L. Anderson, ed., "Cherokee Clay, from Duché to Wedgwood: The Journal of Thomas Griffiths, 1767-1768," *North Carolina Historical Review* 63 (October 1986): 502-503. "Ayoree" is Ioree; "this Fort" is Fort Prince George.

With the disappearance of the Roanoke colonists by 1590, the first Englishmen to actually establish permanent settlements in what is now North Carolina moved into the Albemarle region from Virginia in the seventeenth century. Some landholders, like Henry Plumpton (1648) and Nathaniel Batts (1660), bought acreage from the Indians. After Charles II created the colony of Carolina in 1663, its owners, the Lords Proprietors, prohibited such purchases.

Henry Plumpton aged eighty Six years or thereabouts Deposeth that he hath lived in the County now called Nansemond formerly Upper Norfolk about Seventy four years and that after the Right Honorable Sir Wm. Barkley was made Governor of Virginia he was amongst divers others at Severall Times sent out against the Southern Indians once particularly by Land under the Command of Major Generall Bennett and once by Water under Collonel Dewwhist to the best of his Remembrance was about the year 1646 In which expedition he well remembers that after they had entered Corratuck they proceeded up the Sound or Chowan as far as the mouth of Weyanoake Creek, Where they had a fight with the Indians and had a man killed by them And also about two years after a peace being concluded with the Indians the said Deponent with one Thomas Tuke of the Isle of Wight County and Several others made a purchase from the Indians of all the land from the mouth of Morattuck River to the mouth of Weyanoake Creek aforesaid Which the Indians then Shewed them, Which the deponent knew to be the same place where the man abovementioned was killed, and lyes (to the best of his Judgement and remembrance) about twenty or twenty-five miles above the mouth of Morattuck River: but the Deponent never heard the Blackwater Nattoway or Maherine Rivers or either of them called by the name of Weyanoake Creek.

Deposition, March 25, 1708, in Robert J. Cain, ed., *Records of the Executive Council, 1664-1734*, Volume 7 of *The Colonial Records of North Carolina [Second Series]*, eds. Mattie Erma Edwards Parker, William S. Price Jr., Robert J. Cain, and Jan-Michael Poff (Raleigh: Division of Archives and History, Department of Cultural Resources, [projected multivolume series, 1963–], 1984), 427. "Morattuck River" later became known as the Roanoke River.

To all to Whome these Presents shall come greeting.

These are to Certifie that I Kisentanewh Kinge of Yansapin River sold and alienated from my selfe my heirs or assigns the Land which Mr. Mason and Mr. Willoughby formerly bought of me but never paid me for, to Mr. Nath. Batts for a valuable Considerason in hand evnewd Vizt. all the Land on the southwest side of Pascotanck River from the mouth of the said River to the head of new Begin Creeke, to have and to hold to him and his heirs for ever, and Witness my hand this twentieth fourth of Septembr 1660.

Deed, Kisentawah, king of Yansapin River, to Nathaniel Batts, September 24, 1660, Nathaniel Batts Papers, State Archives, Office of Archives and History, Raleigh. "Yansapin River" is now known as Yeopim River; "new Begin Creek" is New Begun Creek.

102. No person whatsoever shall hold or claim any land in Carolina, by Purchase or gift or otherwise, from the Natives or any other person whatsoever, but merely from and under the <Lords> Proprietors, upon pain of forfeiture of all his Estate, moveable or unmoveable, and perpetual Banishment.

Fundamental Constitutions, July 21, 1669, in Mattie Erma Edwards Parker, ed., *North Carolina Charters and Constitutions, 1578-1698*, Volume 1 of *The Colonial Records of North Carolina [Second Series]*, ed. Mattie Erma Edwards Parker, William S. Price Jr., Robert J. Cain, and Jan-Michael Poff (Raleigh: Carolina Charter Tercentenary Commission, [projected multivolume series, 1963–], 1963), 150-151.

The settlers' encroachment upon lands inhabited or used by Native Americans soon became, and long remained, a major source of friction. Indians especially resented the loss of valuable hunting grounds and the increased competition for game. Some continued to hunt on acreage cultivated by whites, ruining their crops and destroying livestock. Christopher Dudley bludgeoned Sighacka Blount when he attempted to hunt on Dudley's land in 1723. For a time, North Carolina

governor Gabriel Johnston resorted to licensing to regulate Indian access to game lands.

The whole Business of an Indians life is War and Hunting. As Hunters they require a much greater extent of Territory, in proportion to their Numbers than Nations that Subsist by Agriculture: which makes them extreamly tenacious of their Lands and Jealous of encroachments. Each Individual has a right to, and looks upon himself as Proprietor of all the Lands claimed by the whole Nation. This will Account for the Umbridge taken by Indians at purchases made and Titles obtained by private Persons and even by Provinces: since no Indian whatsoever, let his influence or Power in His own Country be ever so great, can give away any more than his own right in any peice of Land; [. . .]

> John Stuart to the Board of Trade, March 9, 1764, in Colonial Office 323/17, British Records, State Archives.

North Carolina ss. Att a Councill holden at the house of Capt. Richd. Sanderson at Litle River on Thursday the 10th day of Mar. 1714/15. Present the Honorable Charles Eden Esqr. Governor Capt. Generall and Admirall. [. . .]

Upon Petition of the Porteskyte Indyans shewing that the Inhabitants of Corratuck Banks have and doe hinder the Said Indyans from hunting there and threatn them to breake their guns and that they Cannot Subsist without the liberty of hunting on those their usuall grounds.

Whereupon it is hereby ordered that the Said Indyans from henceforward have Liberty to hunt on any of the Said Banks And that noe English man presume to disturbe them therein without application made to this Board.

> Entry of March 10, 1714/15, in Cain, *Records of the Executive Council, 1664-1734*, 52, 53.

North Carolina ss. The Deposition of Richard Nixson being of full Adge and Sworne on the Holy Evangelist before us Gyles Shute and Joshua Porter Esqrs. Two of his Magisties Justices of the peace of the precincts of Beaufort and Hyde Saith that four or five Indians Came up to his house and that Mr Dudley was at his house when they Came so when they Came up he asked them where are you a Goeing and the Indians Satt down without Giveing him any Answer; then one Old Indian, Named Sighacka Blount Came up After the Rest and when he Came up he Asked what is the matter and Replyd English men here Allways Scold, then mr Dudley said you shall not hunt here, for this Land is all mine, then old Sighacka Said, that he would Goe hunt, and Catch Beavers, with that mr Dudley, Catched up a board, and said will you Goe, and struck him upon the head, and Caused the Blood to Run, and then the aforsaid Sighacka held up his Arm to Defend the Blow: and Recd a Blow upon his Arm and mr John Gardiner, Stept in Between them and parted them And the Indian satt down on a block, and said that mr Dudley had broake his Arm And with that I went to the Indian and took hold of his arm and felt on it and to the best of my understanding that there was one bone Broak Between the Elbow and [*wrist*] two dayes after I see the Indian Again And his hand and arm was very much swelld and the Indian told me that the Bone was Broak and nine or tenn dayes after I see the Indian Goeing home and his arm was Splintered; and he said he would goe, and tell king Blount; [. . .]

> Deposition of Richard Nixson, March 1722/23, Treaties, Petitions, Agreements, and Court Cases, Indians, 1697-1758, 1769, Miscellaneous Papers, 1677-1775, Colonial Court Records 192, State Archives, Office of Archives and History, Raleigh.

We the Members of the Lower House of Assembly humbly beg leave to lay before your Excellency the several grievances represented to us by the Committee appointed for that purpose which are in the words following [. . .]

Upon the complaint of Beaufort and Bertie Precincts setting forth that the Indians, contrary to the Treaty of Peace, burnt upon their lands, and kill and disturb their Cattle, and they pretend to hunt by virtue of a lycence from His Excellency the Governour.

Resolved by this Committee that the House be moved to address His Excellency to withdraw the said Lycence.

[Governor Gabriel Johnston:] I shall take care to recall all the Licenses given to the Indians, and strictly charge them not to presume to hunt within any plantation in this Government.

> Message from Lower House of Assembly to Governor Gabriel Johnston of North Carolina, and the governor's response, October 7, 1736, in William L. Saunders, ed., *The Colonial Records of North Carolina*, 10 vols. (Raleigh: State of North Carolina, 1886-1890), 4:237, 239.

Native American resistance to encroachment was not limited to trespassing upon land claimed by whites. The Tuscaroras attacked settlers on the Chowan River and the south side of Albemarle Sound in the mid-1660s. In 1675 the Chowan nation, influenced by Indians who had been ravaging white settlements in Virginia, broke the friendship treaty of 1663 and began a two-year struggle to expel colonists from the Albemarle region. Defeated, the Chowans lost their lands on the Meherrin River and were relegated to a reservation on Bennett's Creek in what is now Gates County.

Richard Saunderson, Sr., Esq., aged Seventy years or thereabout, being sworn on the holy Evangelist, saith:

[. . .] that when Mr. Drummond was Governr of North Carolina, The Inhabitants thereof went out against the Tuskeruro Indians who had killed some English dwelling on the So. Shore in Carolina, & that at the same time severall people dwelling on the back bay & to the Norward of Currituck Inlett some twelve or fourteen miles were pressed to go out against the said Indians in behalf of the government of North Carolina, & further saith not.

William G. Stanard, ed., "The Indians of Southern Virginia, 1650-1711: Depositions in the Virginia and North Carolina Boundary Case," *The Virginia Magazine of History and Biography* 7 (April 1900): 347, 348. William Drummond was governor of the county of Albemarle in Carolina province, 1664-1667.

We received yours containing the complaints of the Maherine Indians pretending encroachments made on them by the Inhabitants of this Government &c Upon consideration of which we thought we could not better answer yours than by sending you the true state of that matter being always as willing to give all reasonable satisfaction concerning our proceedings as Zealous to assert the undoubted Right of the Lords proprietors and her Majestys Subjects of this Governments Of a long time before the memory of man the Lands on the Southside of that River which is now called Maherine were in the Rightfull possession of the Chowanoake Indians by Virtue of a Grant from the Yawpin Indians and no other Indians (as plainly appears by successive accounts of that Nation by Original Writings and undoubted evidences) has had any Right to any Land there to this day and when first the Lords Proprietors of Carolina by Virtue of their Charter from his late Majesty King Charles the 2d took possession of this province that nation submitted themselves to the Crown of England under the Dominion of the Lords proprietors and continued peaceably till about the year 1675 about which time by incitements of the Rebelious Indians of Virginia who fled to them they committed hostility upon the Inhabitants of this Government in Violation of their Treaty Whereupon by virtue of the Authority for making peace and Warr granted to the Lords proprietors by their Charter, open war was made upon the said Indians in prosecution whereof (by Gods assistance though not without the loss of many men) they were wholly subdued and had Land for their habitation assigned them where they remained to this day so that all the tract of Land on the Southside of the Maherine River was at that Time resigned into the immediate possession of the Lords Proprietors of Carolina as of their province of Carolina and has been peaceably by them held without any Claime now thirty years [. . .]

North Carolina Executive Council to Virginia Executive Council, June 17, 1707, in Saunders, *Colonial Records*, 1:657-658.

South of Albemarle Sound, smallpox almost wiped out the Pamlico Indians in 1697. The Executive Council, the governing body entrusted by the crown to confirm Carolina land patents, in 1700 opened to white settlement the areas of Bath County that the epidemic had made vacant. As increasing numbers of colonists occupied that land, they were harassed by the Core, Neuse River, Machapunga, and Bear River Indians, as well as the remaining Pamlicos.

1700. Att a Councell Holden att the house of the Honorable Major Saml. Swann.

[. . .]

Ordered that the Secretarys Office be opened to grant patents on the North shore as allso on all Lands on the w. shore and s. shore that was seated att the time when the Lords proprietors Deed was Granted.

> Entry from 1700, in Cain, *Records of the Executive Council, 1664-1734*, 3.

Upon complaint of the Inhabitants of the County of Bath that many robereys outrages and injurys are dayly committed by the Core Indians Who as it is represented to this board are slaves to the Tuscorouda Indians. For Remidy wherof Ordered that Capt. Henderson Walker by such Method as he shall see convenient doe send to the Cheifs of the Tuscaroura Indians to give them account thereof and demand satisfaction for the Injurys done and to signify to them that if they doe not take speedy care to make restitution restrain them from the like injurys this Government will forthwith take [*illegible*] to suppress them with force.

> Entry from 1698, in Mattie Erma Edwards Parker, ed., *North Carolina Higher Court Records, 1697-1701*, Volume 3 of *The Colonial Records of North Carolina* [*Second Series*], eds. Mattie Erma Edwards Parker, William S. Price Jr., Robert J. Cain, and Jan-Michael Poff (Raleigh: State Department of Archives and History, [projected multivolume series, 1963–], 1971), 511-512.

To the Honorable Landgrave Robert Daniell Esqr. Lieftenant Generall Vice Admirall and Deputy Governor of No. Carolina and to the Honorable Councell.

The Humble Petition of the Inhabitants of Neus Rivir. Sheweth

[*torn*] two years agon seated this place [*torn*] sitting [*torn*] stocks A Neus Indian with 4 more in his Company killed [*torn*] hog of Adam Luess and being demanded proof for pay according to their Articles Receaved nothing but Reprochfull Language in respect to the Honorable Governor and to the rest of the English. Having likewise broke two Locks att two severall times, from one house taking thence to the Value of 250 skins and this publickly; and stealing the boards and nails from another, they likewise are seated in severall

Commodious places of this River to the great disadvantage thereof. Demanding unreasonable prices for their Land which we are neither willing or able to give them all which hinders the Speedy and well settling so Commodious a River [. . .]

Petition of Thomas Leppar et al., [1703-1705], in Cain, *Records of the Executive Council, 1664-1734*, 396-397.

To the Honourable Robert Daniell Esqr. Deputy Governour and the rest of the Honourable members in Counsil

The humble petition of the Inhabitants of Matchapungo.

May it please your honours.

Wee whose names are hereunto Subscribed do [H]umbly adresse your honours not only in behalfe of ourselves the Subscribers but of all the Inhabitants of this place most humbly praying that Some Speedy and Effectual Method may bee taken for restraining the Insolency and Continued abuses of the Matchapungo Indians by Killing and destroying our hoggs and beating one of our neighbours for Endeavouring to prevent the Same As Likewise the threatning to take our lives away for discovery of these there Villanies, to prevent which King Charles in his own person (Whether out of policy to See how wee would resent it or out of Reall Kindness to us wee Know not) came down in the night to give us [*torn*] since which and to this Instant they Continue unpardonably [*torn*] both in there Speeches and Actions, In all things rather [*torn*] desire to a War with us than a peace, And have Accordingly [*torn*] themselves nigh a Willdernesse whereupon the least [*torn*] they can easily repair without being pursued, Wherefore these things being taken for truthe, As wee are ready to prove, Do therefore hope and Confidently believe that your honours will find it part of your Christian duty to see us defended from these barbarous heathen, And that wee may not live in such dayly Jeapordy of our lives [. . .]

Petition of Nicholas Daw et al., [1703-1705], in Cain, *Records of the Executive Council, 1664-1734*, 397-398.

Honourable Sir:

These Comes to aquaint your honour about the bare river Indians That Came on Thursday Last to my house There was about sixteen with King Louther all with there guns. I was att worke in the Woods and one Cristopher Gold. I made what hast I could but they ware to quick for me for my wife and children had Left the house, they took away severall Things that we miss. they have Taken all my Aminition. [. . .] They stod with there Guns Cocked so that I Could not gett Into my house till they had Done what they pleased. I beleve itt is through the Instegation of one John Elderedge for he told the Indians

When I Brought a Letter to your honour from Mr. Lawson that It was to Cutt them of which made them lay wait for me att Seder Island. As they told me then [. . .] they would burne my house and when itt was Light Moone the would gether my Corne and the Englishmens Corne. Elderedge told them further that the English men would not sell them no Amunition because they would Cutt them of So We humbly Crave that your honour would take some Corse or Other with them or Else here will be no Living So No More to Trouble your honour with but your humble servant to Command.

William Powell

William Powell to Governor Robert Daniel, October 20, 1704, Miscellaneous Records, Albemarle County Papers, vol. 1:fol. 56, State Archives, Office of Archives and History, Raleigh.

In an about the Month of Septembr. 1707

I Being then att Panticough and Archibald Holmes comeing then on board my sloop with severall Others told me that they Expected the Indians Every day to Come and Cutt their throats and that they had no person to head them or Else they would goe and secure all the Panticough Indians, and that the said Holmes Made severall reflecting words on Major Gale which he the said Deponent does not now remember and further saith nott.

Robt Kingman

Deposition of Robt. Kingman, September 1707, Treaties, Petitions, Agreements, and Court Cases, Miscellaneous Papers, 1677-1775, Colonial Courts Records 192, State Archives, Office of Archives and History, Raleigh. The "Panticough Indians" are the Pamlicos; "Major Gale" is Christopher Gale.

In an effort to keep the Indians of eastern North Carolina from making further trouble, whites began denying them guns and ammunition—a state of affairs which the Indians interpreted as a signal that the colonists were planning to go to war against them. As a result, rumors circulated that the Tuscaroras and their allies, such as the Bear River Indians, were preparing a preemptive attack. Settlers petitioned the governor and council to act to defuse the situation.

Febry. 29th 1703/4. Pamlico in North Carolina. To the Honorable the Governor and Councill wee whose names are under written Doe Humbly present to your Honors

That wee have great reason to believe that the neighbouring towns of the Tuscororah Indians are of late Dissatisfied with the Inhabitants of this place and Severall actions and Discorses of the beare river Indians and more then ordinary familiarity of Late that is between them and the Tuscorodos: Induses us to beleve that they are Indevouring to perswade them that the English here designs a war against them the which occations us to that if your Honors dus not Speedily take Sum Care in the matter; we may receive Sum preiudice from them the which wee Suppose might bee prevented and that Sum of the Chiefs of the Indians would Cum in to your Honors if you would Spedily please to Send a good Interpreter here with orders what to doe and Such of us as your Honors Shall appoint are ready to goe with Such an Interpreter wee pray your Honors will take Sum Speedy Care in the Premesses for our preservation as to your wisdoms Shall Seem meet and remaine your Humble Servantts. [. . .]

[*Endorsed*:]
Mr. Reading Sayes that the Indians of Late are more Impudent in Killing there Creatures then formerly and openly brags of it Mr. Birkenhead Sayes the like[.]

> Petition of Lyonell Reading et al., February 29, 1703/4, in Cain, *Records of the Executive Council, 1664-1734*, 401-402.

The Tuscaroras, the largest and most powerful Native American nation in eastern North Carolina, had been contending with the effects of encroaching white settlement for years. In fact, the colonists' expanding presence caused the nation of normally independent towns to form two major confederations: the northern Tuscaroras, situated primarily between the Roanoke and Pamlico rivers; and the southern Tuscaroras, concentrated between the Pamlico and the Neuse. Like the Indians of the smaller neighboring nations, the Tuscaroras had become increasingly disturbed by the loss of land and game, the dishonesty of traders, and the colonists' kidnapping and enslavement of their people. The arrival of the first wave of settlers upon 17,500 acres of land purchased by Baron Christopher De Graffenried at the confluence of the Neuse and Trent rivers—New Bern was established there in 1710—heightened tensions further. By then it was apparent that the Tuscaroras were considering two courses of action: depart North Carolina or stay and fight. In June 1710 they sought permission from the colony of Pennsylvania to settle within its boundaries. Pennsylvania was prepared to accept them if their headmen could produce a voucher, from the government of North Carolina, of past good conduct. Unfortunately, they were unable to obtain such a document. Distressed by the growing number of settlers at New Bern, the southern Tuscaroras and their allies took advantage of the disarray left in the wake of the Cary Rebellion (a civil war that erupted between the adherents of rivals for governor), and attacked white settlements in the Neuse-Pamlico region at sunrise on September 22, 1711.

At a Council held at Philadia., the 16th of June, 1710.
[. . .]
The Govr. laid before the board the report of Coll. French & Henry Worley, who went on a message to Conestogo, by his Order, wch. follows in these words:

At Conestogo, June 8th, 1710.

Present: John French. Henry Worley. Iwaagenst Terrutawanaren, & Teonnottein, Chiefs of the Tuscaroroes, Civility, the Seneques Kings, & four Chief more of yt nacon, wth. Opessa ye Shawanois King.

The Indians were told that according to their Request we were come from the Govr. & Govmt., to hear what proposals they had to make anent a peace, according to the purport of their Embassy from their own People.

They signified to us by a Belt of Wampum, which was sent from their old Woman, that those Implored their friendship of the Christians & Indians of this Govmt., that without danger or trouble they might fetch wood & Water.

The second Belt was sent from their children born, & those yet in the womb, Requesting that Room to sport & Play without danger of Slavery, might be allowed them.

The third Belt was sent from their young men fitt to Hunt, that privilege to leave their Towns, & seek Provision for their aged, might be granted to them without fear of Death or Slavery.

The fourth was sent from the men of age, Requesting that the Wood, by a happy peace, might be as safe for them as their forts.

The fifth was sent from the whole nation, requesting peace, that thereby they might have Liberty to visit their Neighbours.

The sixth was sent from their Kings & Chiefs, Desiring a lasting peace with the Christians and Indians of this Govmt., that thereby they might be secured against those fearful apprehensions they have these several years felt.

The seventh was sent in order to intreat a Cessation from murdering & taking them, that by the allowance thereof, they may not be affraid of a mouse, or any other thing that Ruffles the Leaves.

The Eight was sent to Declare, that as being hitherto Strangers to this Place, they now Came as People blind, no path nor Communicacon being betwixt us & them; but now they hope we will take them by the hand & lead them, & then they will lift up their heads in the woods without danger or fear.

These Belts (they say) are only sent as an Introduction, & in order to break off hostilities till next Spring, for then their Kings will Come & sue for the peace they so much Desire.

We acquainted them that as most of this Continent were the subjects of the Crown of Great Brittain, tho' divided into several Govmts.; So it is expected their Intentions are not only peaceable towards us, but also to all the subjects of the Crown; & that if they intend to settle & live amiably here, they need not Doubt the protection of this Govmt. in such things as were honest & good, but that to Confirm the sincerity of their past Carriage towards the English, & to raise in us a good opinion of them, it would be very necessary to procure a Certificate from the Govmt. they leave, to this, of their Good behaviour, & then they might be assured of a favourable reception.

The Seneques return their hearty thanks to the Govmt. for their Trouble in sending to them, And acquainted us that by advice of a Council amongst them it was Determined to send these Belts, brought by the Tuscaroroes, to the five nations.

Pursuant to your honrs. & Council's Orders, we went to Conestogo, where the forewritten Contents were by the Chiefs of the Tuscaroroes to us Deliver'd; the sincerity of their Intentions we Cannot anywise Doubt, since they are of the same race & Language with our Seneques, who have always proved trusty, & have also for these many years been neighbours to a Govmt. Jealous of Indians, And yet not Displeased with them; wishing your honr. all happiness, we remain, Your honrs. Most humble & Obliged servants,

John French, Henry Worley. [. . .]

Minutes of the Provincial Council, June 16, 1710, in Samuel Hazard, ed., *Colonial Records of Pennsylvania*, 16 vols. (Harrisburg, Pa.: printed by T. Fenn & Company, 1851-1853), 2:511-512. The Shawnee faction led by Opessa had settled on Pequea Creek in present-day Lancaster County, Pennsylvania.

Motives or causes of the Indian War.

What kindled that Indian or Savages' war were, above all, the slanders and insinuations of a *few rioters* against Govr Hyde and against me. They made the savages believe that I had come to expel them from their lands, and that they would be compelled to settle much further, towards, or even in, the mountains; I convinced them that such was not my intention, and they could ascertain it by the gentleness and civility of my behaviour towards them, and by the payment which I made to them of the lands where I had settled at first, and where I had founded the small town of Newbern, although I had already paid double their worth to the Surveyor Lawson, who sold them to me as free of whole incumbrance, not telling to me that there were Indians. Again, I had made peace and alliance with the King and his Indian dependents, which were well satisfied with me; (3) an important cause was the carelessness, negligence, and lack of precaution of the Carolinian residents; (4) it was the rough treatment of some turbulent Carolinians, who cheated those Indians in trading, and would not allow them to hunt near their plantations, and under that pretence took away from them their game, arms, and ammunition. There even was an Indian killed, which most incensed them, and not unjustly.

> Christopher De Graffenreid, "De Graffenried's Manuscript," in Saunders, *Colonial Records*, 1:921-922. De Graffenreid was a member of the colonial council. "Govr Hyde" is Edward Hyde; the "few rioters" are the supporters of Thomas Cary, leader of the rebellion against Hyde; "Surveyor Lawson" is John Lawson.

The crushing defeat, in 1713, of the southern Tuscaroras and their allies in the Tuscarora War effectively suppressed Native American resistance in eastern North Carolina. Settlers poured into the region. Several thousand southern Tuscaroras fled to Virginia, then moved farther north to reunite with the Iroquois Confederacy in western New York. North Carolina assigned many of the remaining eastern Indians to reservations, and in 1715 enacted a law which addressed the land issues that brought about the war. Militia returns show that, by 1754, the populations of the nations that once occupied eastern North Carolina had shrunk significantly.

Brother Corlaer

We acquaint you that the Tuscarore Indians are come to shelter themselves among the five nations they were of us and went from us long ago and are now returned and promise to live peaceably among us and since there is peace now every where we have received them, do give a Belt of Wampum, we desire you to look upon the Tuscarores that are come to live among us as our Children who shall obey our commands & live peaceably and orderly[.]

They gave some Bevers & other Skins to His Excellency[.]

> Conference between Governor Robert Hunter of New York and the Indians, Albany, September 25, 1714, in E.B. O'Callaghan and Berthold Fernow, eds., *Documents Relative to the Colonial History of the State of New York*, 15 vols. (Albany, N.Y.: Weed, Parsons and Company, printers, 1853-1887), 5:385, 387. "Brother Corlaer" was the title given by the Iroquois to the governors of New York. The Iroquois bestowed the name in honor of Arent Van Corlaer, governor of New Netherlands until 1667, a man they respected for fair dealing.

CHAPTER LXIX.

An Act for Restraining the Indyans from molesting or Injureing the Inhabitants of this Government and for Secureing to the Indyans the right and property of their own lands.

I. Whereas (before ye late war) dayly and grievous Complaints of Depredations & Insults of ye Indyans were Exhibited against them by Divers persons bordering upon and residing near to ye Inhabitants of ye said Indyans for ye prevention of ye like Disorder for ye time to come and for Cultivating a better Understanding with ye said Indyans the want of which has been so Injurious to the Government.

II. Be It Enacted by his Excellency the Pallatine, &c. And It Is Hereby Enacted that whoever shall Discover or find any Indyan or Indyans Killing, Hunting or in pursuit of any horses, Cattle or hogs the right and property whereof is in any white man inhabiting within this Government every such person or persons on Discovery or Sight thereof may & he is hereby Impowered to apprehend every such Indyan or Indyans & him or them so apprehended & taken to Convey before Some one of the Commissioners to be appointed for Indyan affairs (& for want of such before ye nearest Magistrate) which said Commissioners or Magistrate together with the ruler or head man of the Town to which such Indyan Delinquent may belong is and are hereby Impowered to punish every such Delinquent in such manner as the nature of the offence may require and to award satisfaction to the party injured for all Damages by him Sustained (saving always the right of appeal to the Governor & Council) if either party shall think themselves aggrieved or wronged thereby.

III. And Be It Further Enacted by the Authority aforesaid that if any difference shall for the future Arise between any whyte man and Indyan concerning trade or otherwise howsoever, Every such Difference shall be heard, Tried and Determined by such Commissioners as the Governor or Commander in Chief for the time being shall appoint together with the ruler or head man of the town to which the Indyan belongs (Saving only the right of appeal as is herein before Saved & Excepted).

IV. And whereas we have too great reason to believe that disputes concerning land have already been of fatall Consequence to the peace and wellfare of this Colony.

V. Be It Further Enacted by the Authority Aforesaid that no whyte man shall for any Consideration whatsoever Purchase or buy any tract or Parcell of Land claimed or actually in possession of any Indyan without special liberty for so Doing from the Governor And Councill first had and obtained under the penalty of Twenty pounds for every hundred acres of Land so bargained for and purchased one halfe to the Informer & the other halfe to him or them which shall sue for the same to be recovered by Bill, Plaint or Information in any Court of Record within this Government wherein no Essoign, protection, Injunction nor Wager of Law shall be allowed or admitted of.

VI. And Be It Further Enacted by the Authority aforesaid that whatever whyte man shall Defraud or take from any of the Indyans his goods or shall beat or abuse or Injure his person each and every person so offending shall make full satisfaction to the party Injured and shall suffer such other punishment as he should or ought to have done had the offence been Committed to any Englishman.

Laws of North Carolina, 1715, in Walter Clark, ed., *The State Records of North Carolina*, 16 vols. (11-26) (Raleigh: State of North Carolina, 1895-1906), 23:88.

Bladen Troop, [. . .] No Indians. [. . .]

Coll. Robert West's Regim't in Bertie County, [. . .] Tuskaroro Indians, 100 men & 201 women & children, in all 301.

Col: Wm. Dry's Returns for Coll. G. Innis' Regim't in New Hanover County, [. . .] No Indians in the County; [. . .]

Coll. Craven's Regiment, in Chowan, [. . .] There is but one Indian nation, the Chowans, in the County; only 2 men and 5 women and children; ill used by their neighbors. [. . .]

Coll: Thom's Lovick, Collector of Beaufort, in Carteret County. [. . .] No Indians in the County.

Will'm Eaton, Esqr., Coll. of Granville County. [. . .] There are about 12 or 14 Sa[p]ora men, and as many women & children in the County.

Capt'n Evan Jones returns for Tyrrell County Militia, [. . .] No Indians in the County.

Coll: John Heywood's returns for Edgecomb County. [. . .] No Indians in the County, [. . .]

Perquimmans County, Coll: John Riusset's Regim't, [. . .] No Indians; [. . .]

Pasquotank County, Coll: R't Murdens. [. . .] no Indians. [. . .]

Northampton County, John Dawson, Coll: [. . .] No Indians but the Meharins, about 7 or 8 fighting men.

Granville County, Capt'n Hurst's Troop, [. . .] A few Sa[p]ora Indians. [. . .]

Coll: DeRosset's Regiment in Johnston County, [. . .] No Indians. [. . .]

Onslow County, Coll: John Starky. [. . .] No Indians. [. . .]

Coll: Barrows' Regim't, for Beaufort County, [. . .] No Indians. [. . .]

Col: Rutherford's Regim't of Troop in Bladen County, [. . .] No arms, stores or Indians in the County.

Militia Returns, 1754-1755, in Clark, *State Records*, 22:311-312, 313, 314.

Immigrants who traveled south along the Great Wagon Road from Virginia and Pennsylvania began settling the North Carolina Piedmont as prime acreage in the east filled. Speculators like Murray Crymble and James Huey positioned themselves to satisfy the demand for land.

At the Court at St. James's the 19th day of May 1737. Present the Kings most Excellent Majesty, Arch Bishop of Canterbury, Lord President, Lord Chamberlain, Duke of Athol, Duke of Ancaster, Earl of Cholmondiley,

Earl of Selkirk, Mr. Comptroller, Lord Chief Justice Willes, Sir Charles Wills, Sir William Yonge, Stephen Poyntz Esqr.

Upon reading this day at the Board the Report from the Right Honourable the Lords of the Committee of Council for Plantation affairs dated the fifth of this Instant in the words following Videlicet

In Obedience to an Order in Council of the 28th of May 1736 referring to this Committee the humble Petition of Murray Crymble and James Huey of London Merchants, in behalf of themselves and several others praying for a Grant of Lands upon the heads of Pee Dee, Cape Fear and Neuse River in North Carolina and proposing to make a settlement thereon of six thousand Swists, Palatines and other foreign Protestants within the space of ten Years from the date of their Grant. The Lords of the Committee have taken the said Petition into their consideration and have received the opinion of the Lords Commissioners for Trade and Plantations thereupon, and having been several times attended by the Petitioners, do find that they are willing to undertake the settlement upon the following conditions Videlicet,

That they be allowed One Million two hundred thousand acres of Land to be surveyed in twelve different parcels of one hundred thousand acres each.

The Lords of the Committee having considered the said proposals Do [humbly] Report to Your Majesty that although the quantity of Land proposed to be settled is very great, amounting to the proportion of two hundred acres for each Person to be settled hereon, yet their Lordships do not apprehend that any inconvenience can arise from the granting the same to the Petitioners in regard the said Lands are situated in the extremity of the [Province near] to the Cherokee Mountains, and at a very great distance from the seat of Government [And that] there are several million of acres of vacant Land between the sid Land prayed for and the Land already settled. That this Province being by its situation liable to the excursions of the Indians, a settlement formed in this part will be of great service to the said Province in protecting their Frontiers as well as encouraging the further settlement of the said Vast Tract of Vacant Lands, [. . .]

Order in Council, May 19, 1737, in Robert J. Cain, ed., *Records of the Executive Council, 1735-1754*, Volume 8 of *The Colonial Records of North Carolina* [*Second Series*], eds. Mattie Erma Edwards Parker, William S. Price Jr., Robert J. Cain, and Jan-Michael Poff (Raleigh: Division of Archives and History, Department of Cultural Resources, [projected multi-volume series, 1963–], 1988), 337-338. The "Cherokee Mountains" were the Great Smoky Mountains.

As colonists claimed more of the Piedmont, their settlements began to impinge upon the lands of the Catawbas, some of whom reacted to the influx by ransacking the homes and fields of the intruders. The Catawbas were linked by trade and treaty to South Carolina; its

governor, James Glen, warned Matthew Rowan, president of the North Carolina council, that continuing encroachment and the high-handed actions of some North Carolinians risked open warfare. President Rowan complained to British officials of Glen's meddling and the Indians' demands for land, while Anson County residents asserted that the Catawbas allowed raiders from other nations to carry out attacks against them. North Carolina commissioners and King Hagler of the Catawbas met for talks in 1754.

I have very often charged our young Fellows not to molst [*sic*] nor rob the white People. What they have done I could not prevent, but if they commit any more Acts of Violence, shall immediately acquaint you. What they took was mostly Eatables and they were mighty hungary. I complained already by the Bearer Robert Steill in a Letter sent you by him that the white People were settled too near us, but had no Answer to it. If they want Lands we are willing to sell them. By their being settled so near us our Horses are stole from us, and when any of our People dye or are killed by their Enemy, there is Nothing left to pay their Debts. I want much an Answer to the above, particularly relating to the white People's settling so near.

> Catawba King and others to Governor James Glen, November 21, 1752, in William L. McDowell Jr., *Documents Relating to Indian Affairs, May 21, 1750-August 7, 1754*, in *The Colonial Records of South Carolina, Series 2* (Columbia: South Carolina Archives Department, 1958), 361.

Thomas Little 400 [acres] Anson on the South side of the Cataba River Oppsit to the Cataba Nation Joyning David Tempeltons Entrys for Complement.

> Entry of Thomas Little, March 28, 1753, John Rice's Book of Entries for Warrants, Land Office (Colonial), Court of Claims, Secretary of State Records, State Archives, Office of Archives and History, Raleigh.

So Carolina Charles Town the 13th March 1754

The intention of this Letter, is to represent to You the violent and unjust Proceedings of some Persons said to belong to North Carolina, I have formerly Written on that head, and it is with Concern What I see the necessity of renewing my Representations; But unless Your Government apply some speedy remedy, the Harmony and good Correspondence betwixt the Provinces, will unavoidably be interrupted, and even the Peace of both endangered for I truely think that the Consquence may be, that if Your Officers go on unrestrained they will draw on an Indian War; They come into this Province in a forcible manner, disturb our Inhabitants, drive them from their Habitations, destroy their Fences, and cut up their Corn, and threaten their Lives, it is hardly credible that there should be a Breach of Hospitality, betwixt the Subjects of the same Prince; But really Sir to call these Actions by their proper name, they are Acts of Hostility, and had any Nation of Savage Indians used our People in such manner, this Province would have thought it necessary [torn] restrained them by an armed Force; But these Proceedings [torn] [ins]trumental to many Inhabitants, are not so dangerous [to this] Province, as the Conduct of Your People to the Catawba In[dians] may prove, unless You Immediately correct it; That [torn] has been in Treatie with this Government for forty years [.] They are very Brave and have been faithfull to us, but [torn] have some times complained, that our People settled too [close to] them, and said it would breed ill Blood, for as They had [no] other way of subsisting but by hunting, they required a [torn] round their Towns, and this Government thought that thi[rty] miles all around was the Least that they could have. We accordingly restrained our Surveyors from running an[y] nearer, but some from Your Government, have most un[torn]ably and indiscreetly surveyed up to their very Towns, which would cut off all their hunting grounds, and the Nation itself may be cut off with equal Justice, These iniquitous Proceedings may be productive of much Mischief, The last Indian War that this Country was involved in, broke out upon less Provocation, and had like to have proved fatal to it, and tho the Catawba Nation, be not very numerous, yet an Indian war might soon prove General, and therefore out of Prudence and good Policy, as well as from a Principle of Justice, their Grievance in this particular ought to be redressed; [. . .]

Governor James Glen of South Carolina to North Carolina Executive Council president Matthew Rowan, March 13, 1754, in Colonial Office 5/14, British Records, State Archives, Office of Archives and History, Raleigh. The "last Indian War" to which Glen refers is the Yamasee War (1715-1717).

Last week I received a letter from several of the Inhabitants of Anson County near the Cattaboes with a Copy of a letter from Mr. Glen Governor of South Carolina to the King and Great men of the nation dated the 8th of April last telling them that he and the Council had given Orders that no white men should settle within thirty miles of their town and that he had ordered all the white men within that distance to remove, there is settled within that bounds at least five hundred familys of white people that have the Kings Patents It is as fine a Country as any in America, the Cattaboes are about three hundred men, the tuskarora Indians are as numerous as the Cattaboes and are very well satisfied with ten thousand acres of land this is upwards of two millions of acres. What power he and his Council has to do this I cannot say [. . .]

Matthew Rowan to the Board of Trade, June 3, 1754, in Saunders, *Colonial Records*, 5:124.

To His Excellency Arthur Dobbs Esqr. Co. General and Governour in Chief in and over the Province of North Carolina.

The Humble Petition of the Inhabitants on the frunteers of Anson County in This Province Most Humbly Sheweth.

Whereas Many of your Petitioners, have Been Robbed, and assaulted, By the Indians who Calls themselves Shanaws, and Sometimes Sinakers and at other times Cherekees which we Doubt not but they are a Mixter of the Three; and By them our Cattle is Killed and Horses and Houshold Goods Dayly as taking away from us; and our Houses By them Burning and threatning to take Your Petitioners Lives, and very often abusing our women and Children. So that Severals of your Petitioners was obliged to fly from our Livings, and Leave our Crops which seem'd to be aplentiful appearance of a Large Harvest which is all Lost By the Barbarous and Cruel Enemy which is Daily Making Prays of Your Petitioners and others. We Your Petitioners Being at a loss, By not having authority from your Excellency to Proceed against our Enemys, the Shanaws, and their asociates, which are Daily amongst us, Discovering of our Defenceless and Naked Condition which Enemy we have Great Reason to fear is harboured, and Countenanced Both by the Cherekee, and Catauba Indians, and Doubts not but the End will be Dangerous, if not prevented, By your Exelencies Wise and Prudent Means. Therefore we Your Petitioners Most Humbly Begs that Your Excellency will take your Petitioners Cases into Your wise and Prudent Consideration; and grant your Destressed Petitioners Relief, by appointing us a scout for our Safegaurd and Defence and to be stationed Between Enoree River, and the Head Waters of Thickety and [*torn*]las your Petitioners Mutualy agree and nominate the Bearer Capt Wm Green to be Captain of the Scout if [*torn*] [*illegible*] with your Excellencies Will and pleasure. We [*illegible*] [*torn*] Conduct and Courage and well aquainted with the Woods, also your Petitioners Does think it will be highly Convenient that a fort should be forthwith Erected, in Such a Place in the Bounds aforesaid, as Your Excellency and the Bearor Shall think Proper which Countenanced By your Excellency will be a mean to Encourage your Petitioners to abide By the Rights and will be a very Great Encouragment to others, to Come and Settle, there being Large Bodies of Good Land to Settle, in your Excellencies Bounds Therefore we your Petitioners most Humbly Pray Your Excelency would be pleased to take our Present Condition under your wise and Prudent Consideration and Endeavour our Relief by such prudent Means as your Excellency will think most Proper and with all the Speed the Nature of the Case will admit of, many of us almost Resolved to Leave our all and go where we may Most Reasonably Expect to Enjoy peace, But as we have purchased our Lands in the Goverment we most Humbly Begg and pray Your

Excellencies Protection and Your Petitioners as in Duty Bound shall Ever Pray.

Petition, [1754], Miscellaneous Papers, Council Papers, Governors' Office Records, State Archives, Office of Archives and History, Raleigh. "Shanaws" are the Shawnees; "Sinakers" are the Senecas.

<*North Carolina Rowan and Anson County's*> At a Treaty held on Thursday the Twenty Ninth day of August one Thousand Seven Hundred and Fifty four at the house of Mr. Matthew Tool, Between Alexander Osburn and James Carter Esqrs. Commissioners, and the Cataba Indians.
Present James Carter and Alexdr. Osburn Esqrs. Commissioners etc.
King Hagler and Sundry of his headmen and Wariors
[. . .]

<*Commissioners*> You Remember in the Letter the President wrote to You by Capt McClenachan and the other Gentlemen he told You that he had undersood that Mr. Glen the Governor of South Carolina Incouraged You to Drive, all the white people from the Lands within Thirty miles of Your Nation, if he has Told You so You Cannot Expect that this man Loves You or the white people, Because he well knows that the great king Your Father and ours gave those Lands to his Children and also he Gave it into the Care of the President of North Carolina to Divide According to his Discretion Among his people and not to the Governor of South Carolina and it is his desire and pleasure to do Justice Between You and us, for he Looks up[on] You and us as his own [people] and would rejoce to here of our Unity and Frien[dship] to Each Other, for whilst we behave thus to Each o[ther] and stand by Each other we need not fear any opp[onent] that should attempt or Come to Dismay us.[. . .]

<*King*> As to our Liveing on those Lands we Expect to live on those Lands we now possess Dureing our Time here for when the Great man above made us he also made this Island he also made our forefathers and of this Coulor and Hue (Shewing his hands and Breast) he also fixed our forefathers and us here and to Inherit this Land and Ever since we Lived after our manner and fashion we in those Days, had no Instruments To support our living but Bows which we [*torn*]cated with stones, knives and had none, and as it [was our] Custom in those days [to] Cut our hair, which we Did by Burning it of our heads and Bodies with Coals of Fire, our Axes we made of Stone we bled our selves with fish Teeth our Cloathing were skins and Furr, instead of which we Enjoy those Cloaths which we got form the white people and Ever since they first Came among us we have Enjoyed all those things that we were then Destitute of for which we thank the white people, and to this Day we have

Lived in a Brotherly Love and peace with them and more Especially with these Three Goverments and it is our Earnest Desire that Love and Friendship which has so Long remain'd should Ever Continue.

Meeting between Commissioners James Carter and Alexander Osburn and King Hagler, August 29, 1754, Matthew Rowan, Colonial Governors' Papers, State Archives, Office of Archives and History, Raleigh.

The border across the Piedmont had yet to be finalized between the two Carolinas, and unrest, as described in Glen's letter of March 13, 1754, above, prevailed. Land-hungry colonists who claimed acreage under one government clashed with those who held it under the other. Caught in the boundary dispute were the Catawbas, whose territory in the central Piedmont straddled the potential line; as long as that line remained to be drawn, jurisdiction over the area and the Catawbas was in doubt and the threat to peace remained. Neither Britain nor the Carolinas wanted to provoke the nation. Except for a few flare-ups, relations with the Catawbas generally had been stable; their presence served as a security buffer between the frontier settlements and hostile forces; and they provided warriors for campaigns against the French and other common enemies. However, Governor Arthur Dobbs of North Carolina had obtained large tracts of Piedmont land from Crymble and Huey that he hoped to sell to settlers. Like Matthew Rowan, he dismissed as extravagant the reservation of thirty miles' radius that South Carolina attempted to enforce. Considering their total number, Dobbs believed that the Catawbas should be content to live on less. They eventually were: seriously weakened by small pox, and in exchange for a fort to be built by South Carolina for their protection, the Catawbas agreed in 1760 to reduce the size of their reservation to "15 Miles Square."

Mr. Glenn having buoyed up the Catawba Indians, whom I found to be about 300 Warriors and are computed at about 700 souls in the whole, that he would grant to them and have it confirmed by the Crown a Circle of 30 miles round their Towns within which radius no white man should settle, and Governor Lyttleton having acquainted me that the Catawba King Haglar had complained to him that the English were settling within their Bounds, it will be proper when the Boundary is fixed to consider how much Land to allow to them in proportion to their Numbers, as we are now building a Fort in the midst of their Towns at their own Request we can the better fix their Lands. I find that when the Tuskerora Lands were fixed, who where then more numerous than the Catawbas are now, that they were content with a tract less than 10 miles radius round their towns. I find that in a Circle of Ten miles radius is contained 200,960 acres, and in a Circle of 30 miles radius it contains 1,808,640 acres the least Tract divided among 700 souls would be 287 acres to each person, and in the larger Circle 9 times as much above 2,500 acres to each person. [I]n whatever way his Majesty is pleased to determine it, I humbly think it ought to be done by a publick Treaty with them to please them, by both the Colonies in which the several lands may lie, and in case they should make any large demand, that then the several Governments may be empowered to purchase from them by their free consent whatever may exceed a sufficient Competency for their numbers to be paid out of His Majestie's Quit rents, as the Crown will be reimbursed by the Quit rents, at the same time allowing them to hunt on the English adjoining Lands equally as the English Subjects which may be purchased for a small sum, in goods which they should choose, and what ever they have granted to them should not afterwards be purchased from them, altho' their numbers should greatly diminish, by any private person or planter, but should only be purchased by Agreement from the Crown, and then they would not be defrauded out of their remaining Lands.

Governor Arthur Dobbs of North Carolina to the Board of Trade, January 20, 1757, in Saunders, *Colonial Records*, 5:739, 742.

CHARLES TOWN (South Carolina) August 9.

[. . .]

The same Day the Hon. Edmond Atkin, Esq; His Majesty's Agent for, and Superintendant of, Indian Affairs, &c. arrived in Town from the Cherokee Country (whether he went with the Army) but last from Pine Tree Creek, on Wateree, where, we are told, he has happily settled the Affair of their Lands, so many Years depending between the Catawba Nation, and this Province and North Carolina: Almost the whole Nation was present, and unanimously approved of what was done; whereby both Provinces may reap great Benefit, as well as Individuals, and the Public in general, especially at this Juncture, because the Dissatisfaction of the Catawbas, on Account of the Lands they claimed, might have been the Means of our losing that brave and faithful Nation, who tho' now reduced to about 100 fighting Men, are still important to the Welfare and Security of our Back Settlements.

Pennsylvania Gazette, August 28, 1760. The agreement reached by Atkin and the Catawbas in July 1760 is known as the Treaty of Pine Tree Hill. Pine Tree Hill is current-day Camden, South Carolina.

I must beg your Lordships indulgence while I relate some account of the Catawba Lands, tho' it may perhaps have heretofore been given. Some years ago on the complaint of the Catawbas that their Settlements and Stocks of

Horses and Cattle were disturbed by incroachments of Surveyors and Settlers from both Provinces; This Government issued an Order that no Deputy Surveyor should go within 30 Miles of the Catawba Towns. These Orders were duly observed by the Surveyors of South Carolina because they knew their Surveys would be void as no Grants would be obtained thereupon; but the North Carolina Surveyors could not be controll'd, as the Line of Jurisdiction was not ascertained. But in the Year 1760. The Catawbas having been harassed by the Cherokees and the Northward Indians and by the great ravages which the Small-Pox made among them reduced to only 75 Men, they were desirous of removing lower and nearer our Settlements. At a Conference which Mr. Atkin His Majesty's Superintendant for Indian Affairs had with their Nation in their Town, it was agreed that if this Province would build a Fort to Cover their Women and Children from the Enemy, they would be satisfied with an Extent of 15 Miles Square which they judged sufficient for the wants of their Number. Upon this information from Mr. Atkins I prevailed on the Assembly to build a Fort, and one was built in 1760 and their whole Tribe were fed and cloathed at the Expence of this Government during the whole Cherokee War.

Lieutenant Governor William Bull of South Carolina to the Board of Trade, December 10, 1764, in Colonial Office 5/378, British Records, State Archives, Office of Archives and History, Raleigh.

Despite the Catawbas' agreement with Superintendent Edmond Atkin to reduce their reservation by half, Governor Dobbs was still not satisfied. He wrote to Governor Thomas Boone of South Carolina, objecting to Atkin's actions and stating that all of the Catawba land to be surveyed could lay in North Carolina once the trans-Piedmont boundary was run. North Carolinians were already occupying the territory the nation had abandoned during the small-pox epidemic; demands that settlers vacate those holdings "would occasion much Confusion." Boone urged patience and defended the Catawbas' position. Dobbs argued that settlers had a right to land, including hunting grounds, that was not under cultivation or enclosed by the Indians—a rationalization often used by acquisitive officials. Both governors agreed that colonists must not disturb the Indians' burial places, the sanctity of which the Catawbas were determined to defend.

After writing my Letter of Yesterdays date to your Excellency Mr. Samuel Wyley arrived here and informs me he had directions from Mr. Bull to run out Lines of the Lands alloted for the Catauba Nation a Tract of fifteen Miles Square Commencing at the Southward from 12 Mile Creek to the Northward 15 Miles from East to West 7 Miles and half On each Side of Catabaw River pursuant as he says to an Agreement made with the Catawbaw Nation about a Year ago between Mr. Atkins agent for Indian affairs with King Heglar, and Heglar with three Indians have arrived here the same day upon the same Account.

It does not a little Surprise me to find that Mr. Atkin should peremtorily have taken upon him to have fixed so large a Tract of Land to them without first acquainting me with it, as there is the highest probability that all these Lands will be within this province by the parrellel Lines which will determine our Boundary without ever shewing his power to me of determining it without His Majesty's approbation or Consulting the Government of this province, and still more so in having never communicated his agreement to me since he concluded it if it can be yet said to be concluded without his Majestys Consent and Approbation of which I never had the least intimation till yesterday from Mr. Wyley. And this Survey if perfected would ascertain the Catawba's Claim hereafter would at present occasion much Confusion among those who had taken Warrants and Patents upon these Lands. For upon the Indians removal from Sugar Creek Town to 12 Mile Creek many of the Lands Northward from Sugar town upon the Catawba River have been Surveyed and some patents issued as I apprehended upon their removal they had Chosen and Accepted of other Lands more Southerly and more so as their Number of Warriors have been Reduced In a few Years by Heglars Confession from 300 to 50 and all their Males dont exceed 100 Old and young included so they are now scarse a Nation but a Small Village the Lands alloted to them since their Reduction by Mr. Atkin is 144,000 Acres and the Tuskororars who had and still have 300 Warriors were Content to enjoy a Township of 40,000 Acres to the best of my Remembrance having not the Law nowhere as the Catawbaus have behaved well though their Members are reduced I would agree to their having a Larger Tract and Proportion of Land would not think it imprudent to Advise his Majesty to allow them a Tract of 12 Miles Square which would contain 96,000 Acres a Sufficient Quantity for so Small a Number and then their Bounds might be Limitted between 12 Mile Creek and Sugar Creek on the East Side of Catawba and as much more to the westward as shall make up the Compliment till his Majesty's approbation is obtained, and therefore at present should advise that the Surrounding Lines should be suspended and only the Distance Run from 12 Mile Creek to Sugar Creek to asscertain that distance and in the mean time I shall Suspend the issuing of any more patents within that Limit and think it reasonable that Captain Stewart who Succeeds Mr. Atkins should send me a Copy of Mr. Atkins power by which he acted in fixing their Limits without his Majesty's Approbation or the Consent of this province and then when the Limits are ascertained no private purchase should be allowed though their Numbers should diminish without the Approbation of the Government of the province in which the Lands may lay and the General Consent of the Catawba Nation.

These are my present thoughts as I have none of the Council to Consult which I hope will meet with your approbation, as I have acquainted King Haglar that the agreement could not be Confirmed untill after the peace when we Should have his Majesty's pleasure known upon it and in the mean time I would endeavour to prevent any Encroachments below Sugar Creek.

Governor Arthur Dobbs to Governor Thomas Boone of South Carolina, July 6, 1762, in Robert J. Cain, ed., *Records of the Executive Council, 1755-1775*, Volume 9 of *The Colonial Records of North Carolina* [*Second Series*], eds. Mattie Erma Edwards Parker, William S. Price Jr., Robert J. Cain, and Jan-Michael Poff (Raleigh: Division of Archives and History, Department of Cultural Resources, [projected multivolume series, 1963–], 1994), 108-109.

Sir

I Duly received your favour by Mr. Smith a little before which the Catabas had been down with me to complain of the encroachmen made on their Lands by the Inhabitants of your province, and I waited to know how well grounded these Complaints were before I answered your Letter. I was two days ago favoured with your Letters of the 5th and 6th and have according to your request laid all of them before His Majestys Council of this province, and I shall now communicate to you the result of our delibertations on the several Subjects: with regard to the Catawbas, which we cannot help looking on as a matter of Consequence it is our opinions that all foundation for their Complaints should be absolutely removed whether they are agrieved by the Inhabitants of this province or the next, they are certainly the original possessers of the Soil and have not Conveyed it away, they are very Serious in Claiming their Rights and deserve that Justice should be done them, if they were disposed to be Satisfied with what Mr. Atkins promised, who no doubt had authority for what he did, though none from either Government for he was Independant of any: it is highly incumbent on both provinces to make them easy, nor can it be said at whose expence their Tranquility will be purchased untill the Boundary Line is Run; with regard to what might be Sufficient for them as a Nation that is not what we are to determine but to do them Justice and leave the Burying place of their Ancestors undisturbed, I flatter my self therefore that you will prevent any further encroachments upon their Limits agreed upon with Mr. Atkin.

Governor Thomas Boone to Governor Arthur Dobbs, July 23, 1762, in Cain, *Records of the Executive Council, 1755-1775*, 111-112.

Sir

I received your Excellencys Letter of the 23 July by Capt. Ellis in Answer to my Several Letters as I can't Summon a Council upon it without sending

Messengers near two hundred Miles to make a Sufficient Number I can Only Answer such parts of it untill our next Council meets at next Superior Court and Court of Claims when they must attend, and therefore shall pass Slightly over what Concerns the Catawbas Claim till we meet but think your Claim on Account of the Indians is much too extensive as almost all the Lands we possess in America ought to have been purchased from them, but I think no Occupancy gives us a right to what they dont Cultivate or inclose for if a Liberty of hunting upon unimproved Lands gives them a Title we ought to quit all our Lands to them for they hunt down to the Sea coast nor can I allow of Mr. Atkins Settlement of their Lands untill his Commission is produced and Registered in this province otherwise any one may pretend to have a Commission or exert powers never Granted to them which it is every Governors duty to disallow till produced, and therefore I have a right to see it before I can Submit to it at the same time I am far from doing Real prejudice to the Catawbas or entering upon their Burial Grounds which ought always to be Excepted.

> Governor Arthur Dobbs to Governor Thomas Boone, August 28, 1762, in Cain, *Records of the Executive Council, 1755-1775*, 109.

My Lords

I am under a necessity of applying to your Lordships upon a Subject of some Consequence to both Colonies of So. and No. Carolina, having used fruitless Endeavours with Governor Dobbs to keep everything quiet till his Majesty's determination upon our Boundary was signified. The Catawba Indians a brave and faithfull people, that have constantly hitherto, and are always ready to deserve [well] of the English, have made frequent complaints of the Encroachments of No. Carolinians upon those lands which the Catawba's call theirs, and which either by the Justice or Indulgence of this Colony have been set apart for their Hunting; these lands if the Indian Claim is not allowed, are by no means acknowledged by us to be in the No. Government, but as I am no stranger to a late Instruction of his Majesty to the Governor of New York upon a similar Complaint from the five nations, I am in no doubt neither, but it will be equally the King's pleasure, that these Catawbas should be quieted either by purchase or possession, but the Lands in question fall within the boundary of either Goverment. Till June or July last they had contented themselves with Complaining only, but an Attempt of the No. Carolina Surveyors to Run out even their Burial places so Exasperated them that they pursued with an Intention to Murder them.

> Governor Thomas Boone to the Board of Trade, October 9, 1762, in Colonial Office 5/377, British Records, State Archives, Office of Archives and History, Raleigh.

The land concerns of the Catawbas were addressed soon after the French and Indian War ended in 1763. With its defeat of France, Great Britain won a vast swath of North America that stretched from Canada to Florida and westward to the Mississippi River. It also assumed the oversight of Indian nations formerly allied with its enemies. To preserve the peace, amicable relations with the Indians were vital. Lord Egremont, secretary of state for the southern department, instructed Superintendent John Stuart and the governors of Georgia, Virginia, and the Carolinas to meet with the southern nations at Augusta, Georgia: there they were to act upon the Indians' grievances and explain royal policies. Approximately 700 Indians from five nations attended the Augusta Congress of November 1763. Speaking on behalf of the Catawbas, headman Colonel Ayres told officials that white encroachment had ruined the hunting grounds for one hundred miles around their town, a loss for which the nation had never been compensated. He asked that boundaries be established to protect their remaining land. Colonel Ayres got his wish, and the reservation approved in 1760 by South Carolina, Edmond Atkin, and the Catawbas was laid out by the end of 1764. The trans-Piedmont border, completed in 1772, placed the Catawbas and their territory in South Carolina.

Colonel Ayres chief of the Catawbas said (in English) he always minds the White People the King George's Talk and four Governors are all good, to day all the people meet here, he hears all the Red people and the White right well and they Talk good (Gives a String of Beads) these are white beads all none black all for King George and the four Governors they all send a Talk a good Talk to the Red People he and his People are as White Men and is well pleased with what he has heard he did and will keep it to his heart he goes to sleep and rises but never loses the Talk of the White People The Catawbas and he are all of one mind. All the Indians that are now good their children should be suffered to grow up he has very little to say he lives among the White People and came to hear the Talks of Others he holds fast his commission receives none from the French and in consequence of his commission from his Brethren the White People he came to hear the Talks of others.

He informed the Governors his Land was spoilt he had lost a great deal both by scarcity of Buffalos and Deer they have spoiled him 100. Miles every way and never paid him his hunting Lands formerly extended to Pedee Broad River etc. but now is driven quite to the Catawba Nation if he could kill any deer he would carry the meat to his Family and the skins to the White People but no Deer are now to be had he wants 15. miles on each side his Town free from any encroachments of the white People who will not suffer him to cut Trees to build withal but keep all to themselves.

Augusta Congress, November 7, 1763, in Clark, *State Records*, 11:189.

To Colo Ayres and Brothers of the Catawbas.

It gives us great pleasure and satisfaction to find that the good Talk which we gave you from Our Great King and Father of both the Red and White Children is so satisfactory to you as you have always been fast Friends to all his White children so our King and Father holds out his arms to receive and protect you from all your enemies and it is very sensible of your constant Love and Friendship for all your White Brothers and you may be assured of his confirming to you all your just claims to your Lands and Hunting Grounds pursuant to the Agreement made between your Nation and his Governor of South Carolina and Mr Atkins his Superintendant of Indian Affairs upon your having a Fort built for your Protection from your Enemies when you deserted your old Towns which was then agreed upon on both sides to be a square of Fifteen Miles to be laid out on both sides of the Catawba River and part of the Line was actually surveyed. [. . .]

The Catawbas upon appearing satisfied of the Line of 15. Miles square were informed that a new Survey should be made and when the Line was run the People settled within should be removed and no new Warrants granted them or any others to settle within those Limits. Upon which they desired a new Line should be run out immediately.

Augusta Congress, November 9, 1763, in Clark, *State Records*, 11:191, 198.

This Treaty was confirmed at the Congress of Governors at Augusta in 1763 and the 15 Mile Square actually run out.

Lieutenant Governor William Bull of South Carolina to the Board of Trade, December 10, 1764, in Colonial Office 5/378, British Records, State Archives. "This Treaty" refers to the Treaty of Pine Tree Hill.

Like the Augusta Congress, the Royal Proclamation of 1763 was conceived by the British to reassure the Indians and promote peace. To reduce the chances for conflict between whites and Native Americans, the document prohibited governors from granting land within the Indian nations and barred settlers from moving west of the crest of the Appalachian Mountains.

Whereas we have taken into our Royal consideration the extensive and valuable acquisitions in America, secured to our Crown by the late Definitive Treaty of Peace concluded at Paris the 10th day of February last; and being desirous, that all our loving subjects, as well of our kingdoms as of our colonies in America, may avail themselves, with all convenient speed, of the great benefits and advantages, which must accrue therefrom to their commerce, manufactures and navigation; we have thought fit, with the advice of our Privy Council, to issue this our Royal Proclamation, [. . .]

And whereas it is just and reasonable, and essential to our interest and the security of our colonies, that the several nations of tribes of Indians, with whom we are connected, and who live under our protection, should not be molested or disturbed in the possession of such parts of our dominions and territories as not having been ceded to or purchased by us, are reserved to them or any of them as their hunting grounds, we do therefore, with the advice of our Privy Council, declare it to be our Royal Will and Pleasure, that no Governor or Commander in Chief in any of our colonies of Quebec, East Florida, or West Florida, do presume, upon any pretence whatever, to grant warrants of survey or pass any patents for lands beyond the bounds of their respective governments, as described in their commissions; as also that no Governor or Commander in Chief in any of our other colonies or plantations in America, do presume for the present, and until our further pleasure be known, to grant warrant of survey, or pass patents for any lands beyond the heads or sources of any of the rivers which fall into the Atlantick Ocean from the West and North West; or upon any lands whatever, which not having been ceded to or purchased by us as aforesaid, are reserved to the said Indians, or any of them.

And we do further declare it to be our Royal Will and Pleasure for the present as aforesaid, to reserve under our sovereignty protection, and dominion, for the use of the said Indians, all the lands and territories not included within the limits of our said three new Governments, or within the limits of the territory granted to the Hudson's Bay Company; as also all the lands and territories lying to the Westward of the sources of the rivers which fall into the sea from the West and North West as aforesaid; and we do hereby strictly forbid, on pain of our displeasure, all our loving subjects from making any purchases or settlements whatever, or taking possession of any of the lands above reserved, without our especial leave and licence for that purpose first obtained.

And we do further strictly enjoin and require all persons whatever, who have either wilfully or inadvertently seated themselves upon any lands within the countries above described, or upon any other lands, which not having been ceded to or purchased by us, are still reversed to the said Indians as aforesaid forthwith to remove themselves from such settlements.

And whereas great frauds and abuses have been committed in the purchasing lands of the Indians, to the great prejudice of our interests, and to the great dissatisfaction of the said Indians; in order therefore to prevent such irregularities for the future, and to the end that the Indians may be convinced of our justice, and determined resolution to remove all reasonable cause of discontent, we do, with the advice of our Privy Council strictly enjoin and require, that no private person do presume to make any purchase from the said Indians of any land reserved to the said Indians within those parts of our colonies, where we have thought proper to allow settlements; but that if at any time any of the said Indians should be inclined to dispose of the said lands, the same shall be purchased only for us, in our name, at some public meeting or assembly of the said Indians, to be held for that purpose by the Governor or Commander in Chief of our colony respectively, within which they shall lie: And in case they shall lie within the limits of any proprietary Government, they shall be purchased only for the use and in the name of such proprietaries, conformable to both directions and instructions as we or they shall think proper to give for that purpose: [. . .]

Royal Proclamation of 1763, October 7, 1763, *Boston Gazette*, December 19, 1763.

White encroachment across the North Carolina Piedmont continued without abatement. Within two years of the issuance of the Proclamation of 1763, settlements had been established near the Lower Cherokees. Within three years, colonists had advanced into the Blue Ridge, seventy miles west of Fort Dobbs.

[. . .] I hear the People of North Carolina are making quick advances to the foot of the Cherokee Mountains, which is the Chief Hunting Ground for the Lower Cherokees.

Lieutenant Governor William Bull to the Board of Trade, March 15, 1765, Colonial Office 5/378, British Records, State Archives.

Fort Johnston is the only fort in this province. Fort Granville was never finished and what was done to it is now in ruins. Fort Dobbs in Rowan County is likewise neglected and in ruins, if this last fort had been kept up it could not have been of further service against the Indians as the inhabitants of this province have since the last war extended their settlements upwards of seventy miles to the westward of the fort.

Governor William Tryon of North Carolina to the Board of Trade, April 30, 1766, in Saunders, *Colonial Records*, 7:203. Fort Johnston is located in Southport, North Carolina. Fort Granville had been begun at Ocracoke Inlet on the Outer Banks. Fort Dobbs was built approximately four miles north of present-day Statesville, North Carolina.

Having lost the Cherokee War in 1761 (a conflict to be discussed later), the Cherokees desired to limit contact with whites. The nation, troubled by the intrusion of colonists into the mountains, believed it had obtained a halt to settlement beyond Long Canes Creek at the Augusta Congress. It had not. South Carolina maintained that the treaty ending the war had established a boundary farther west and persisted in granting lands between that line and Long Canes. North Carolinians also had been claiming acreage deep in Cherokee territory. Resentment among the Indians grew, and Lieutenant Governor William Bull began negotiating a boundary agreement between South Carolina and the Cherokees. Superintendent Stuart was "mortified" to learn of the uneasy relationship with the Indians during a July 1765 visit to South Carolina; although the Cherokees were eager to fix a border with the Carolinas and Virginia, Bull's efforts displeased him.

When I embarked for this Province the 15th June, I rejoiced in the Prospect of Peace and good Order in this Department, [. . .] The Cherokees I considered as firmly attached to us, and I depended on my own Influence and intimate Acquaintance with them, for introducing amongst them any necessary Arrangement; But I was greatly mortified on my Arrival here the 19th July to find the greatest Appearance of Disorder in that Quarter; where it was least expected.

At the Congress with the different great Nations at Augusta 1763, the Cherokees requested that no Lands should be granted beyond, or to the Westward of what was then inhabited by the White People; They represented that they were a Nation of Hunters, who depended on Game, with whose Meat they supported themselves and Families, and with their Skins ands Furrs they purchased such Utensils and Necessaries as they stood in Need of, and could not subsist without.

That although they were already much limited by the Encroachments of the White People on their Hunting Grounds, and their Game drove away; yet they would be very well satisfied, that the Settlements should remain as they were, provided none should be allowed for the future to advance and settle nearer their Towns; to this they were answered, that the Settlements beyond Long Canes were agreed to in the Treaty of Peace signed at the Close of last War by Lieutenant Governor Bull and Attakullakulla between the White People and their Nation.

The Cherokees still desired and expected that no further Encroachments should be made on their Lands, which has not however been attended to; Large Tracts have since that Time been granted by this Government far beyond what was then settled; and an Indian of Note called the Turrepine belonging to the Lower Cherokee Towns, who was hunting, having passed the Line fixed by Governor Bull's Treaty, was surprised in his Camp by a Justice of the Peace, who bound him with Ropes, and kept him Prisoner several Days.

To the Northward, the Province of North Carolina granted Lands as far back as the Mountains, and deprived the Indians of the Lower Cherokee Towns of the most Valuable Part of their hunting Grounds. [. . .]

The fixing and ascertaining a distinct Boundary between the Indians and all the Provinces is essential to the Tranquility of this District; it is a Point which greatly concerns them, and to which they are extreamly attentive.

The Murder of their People by the back Settlers of Virginia has not so bad an Effect, and the Consequences are not so much to be apprehended as of Encroachments on their Lands. The Indians can comprehend that the wicked Actions of a few Individuals ought not to be considered as a Proof of the Intentions of the whole Community, and will be well satisfied to have the Perpetrators brought to Justice. But grants of Land claimed by them, they know to be the Acts of Whole Provinces, which alarms them, and they consider as incontestable Proofs of our bad Intentions and Want of Faith.

It is not the Cherokees alone, who think themselves injured; the Jealousy of all the Nations is awakened, [. . .]

The Settlement of these Differences with the Cherokees and the Establishing a fixed Boundary, as well as making such Arrangements as may be judged convenient by their Lordships, may render it necessary to have a Meeting with their Chiefs, relative to which I hope to be honored with their Lordships Commands. [. . .]

I cannot inform you particularly of Mr. Bull's Negociations with the Cherokee Indians relative to a Boundary Line, as they have all been carried on entirely independant of me, my having any Concern in that Matter being thought quite unnecessary by the Lieutenant Governor.

I humbly offer it as my Opinion, that it cannot be done properly but with the Consent of all the Nation: any Grant from a Part will be productive of perpetual Grumbling and Disputes; and I humbly submit to their Lordships, if such Matters should not be transacted with the Participation of the Superintendant, or some Person acting for him, as he will be applyed to by the Indians in Case of any Dispute, and therefore it seems proper that he should be acquainted with the Circumstances of such Transactions.

I beg Leave to observe, that the far Extension of our Boundaries backwards, by approaching too near the Indian Nations, will expose us to perpetual Broils. The Inhabitants of those back Countries are in general the lowest and worst Part of the People; and as they and the Indians live in perpetual Jealousy and Dread of each other; so their rooted Hatred for each other is reciprocal.

The Laws in the American Provinces are not strong enough to operate with necessary Vigor, amongst People living so remote, and who require to have the Hand of Justice perpetually stretched over them; [. . .]

John Stuart to John Pownall, secretary to the Board of Trade, August 24, 1765, in Colonial Office 5/66, British Records, State Archives, Office of Archives and History, Raleigh.

The new boundary between the Cherokees and South Carolina was drawn in the spring of 1766, and Stuart relayed to Governor William Tryon the nation's desire to extend it across western North Carolina. Tryon and the Cherokees, led by Ostenaco (Jud's Friend), met in early June 1767 to discuss the line. It was finalized on the thirteenth.

Copy of a Talk from the Cherokees at Fort Prince George dated 8 May 1766.

At a Congress at Fort Prince George 8th. May 1766. Present Alexander Cameron Esqr. Deputy Agent for the Cherokee Indians, Ensign George Price commanding Officer of Fort Prince George, Kittagusta or the Prince of Choteh Head beloved Man of the Cherokee Nation Juds friend, and many other Headmen and Warriors of the upper, middle and lower Cherokee Towns. When Kittagusta addressed himself to Mr. Cameron and Mr. Price as follows.

Brothers,

I am to utter the united Voice of my Nation to you, and to desire you to make Our father Captain Stuart His Majesty's Agent and Superintendant of Indian Affairs, acquainted, as soon as possible, with my Speech.

We returned yesterday from making the Line between South Carolina and our Country; a Task of Fatigue, but nevertheless agreeable, as our Brothers, who are settled on the Frontiers of that Province, and we can never more have any Disputes about Land.

At Our Meeting with you here in October last we proposed also a Boundary Line on the North Carolina and Virginia Side; we repeat it once more, and desire to have it extended from where that of South Carolina terminates upon Reedy River, a streight Course to Colonel Chiswell's Mines, which will be a just Boundary, and the only one we can allow of. The Number of Families that have come from North Carolina, and Virginia, and settled upon a great part of Our best Lands, and the bold Inroads of a few that are within an easy Day's March of some of Our Towns, are Circumstances very alarming to us; therefore we shall be ready at the End of the 5th. Moon (Sept.) from this Time to attend at the marking a Line; Our Minds will not be easy 'till it is compleated; and, if our Brothers will not be assisting we must [*illegible*] effect it ourselves.

When our Father Captain Stuart remembers, that he was at the Congress at Augusta held in 1763, where were also present the four Governors of

Virginia, North and South Carolina, and Georgia, when the Great King's Proclamation relative to his red Children was read to us, and we were promised quiet possession of our Lands and Redress of Our Grievances, that we might claim the Land a great way beyond where we propose the Line to be run; but chuse much rather to part with it than have any disputes concerning it; and that we are poor people dependant upon the Woods for our Support, and without the means of redressing ourselves, but by Violence, which we do not chuse to exercise against our Brothers, he will certainly write to the Governors of Virginia and North Carolina, urging strongly the reasonableness of our Demand, and the Necessity of sending People of Consequence to meet us to put it in Execution.

Here a String of Beads was given. [. . .]

Talk from the Cherokees, May 8, 1766, Colonial Office 5/67, British Records, State Archives, Office of Archives and History, Raleigh. The lead mines owned by Colonel John Chiswell are located in present-day Austinville, Wythe County, Virginia.

June 2d 1767.

Jud Friend's Talk to Governor Tryon in answer to his Excellency's Talk delivered Yesterday at Tyger River Camp.

We have met here and smoked together as Brothers in the presence of him who sees above and in remembrances of great George over the Water.

I am going now to give you a Talk. Listen well & remember what it is, my Intention is good and the Man above is Witness to it. My Talk is straight and good.

I met you here and heard your Talk already, and you have met Warriours.

You have left your place of Residence, and we have also left ours and met here to remember His Majesty's Talks.

The Man above is Witness here, You are not the first Governor I have had Talks with, I have met Governors before and had Talks with them and have not forget them, but hold them fast.

Gave a string of White Beeds

I remember the meeting at Augusta with four Governors, where were the Chicasahs, the Choctahs, Creeks and Catawbas, where I heard His Majesty's Talk which I have not forgot, nor never shall.

I have come here with a few of my People, but they remember His Majesty's Talks The Man above is Witness that my Talk is straight and good and that it is my desire that there shall be nothing dark no more but all straight and Right.

I have met your Excellency here, and it is the first meeting I ever had from your Government. I hope our Talks will be straight and Right.

My Talk is the Sentiments of all our Nation, as well as those who are present of the head beloved Man in Chota, and of them all that I deliver here.

The Talks of your Excellency, the Governor of South Carolina, our Father Stewart and the Governors of Virginia and Georgia all agree

Gave a Stran of Beeds.

All the Towns in the Cherokee Nation are as one, they are all my People and We remember His Majestys Talk, that he told us to be all good.

His Majesty told me when I was there, that the white People and ourselves should be all one, that we were all his, and should be as one People. As His Majesty desires so I hope we shall look with one Eye, speak with one Tongue and be as one People.

Gave a stran of Beeds.

I am going to Talk more. The Man above is he who made the Land and His Majesty over the Water desires that the White People and themselves should mutually possess it.

As I said before the Man above is head of all, He made the Land and none other, and he told me that the Land I stand on is mine, and all that is on it. True it is the Deer and Buffaloe and the Turkeys are almost gone. I refer all to him above. The white people eat Hogs, Cattle, and other Things which they have here, but our Food is further off.

The Land here is very good Land, it affords good Water, good Timber and other good Things, but I will not love it. My Talk is very good, I do not love the Land as we are going to make a Division, I want to do what is fair and right.

I desire that your Excellency nor your Warriours will forget my Talk and that my Men also may not forget it but remember it well. I recollect the Talk we had from our Father Stewart about the Line and am accordingly come, and am ready to run it, for the white people to live on one side, and ourselves on the other, all in peace, our hunting grounds are but small and but a little way from the Nation.

There are Rogues among your People and among my people, but I will give my People a good and a strong Talk to be so no more, and I hope your Excellency will also give your People a Talk to be honest.

His Majesty told me when I was there and I have since heard that he desires a Line may be run between us, & that neither shall encroach on the other. I am now come to run it, and it must be done without alteration, I never indeed heard any proposed before a little last Night. I determine to have it run from the place it Terminated in South Carolina a straight course according to what has been agreed on. I remember the Talk from His Majesty and the head beloved at Augusta, concerning what course the Line should run. I am now come to run it and the Land that is on this side I wont love, I give it to the white People. The Price the white People give for Land when they buy is very small, they give a shirt, a match Coat and the like which soon wears out but Land lasts always.

I am now done talking, the Land is given when the Line is run and I quit all pretensions to it.

Layed down a string of Beeds on the Course the Line was to run.

I am now done and I wish to see the White People live well, increase and have Children and that we may do so to.

My People are here, come a great way naked, I expected to have had Things here for them, but as they are not come whether will they be sent for, or what will be done?

In answer to which His Excellency proposed, that a Sergeant & six Men from his detachment should Escort six of the Indians to Salisbury to receive the Presents and return back again with them as far as Loves Ford on Broad River, where the Presents should be delivered to the Indians, Which proposal Jud's Friend (on behalf of the Indians) complyed with, and the Detachment and Indians marched off immediately to Salisbury.

Cherokees' Reply to William Tryon, June 2, 1767, in William S. Powell, ed., *The Correspondence of William Tryon and Other Selected Papers*, 2 vols. (Raleigh: Division of Archives and History, Department of Cultural Resources, 1980-1981), 1:498-500.

Be it Remembered that on the 13th. Day of June in the seventh year of the Reign of our sovereign Lord King George the Third by the Grace of God of Great Britain France and Ireland King Defender of the Faith etc., and in the Year of Our Lord One Thousand Seven Hundred and Sixty Seven it was agreed in Behalf of His Most Excellent Majesty of the one Part and the Head Beloved Men and Warriors of the Cherokee Nation of the other part, Witnesseth, that whereas by a Talk had between the Head Beloved Men and Warriors of the Cherokee Nation and the Honorable John Stuart Esquire, His Majesty's Superintendant of Indian Affairs for the Southern Department dated the 20th day of October One Thousand Seven Hundred and Sixty five concerning the Boundary Line between the Frontiers of the Province of North Carolina and the Cherokee Hunting Grounds, to avoid All further Disputes was unanimously agreed as follows, By the Prince of Chote Juds Friend and All the Head Warriors and Head Beloved Men of the over Hills, Middle Settlements and Lower Towns that a Line on the North Carolina Side should be run, to Commence where that on the South Carolina terminates and to be run a North Course into the Mountains whence a Straight Line to the Lead Mines of Colonel Chiswell should fix the Boundary, in which Talk His Excellency William Tryon Esquire Governor and Commander in Chief in and over His Majesty's Province of North Carolina etc. by Commission under his Hand and Seal appointed The Honorable John Rutherford, the Honorable

Robert Palmer Esquires and John Frohock Esquire Commissioners to run the said Boundary Line between the Frontiers of North Carolina and the Cherokee Hunting Grounds: The Commissioners aforesaid with Alexander Cameron Esquire, Deputy Superintendant and the Head Chiefs and Warriors of the said Nation. To Wit Juds Friend, Tifftoe, Sallowee or the Young Warrior of Estatoe, Ecoy, Chinesto of Sugar Town and the Wolf of Keowee and others met on the Fourth day of June one Thousand Seven Hundred and Sixty Seven at Reedy River and run the Line as follows Beginning at a Waughoe or Elm Tree on the South Side of Reedy River standing on the Bank of the River where the South Carolina Line terminates and runs thence a North Course about Fifty Three Miles into the Mountains to a Spanish Oak marked with the Initial Letters of the Commissioners Names and Several other Trees with the Names and marks of Juds Friend, Sallowee Ecoy and others standing on the Top of a Mountain called by Us Tryon Mountain on the Head Waters of White Oak and Packlet Creeks, White Oak running into Green River and Packlet running into Broad River and as it was found impracticable that a Line should be run and marked thro' the Mountains to Colonel Chiswell's Mines it is further agreed between the said John Rutherfurd, Robert Palmer and John Frohock Commissioners as aforesaid in behalf of His Most Excellent Majesty and the said Alexander Cameron Esquire Deputy Superintendant as aforesaid and Juds Friend Tufftoe, Sallowee Ecoy, Chenesto and the Wolf of Keowee in behalf of Themselves and the Head Beloved Men and Warriors of the Cherokee Nation that the Line between the Frontiers of the Province of North Carolina and the Cherokee Hunting Grounds be continued as follows running from the Top of Tryon Mountain aforesaid beginning at the Marked Trees thereon by a direct Line to Chiswell's Mines in Virginia shall and is hereby declared to be the Boundary Line between the Said Frontiers of North Carolina and the Cherokee Hunting Grounds and the Commissioners aforesaid in behalf of His Excellent Majesty and the said Alexander Cameron Esquire, Juds Friend, Tufftoe, Sallowee, Ecoy, Chenesto and the Wolf of Keowee in Behalf of Themselves and the Head Beloved Men and Warriors of the Cherokee Nation agree determine and conclude that the Boundaries aforesaid herein described shall stand, be and remain the Boundary Line between the Frontiers of this Province and the Cherokee Hunting Grounds untill His Most Excellent Majesty's Pleasure shall be further known thereon. In Testimony of which the several Parties herein mentioned have hereunto Interchangably set their Hands and Seals the day and Year first above Written.

John Rutherford (Seal), Robert Palmer (Seal), John Frohock (Seal), Alexander Cameron (Seal)

Ustenecah Ottassatie or Juds Friend <*his mark*> (Seal), Ecuy, or the Good Warrior of Estatoe <*his mark*> (Seal), Saluy, or the Young Warrior of Estatoe <*his mark*> (Seal), Tifftoe, the Warrior Keowee <*his mark*> (Seal), Wolf of Keowee <*his mark*> (Seal), Chinesto of Sugar Town <*his mark*> (Seal)

> Boundary Line Agreement, June 13, 1767, Colonial Office 5/310, Part II, British Records, State Archives, Office of Archives and History, Raleigh. Tryon Peak is located north of the town of Tryon, Polk County, North Carolina. Sugar Town had stood on the Keowee River near Salem, Oconee County, South Carolina.

The Cherokee boundary line was no impediment to trespassing whites, nor in time was it able to bind the nation to its own land. The Cherokees, in need of trade goods, negotiated the sale of millions of acres to Richard Henderson of North Carolina and his associates. The tract lay in what is now Tennessee and Kentucky. Governor Josiah Martin attempted to forestall the transaction, which he believed violated the Royal Proclamation of 1763 and colonial law. Nevertheless, the Cherokees and the buyers approved the deal at Sycamore Shoals, on the Watauga River, on March 17, 1775.

CHARLESTOWN, *October* 2.

A letter from Fair Forest, on the northwest confines of this province, dated the 20th past, says that seven men of that neighbourhood, in North Carolina government, went to hunt amongst the mountains, and on the 5th of the said month, being upwards of 60 miles beyond the boundary line, about two hours after it was dark, as they were going to sleep, they were fired upon, as they suppose, by Indians; five of them got home again, one was killed on the spot, and they were obliged to leave another on the path mortally wounded.

> *Virginia Gazette* (Purdie and Dixon), December 3, 1767.

North Carolina ss. By His Excellency Josiah Martin Esqr. etc.

A Proclamation

Whereas it hath been represented to me by John Stewart Esquire His Majesty's Superintendant of Indian Affairs that sundry persons supposed to be Emigrants from this Province had settled on the Cherokee Lands, in Violation of the most Solemn Treaties, which had given just Umbrage to the said Indians, and may be attended with the most fatal Consequences. I have therefore thought fit, by and with the advice and Consent of His Majesty's Council to Issue this Proclamation hereby strictly enjoining and requiring the said settlers immediately to retire from the Indian Territories, otherwise they are to expect no protection from His Majesty's Government.

Given etc. 25th April 1774.

Proclamation of Governor Josiah Martin, April 25, 1774, in Cain, *Records of the Executive Council, 1755-1775*, 302.

A Proclamation by Governor Martin against Richard Henderson and the Transylvania Purchase.

Whereas his Majesty by his Royal Proclamation bearing Date at St James's the seventh day of October 1763, did among other Regulations thereby made, declare his Royal Will and Pleasure with respect to his Territory claimed by the Indian Nations in North America in the following words: "And Whereas great Frauds and Abuses have been committed in the purchasing Lands of the Indians to the great Prejudice of our Interests and to the great Dissatisfaction of the said Indians. In Order to prevent such Irregularities for the future and to the end that the Indians may be convinced of our justice and determined Resolution to remove all reasonable cause of Discontent, we do with the advice of our Privy Council strictly enjoin and require that no private person do presume to make any purchase from the said Indians of any Lands reserved to the said Indians within those parts of our Colonies where we have thought proper to allow Settlement; but that if at any time any of the said Indians should be inclined to dispose of the said Lands the same shall be purchased only for us in our name at some public Meeting Assembly of the said Indians, to be held for that purpose by the Governor or Commander in Chief of our Colony respectively within which they shall be: And in case they shall be within the limits of any Proprietary Government they shall be purchased only for the Use and in the Name of such Proprietaries conformable to such Directions or Instructions as we or they shall think proper to give for that Purpose."

And Whereas in and by an Act of the General Assembly of this Province intituled "An Act for restraining the Indians from molesting or injuring the Inhabitants of this Government and for securing to the Indians the Right and Property of their own Lands"; it is, among other things, "Enacted, That no white Man shall, for any consideration whatsoever, purchase or buy any Tract or Parcel of Land claimed or actually in possession of any Indian without special Liberty for so doing from the Governor and Council first had and obtained under the Penalty of Twenty pounds for every hundred Acres of Land so bargained for and purchased; one half to the Informer, and the other half to him or them that shall sue for the same."

And Whereas I have information that a certain Richard Henderson, late of the County of Granville in this Province, confederating with divers other

Persons, hath, in open violation of his Majesty's said Royal Proclamation and of the said act of the General Assembly of this Province, entered into Treaty with certain Indians of the Cherokee Nation for the Purchase and Cession of a very large Tract of Country, by some reported to be Two Hundred Miles Square, by others Three Hundred Miles Square, and said to be part of the hunting Grounds of the Cherokee Nation, and actually comprized within the limits of the Colony of Virginia and the Royal Grant to the Right Honorable the Earl Granville.

And whereas, this daring, unjust and unwarrantable Proceeding is of a most alarming and dangerous Tendency to the Peace and Welfare of this and the neighboring Colony inasmuch as it is represented to me that the said Richard Henderson and his Confederates have conditioned to pay the Indians for the Cession of Land before mentioned a considerable quantity of Gunpowder, whereby they will be furnished with the means of annoying his Majesty's subjects in this and the neighboring Colonies; and that he hath also invited many Debtors, and other persons in desperate circumstances, to desert this Province and become Settlers on the said Lands, to the great injury of Creditors.

And whereas, it is to be apprehended that if the said Richard Henderson is suffered to proceed in this his unwarrantable and lawless undertaking, a settlement may be formed that will become an Asylum to the most abandoned Fugitives from the several Colonies, to the great Molestation and Injury of his Majesty's subjects in this Province in particular and to the manifest Detriment of the Interest of Earl Granville, within whose proprietary District the Lands treated for as aforesaid by the said Richard Henderson with the Cherokee Indians are deemed and reported to be in part comprehended: I have thought proper to issue this Proclamation hereby in his Majesty's Name and also in Behalf of the Earl Granville, as his Agent and Attorney strictly to forbid the said Richard Henderson and his Confederates, on pain of his Majesty's highest displeasure, and of suffering the most vigorous Penalties of the Law, to prosecute so unlawful an Undertaking, as also to enjoin all his Majesty's liege subjects to use all lawful means in their Power to obstruct, hinder and prevent the Execution of his Design of settlement, so contrary to Law and Justice and so pregnant with ill consequences. And I do hereby forewarn all, and all manner of persons against taking any part or having any concern or dealings with the said Richard Henderson, touching the Lands for which he is said to have entered into Treaty with the Indians as aforesaid or with any other Person or Persons who have engaged or may engage in Projects of the like Nature, contrary to the Tenor of his Majesty's Royal Proclamation aforesaid, as every Treaty, Bargain and Agreement with the Indians repugnant thereto is illegal, null and void, to all Intents and Purposes, and that all partakers therein will expose themselves to the severest Penalties. And as it is necessary for the more effectual Prevention of such illicit and fraudulent dealings with the Indians, to advertise them of the Rules and Regulations established by his Majesty's Proclamation; it is hereby required of his Majesty's subjects having intercourse with the Indians and particularly of the Officers appointed to superintend Indian Affairs, that they do fully explain to them the beneficial Nature and Design of the said Royal Proclamation to themselves and that they do make the Indians sensible of the high Offence they commit against his Majesty in doing anything contrary to the directions thereof.

Given under my Hand, and the Great Seal of the said Province, at Newbern, the 10th day of February, Anno Dom 1775, and in the 15th year of his Majesty's Reign.

JO. MARTIN.

God save the King.

Proclamation of Governor Josiah Martin, February 10, 1775, in Saunders, *Colonial Records*, 9:1122-1125. In the second paragraph, above, Martin quoted Laws of North Carolina, 1715, c. 64, s. 5; see p. 154 of this volume.

This Indenture made this Seventeenth day of March in the year of our Lord Christ One thousand Seven hundred and seventy five, Between Oconistoto, chief warrior and first representative of the Cherokee Nation or Tribe of Indians and Attacullacullah and Savanooko otherwise Coronoh for themselves and in behalf of the whole nation, Being the aborigines and sole owners by occupancy from the beginning of time of the Lands on the Waters of Ohio river from the mouth of the Tenesee river up the said Ohio to the mouth or emptying of the great Canaway or new river and so across by a Southward line to the Virginia line by a direction that shall strike or hit the Holstein river six english miles above or Eastward of the long Island therein, and other lands and Teritories thereunto adjoining, of the one part, and Richard Henderson, Thomas Hart, Nathaniel Hart, John Williams John Luttrell, William Johnston, James Hogg, David Hart and Leonard Henley Bullock of the province of North Carolina of the other part,

Witnesseth that the said Oconistoto for himself and the rest of the said nation of Indians for and in Consideration of the Sum of Ten thousand pounds of Lawful money of Great Britain to them in hand paid by the said Richard Henderson, [et al., . . .] the Receipt whereof the said Oconistoto and his said whole nation, do and for themselves, and their whole Tribe of people, Have granted, bargained and Sold, aliened, enfeoffed, released and confirmed and by these presents Do grant, bargain and sell, alien, enfeoff, release and confirm unto the[m] the said Richard Henderson, [et al., . . .] their Heirs and assigns forever, all that Tract, Territory or parcel of land situate, lying and being in North America, on the Ohio river one of the East branches of the

Mississippi. Beginning in the said Ohio River at the mouth of Cantuckey Chinoca, or what by the English is called Louisa river, from thence running up the said river, and the most Northeasterly branch of the same to the head spring thereof, thence a South East course, to the top ridge of Powels mountain, thence Westwardly along the ridge of said Mountain into a point from which a North west course will hit or strike the head spring of the most Southerly branch of Cumberland river, then down the said river including all its waters to the Ohio river, thence up the said river as it meanders to the beginning etc. [. . .]

In Witness whereof the said Oconistoto, Attacullacullah and Savonocko, otherwise Coronoh, the three Chiefs appointed by the Warriors and other head men to Sign for and on behalf of the whole Nation, hath hereunto set their hands and Seals the day and year first above written.

> Copy, Transylvania Company deed, Session of April-May 1783, General Assembly Session Records (Oversized), State Archives, Office of Archives and History, Raleigh. The "great Canaway or new river" is the Kanawha River. The Long Island is located in the Holston River at present-day Kingsport, Tennessee. The Cherokees considered it a sacred treaty and council place as well as a refuge. "Louisa river" is the Kentucky River.

The lands opened by the Transylvania Company, as Henderson and his associates became known, enticed more settlers to join the westward march into the Appalachians as the American Revolution unfolded. The Raven of Chota told Henry Stuart, in May 1776, that a considerable number of Cherokees wanted their hunting grounds restored to them. The brother of Superintendent John Stuart, Henry had visited the nation to ensure its attachment to the British. Not long afterward, Cherokee war parties attacked backcountry homesteaders on a wide scale.

At a meeting of the principal chiefs of the Upper, Middle and Lower Settlements of Cherokees, at Choeto, on the second day of May, 1776, the Raven of that town being the chief speaker and addressing himself to Mr. Henry Stuart, spoke as follows:

You have been told that we disposed of our land contrary to the advise and desire of our father and our repeated promises to him. 'Tis true, we suffered the people who first settled themselves on our land on Watauga [River] to remain there some years, they paying us annually in guns, blankets and rum, etc. But we are informed lately that they gave out publicly that we sold the land to them forever and gave them a paper for it. If they have any paper of this kind, it is of their own making, for we have never given them any, as it was contrary to our thoughts. Now, we look upon you as our father, and rejoice that you are here, and desire that you will write to the white people of

Watauga, Nanachucket and all others that settled this side of the great boundary line, which was marked at the desire of the Great King, to move to some other land within the white people's bounds. We hope and wish they may hear and prevent any mischief that may happen between them and our people, many of whom we find uneasy already for the recovery of their hunting ground.

> The Raven to Henry Stuart, May 2, 1776, in Clark, *State Records*, 22:995. Savanukah was also known as the Raven of Chota ("Choeto"). "Nanachucket" was the Nolichucky River.

Land fever re-intensified after the combined militias of the Carolinas, Georgia, and Virginia defeated the Cherokees in the autumn of 1776. It was further encouraged by the concessions the victors obtained in the peace agreements the following year. The Treaty of DeWitt's Corner, signed May 20, 1777, deprived the Lower Cherokees of most of their towns and hunting grounds in northwestern South Carolina. The Treaty of Long Island of Holston, concluded on July 20, took away the Overhill Cherokees' hunting grounds east of the Blue Ridge Mountains. Although the new state of North Carolina attempted to manage the settlement of its western lands, it could not prevent encroachment beyond the boundary specified in the Treaty of Long Island of Holston. South Carolina president Rawlins Lowndes warned Governor Richard Caswell that expansionist pressure on the Cherokees, coupled with the "machinations of the King's Superintendent of Indian affairs," would lead to trouble.

Section XLII. That no Purchase of Lands shall be made of the Indian Natives, but on Behalf of the Public, and by Authority of the General Assembly.

> North Carolina Constitution, 1776, in Clark, *State Records*, 23:984.

<No 316 Transfered to Wm Sharpe and Test D Vance> David Dickey enters in Burke County four hundred acres of land in the forks of the Middle fork Ivey River including larg Indian incampments and a Small Cane brake Entered this 28th Day of March 1778.

> Land entry of David Dickey, Entry no. 316, March 28, 1778, Burke County Land Entries, Transcriptions of County Land Entry Books, Land Office (State), Secretary of State Records, State Archives, Office of Archives and History, Raleigh.

April 14th 1778.

Indian talk addressed to Gov. Caswell: My Brother you are the man that hears my talk, tho' I think I am speaking to the great beloved man of North Carolina through you. I understand he is head of that State. I was at a treaty with him, I looked on it so, tho it was some of his warriers, that touched flesh with me, but through him I thought I had him by the hand. That treaty seems to me but yesterday, I have been at Long Island, I wonder I did not see one of the warriors, from North Carolina, and one from Virginia, to strengthen the friendship. I remember at the treaty, we were never to forget what was said on both sides, and what was said came from our hearts, how can your people be so forgetful, while it seems but yesterday to me and my people, what ever I hear I do not mind, as yet, I am determined, to keep strong my promise, I have sent my father Capt. Robertson, whom you gave me to assist in hard matters, he will bring me the truth. I promised you by your warriors, as I was head of my nation, if my people were bad, I would alter them. I have cleansed their hearts, this you hear from me. I hope to hear from you, better news than is now going. My people have been lying very still. They had good ears at the treaty, I wonder at your people of Wataugah, that they should be so forgetful, they are marking trees all over my country, and near to the place I live, and are killing my stock near by beloved towns, now I give you this from my heart, I promised you my people should do no harm. You told me you could do anything with your people. I hope you will put a stop to your people cutting our trees, and let the mark grow out. We were promised I looked on it from your mouth, that your people should not cross the boundary made by your warriors, and by me and my people, except on business, and then only in the path, and if they should do it you would punish them. If there was any such orders given surely the people would not go on at the rate they do, I hold fast my end of the chain of friendship, and keep it bright, there is a small speck of rust on that chain, I hope you will help me to rub it off. I shall give you but a short talk, as I will say nothing but truth, in a long talk there is apt to be lies. I send you a white string of beads, in confirmation of what I have said. I have mentioned having talks with you before, and promises from your mouth. I looked on it so, because I got it from your warriors. There is some bad people at Wataugah, I hope you will move them lower down the country, or they will keep bad talk always going. This from your younger Brother Savanuca or the Raven of Cho[t]a.

<*his mark*>

N.B. This talk was given at the house of Capt. James Robertson by the Raven, on his return from Long Island.

Savanukah, or the Raven of Chota, to Governor Richard Caswell of North Carolina, April 14, 1778, in Clark, *State Records*, 13:90-91.

State of North Carolina.

His Excellency Richard Caswell Esq., Captain General and Commander in Chief of the said State,

To Savanuca or the Raven of Cho[t]a, Head Man of the Cherokee Nation. Friend and Brother:

I received your talk of the 14th of last month, by your father and my brother Captain Robertson. It made my heart glad to receive a talk from your own mouth addressed to myself, for although you have held a treaty with the Commissioners appointed by this State who had authority from the people to speak to you and your people for me and for all the people in this State, yet your talk to me through them was not so powerful as that now delivered to myself.

The treaty you speak of appears to me and all the good people of this State only as of yesterday. I did not know of any public meeting at Long Island at the time you mention or I would have sent one at least of our warriors to meet you there, to strengthen the friendship and brighten the chain between our good Brothers your people and this State; you will do well whenever you propose a public meeting of your people in which you wish to have the presence or assistance of any of our people to give me notice, which you may always do by applying in time to your Father and my good brother Captain Robertson whom we sent to live among our good Brethren your people for that purpose, and whom I hope you have no cause to believe would do other than serve you and your people in the trust we repose in him.

I am sorry you should have cause to complain of the conduct of any of our people towards you or yours, and particularly in the matter you complain of regarding their marking and cutting your trees. I fear these people have been misled in supposing they had liberty from the wise men of this State (the General Assembly) to enter your lands and make them their own. Their conduct has been represented to our wise men who lately sat in Council here who disapproving the measures determined to prevent such mischief for the future, and have directed that no such trespasses shall be committed by our people on your lands nor are they on any pretence to go into your country or cross the boundary line for any other purpose than what is expressed in the treaty. This you have from my mouth, and whilst I am to speak for the people of this State as the Head Man thereof, you may rely on my promise to use my best endeavor to see that this resolution of the wise men of the State be put into execution, and I trust it will be properly observed by all our people. To that end I have issued a proclamation to let the people know this and forbid their trespassing on your property by killing your stock or otherwise. That if they do they will be punished in confidence that you will not suffer your people to do any injury to our people.

You say, "you give me but a short Talk for that in long Talks there generally are lies," you say true, and therefore I follow your example.

You say, "there is a small speck of Rust on the Chain and hope I will help you to rub it off." What I have now done, with what has been done by the wise men of the State, I hope will be sufficient for removing the Rust. If these do not prove effectual, no effort on my part shall be wanting to rub it off, and continue the chain bright. To confirm this truth, I send you a string of white Beads, and give my right hand to your Father Capt. Robertson, that through him I may touch your Flesh and salute you as my Brother.

Given at New Bern under my hand and the seal now used for the said State the 5th day of May, Anno Domini 1778, and in the second year of the Independence of the Said State.

R. CASWELL.

Governor Richard Caswell to Savanukah, May 5, 1778, in Clark, *State Records*, 13:117-118.

Sir:

I think it necessary to inform your Excellency that I have received letters from our Commissioner of Indian affairs for the Cherokee Department, Col. Hammond. That the Prince of Notley and some other head men from the valley and middle settlements at a meeting lately held with the Commissioners complained that many people of your State had lately run out Tracts of Land in their Hunting Grounds, that lies that way. Some have taken in Tracts close to their Towns. They loudly remonstrate against this grievance. The Commissioner writes that he examined the Traders on this head and that they confirm the Indians' information, and add further that several of the Towns were entered by the people of No. Carolina, and some Towns even over the Hills were surveyed by them; and that a Fort was building on the Northern parts of our Frontier. The Indians attribute this encroachment to a hostile disposition in the North Carolinians. At a time Sir, when this State is suffering the greatest inconveniences; and exerting their most extreme efforts, to supply the Indians with goods in order to keep them quiet, and disappoint the designs and machinations of the King's Superintendent of Indian affairs, who leaves no stone unturned to ruin our interest with those people, and represent us as combined to destroy them, it gives great uneasiness and concern to find our sister Colony, or rather some of her subjects, (for we cannot suppose a measure of such fatal tendency can have the countenance or sanction of Government) pursue a conduct that may frustrate our well meant endeavours and bring upon us all those evils and calamities which at so great an expense we are so assiduous to avoid. I have therefore Sir thought it my indispensable duty to lay those matters before your Excellency, not doubting but your Excellency will view them in a proper light, and interpose your authority to remove the unfavorable impressions this conduct had made on the Indians, and prevent any ill effects that may result from their harboring suspicions injurious to the Honor of the American State, now in alliance with these people. This country have observed the most cautious conduct in respect to giving any umbrage to the Indians, and we are hopeful the State of North Carolina will judge it prudent to adopt the same policy.

Rawlins Lowndes, president of South Carolina, to Governor Richard Caswell, July 2, 1778, in Clark, *State Records*, 13:184-185.

Cherokees had begun raiding western settlements by late 1780, but the attacks were quickly quelled. To prevent new outbreaks of violence, the North Carolina House demanded the removal of settlers from Indian lands in Rutherford County. However, it soon became apparent that the state needed to do more to discourage trespassing. Old Tassel, headman of the Overhill Cherokees, begged Governor Alexander Martin for relief from the tide of homesteaders that was overtaking them. Virginia governor William Harrison worried that encroachment by North Carolinians would have fatal repercussions on his side of the border. Suggesting to Martin that the Carolinas and Virginia meet with the Cherokees and other nations to establish tenable boundaries, Harrison declared: "Indians have their rights and our Justice is call'd on to support them, whilst we are nobly contending for Liberty, will it not be an eternal blot in our National Character if we deprive others of it who ought to be as free as ourselves." North Carolina passed a law to reserve land for the Cherokees in 1783.

Ordered that the following Message be sent to the Senate:
[. . .]
Whereas sundry entries have been made in the entry taker's office in the County of Rutherford for Lands which lie to the westward of a line formerly agreed on as a boundary between the people of this State and the Cherokee Indians, and which said Land was by treaty reserved to the Cherokees for places of residence, hunting grounds, etc.

Resolved, that all such entries are null and void, and that the Money or Monies paid into said office on account thereof except the Entry taker's fees, be immediately returned to the person or persons intituled thereto, and the Entry taker is hereby ordered to repay the same.

North Carolina House Minutes, July 7, 1781, in Clark, *State Records*, 17:942. The "sundry entries" violated the boundary established by the Treaty of Long Island of Holston.

Virginia In Council Nov: 12th: 1782.

Sir

Since I did myself the Honor of writing to you last I have receiv'd by Colo. Martin our Indian Agent a Talk from the Cherokees, a paragraph of which I enclose you. These poor wretches seem to be in the deepest distress from an apprehension that the people of your State mean to deprive them of their hunting grounds which have been long since saved to them by solemn Treaty, if the Information is true I doubt not but the encroachments must be made without the privity or consent of your Excellency, or the legislature of your State, and that you will give immediate orders for the Lands being evacuated; I should in no Manner interest myself in this Affair if I did not see clearly that the farther prosecution of it will be attended with the greatest Inconvenience to this State and perhaps with the loss of the lives of very many of our back Inhabitants, the Nature of Indians being such as to revenge an Injury done by one State, on another, altho' they are altogether innocent of the Wrongs they receive. The Friendship which subsists between this State and yours and which I hope will ever remain inviolate induces a wish that you would call the Attention of your Assembly to the subject and to use your Endeavours that they fall on some Means for settling a Boundary between your State & the Indians, if this proposal meets with your Excellencys approbation I will immediately take the same steps with our Assembly who will no doubt concur in any measure that shall be proposed for having their own Boundaries fixed at the same Time; the most proper Mode that I can think of will be the appointing Commissioners (Men of Honor & disinterested) from the two Carolina's and this State to meet the Indians of the different Tribes on the frontiers of the several States, to have the Boundaries of each firmly fixed, till the Indians shall be disposed to sell, when each State shall have the exclusive right of purchasing within it's charter'd Bounds, this being done, and our people forced to observe the Treaties that shall be made there will probably be no more cause for Indian Wars, if there should be making a common cause of it they might soon be brought to reason. The Importance of the subject will plead my excuse for entering on it, Indians have their rights and our Justice is call'd on to support them, whilst we are nobly contending for Liberty, will it not be an eternal blot in our National Character if we deprive others of it who ought to be as free as ourselves. The subject is copious but I shall not enlarge on it to you[r] Excely. whose Justice & humanity are too well known to me to occasion a Thought of it's being necessary.

Governor William Harrison of Virginia to Governor Alexander Martin of North Carolina, November 12, 1782, in Henry Read McIlwaine, ed., *Official Letters of the Governors of Virginia*, 3 vols. (Richmond, Virginia: D. Bottom, superintendent of public printing, 1926–), 3:375.

An Act for opening the Land Office for the redemption of specie and other certificates, and discharging the arrears due to the army.

I. Whereas, opening the land office, and granting the lands within this State would not only redeem the specie and other certificates due from the public, but greatly enhance the credit thereof:

II. Be it therefore enacted by the General Assembly of the State of North Carolina, and it is hereby enacted by the authority of the same, that so much of an Act of the General Assembly, passed at Wake, intituled, An Act to regulate and ascertain the several officers fees therein mentioned, as prohibits the future entering of lands with any entry-taker in this State, and declares void so much of an An Act for establishing offices for receiving entries of claims for lands in the several counties within this State, for ascertaining the method of obtaining titles to the same, and for other purposes therein mentioned, shall be null and void; and the Act last above recited is hereby declared to be in full force and efficacy, except so much thereof as comes within the purview and meaning of this Act.

III. And be it further enacted by the authority aforesaid, that the western boundary be enlarged and established by a line beginning in the line which divides this State from that of Virginia, at a point due north of the mouth of Cloud's creek, running thence west to the Mississippi, thence down the Mississippi to the thirty-fifth degree of north latitude, thence due east until it strikes the Apalachian mountains, thence with the Apalachian mountains to the ridge that divides the waters of French Broad river, and the waters of Nollichuckei river, and with that ridge until it strikes the line described in the fifth section of an Act, intituled, An Act to amend an Act for establishing offices for receiving entries of claims for lands in the several counties within this State, for ascertaining the method of obtaining titles to the same, and for other purposes, and with that line, and those several water courses, to the beginning.

IV. And be it further enacted, by the authority aforesaid, that all entries of land heretofore made, or grants already obtained, or which may be hereafter obtained in consequence of the aforesaid entries for land, to the westward of the line last above described in this Act, be, and the same are hereby declared to be null and void to all intents and purposes, as if such entries and grants had never been made or obtained.

V. And be it further enacted, by the authority aforesaid, that the Cherokee Indians shall have and enjoy all that tract of land bounded as follows, to wit: Beginning on the Tenasee where the southern boundary of this State intersects the same, nearest to the Chickamawga towns, thence up the middle of the Tenasee and Holston to the middle of French Broad, thence up the middle of French Broad river (which lines are not to include any island or islands in the said river) to the mouth of Big Pidgeon river, thence up the same to the head thereof, thence along the dividing ridge between the waters of Pidgeon river and Tuckasejah river, to the Southern boundary of this State; and that the lands contained within the aforesaid bounds shall be, and are hereby reserved unto the said Cherokee Indians and their nation for ever, anything herein to the contrary, notwithstanding.

VI. And be it further enacted by the authority aforesaid, that no person shall enter and survey any lands within the bounds set apart for the said Cherokee Indians, under the penalty of fifty pounds specie for every such entry so made, to be recovered in any court of law in this State, by and to the use of any person who will sue for the same; and all such entries, and grants thereupon, if any should be made, shall be utterly void.

VII. And be it further enacted, by the authority aforesaid, that no person, for any consideration whatever, shall purchase or buy, or take any gift or lease of any tract of land within the said bounds, of any Indian or Indians, but all such bargains, sales, gifts, and leases shall be, and are hereby declared to be null and void; and the person so purchasing, buying, leasing, or taking any gift of any land, of any Indian or Indians, as aforesaid, shall moreover forfeit the sum of one hundred pounds specie for every hundred acres so purchased, bought, leased or taken as aforesaid, one half to the use of the State and the other half to him that will sue for the same, to be recovered in the manner as aforesaid.

VIII. And whereas the said Indians may receive injuries from people hunting, ranging or driving stocks of horses, cattle or hogs, on the lands hereby allotted to them; for remedy whereof, Be it enacted by the authority aforesaid, That it shall not be lawful for any person or persons whatsoever to hunt or range on the said lands, or to drive stocks of cattle, horses, or hogs thereon, on pain of forfeiting the sum of fifty pounds specie for every such offence, together with such stock or stocks of horses, cattle or hogs, so driven; to be recovered by any person who shall sue for the same, in the manner aforesaid. [. . .]

XII. [. . .] that it shall not be lawful for any person or persons to claim, enter or survey the great island in Holston river; and if any such entry be made; (the same having been made in open violation of treaty) is hereby declared void. And be it enacted, That the said island shall be, and hereby is reserved and appropriated to the sole purpose of holding the beloved talks and treaties on, with the said Cherokee Indians, and shall not be granted, sold or disposed of, to any person or persons whatever. [. . .]

XXIII: And be it further enacted by the authority aforesaid, that all the lands lying between the Iron mountain and the present Indian boundary, as far as a point opposite to the line already extended betwixt Burke and

Rutherford counties, shall be entered in the county of Burke; and all the lands south of the last mentioned line to the south line of this State and the Indian boundary, from the aforesaid point, shall be entered in the county of Rutherford.

XXIV: And be it further enacted by the authority aforesaid, that this Act shall be in force, and take effect in the respective counties in this State, on the first day of August next, excepting for the lands appropriated by sundry Acts of this Assembly, lying to the westward of the present Indian boundary line, which said lands shall not be liable to be entered until the twentieth day of October next.

Laws of North Carolina, May 1783, in Clark, *State Records*, 24:478, 479, 480, 482. "Chickamawga towns" is a reference to the Chickamauga Cherokees. Scorning the land cessions that their headmen had made to whites, some Cherokees moved westward and settled along Chickamauga Creek in present-day northern Georgia during the American Revolution. The Chickamauga Cherokees fought the American forces until 1794.

War

The decision to go to war was not made lightly. Although observers such as Superintendent John Stuart commented on the vengeful nature of the Indians of Carolina, it was also noted that they resorted to combat only after the merits of pursuing such a course had been fully considered in a council of war. In addition to satisfying the need for revenge, war served a religious purpose: the spirit of a victim would never find peace unless the people accountable for his or her death had been destroyed. Stuart wrote that warriors were "carefull to kill the same Number which they lost."

They are very politick, in waging, and carrying on their War, first by advising with all the ancient Men of Conduct and Reason, that belong to their Nation; such as superannuated War-Captains, and those that have been Counsellors for many Years, and whose Advice has commonly succeeded very well.

John Lawson, *A New Voyage to Carolina*, ed. by Hugh T. Lefler (Chapel Hill: University of North Carolina Press, 1967), 208.

When any Number of their people are killed by those of a Nation at peace with them: such a meeting is, commonly called. They then depute some person to go and demmand satisfaction in the Name of the whole; which, if refused, and they think themselves able to undertake a War with the aggressors, a Sufficient Number of Men generally Relations to the people killed, go against them for revenge, and are carefull to kill the same Number which they lost. They commonly leave a Token, by which it may be known who they are, and that they are satisfyed. But if acts of Hostility are repeated by either side a general war ensues. When the temper of the Nation in general is Pacifick and Averse to War; offences against Neighbouring nations that may involve the whole are Capitally punished, by way of Satisfaction. Which act of Justice is also performed by a near Relation only. The Criminal, never knows his condemnation till the Moment his sentence is put in execution which often happens, when he is dancing the War dance in the Town house and bragging of the very exploit for which he dyes.

John Stuart, superintendent of Indian Affairs for the southern district, to the Board of Trade, March 9, 1764, in Colonial Office 323/17, British Records, State Archives, Office of Archives and History, Raleigh.

Warriors volunteered for combat, according to trader James Adair, and followed strict purification rituals to ensure victory in the coming campaign. Before going into battle, eastern North Carolina Indians painted their faces. The Chowans inspired their young men to greatness by recounting past injustices: traveling through what is now

Northampton County, Edward Bland witnessed a curious custom tied to one of those stories.

In the first commencement of war, a party of the injured tribe turns out first, to revenge the innocent crying blood of their own bone and flesh, as they term it. When the leader begins to beat up for volunteers, he goes three times round his dark winter-house, contrary to the course of the sun, sounding the war-whoop, singing the war-song, and beating the drum. Then he speaks to the listening crowd with very rapid language, short pauses, and an awful commanding voice, tells them of the continued friendly offices they have done the enemy, but which have been ungratefully returned with the blood of his kinsmen; therefore as the white paths have changed their beloved colour, his heart burns within him with eagerness to tincture them all along, and even to make them flow over with the hateful blood of the base contemptible enemy. Then he strongly persuades his kindred warriors and others, who are not afraid of the enemies bullets and arrows, to come and join him with manly cheerful hearts: he assures them, he is fully convinced, as they are all bound by the love-knot, so they are ready to hazard their lives to revenge the blood of their kindred and country-men; that the love of order, and the necessity of complying with the old religious customs of their country, had hitherto checked their daring generous hearts, but now, those hindrances are removed: he proceeds to whoop again for the warriors to come and join him, and sanctify themselves for success against the common enemy, according to their ancient religious law.

By his eloquence, but chiefly by their own greedy thirst of revenge, and intense love of martial glory, on which they conceive their liberty and happiness depend, and which they constantly instil into the minds of their youth—a number soon join him in his winter-house, where they live separate from all others, and purify themselves for the space of three days and nights, exclusive of the first broken day. In each of those days they observe a strict fast till sun-set, watching the young men very narrowly who have not been initiated in war-titles, lest unusual hunger should tempt them to violate it, to the supposed danger of all their lives in war, by destroying the power of their purifying beloved physic, which they drink plentifully during that time. This purifying physic, is warm water highly imbittered with button-rattle-snake-root, which as hath been before observed, they apply only to religious purposes. Sometimes after bathing they drink a decoction made of the said root— and in like manner the leader applies aspersions, or sprinklings, both at home and when out at war. They are such strict observers of the law of purification, and think it so essential in obtaining health and success in war, as not to allow the best beloved trader that ever lived among them, even to enter the beloved ground, appropriated to the religious duty of being sanctified for war; much less to associate with the camp in the woods, though he went (as I have known it to happen) on the same war design;—they oblige him to walk and encamp separate by himself, as an impure dangerous animal, till the leader hath purified him, according to their usual time and method, [. . .]

James Adair, *A History of the North-American Indians, Particularly Those Nations Adjoining to the Mississippi* [sic], *East and West Florida, Georgia, South and North Carolina and Virginia* (1775; reprint, Ann Arbor, Michigan: UMI Books on Demand, 2002), 159-161.

Their Dress in Peace and War, is quite different. [. . .] when they go to War, their Hair is comb'd out by the Women, and done over very much with Bears Grease, and red Root; with Feathers, Wings, Rings, Copper, and *Peak*, or *Wampum* in their Ears. Moreover, they buy Vermillion of the *Indian* Traders, wherewith they paint their Faces all over red, and commonly make a Circle of Black about one Eye, and another Circle of White about the other, whilst others bedawb their Faces with Tobacco-Pipe Clay, Lampblack, black Lead, and divers other Colours, which they make with the several sorts of Minerals and Earths that they get in different Parts of the Country, where they hunt and travel. When these Creatures are thus painted, they make the most frightful Figures that can be imitated by Men, and seem more like Devils than Humane Creatures. You may be sure, that they are about some Mischief, when you see them thus painted; for in all the Hostilities which have ever been acted against the *English* at any time, in several of the Plantations of *America*, the Savages always appear'd in this Disguize, [. . .]

Lawson, *New Voyage to Carolina*, 201.

After we had passed over this River we travelled some twenty miles further upon a pyny barren Champion Land to *Hocomawananck* River, South, and by West: some twelve miles from *Brewsters* River we came unto a path running crosse some twenty yards on each side unto two remarkable Trees; at this path our Appamattuck Guide made a stop, and cleared the Westerly end of the path with his foote, being demanded the meaning of it, he shewed an unwillingnesse to relate it, sighing very much: Whereupon we made a stop untill *Oyeocker* our other Guide came up, and then our Appamattuck Guide journied on; but *Oyeocker* at his comming up cleared the other end of the path, and prepared himselfe in a most serious manner to require our attentions, and told us that many yeares since their late great Emperour *Appachancano* came thither to make a War upon the *Tuskarood*, in revenge of three of his men killed, and one wounded, who escaped, and brought him word of the other three murthered by the *Hocomawananck* Indians for lucre of the *Roanoke* they brought with them to trade for Otter skins. There accompanyed *Appachancano* severall petty Kings that were under him, amongst which there was one King of a Towne called *Pawhatan*, which had long time harboured a grudge against the King of *Chawan*, about a yong woman that the King of *Chawan* had detayned of the King of *Pawhatan*. Now it hapned that the King of *Chawan* was invited by the King of *Pawhatan* to this place under pretence to present him with a Guift of some great vallew, and there they met accordingly, and the King of *Pawhatan* went to salute and embrace the King of *Chawan*, and stroaking of him after their usuall manner, he whipt a bow string about the King of *Chawans* neck, and strangled him; and how that in memoriall of this, the path is continued unto this day, and the friends of the *Pawhatans* when they passe that way, cleanse the Westerly end of the path, and the friends of the *Chawans* the other. And some two miles from this path we came unto an Indian Grave upon the East side of the path; Upon which Grave there lay a great heape of sticks covered with greene boughs, we demanded the reason of it, *Oyeocker* told us, that there lay a great man of the *Chawans* that dyed in the same quarrell, and in honour of his memory they continue greene boughs over his Grave to this day, and ever when they goe forth to Warre they relate his, and others valorous, loyall Acts, to their yong men, to annimate them to doe the like when occasion requires.

Entry of August 31, 1650, in Edward Bland, *The Discovery of New Britain* (1651; reprint, Ann Arbor: William L. Clements Library, University of Michigan, 1954), 8-9. "Hocomawananck River" is the Roanoke River; "Brewsters River" is believed to be Gumberry Creek, Northampton County, North Carolina.

A conjurer could prevent the departure of a war party if he believed no good would come to it. George Turner, commissioner for Virginia, was thwarted in his attempt to enlist Cherokee aid during the French and Indian War for such a reason.

When the Great Warriour [Oconostota] and his Brother [Prince of Chota] came to the Fort and upon Captain [Paul] Demere's saying he was glad of the Oppertunity to wish them a good Journey, they replyed that they could not tell that all depended upon their Conjurers, which I confess greatly alarmed me and more when I was told that no Body had observed any Preparation for their parch Corn-Flower and Bread which they always carry with them. However on the Day appointed my Horses were sadling and packing, when the Little Carpenter came into the Fort. I told him that I was just ready. He desired me not to take my Baggage to Chota that Day, as we should come back that Evening. I told him, he had promised me to stay at Chota (the general Rendezvouze) that Night and all to march for Virginia the next Day. He said it was very true but one Day would break no Squares, and I went over with him without my Baggage, and their at Old Hop's meet all the Warriours and Conjurers and Beloved Men, and then (I believe your Excellency will be greatly surprised at it) they told me that several bad Omens had appeared in their Conjurations and they were threatened with Sickness and Death to many and vast Fatigue to the Whole if they went in, and possitively refused to go till the Fall and wanted me to wait till then.

I told them that their Treatment had so much astonished me that I could not tell what to say. I reproached them with their Ingratitude to you, who had by their own Confession treated them nobly. I put them in Mind of the Presents that Colonel Byrd had distributed amongst them and of the Presents that I had sent but eight Days before and told them that when I reported this I should hardly be credited, that so many Men who had given so many Proofs of their Valour and Resolution, should now be diverted from their Purpose by a Conjurer. The Little Carpenter who was the Mouth of the Company, said that when he had promised to go, that he intended it, but they never undertook any Thing of Consequence, but they consulted their Conjurers to know the Pleasure of the Great Men above and they never depared [sic] from his Opinion. The Conjurers repeated that the two first Moons they would be very well, but afterwards that a pestilential Distemper would get among their young Men, that they would loose a great many and the Rest would be so harrased with Fattigue and Sickness that they would gett in very late if at all.

I told them that I would take care they should not go into no Towns, nor encamp among the Whites and I would not desire a Man of them to go a Foot further then I went my self, but all to no Purpose. I could not prevail upon them to stir before the Fall, so I [concluded] my Visit by desiring that their Chiefs would come over to the Fort and say all this before Captain Demere and the Officers of the Garrison who might testify it for my Justification, for I was liable to be called to an Account of the Loss of so much Time and the Wast [sic] of so much public Money. They came at my Request and did repeat all which I have wrote to your Excellency and much more. I got a Gentleman to take it down in Writing and the Carpenter, Old Hop, Standing Turkey, Great Warriour, and Prince [of Chota], his Brother, the Conjurer and two more did put their Marks to it in the Presence of the whole Garrison and the Officers and three Interpreters witnessed.

It would be tedious to trouble your Excellency with any more Repititions of this though it took up several Hours. The Little Carpenter made Use of a poor, dirty Evasion by saying that I brought no Wampum and that the Talks were often Lies, but that their Belts never lied. Before I could answer this, Captain Demere took up the Conversation and [made] a downright Quarrel with the Carpenter, who I thought seemed to have the best of the Dispute, but however it prevented my answering him and I rose and left them, and immediately sent about to get an Express that I might let the Commanding

Officer in Virginia know my Disappointment, least he should have any Dependance upon me.

George Turner to Governor William Henry Lyttelton of South Carolina, July 2, 1758, in William L. McDowell Jr., ed., *Documents Relating to Indian Affairs, 1754-1765*, in *The Colonial Records of South Carolina*, Series 2 (Columbia: South Carolina Archives Department, 1970), 470-472. The "Fort" is Fort Loudoun.

Native American warfare typically took the form of a raid, and warriors employed considerable skill in its execution. After a boisterous departure from town, they relied upon stealth, surprise, and superiority in numbers to guarantee success against their opponents.

They have likewise their Field Counsellors, who are accustomed to Ambuscades, and Surprizes, which Methods are commonly used by the Savages; for I scarce ever heard of a Field-Battle fought amongst them.

Lawson, *New Voyage to Carolina*, 208.

When they have finished their fast and purifications, they set off, at the fixed time, be it fair or foul, firing their guns, whooping, and hallooing, as they march. The war-leader goes first, [. . .]: he soon strikes up the awful and solemn song before mentioned, which they never sing except on that occasion. The rest follow, in one line, at the distance of three or four steps from each other, now and then sounding the war whoo-whoop, to make the leader's song the more striking to the people. In this manner they proceed, till quite out of the sight, and hearing of their friends. As soon as they enter the woods, all are silent; and, every day they observe a profound silence in their march, that their ears may be quick to inform them of danger: [. . .]

The common number of an Indian war company, is only from twenty to forty, lest their tracks should be discovered by being too numerous: but if the warring nations are contiguous to each other, the invading party generally chuses to out-number a common company, that they may strike the blow with greater safety and success, as their art of war is chiefly killing by surprise; confident that in case of a disappointment, their light heels will ensure their return to their own country. When a small company go to war, they always chuse to have a swamp along side of them, with a thick covert for their shelter, because a superior number will scarcely pursue them where they might reasonably expect to lose any of their warriors. When they arrive at the enemies hunting ground, they act with the greatest caution and policy. They separate themselves, as far as each can hear the other's travelling signal, which is the mimicking such birds and beasts as frequent the spot. And they can exactly imitate the voice and sound of every quadruped and wild fowl through the American woods. In this way of travelling, they usually keep an hundred yards apart on the course agreed upon at camp. When the leader thinks it the surest way of succeeding against the enemy, he sends a few of the best runners to form an ambuscade near their towns: there, they sometimes fix the broad hoofs of buffalos, and bear's paws upon their feet, to delude the enemy: and they will for miles together, make all the windings of these beasts with the greatest art. But, as both parties are extremely wary and sagacious, I have known such arts to prove fatal to the deluders. At other times, a numerous company will walk in three different rows, by way of a decoy, every one lifting his feet so high, as not to beat down the grass or herbage; and each row will make only one man's track, by taking the steps of him who went before, and a gigantic fellow takes the rear of each rank, and thereby smooths the tracks with his feet. When they are convinced the enemy is in pursuit of them, at so considerable a distance from the country, as for themselves not to be over-powered by numbers, they post themselves in the most convenient place, in the form of an half-moon, and patiently wait a whole day and night, till the enemy runs into it; and in such a case, the victory at one broad-side is usually gained.

When they discover the tracks of enemies in their hunting ground, or in the remote woods, it is surprising to see the caution and art they use, both to secure themselves, and take advantage of the enemy. If a small company be out at war, they in the day time crawl through thickets and swamps in the manner of wolves—now and then they climb trees, and run to the top of hills, to discover the smoke of fire, or hear the report of guns: and when they cross through the open woods, one of them stands behind a tree, till the rest advance about a hundred yards, looking out sharply on all quarters. In this manner, they will proceed, and on tiptoe, peeping every where around; they love to walk on trees which have been blown down, and take an oblique course, till they inswamp themselves again, in order to conceal their tracks, and avoid a pursuit. [. . .]

When the invaders extend themselves cross the woods, in quest of their prey, if they make a plain discovery, either of fresh tracks, or of the enemy, they immediately pass the war-signal to each other, and draw their wings toward the centre. If the former, they give chace, and commonly by their wild-cat-method of crawling, they surround, and surprise the pursued, if unguarded—however, I have known them to fail in such attempts; for the Indians generally are so extremely cautious, that if three of them are in the woods, their first object is a proper place for defence, and they always sit down in a triangle, to prevent a surprise. When enemies discover one another, and find they can take no advantage, they make themselves known to each other; and by way of insulting bravado, they speak aloud all the barbarities they ever committed against them;—that they are now, to vindicate those actions, and make the wound for ever incurable; that they are their most bitter enemies, and equally contemn their friendship and enmity. In the mean while, they throw down their packs, strip themselves naked, and paint their faces and breasts red as blood, intermingled with black streaks. Every one at the signal of the shrill-sounding war-cry, instantly covers himself behind a tree, or in some cavity of the ground where it admits of the best safety. The leader, on each side, immediately blows the small whistle he carries for the occasion, in imitation of the ancient trumpet, as the last signal of engagement. Now hot work begins—The guns are firing; the chewed bullets flying; the strong hiccory bows a twanging; the dangerous barbed arrows whizzing as they fly; the sure-shafted javelin striking death wherever it reaches; and the well-aimed tomohawk killing, or disabling its enemy. Nothing scarcely can be heard for the shrill echoing noise of the war and death-whoop, every one furiously pursues his adversary from tree to tree, striving to incircle him for his prey; and the greedy jaws of pale death are open on all sides, to swallow them up. One dying foe is intangled in the hateful and faltering arms of another: and each party desperately attempts both to save their dead and wounded from being scalped, and to gain the scalps of their opponents. On this the battle commences anew—But rash attempts fail, as their wary spirits always forbid them from entering into a general close engagement. Now they retreat: then they draw up into various figures, still having their dead and wounded under their eye. Now they are flat on the ground loading their pieces—then they are up firing behind trees, and immediately spring off in an oblique course to recruit—and thus they act till winged victory declares itself.

Adair, *History of the North-American Indians*, 381, 384-387.

Their foes vanquished, the victors peeled away the scalps of those whom they had slain. The taking of scalps confirmed the number of opponents who had been killed and gave irrefutable evidence to the spirits of the deceased tribesmen, for whom the war was waged, that they had been avenged. It also disfigured the corpse, which communicated both a taunt and a threat to the enemy. Adair described the act of scalping; the preservation of the trophy; and the custom of some warriors to sever an appendage of the victim in addition to taking a scalp. Colonists adopted the practice of scalping enemy Indians at the encouragement of their government: the North Carolina Committee of Public Claims paid a £10 bounty to Henry Harmon in 1760, during the French and Indian War.

[. . .] the victors begin, with mad rapture, to cut and slash those unfortunate persons, who fell by their arms and power; and they dismember them, after a most inhuman manner. If the battle be gained near home, one hero cuts off and carries this member of the dead person, another that, as joyful trophies of a decisive victory. If a stranger saw them thus loaded with human flesh, without proper information, he might conclude them to be voracious canibals; according to the shameful accounts of our Spanish historians. Their first aim however is to take off the scalp, when they perceive the enemy hath a proper situation, and strength to make a dangerous resistance. Each of them is so emulous of exceeding another in this point of honour, that it frequently stops them in their pursuit.

This honourable service [scalping] is thus performed—They seize the head of the disabled, or dead person, and placing one of their feet on the neck, they with one hand twisted in the hair, extend it as far as they can—with the other hand, the barbarous artists speedily draw their long sharp-pointed scalping knife out of a sheath from their breast, give a slash round the top of the skull, and with a few dexterous scoops, soon strip it off. They are so expeditious as to take off a scalp in two minutes. When they have performed this part of their martial virtue, as soon as time permits, they tie with bark or deer's sinews, their speaking trophies of blood in a small hoop, to preserve it from putrefaction, and paint the interior part of the scalp, and the hoop, all round with red, their flourishing emblematical colour of blood.

Adair, *History of the North-American Indians*, 387-388.

Your Committee recommends to the House that a proper allowance be made for the taking of an Indian scalp, produced by Mr. John Frohock, taken by Henry Harmon, who went with a party under the command of Captain Teague; allowed by the House £10 0 0.

Report of the Committee of Public Claims, November 18, 1760, in Walter Clark, ed., *The State Records of North Carolina*, 16 vols. (11-26) (Raleigh: State of North Carolina, 1895-1906), 22:826.

A Cherokee who proved his mettle in combat earned a "war Name," while one who shirked his duties was chastised and surrendered any possible chance of becoming the head warrior of his town until he demonstrated singular courage in the face of the enemy.

A young Fellow who deserts or dissobeys a Leader under whom he goes to War, cannot be punished: but he certainly loses his Reputation and forfeits all Hopes of being one Day head Warrior of his Town, (hopes which every Young man in the Nation entertains), Except by some extraordinary Exploit he wipes off the Stain. And a Reprimand by the Beloved man, in the Town House, for an irregular or dishonest Action is considered as Most shamefull. [. . .]

No Indian can attain any Rank in the Community except by some Warlike Exploit. This is the Source of perpetual Bloodshed. Young men plunge their Country into War with their Neighboring Tribes that they may have an opportunity of making themselves considerable and if we cannot point this propensity to other objects, we must often feel the bad Effects of it. [. . .]

There are besides in each Town a Number of Men who in recompense of their War Exploits are dignifyed with war Names: Such as the Raven or person who discovers the Enemy in Ambush: The Slave catcher: The Man-killer: and the Highest Skyagusta or War Captain. Each Name is accompanyed with a certain degree of Respect and Influence: which with the Number of his Followers and Adherents increase in proportion to the Eloquence and other abilities of the Bearer.

John Stuart to the Board of Trade, March 9, 1764, in Colonial Office 323/17, British Records, State Archives.

The Native Americans of early Carolina employed various methods to commemorate past battles or fallen combatants. One was to scratch easily decipherable "Hieroglyphicks" upon various objects in the woods. Another was to build a cairn over the grave of a warrior. When encountering a cairn it was customary for Indians to add a rock "according as he likes or dislikes the occasion, or manner of the death of the deceased." Over time, some of those rock piles became sizeable.

Besides, in their War Expeditions, they have very certain Hieroglyphicks, whereby each Party informs the other of the Success or Losses they have met withal; all which is so exactly perform'd by their Sylvian Marks and Characters, that they are never at a Loss to understand one another.

Lawson, *New Voyage to Carolina*, 213-214.

To perpetuate the memory of any remarkable warriors killed in the woods, I must here observe, that every Indian traveller as he passes that way throws a stone on the place, according as he likes or dislikes the occasion, or manner of the death of the deceased.

In the woods we often see innumerable heaps of small stones in those places, where according to tradition some of their distinguished people were either killed, or buried, till the bones could be gathered: there they add *Pelion* to *Ossa*, still increasing each heap, as a lasting monument, and honour to them, and an incentive to great actions.

Adair, *History of the North-American Indians*, 184. *Heaping Ossa upon Pelion*: "Adding difficulty to difficulty, embarrassment to embarrassment, etc. When the giants tried to scale heaven, they placed Mount Ossa upon Mount Pelion for a scaling ladder." *Dictionary of Phrase and Fable*, s.v. "Pelion."

Warriors sometimes took prisoners, who could be adopted into the clan or tortured. Antoine Bonnefoy, an adult whose adoption by the Cherokees is recounted earlier in this volume, was fortunate; and a Catawba, captured and adopted as a boy by the Shawnees ("Shawnoise") and later the topic of peace negotiations, seemed reluctant to return to the nation of his birth. Torture was a notable ritual among Native Americans: when performed by women and youngsters, it allowed them the opportunity to avenge the killings of clan members, since their gender or age prohibited active participation in war parties. Captives sentenced to die by torture often succumbed to fire. Lawson describes the insertion of pine splinters, which captors then ignited—a method by which he is rumored to have died just before the Tuscarora War erupted. Adair gives vivid details of the selection of victims and the actions of torturers.

The Shawnoise & all the Indians present were further askt whether they had any prisoners of the Catawba Nation, or of any other Nation in Friendship with Virginia. The Shawnois answered that they had one prisoner, a young man taken some years agoe, whom they Produced; but all the Others answered they had none.

It was demanded of the Shawnois that this prisoner shou'd be Return'd to the Catawbas, from whence he was taken. Their King or Chief answered that they had taken him several years agoe, when he was but a little Lad; that he had now forgot his Native Language, & spoke theirs, and that they did not think themselves Obliged to Return him at this time.

Being further prest to it, The Chief answered that if the King of the Catabaws, whom he now understood were in League with Virginia, would come hither & make a peace with him and his people, (the Shawnois,) he might have that young man Back with him, if it was desir'd; but that the Catawbas were a people of Great Extent, & there were many Nations under that name.

The Young Man was askt whether he was willing to Return, but would give no Answer.

Pennsylvania Provincial Council Minutes, July 19, 1717, in Samuel Hazard, ed., *Colonial Records of Pennsylvania*, 16 vols. (Harrisburg, Pennsylvania: Printed by T. Fenn and Company, 1851-1853), 3:23.

Those Captives they did intend to burn, few Prisoners of War escaping that Punishment. The Fire of Pitch-Pine being got ready, and a Feast appointed, which is solemnly kept at the time of their acting this Tragedy, the Sufferer has his Body stuck thick with Light-Wood-Splinters, which are lighted like so many Candles, the tortur'd Person dancing round a great Fire, till his Strength fails, and disables him from making them any farther Pastime.

Lawson, *New Voyage to Carolina*, 53.

When the company return from war, [. . .] They camp near their town all night, in a large square plot of ground, marked for the purpose, with a high war-pole fixed in the middle of it, to which they secure their prisoners. Next day they go to the leader's house in a very solemn procession, but stay without, round his red-painted war-pole, till they have determined concerning the fate of their prisoners. If any one of the captives should be fortunate enough to get loose, and run into the house of the arch-magus, or to a town of refuge, he by ancient custom, is saved from the fiery torture—these places being a sure asylum to them if they were invaded, and taken, but not to invaders, because they came to shed blood.

Those captives who are pretty far advanced in life, as well as in war-gradations, always atone for the blood they spilt, by the tortures of fire.—They readily know the latter, by the blue marks over their breasts and arms; they being as legible as our alphabetical characters are to us. [. . .]

The young prisoners are saved, if not devoted while the company were sanctifying themselves for the expedition; but if the latter be the case, they are condemned, and tied to the dreadful stake, one at a time. The victors first strip their miserable captives quite naked, and put on their feet a pair of bear-skin maccaseenes, with the black hairy part outwards; others fasten with a grape-vine, a burning fire-brand to the pole, a little above the reach of their heads. Then they know their doom—deep black, and burning fire, are fixed seals of their death-warrant. Their punishment is always left to the women; and on account of their false standard of education, they are no way backward in their office, but perform it to the entire satisfaction of the greedy eyes of the spectators. Each of them prepares for the dreadful rejoicing, a long bundle of dry canes, or the heart of fat pitch-pine, and as the victims are led to the stake, the women and their young ones beat them with these in a most barbarous manner. Happy would it be for the miserable creatures, if their sufferings ended here, or a merciful tomohawk finished them at one stroke; but this shameful treatment is a prelude to future sufferings.

The death-signal being given, preparations are made for acting a more tragical part. The victims arms are fast pinioned, and a strong grape-vine is tied round his neck, to the top of the war-pole, allowing him to track around, about fifteen yards. They fix some tough clay on his head, to secure the scalp from the blazing torches. Unspeakable pleasure now fills the exulting crowd of spectators, and the circle fills with the Amazon and merciless executioners—

The suffering warrior however is not dismayed; with an insulting manly voice he sings the war-song! and with gallant contempt he tramples the rattling gourd with pebbles in it to pieces, and outbraves even death itself. The women make a furious on-set with their burning torches: his pain is soon so excruciating, that he rushes out from the pole, with the fury of the most savage beast of prey, and with the vine sweeps down all before him, kicking, biting, and trampling them, with the greatest despite. The circle immediately fills again, either with the same, or fresh persons: they attack him on every side—now he runs to the pole for shelter, but the flames pursue him. Then with champing teeth, and sparkling eye-balls, he breaks through their contracted circle afresh, and acts every part, that the highest courage, most raging fury, and blackest despair can prompt him to. But he is sure to be over-power'd by numbers, and after some time the fire affects his tender parts.—Then they pour over him a quantity of cold water, and allow him a proper time of respite, till his spirits recover, and he is capable of suffering new tortures. Then the like cruelties are repeated till he falls down, and happily becomes insensible of pain. Now they scalp him, in the manner before described: dismember, and carry off all the exterior branches of the body, [. . .] in shameful, and savage triumph. This is the most favourable treatment their devoted captives receive: it would be too shocking to humanity either to give, or peruse, every particular of their conduct in such doleful tragedies—nothing can equal these scenes, but those of the merciful Romish inquisition.

Not a soul, of whatever age or sex, manifests the least pity during the prisoner's tortures: the women sing with religious joy, all the while they are torturing the devoted victim, and peals of laughter resound through the crowded theatre—especially if he fears to die. But a warrior puts on a bold austere countenance, and carries it through all his pains: —as long as he can, he whoops and out-braves the enemy, describing his own martial deeds against them, and those of his nation, who he threatens will force many of them to eat fire in revenge of his fate, as he himself had often done to some of their relations at their cost.

Though the same things operate alike upon the organs of the human body, and produce an uniformity of sensations; yet weakness, or constancy of mind derived from habit, helps in a great measure, either to heighten, or lessen the sense of pain. By this, the afflicted party has learned to stifle nature, and shew an outward unconcern, under such slow and acute tortures: and the surprising cruelty of their women, is equally owing to education and custom.

Adair, *History of the North-American Indians*, 388-391.

CHARLESTOWN, *May* 24.

[. . .]

From Waxsaws, about 12 miles from the Catawba settlement, we have the following account. "On Sunday the 1st of May the Catawba Indians had notice that a party of the Shawanese, who have been long their enemies, had been seen near their town; on which they immediately raised a party go out against the enemy, with whom they came up next morning, and found them to be seven in number, and all asleep. The Catawbas immediately fired and killed three on the spot, and took three prisoners; one escaped wounded, but has been since found dead in the woods. Among the prisoners is the Indian who killed King Heigler; they were all delivered to the Families who have had their relations killed by the Shawanese, who put them to death in the inhuman barbarous manner common to the Indian nations. One of the prisoners was very young, and pleaded hard for his life, begging them to consider his tender age, assuring them he was brought by his brother against his own inclinations, and that he had never killed or hurt any body; but nothing could prevail."

Virginia Gazette (Purdie and Dixon), June 23, 1768.

Some Cherokee women accompanied war parties to tend the camps, cook for the warriors, and perform other support roles. A person who distinguished herself in those ways could be granted the title of war woman by the clan matriarchs of her town. One of the war woman's responsibilities was to receive captives for adoption into the clan. Sometimes she would disguise herself in order to intercept and claim prisoners before vengeful warriors killed them.

The Deputy Governour having desired the Board to supply the Publick, with seven Yards and 7/8 of a Yard Strouds, for a Present to nine Charikee Indian Women, who have promised his Honour to follow their Warrier's Camp, to the War against the Yamasees, and having drawn his Order on the Commissioners for Payment of the Charges of the Charikee Indians &c. for Paying the Sum of eight Pounds, five Shillings for the said Cloth, [. . .]

Entry of January 30, 1716/17, in William L. McDowell Jr., ed., *Journals of the Commissioners of the Indian Trade, September 20, 1710-August 29, 1718*, in *The Colonial Records of South Carolina, Series 2* (Columbia: South Carolina Archives Department, 1955), 155.

This Woman, after some Campaigns is raised to the Dignity of War Woman, to which all Prisoners must be delivered alive (without any Punishment) as her Slave, if she requires it, which is a Privilege no Man can enjoy, not even their Emperor, Kings, or Warriors; there are but few Towns in which is a War Woman; and if she can come near enough to the Prisoner as to put her hand upon him, and say, this is my Slave, the Warriors (tho' with the greatest Reluctancy) must deliver him up to Her, which to prevent they in a great hurry drive a Hatchet in the Prisoner's Head, before the War-Woman can reach him; therefore the War Women use that Strategem to disguise themselves as Traders, and come in Company with them, as if out of Curiosity to see the Spectacle of the cruel War-dance.

> Louis De Vorsey, Jr., ed., *De Brahm's Report of the General Survey in the Southern District of North America* (Columbia: University of South Carolina Press, 1971), 109.

From the late seventeenth to the early eighteenth century, the Indian captives of warriors were more likely to be sold to European traders than surrendered for adoption. The Indian slave trade was at its height and war parties roved throughout the Southeast, capturing as many of the enemy's women and children as possible, who then were bartered for highly desirable manufactured goods. (Adult males, deemed refractory, would be killed.) Until the demand for African slaves overwhelmed it, the Indian slave trade was a very lucrative plum that Carolina colony attempted to protect, as an edict from 1692 indicates. In North Carolina, funds from the sale of Indians were used to pay a debt. Eleazer Wiggan and Alexander Longe, traders among the Cherokees, spurred their customers to engage in slave raids.

Whereas ye: Rt: Honoble the Lords and absolute Proprs: of this Province have taken all the Indians into theire protection wth: in four hundred miles of Charles towne and Likewise have by theire order Required that noe Such Indian be Sold as a Slave and Sentt out of the Country.

It is therefore ordered for the better preservation thereof that noe person or persons whatsoever from and after the publication hereof presume to take or Ship one board or Carry away in any Ship or vessel that Shall depart out of and from this part of the Province that Lyes South and west of Cape ffeare any Indian or Indians whatsoever wth:out due Lysence first had and obtained from ye: honoble: ye: Governor: for the time being for soe doeing as he or they will answere the Contrary att theire uttmose perill.

> Entry of June 22, 1692, in Alexander S. Salley, ed., *Journal of the Grand Council of South Carolina*, 2 vols. (Columbia: The Historical Commission of South Carolina, 1907), 2:45-46.

North Carolina General Court

Nath. Chevin Esqr. Is plaintiff against [*illegible*] Wm. Reed Esqr. Defendant in a plea of the loss.

[. . .] that whereas at a committy of both houses of assembly holden at the house of Captain John Hecklefeild in Little river on the 20th of march anno 1711 i[t] was Taken into Consideration that Certaine Indians Captives belongen to the Town of Bare river should be Exposed to Sale to such persons as should bid Highest for them and that the money thereby arising upon the sale of the said Indians should be paid unto the hand of the said Plaintiff on or before the forth of march then next Ensueing, at which time and place the aforesaid Defendant for and in consideration of five of the aforesaid Indian Slaves [. . .]

March 1713, Treaties, Petitions, Agreements, and Court Cases, Indians, Miscellaneous Papers, 1677-1775, Colonial Court Records 192, State Archives, Office of Archives and History, Raleigh. John Lawson reported in 1701 that the Bear River Indians had one town, called Raudauqua-quank, that contained fifty warriors. It was probably located in present-day Craven County, North Carolina. Lawson, *New Voyage to Carolina*, 242.

Mr. Benja. Clea being sworn said he heard Capt. [Robert] Card say there was a Design among the Cherikees to cut off Chestowee 10 Dayes before the said Town was cut off, and that the Cherikees designed to invite the Euchees to a Ball Play in order to cut them of. That he heard from Mr. [Garrett] Dillon that the Indians gave an Account of some white People that pretended the Governor's Order for cutting off Chestowee. That Mr. Long had some Difference with an Euche Indian who had puled of sum of his Hair. [. . .]

That itt loockt suspitious that the Governour's Letter to Capt. Card was detained behind the Mountains till the Euchees were cut off. That he was informed, by Mr. Dillon, the Euches before the Disturbance killed one Cherikee.

That Mr. Dillon also told him the Indians related that Mr. Long told them the Governour had ordered the Euchees to be cut off. That Partridg did not consent to act against Chestowe because there was no Order from the Governor. That Mr. Long and, as he thincks, Mr. Wiggen told him there would be a brave Parcel of Slaves if Chestowe were cut off. That the Cherikees voluntarily paid what Debts were due to Long and Wiggen from the People of Chestowee after they were cut off. That an Indian told Mr. Wiggen that Mr. Long said the Euchee shoold be cut off before green Corne Time. That he heard John Chester say he heard G. Sheld declare he heard Long say he would be revenged of the People of Chestois. That Mr. Long and Wiggen['s] Cargo was £320 but their Debts helped to purchase the Slaves.

Entry of May 4, 1714, in McDowell, *Journals of the Commissioners of the Indian Trade*, 53, 54-55, 56. In the early eighteenth century, the Yuchi Indians ("Euchees") primarily inhabited parts of northwestern Florida, the Savannah River Valley, and southeastern Tennessee. Their town of Chestowee was located on the north bank of the Hiwassee River, near its junction with Chestuee Creek, in present-day Polk County, Tennessee.

Warriors did not hold a monopoly in capturing Indians for the slave trade. Settlers in short-lived Clarendon County (1665-1667), who were at war with the peoples indigenous to that part of the Cape Fear Valley, also sold captives into servitude.

[. . .] they knew wee were in actuall warre with the Natives att Clarendon and had killed and sent away many of them [. . .]

> Robert Sandford, "The Port Royal Discovery . . . ," 1666, in William L. Saunders, ed., *The Colonial Records of North Carolina*, 10 vols. (Raleigh: State of North Carolina, 1886-1890), 1:137.

Elsewhere in North Carolina, white raiders began kidnapping Native American women and children to meet the colonists' demand for slaves. The widespread abductions were a primary cause of the discontent that fueled the outbreak of the Tuscarora War. Coordinated among the southern Tuscaroras and their allies, the surprise attacks upon settlers in the Neuse-Pamlico area that launched the war in 1711 were unprecedented in scope and severity. The colony reeled. North Carolina receiver-general Christopher Gale, in Charleston to plead for military aid from South Carolina, described to his sister the destruction wrought by enraged warriors in the vicinity of Bath.

On Sunday Octobr. 21. I arrived here in the quality of an Agent, and in order to procure the assistance of the Government to destroy our Enimies which I doubt not in a little time to effect. The Family I left in Garison at Bathe Town my wife and Brother pritty well recovered, but what has hapned since I know not. Two days after I left the Town, at daybreak (which is the Indians' usual time of attack) above 100 Gunns were heard, which must have been an attack made by the Indians upon some of our Garisons, which are in all eleven in number, but cannot hear the success of it, though a small vessel came from the out part of our Government here the other day, by which I have the following newes:

That on my coming away Captain Brice detached from our out-Garisons fifty men, and in the woods met with a Body of Indians, who fought them three days, and forc'd them at last to retire into their Garison. The Indians lost in this engagement fifteen men, and we two, one of which was killed by one of our own men. During this engagement, another Body of Indians, being advised that the Garison was weakned by this detachment, came and attacked the Garison, and at the same time a number of Indian Prisoners of a certain nation, which we did not know whether they were Friends or Enimies, rose in the Garison, but were soon cut to peices, as also those on the outside repelled.

In the Garison were killed nine Indian Men, and soon after thirty-nine women and children sent of[f] for slaves. This is the condition we at present labour under. I shall not trouble you with a particular relation of all their Butcheries, but shall relate to you some of them, by which you may suppose the rest. The Family of one Mr. Nevil was treated after this manner. The old Gentleman himselfe after being shott, was laid on the House Floor, with a clean Pillow under his Head, his wives headclothes put upon his Head, his stockings turned down over his Shoes, and his Body covered all over with new linnen. His wife was set upon her knees, and her hands lifted up as if she was at prayers, leaning against a Chair in the Chimney Corner, and her Coates turned up over her head. A son of his was laid out in the Yard, with a Pillow under his head, and a bunch of Rosemary laid to his Nose. A Negroe had his right hand cut of[f], and left dead. The Master of the next House was shott, and his body laid flat upon his wives grave. Women were laid on their House Floors, and great stakes run up their bodies. Others bigg with child, the Infants were ript out, and hung upon Trees. In short, their manner of butchery, has been so various and unaccountable, it would be beyond credit to relate them. This blow was so hotly followed by the hellish crew, that we could not bury our dead, so that they were left for prey to the Doggs and Wolves, and Vultures, whilst our care was to strengthen our Garison to secure the living.

Christopher Gale to his sister, November 2, 1711, in Saunders, *Colonial Records*, 1:826-827.

South Carolina dispatched Colonel John Barnwell, with a force comprised mostly of Yamassee and other Indians, northward to repulse the Tuscaroras. Burning towns and wreaking havoc, his army advanced into the heart of their nation. Barnwell's men vanquished the Tuscaroras' fort at Torhunta—which he called "Narhantes"—near what is now Goldsboro, North Carolina, in January 1712. On March 5, he described the initial attack upon the stronghold of King Hancock, leader of the southern Tuscaroras. It was built approximately thirty miles east of Torhunta at Catechna, on Contentnea Creek, in the vicinity of present-day Grifton.

My next work was to take of one ye forts, and while I was preparing [. . .] to do the same orderly, some of my Yamasees were so mettlesome as to advise to force it by Assault, willing to flesh while they were hot, I immediately ordered the Attack, the Indians were first up, but dropping, they began to cool, when my too few valiant white men reinforced them and broke into the fort in three places. Captain Steel was the first in, and I to encourage the men followed, then my Yamassees; but to our great surprise, within the Fort were two Houses stronger than the fort which did puzzle us & do the most damage, but now it was too late to look back, we forced them but the enemy were so desperate, the very women shooting Arrows, yet they did not yield until most of them were put to the sword. [. . .] when I found ye Enemy terrified at the quick work made here, quitted all their forts, & left a fine Country open full of provisions, Our Indians presently loading themselves with English plunder of which these Towns are full, and running away from me, nothing left for the white men but their horses tired & their wounds to comfort them.

> January 30, 1712, in John Barnwell, "Journal of John Barnwell," pt. 1, *Virginia Magazine of History and Biography* 5 (April 1898): 395, 396.

5 [March]. [. . .] I imeadiately viewed the Fort with a prospective glass and found it strong as well by situation on the river's bank as Workmanship, having a large Earthen Trench thrown up against the puncheons with 2 teer of port holes; the lower teer they could stop at pleasure with plugs, & large limbs of trees lay confusedly about it to make the approach intricate, and all about much with large reeds & canes to run into people's legs. The Earthern work was so high that it signified nothing to burn the puncheons, & it had 4 round Bastions or Flankers; the enemy says it was a runaway negro taught them to fortify thus, named Harry, whom Dove Williamson sold into Virginia for roguery & since fled to the Tuscaruros. Yet hoping to finish the war by this stroke, where now all the principal murderers were in a pen, I encouraged my men by promises, &c. I ordered 200 Fashines to be made which ye palatines well understood to do. I had them presently done. It is too tedious to inform yor Honr all the particulars how I ordered the Attack; but in short, when we were got within 10 or 12 yards of the Fort the enemy made a terrible fire upon us without the least damage in the world, but this country base, cowardly people hearing the shott strike their Fashines, threw both them & their arms away & run for life, wch not only left themselves exposed but also all those that went under their shelters; this encouraged the enemy to renew the firing, [. . .] In the mean time my brave South Carolina men 23 of this country undauntedly kept their order. I ordered them to keep their stations until I brought up the runaways. But all my endeavour was in vain, tho' I mauled sevll wth my cutlass, and as soon as they saw me running towards them they would scamper into the swamp that was hard by. I, seeing the confusion & being afraid that the number that drew the enemy's fire was insufficient to come at the Fort by assault, I ordered a retreat which was bravely managed, for every man got his Fashine on his back, and of my own number I had but one wounded; the most of them had 10 or more shott in his Fashine, but of the runaways there were 1 killed & 18 wounded, and of the 23 that stood by my men there were 3 killed & 2 wounded, in all 4 killed and 20 wounded.

> March 5, 1712, in John Barnwell, "Journal of John Barnwell," pt. 2, *Virginia Magazine of History and Biography* 6 (July 1898): 44-45. A *fascine* ("Fashine") is a long cylindrical bundle of sticks or brush, tightly tied, used to fill trenches.

Failing to seize Hancock's fort on March 5, Barnwell and his men returned on April 7 to besiege it a second time. But his forces' dwindling supplies, and a rising concern for the hostages confined by his enemies, obliged the colonel to relent after ten days and conclude a treaty. In early June he invited the southern Tuscaroras and their allies—the Bear River, Machapunga, Core, and Neusiok Indians—to exchange their prisoners for presents. When his guests arrived, Barnwell's forces struck, killing as many as fifty men; he also had several hundred Indian women and children enslaved and removed to South Carolina for eventual sale, apparently as payment for the uncompensated costs he incurred during the campaign. Outraged by that act of duplicity, Hancock's Tuscaroras and their confederates resumed their attacks.

I presume you are no Stranger to the Indian War, which has some time Since begun and continues in the Barbarous Massacres of so many English Inhabitans, Most Families of Pamlico hourly feeling the Effects of their Cruelty. <421> Nor Truly can the Governor promise himself one hours safety, being continually Allarm'd by the Tuskarora Spies in his Own Quarters. Colonel Boyde was the other day sent out with a Party against the Indians, but was unfortunately Shot thro' the Head, and few of his men came home, but what shar'd in his fate and fell Sacrifices in the same common Misfortune. They Sculck so in Parties in the Woods, that common prudence obliges the Inhabitants (as the surest method of preservation) to keep to their Plantations and Several of them told me, that when they lye down in their beds, (they are so often Invaded) that they can't say they shall rise to see morning.

> Reverend Giles Ransford to Secretary, SPG, July 25, 1712, in Robert J. Cain, ed., *The Church of England in North Carolina: Documents, 1699-1741*, vol. 10 of *The Colonial Records of North Carolina* [*Second Series*], eds. Mattie Erma Edwards Parker, William S. Price Jr., Robert J. Cain, and Jan-Michael Poff (Raleigh: State Department of Archives and History, [projected multivolume series, 1963–], 1999), 144.

Beleaguered North Carolina ultimately took two steps to quell Hancock. First, it enlisted the support of the previously neutral northern Tuscaroras, via a pact signed on November 25, 1712. The headman of the northern Tuscaroras, Tom Blunt, captured Hancock, who was put to death. Second, South Carolina was persuaded to send another expedition, this one under Colonel James Moore, to assist its neighbor. Moore met with more success than Barnwell: with an army of Indians and a relative handful of whites, he destroyed the southern Tuscarora stronghold of Neoheroka in late March 1713.

North Carolina ss.

Preliminary Articles and order to a General peace had made Concluded and Agreed upon this 25th day of Novr. Ano Dom 1712 Between Tom Blount, Saroonka Heust he noh neh, Cheust hartuithoo, Neuroout tootsere. Chief men of several of the Tuskerora Towns for and on behalf of themselves and the Townes of Eukuiknoreuit Rarookakeo, Tostohant, Reuroota, Tasttuith, Kenta Toherooka Juninits and Caunookeha of the one part And the Honorable Thos Pollock Esqr. President and the rest of the Counsill for and on behalf of themselves and this Goverment of North Carolina on the other part

Witnesseth

<Imprimis> The aforsaid great Men Doe here by Covenant and agree to and with the said president and Counsill that they shall and will with the utmost Expedition and Dilligence make War against all the Indyans belonging to the Towns or Nations of Catachny Cores Nuse and Bare River and pamplico and that they shall not nor will not give any Quarter to any Male Indyan of those Towns or Nations above the Age of Fourteen Years And also that they shall and will Sell off and Dispose of all the Males under that Age, And that further after they shall have destroy'd those townes or too Soone as this Goverment shall think proper to require it the said great Men doe hereby promise to Joine the English with Soe many Men as may be thought proper to destroy and Cutt off all the Matchepungo Indyans.

<2dly> The aforsaid Great Men doe hereby Covent and agree that if in this Warr they shall take any Armes which shall be proved to have been owned by the English and taken away in the late horrid Massa[cre] such armes shall be delivered to the right owne[rs] thereof.

<3dly> It is hereby further agreed by the said Great Men that they shall and will well and truely deliver up to the English all the White Captives and horses that they shall find among the said Indyans.

<4thly> It is hereby further Agreed by the Great Men aforsaid that the Severall Towns of Tostohant Reuiroota Tarhuntah Kentah Toherooka Juninits and Caunookehee nor any of the Indyans belonging to those or either of them shall not nor will not Hurt nor range among the English plantations nor Stocks without leave nor then above the number of three at one tyme neither shall they Carrie any property to the Lands on the South Side of Nuse Called Chatooke River nor below Catostery Creek on Nuse nor below Bare Creek at Netaske-turn-heu-rough on the North Side of Pamplico river.

<5thly> It is Mutually agreed by and between all the said partys, to those presents that if any Injury shall hereafter be done on either Side upon Complaints made to such persons as shall hereafter be appointed for that purpose full satisfaction shall be regarde.

<6thly> The aforsaid great Men doe here by agree that from and after the Ratification of a gentle peace they shall and will pay unto this Goverment such a Yearly Tribute and hereafter shall be agreed upon.

<7thly> The said Great Men doe hereby further Agree that for the full and true performance of all and every the above Articles on their parts to be performed the several Townes of Tostehant, Raurooka Tarhunta Kenta Taherooka Juninits and Canusokehee shall bring in and deliver up to this Goverment at the home of Collonel Thos. Pollock Six of the Chiefest Women and Children for each Town for Hostages by the next full Moon provided that they doe not destroy the Enemy after [*illegible*] tyme.

<8thly> The said president and Counsill doe hereby Covenant and Agree to and with the great men aforsaid that upon the Just and true performance of these Articles the Severall Hostages aforsaid shall be well and truely delivered up againe and a free and open trade shall be had with the said Indyans as aforesaid [*illegible*].

<Lastly> The aforsaid Great Men doe hereby agree that they will endeavour to bring in to Some of their [towns] Alive Cannineth quoth keno[*torn*], Ense que re hau, Canninetk[*torn*] Nou reuti quot kau Called Jno pagett Ete koi quost Called Lawson Coret ni ena Called Barbar, Cotsere Called He[*torn*]Lysle Ouns kin nesee Called Squarehooks Touh qui auth Erun tau hy ne and Young Tyler and sends three Runners to Mr. Reading's Garrison. Grant those three troops then shew the White Cloth for a Signall in order to pilott Such persons as wee shall think proper to send to see done upon the aforsaid murderers.

> John Devereux Papers, State Archives, Office of Archives and History, Raleigh. The towns of Eukuiknoreuit, Rarookakeo, and Reuroota could not be identified. "Tostohant" was Toisnot; it was located near the junction of Buck Branch and Toisnot Swamp in present-day Wilson County, North Carolina. Kenta was on Cow Branch, south of Nahunta Swamp, in Wilson County. The town of Neoheroka ("Toherooka") stood along both banks of Contentnea Creek, four miles northwest of present-day Snow Hill, Greene County, North Carolina. Innennits ("Juninits") was on Panther Swamp Creek, north of present-day Snow Hill, Greene County. Caunookehoe stood south of present-day Maury, Greene County. Built in response to the Indian attacks, the fort named for Lionel Reading was located on his plantation on the south bank of the Pamlico River and opposite present-day Washington, North Carolina.

Sr

Ye 20th of this instant I attact No-ho-ro-co fort, on C[ontentnea] Creek & ye 23d In ye morning took itt, with ye Loss of 22 Whit men & 24 more wond'd—35 Indians Kill'd & 58 wond'd—Most of ye Damage wee Reced after wee had Gott ye fort to ye Ground, which we Did in ye first 3 hours—I have Little else to advise ye Honrs but that ye Qut of ye Ememies Destroyed is as follows—Prisoners 392, Scolps 192, out of ye sd: fort—& att Least 200

Kill'd & Burnt In ye fort—& 166 Kill'd & taken out of ye fort on ye Scout, which is all; but My Servis to Capt: Jones, from yr: Honrs obdt Servt

JA: MOORE

Letter from James Moore, March 27, 1713, in William Pitt Palmer et al., eds., *Calendar of Virginia State Papers and other Manuscripts, 1652-1781*, 11 vols. (1875-1883; reprint, New York: Kraus Reprint Company, 1968), 1:165. The Tuscaroras had built Neoheroka ("No-ho-ro-co") Fort near the junction of Fort Run and Contentnea Creek in what is now Greene County, North Carolina.

The southern Tuscaroras never recovered from their defeat at Neoheroka. Those who left North Carolina to rejoin the Iroquois retained a deep animosity toward their enemies.

[. . .] it was designed this Spring to have you among the said Onandine Indians again, but the Interpreter told me it was very dangerous travelling in the Wood that way, because upwards of five hundred families of the Tuskaroris Indians that made War upon South Carolina about 4 or 5 year agoe were come to live among the five Nations beyond us, who have an Implacable hatred against Xtians at Carolina, killing the farmers, Cattle and Hogs as they pass to and again, and when the People speak to them, they tell them theyl serve them the same if they are not Quiet.

Reverend William Andrews to Secretary, SPG, April 20, 1716, Letterbooks, Series A, Society for the Propagation of the Gospel in Foreign Parts, British Records, State Archives, Office of Archives and History, Raleigh. The "Onandine" are the Oneidas.

Iroquois interest in the Native Americans of the South extended beyond the repatriation of the Tuscaroras. Eager for new hunting grounds and martial glory, they had clashed with the Indians of Carolina since the late seventeenth century. The Catawbas in particular were subject to persistent attacks from the Iroquois.

Brother Corlaer

You say that you are informed that there was a warlike Preparation making among the Five Nations which we acknowledge to be true but we know not as yet ourselves where they intend to go. Two years ago Two Tuskarores brought a Belt of Wampum from the Governor of Virginia (as they said) and thereby in the name of the Governor of Virginia desired the five Nations to make War & destroy the Tadirighrones [Catawba], but being informed that the Governor of Virginia was to be at Albany we deferred any resolution about that affair, till we had spoken with him ourselves [. . .]

Conference between Governor William Burnet of New York and the Iroquois, September 1722, in E.B. O'Callaghan and Berthold Fernow, eds., *Documents Relative to the Colonial*

History of the State of New York, 15 vols. (Albany, N.Y.: Weed, Parsons, and Company, 1853-1887), 5:660.

In the Court House Chamber at Lancaster, [Pa.,] June 30th, 1744, A.M.

PRESENT:

The Honourable the Commissioners of Virginia.

The Deputies of the Six Nations.

Conrad Weiser, Interpreter.

Gachadow, Speaker for the Indians, in answer to the Commissioner's Speech at the last meeting, with a Strong Voice and Proper Actions, Spoke as follows:

[. . .]

Brother Assaraquoa:

You Charge us with not acting agreeable to our Peace with the Catawbas; we will repeat truly to you what was done: The Governor of New York at Albany, in behalf of Assaraquoa, gave us several Belts from the Cherickees and Catawbas, and we agreed to a Peace if those Nations would send some of their Great men to Us to confirm it face to face, and that they would Trade with us, and desired that they would appoint a time to meet at Albany for this Purpose, but they never came.

Brother Assaraquoa:

We then desired a Letter might be sent to the Catawbas and Cherikees to desire them to come and confirm the Peace. It was long before an Answer came, but we met the Cherikees and Confirmd the Peace, and sent some of Our People to take care of them untill they returned to their own Country.

The Catawbas refused to come, and sent us word that we were but Women; that they were men and double men [. . .]; that they could make Women of Us, and would be always at War with us. They are a deceitful People; Our Brother Assaraquoa is deceived by him; we don't blame him for it, but are sorry he is so deceived.

Brother Assaraquoa:

We have confirm'd the Peace with the Cherikees, but not with the Catawbas. They have been Treacherous, and know it, so that the War must continue till one of Us is destroyed. This we think Proper to tell you, that you may not be Troubled at what we do to the Catawbas.

Proceedings, Treaty of Lancaster, Minutes of the Pennsylvania Provincial Council, June 30, 1744, in Samuel Hazard, ed., *Colonial Records of Pennsylvania*, 16 vols. (Harrisburg, Pennsylvania: Printed by T. Fenn & Company, 1851-1853), 4:720-721. "Brother Assaraquoa" was the title given by the Iroquois to the governors of Virginia. The Catawbas sought and won peace with the Iroquois in July 1751.

To the Governor of South Carolina

An Account of a Catawbaw Wench which she gives after her Escape from the Mohawkes or the five Nations, by whom she was taken by Mrs. Russetts and carried of[f].

She heard that they intend to cut off every Soul of the Catawbaws for Revenge, as the Catawbaws has formerly cut off some of the above Indians, and killed their Head Man.

This Woman further says that she heard them say, in their House where they talked; that they knew where the Catawbaws fetched their Water and Wood and they would utterly destroy them.

King Hagler says he is not afraid of the People in this Country, but of the French. This Woman came to me two Days before we came from Home and this is the ninth Day we left our Nation.

Catawba Indians to Governor James Glen of South Carolina, 1755, in McDowell, *Documents Relating to Indian Affairs, 1754-1765*, 48-49.

The Catawbas' attackers had been abetted by the Cherokees, who provided sanctuary to the Iroquois and to Indians allied with the French. The Cherokees claimed that they were powerless to resist.

I have already observed to your Lordships that I had sent for some of the Indian Kings and Head men who came according to my desire namely the King of the Catawbaws with about twenty of his People and some of the Headmen and about Forty of the Cherrockees. The Catawbaw King complained loudly that the Cherockees tho' pretended friends permitted his Enemys the French and other Indians to come through their Country to make War upon him, supplying them with Provisions and Ammunition and that they received them and protected them in their retreat. The Cherrockees acknowledged that they permitted them to pass through their Country, but alledged it was impossible for them without drawing destruction upon their own Heads to prevent it. That their over-Hills Towns lay naked and open to the Incursions and Inroads of the French and their Indians from the Mississippi, Wabash and other Rivers, that they had long opposed them by which they were greatly thinned, and no Longer in any condition to make head against them, and that they might now impose what conditions they pleased upon them, that they had hitherto refused them the Liberty to settle amongst them, and to trade with them, but it was now no longer in their power to refuse them whatever they asked, [. . .]

Governor James Glen to the Board of Trade, July 26, 1748, in Colonial Office 5/372, British Records, State Archives, Office of Archives and History, Raleigh.

A nation with strong ties to the French, the Caughnawaga Indians of Quebec sent war parties southward to attack the Catawbas and the Cherokees. A newspaper account of a battle in Rowan County reveals that the Catawbas possessed the ability to prevail over the Caughnawagas.

Sir, Since my last Letter to your Excellency of 7th of this Instant, Col. Johnson, a Gentleman living on his Estate near the Mohawk Lower Castle about 30 Miles from Albany, and has been employed several Years past as Commissioner for Indian Affairs in the Province of New York, which Office he has lately declined, arrived in New York and brought an Account that this Spring above a Month ago several Parties from each of the Six Nations at several Times together with a Body of a Nation near Montreal known by the Name of Cahnuwagaws, who were formerly Part of the Five Nations have marched to the Number of 6 or 700 Men to War against 3 Nations of the Southward Indians, viz., the Catawbas, Cherokees and one they call Geerick Roonee, which I suppose must be the Creeks.

He says they expect to be joined by the Indians living on the Ohio River. The Reason given for their going to War in so large a Body is that they find their small Parties which were heretofore sent were often cut off, and they had no Prospect of conquering their Enemies by such Means. Wherefore they were determined to carry on the War now with such Force as should not be resisted, and at one Blow subdue them. He says they seem to be much exasperated. Severall Parties that were going to War last Spring against the Catawbas were stopt on hearing the Report that they were to give a Meeting to the Six Nations, and to make a Peace, and if they had heard that the Catawbas were to have come to Albany this Summer for that Purpose, he makes no Doubt but this Army would not have assembled or marched notwithstanding the Industry of the French Agents who are very busie among the Nation, particularly called Senecas, who are the westermost of the whole and live next to the Niagara Falls.

Lieutenant Governor William Bull of South Carolina to Governor James Glen, June 1751, in William L. McDowell Jr., ed., *Documents Relating to Indian Affairs, 1750-1754*, in *The Colonial Records of South Carolina, Series 2* (Columbia: South Carolina Archives Department, 1958), 110. "Col. Johnson" is Sir William Johnson, future superintendent of Indian affairs for the northern district; "his estate," Fort Johnson, was located in what is now the town of Amsterdam, New York. "Mohawk Lower Castle" is another name for the Mohawk town of Teatontaloga, located at the junction of Schoharie Creek and Mohawk River in New York. The site was also known as Fort Hunter for the fortification built in the vicinity by the British.

NEWBERN, (in North-Carolina) Aug. 4.

Extract of a Letter from a Gentleman in Johnston *County to his Correspondent in* Newbern, July 25, 1753.

A Gentleman of your Acquaintance dropt in here last Night for Quarters, who has brought Intelligence, That a Body of Indians in the French Interest are in this Province, and commit Depredations; That there has been a skirmish in Rowan County, betwixt a detach'd Party of the Enemy and our Friends the Catawbas, in which our Allies signaliz'd themselves by a compleat Victory: He says he came to the Field of Battle about half an Hour after the Action, and on his Departure, met with the Conquerers, who were busy'd in fitting Scalps, &c. after their Fashion, and had likewise drest themselves with the Spoils of the Slain, which consisted of Silver Crucifixes, Beads, Looking-Glasses, Tomahawks, and other Military Implements of War, which were intirely French, and the Catawba's themselves, upon being ask'd, confirm'd their being so. You may depend on the Truth of this as an absolute Fact.

New-York Mercury, November 12, 1753.

In addition to foes from the north, the Cherokees tangled with the Choctaws, who lived in what is now Mississippi.

February 22nd [1753]. Forty-six Cherokees came here in order to go to war against the Chocktaws. They came down the River in Canoes and coming down the Falls or Breakers, the Rapit running of the Water oversett four of their Canoes with at least twenty Fellows in them. They lost all their Guns, Blankets, and Boots, and had two Men drownded, and the Rest got out with great Difficulty. They came into this Nation in a Manner naked, and stayed but a little while here before thirteen of them fitted out for the Chocktaws, but did not gett to that Nation before they where engaged with about twenty Chocktaws who came upon them about the Midle of the Day. They killed three of them the first Shott, and wounded one. The Rest, after throwing away their Guns, run off. The wounded Man was shot throw the Arm, and him they took alive, and carryed him to the Choctaws, throw several of their Towns, whiping him at every Town for three Days, which is their Custom with Slaves. The fourth Day he was to have been burnt, and they thinking him by this Time secure, they untied his Hands. In the Middle of the Night he made his Escape, and in three Days gott safe here, notwithstanding he was persued by at least a hundred Fellows, and says he was many Times in the Midst of them. The Rest of them are returned to their Land, he only remains here under the Doctor's Hands. Their coming here has been attended with bad Success, and I am apt to think they will hardly attempt War with the Chocktaws any more.

The Chocktaws say they think but little of them since they find they are so easly started.

"Journal of John Buckles," Chickesaw trader, in McDowell, *Documents Relating to Indian Affairs, 1750-1754*, 384.

Separating them from the Choctaws were the Cherokees' rivals to the southwest, the Creek Indians. Hatred of the Cherokees stemmed from the 1716 massacre of a Creek delegation in the Lower Town of Tugaloo. Later the French, backing the Creeks, fomented a sporadic Creek-Cherokee war that began in 1740. It ended in 1753, following a diplomatic offensive by Governor James Glen of South Carolina.

I left Silver Bluff October 18, 1749. I set out from the Creeks in the Beginning of November. About sixteen Miles from the Nation I met some Cusita Indians going out to War against the Cherokees. I told them I thought it was a firm Peace. They say'd they thought so two but that the Cherokees about six Days before had killed 2 Women and had carried four alive, and that some of the People had followed them and retook the Women again that I got in the Nation. Them Indians I met going to War in about a Month returned. They killed 2 and brought one in alive which they bury'd. I did all that lay in my Power to save him but could not. In the Spring about 400 went against the Cherokees and killed between 30 and 40 and brought in seven alive which they burned.

Memorandum from George Galphin to William Pinckney, commissioner of Indian affairs, November 3, 1750, in McDowell, *Documents Relating to Indian Affairs, 1750-1754*, 4. Silver Bluff was George Galphin's trading post and plantation on the Savannah River near present-day Jackson, Aiken County, South Carolina. Cusseta ("Cusita"), a principal town of the Lower Creek nation, sat on the east bank of the Chattahoochee River at present-day Fort Benning, Chattahoochee County, Georgia.

May 3rd, 1752

[. . .] There was some Confusion in the Town of Iwassee occassioned by the Southwards killing a Notcha Fellow the Day before which hindred their writing till Dark, so that I prevailed with Mr. [Anthony] Dean to take the Talk down for me, he having better Eyes with Candlelight than I had, the exact Substance whereof I have sent your Excellency by Mr. [John] Elliott.

The Manner of the Creeks killing the said Notche was somewhat remarkable. There was two of them had gone some Days before a hunting a little Way over the River from the Town where eight of the Enemy came up and fired upon them and wounded one of them in the Thigh so that he sunk down and sat upon the Ground, which the other seeing betook himself to a

Tree with his Gun loaded in his Hand. The Enemy called to them and asked what Town they belonged to, who made Answer, Iwassee. The Enemy said, Iwassee was good and the Raven who was made a King at the English was good, but that the Cauetas, Kewohe, Estertoe, and the other Lower Towns were great Rogues, and desired them to come to them and they would dress the wounded Man. The Fellow who stood by the Tree not willing to trust their fair Promises betook himself to Flight and got Home in the Middle of the Night, and having alarmed the Town they sent out next Morning (being the Day I came there) by the break Day to bring in the wounded Man whom they expected was yet alive. But when they came to the Place where he lay they found his Body shott all over and mangled after a most barbarous Manner, and found that these who killed him were gone Home but that a little Way farther a Body of them had lain, and by their Track had made toward the Middle Settlements of this Nation. However, there has been no farther News of them since, so that it may also be supposed they have missed their Aim and returned Home. The Raven said that the Enemies wanting the 2 Notche Fellows to come to them was a Decoy in order to kill them both, that they might the better come upon the Town undiscovered and do more Mischief. [. . .]

I have sent your Excellency a Letter which I received of Chachetcha, the Warriour of Tuckasega, I believe written by Mr. Crawford. It is most certain that the fronteer Towns of this Nation in general are not capable now in Time of this general Warr to hunt to purchase Ammunition &c. meerly to defend themselves from their Enemies. This constrains them to have Recourse to your Excellency and Province for Succour and Relief which may be of good Consequence for the Future, and may be a substantial Argument for the Government to put them in Mind of their Obligations. They always have layn under to Carolina, and now are obliged to lye under for their Relief.

Ludovick Grant to Governor James Glen, May 3, 1752, in McDowell, *Documents Relating to Indian Affairs, 1750-1754*, 261, 262. "Cauetas" cannot be identified. "Iwassee" is Little Hiwassee.

I-oree, February the 8th, 1753

[. . .] While Mr. Beamer's People were a hunting there came a Coweta Fellow to the Warriour's Camp and told him that his People had heard the Governor's Talk, and that now it was Peace, and his People were ordered to go no more to War against the Cherokees. At which the Estertoe Warrior thanked him, and promised to send through the Nation and forbid his People to go any more to War, and withall gave the Creek Warriour Presents as Usual amongst Indians, Pipes, Beads, and Tabacco in Token of Peace, and desired he should give them to his Warriours and beloved Men.

Since Mr. Elliott came up from your Excellency there were some young Fellows were going to War against the Southwards, but were stoped by the Prince of Ioree and turned back to their Towns on Stecoe River.

Ludovick Grant to Governor James Glen, February 8, 1753, in McDowell, *Documents Relating to Indian Affairs, 1750-1754*, 366, 367. Like Cusseta, Coweta was another principal town of the Lower Creeks; it stood on the west bank of the Chattahoochee River, approximately six miles north of Cusseta, near present-day Phenix City, Alabama. "Stecoe River" is the Tuckasegee River.

Although the Cherokees had differences with the Creeks and Iroquois, together they possessed the balance of power as competition between Britain and France intensified, in the 1740s and early 1750s, for control of the Ohio Valley. To the two European adversaries, trade with the region's indigenous people provided more than an important source of wealth: Indian trading partners were willing to act as military allies as long as they had access to manufactured goods. Agents of both countries established outposts to promote and preserve their commercial and strategic interests in the area. The French capture in April 1754 of a fort being constructed by Virginians at the headwaters of the Ohio River, the site of modern-day Pittsburgh, Pennsylvania, touched off the French and Indian War. Determined to secure their ties to Britain and keep them safe from marauding "French" Indians, Governor Glen invited Cherokee headmen to talks in Charleston.

Charles Town, 12th December 1754

MY GOOD FRIENDS AND LOVING BROTHERS, TACITE OF HYOWASSIE, COLANE OF EURPHORSEE, KING OF THE VALLEY, I hope this Letter will find you and your Spouse, your son Amahetai and George all well and in good Health. You was so kind as to come and see me [at] Keewohee with your old friend Cornelius, and I endeavoured to make you as wellcome as I could. You and I have often met in Charles Town, we have met in the Woods, we have met in your Nation and though both you and I grow older than when we first knew one another, yet I hope we shall meet again and I wish to see you and your Son about the Middle of February in Charles Town with any other of the Headmen of the Valley or Warriours that your please.

I have written to Old Hop for some of the Head-men from Over the Hills, and I expect Chuchitchi and Round O from the Tuccaseagia Parts, and some from the Middle Settlements, and also from the Lower Towns that we may have a great Talk togeather.

I have also sent for some of the Headmen both of the Upper and Lower Creeks and they will be here about that Time. One Part of my Design is to confirm and settle the Peace betwixt your two Nations for the French have been lately endeavouring to make a Breach and to kindle the Flame that I happily extinguished, but I have defeated their Designs. But another great End of my desiring a Meeting with the Headmen of the Cherroekees is to consult what Steps are to be taken to prevent the French, their Indians the Tawasaws, and other Northern Indians from hurting your Nation. They want to bring both the Chactaws and Creeks against you on one Side and they themselves and their northern Friends attack you on the other Side and so by putting you betwixt two Fires they may intirely destroy and consume you. It is to protect your Nation from this that I want to consult with you and to enable you not only to stand your Ground and defend your Towns, but to drive your Enemies before you and I hope I shall unite togeather both Cherroekees, Creeks and Catawbaws like one Man against the common Enemy. You shall not want for Arms and Ammunition and we must consult how to secure your old Men, your Wives and Children not only against any Enemy, that may come against your Towns, but while your Warriors are gone against the Enemy.

You are sensible that there are great Points and Matters of the utmost Importance and therefore though you are old and the Weather will then be cold yet I doubt not but you will come. I want you because you are wise and good and love your People. This is a great and solem Meeting. After this your Son Amehetae may supply your Place, but at present I want you both and I will take no Refusal.

> Governor James Glen to Tacite of Hiwassee and Colane of Eurphorsee, King of the Valley, December 12, 1754, in McDowell, *Documents Relating to Indian Affairs, 1754-1765*, 26-27. The "Tawasaws" are the Miami Indians, who once claimed what is now Indiana and Ohio.

The Catawbas remained steadfast allies of the British throughout the French and Indian War. They assisted colonials in pursuing hostile Indians who had attacked a settlement on Buffalo Creek, in Rowan County, in 1754. Early in 1756, Governor Arthur Dobbs credited their presence with having kept the North Carolina backcountry safe. King Hagler assured the colony's chief justice, Peter Henley, of his nation's support.

An acct brought from Rowan County being occCationed bye sum murder that was Commited on the Inhabitance of bufflo Creek a branch of Broad River on which thare was a mesener sent to his Honour the President the Charge of which amount to £2 15 0

to one Captain at 7/6 42 day	15 6 0
to one Settlement 42 days at 5/0	10 0 6
to 24 men 42 days at 3/0	144 10 0

to bringing Powder and Lead from for the
patarolors from the new store on Cap fare   14 0
to money payed to willis Ellis for Going
to the Catabo nation in order to hire some
of the Indions to persue those that Commited
murder above said.   £1 16 0
                                                                                             £175 3 6

December the 19th 1754
Save Erors by   Jas. Carter

[*Enclosed*:]
Claim of £175.3.6 Collonel George Smith for payment of the Men etc. that
went after the Murderers in Rowan County
Allowed

> Account presented to General Assembly, December 19, 1754, Frontier Scouting and
> Indian Wars, 1758-1777, Military Collection, State Archives, Office of Archives and
> History, Raleigh.

We are also erecting a small fort on our western Frontier, against the Indians,
but Labour is so dear here, and Labourors scarce to be had at any Price, that all
our affairs here are retarded. We have had no attacks or Insults yet upon our
Frontier, owing principally to our frontier Company, and Neighbourhood of
the Cataubas Indians – our friends. I have appointed two Commissioners to
join two sent by Governor Dinwiddie to the Cherokees and Cataubas with a
present to confirm them in their friendship, and to indeavour to procure some
hundreds of their Warriours next Summer to joyn our Virginia Troops; [. . .]

> Governor Arthur Dobbs of North Carolina to Thomas Robinson, secretary of state for the
> southern department, January 5, 1756, in Colonial Office 5/17, British Records, State
> Archives, Office of Archives and History, Raleigh. Upon completion, the "small fort"
> mentioned by the governor was named Fort Dobbs.

[. . .] the King spoke as follows –

The Cherokees We and the White People have been Brothers, and I
desired that the path between us might be kept clear but the Cherokees have
been playing the Rogue at which I am extremely concerned.

All the White People from South to North as far as New York nay beyond
the great Waters under the great King are our Brothers, should the French
come we will stand by our Brethren the English or go down into the Grave
with them.

The Cherokees have told me that they would enter into a Friendship with
the French but be assured that the White People shall still be my Brothers and
I will assist them, these men I have brought here (pointing to his Warriors) are

all come freely and voluntarily to acquaint the English that they will stand by them as long as they live, Mine is a small Nation yet they are brave men, and will be fast friends to their Brothers the White people as long as the sun endures.

I always advise my Men to be kind and obliging to the White People, as they are their Brothers and I shall continue to do so and remain their Brother 'till a sharp thing pierces my Breast so that I die, when that happens they must do as they please.

As I suppose there will soon be a War, I desire the Governour of North Carolina as this Land belongs to him to send us some Ammunition as soon as possible, and that he will build us a fort for securing our old men women and children when we turn out to fight the Enemy on their coming and as we love to wear silver plates on our Breasts and Arms I should be glad he would send us some of them with some Wampum.

Colo Alexander Colo Harris and Capt Berry told me they would make my Warriors a small present for assisting the White People in retaking their Good Horses &c: from the Cherokees which they had plundered them of.

I go very much among the White people and have often my Belly filled by them and am very sorry they should at any time be distracted.

I return the Governour thanks for his care in purchasing Corn for my people which has saved the lives of many of our old men women and children.

As my people and the White people are Brethren I desire that when they go to their houses they may give them victuals to eat, some of the White People are very bad and quarrelsome and whip my people about the head, beat and abuse them but others are very good.

[. . .]

After this the King informed the Chief Justice he had nothing more to say to him but had something to observe to his Warriors and thereupon addressed himself to them and then to his young men and desired them to declare whether in what he had said to his Brethren the English he had expressed their Sentiments as well as his own to which they unanimously answered that he had. Then he added, That should his Brethren of Carolina be engaged in a War as he feared they soon would he would have his Men all ready on the first notice to march to their assistance. He desired them to fight on such an occasion as became Catawbas and do nothing that might lessen the great Character they had obtained by their Military atchievements He added they were under the greatest Obligations to do this for two reasons. First because the English had cloathed them naked and fed them when hungry Secondly because the White people were now seated all round them and by that means had them entirely in their power.

To which the Warriors and young men all answered they would remember what he had given them in charge.

On this the King presented the pipe of Peace to the Chief Justice who as well as the rest of the company accepted it in the usual manner.

Conference between King Hagler and Chief Justice Peter Henley, Salisbury, May 26-27, 1756, in Saunders, *Colonial Records*, 5:580-581, 581-582.

As mentioned in Governor Dobbs's letter of January 1756, above, Virginia and North Carolina sent commissioners to convince the Cherokees to serve with colonial forces on the Virginia frontier. Those officials courted a wary nation. Plagued by white encroachment upon their hunting grounds and the abuses of "English" traders, some wanted to side with the French. However, those loyal to the British were the source of much of the panic in North Carolina's western Piedmont during the spring and summer of 1756. The Cherokees' assault against pro-French Shawnees in the Ohio Valley had failed. Provisions gone, warriors wending their way back to their settlements raided the homes and farms of colonists. Fearful settlers fled the frontier for the Moravian town of Bethabara.

May 18 [1756]. [. . .] many people are again leaving their farms for fear of the Indians. Br. Jacob Loesch, who had ridden out early in the morning to get oil, came home in the evening and reported that he had met 11 Indians, who had a white woman with them. They wanted to take his horse and repeatedly ordered him to dismount, but he refused to do it. They asked if he had rum in the keg which he had taken for the oil, — he said no, and struck the keg to show that it was empty. Then they again told him to dismount, he refused and said he needed the horse, that he could not travel afoot. They looked surly, and he then asked them whether they were hungry, and told them to come to his farm, twelve miles away, and he would fill them full of food. The white woman said he was a fool to tell them where he lived, that they would come and take everything he had. Then they went on their way and he on his, filled his keg, fed his horse, and set out on his return. On the way back he heard that the Indians had been to a farm and seized the horses and saddles, that they had taken Mr. Haltem's horse from him after he left us, and that Mr. Benner and all his family had fled, whereupon he came home at a gallop. After the evening services, having consulted with Br. Christian Henrich and Br. Hofmann, he called some of the Brethren together, told them what he had seen and heard, and that he thought we should be on our guard, and appointed them as a night watch here and at the mill. He also sent Br. Holder "Express" to our neighbor, Justice Edward Hughes, giving him a report of all that had occurred, and that the Indians were going in his direction.

Next day Br. Holder returned bringing the thanks of Justice Hughes, and word that fifteen of the neighbors had already before he left gathered at the home of the Justice to try to capture the Indians. At noon the Brn. Jac. Loesch and Kalberlahn went to see whether Mr. Benner had come home, but they met him, his wife, children and servant, coming to stay with us again for several days. He said that he and his family and servant had been in the corn-field, and the Indians had entered his house and taken the best clothing and all his money. His wife had met one of them, and he had run away, which encourages us to think that they are local Cherokees and not French or other strange Indians.

May 20. We hear that the Indians went to Justice Hughes, and behaved very politely,—probably because there were so many people there. When the Justice heard that they were Cherokees from the fort near Haw River, who had left there because of lack of food, he gave them plenty to eat, and sent them with a strong guard to another fort, seventy miles away. By Br. Loesch's advice Mr. Benner and his family went home; he spoke of moving away, selling his corn in the field, we should be very sorry to have him do this, and hope he will re-consider.

May 25. Today Mr. Benner's wife, children, negress and mulatto arrived again, also the younger Guest and his wife, Mr. Haltem's wife and children, and a Dunkard, or Bearded Man. They asked for a few days lodging, since a troop of Cherokees were marching through, and had frightened and annoyed them. We cleared out the joiner's shop, shoe-shop and strangers' house for them. The Dunkard was sent to the mill, and hardly reached there when a party of eight Indians also arrived there. Our Brethren went quietly on with their work; Br. Jacob Loesch went to them, spoke to them kindly, asked who they were, where they came from, and whither they were going, all of which they answered politely, it appearing that they were Cherokees from the fort. We gave them a few clay pipes, for which they were grateful, and went gravely from one to the other of us shaking hands. Then we gave them food, and they camped in the woods near the mill, spending the night very quietly. Perhaps we were too many for them, for there were several at the mill, and other Brethren went over to see them; twelve Brethren stayed at the mill all night, on guard. They told us, partly by signs, that there were eight more companies on the way. They breakfasted by the mill next morning, then bade the Brethren a polite adieu.

May 29. Br. Kalberlahn, who had been to visit patients, returned with the report that the Irish, helped by the Catawba Indians, had taken from the companies of Cherokees the goods they had stolen, and the white men had taken the things to Salisbury, where any one who had been robbed could go to reclaim his property. [. . .]

July 4. The younger Guest, his wife, and mother-in-law, arrived, and asked permission to stay, as they feared another outbreak of trouble with the Indians. After supper the Brethren gathered for a conference. Br. Christian

Henrich laid the whole matter before them, stating that it seemed to be true that the Cherokees, hitherto our friendly neighbors, had joined the French, and therefore the danger was much increased, families were leaving their farms and retreating, leaving us on the frontier, and therefore likely to be the first point of attack. [. . .]

Next day, after dinner, Br. Jacob Loesch called the Single Brethren together to decide the matter discussed on the 4th, which was quickly done, the unanimous conclusion being that all work, except the harvesting, should be dropped until a palisade had been built around the houses, making them safe before the first incursion of the Indians should take place. Duties were assigned to each man,—felling trees, digging the trench, continuing the harvesting.

> Bethabara Diary, March-December 1756, in Adelaide L. Fries *et al.*, eds., *Records of the Moravians in North Carolina*, 13 vols. (Raleigh: Office of Archives and History, Department of Cultural Resources, 1922-2006), 1:164-165, 166, 170.

Settlers often furnished food and other supplies to Cherokee and Catawba war parties, as they crossed North Carolina on their way to and from the conflict with the French and their Indian allies, and then sought reimbursement from the colony. Martin Phifer's request for repayment was typical. The Hugens family obtained compensation of a different kind at the expense of a Cherokee warrior who stopped to rest.

The Publick of North Carolina to Martain Pifer Dr.

<1756 July the 21> By King hagler and his Compeney on his way
  to Virginia to war To provisions   £ 8 0
<1757 Feby the 14> Capt. John and Eight more Cottaba Ingon
  on thear Return from Virginia for Neseacery Provisions   £ 5 6
<the 17> To 17 Cottabo Ingons on thear way to Virginia For
  Provisions   £ 9 [*torn*]
<the 19> Capt. Bullen and Eight of his men For Provision   £ 5 6
<1757 Febry the 27> King hagler and his Compeney on thear way
  to Virginia To Expenses for Provisions   £1 13 0
<march the 3> Capt. George and Seven more on thear way to
  Virginia To Expences for Provisions   £ 4 0
<March the 20> Mr Richard Smith and 30 od Cherrekes on thear
  way To Virgina To Expences   £1 0 4
<May the 27> King hagler on his Return from Virginia with his
  Compeney to Expenses   £1 1 5
<June the 3> Prenche hura and his Compeney on thear Return from
  Virgina Expences   £ 10 2

<Sepr. the 14> one Creek Ingon and his Interpertor with a
  Express to the Governer of Charles town To Expences   £ 4 8
<Octr. the 4> To 4 Cattabo Ingons on thear Return from Virgina
  To Expences   £ 4 0
                                                           £6 6 [*torn*]

<Anson County North Carolina> this day Came Martin Phifar Before the
Subscriber a majestrate of said County and made oath that the above accompt
is just and true as it stands stated and that he hath Received no part Nor parcil
securety or satisfaction for the same. Sworn Before Nathl. Alexander Alexr.
Cathey.

> Claim of Martin Phifer, October 13, 1757, Joint Committees, Session of November-
> December 1757, General Assembly Session Records, State Archives, Office of Archives
> and History, Raleigh.

The Examination of Thomas Hugens Senior of Granvil County Taken before
Me Robert Hicks Esqr. one of his Maiesties Justices of the peace for said
county [. . .] the Said Thomas Hugens being charged before me [. . .] Did
lately felloniously steal in His own Hous a pack belonging to a choroke Indian
[. . .] Thomas Hugens Did uppon his Examination by me the Said 21th Day
of February Declare as followeth to wit that the Indians under the Conduct of
Richerd Smith onpacked ther Horses and spred There Goods in His yard and
further saith He never knew Smith or the Indian Mist aney thing until the next
Day Smith came Back to make Enquiry aughter the pack that wors Lost But
He could give Him no Intiligenc thereof he the Said Hugen Being Drunk and
not compus mentus all the time the Indian wors at His Haus and further this
Exeminant saith Not.

> Examination of Thomas Hugens Sr., February 21, 1759, Miscellaneous Records, Granville
> County Miscellaneous Papers, State Archives, Office of Archives and History, Raleigh.

The Examination of James Mitchell of Granvil County Taken before Mee
Robert Hicks Esqr. uppon oath the Said James Mitchel Dclareeth he Saw
aughter Hugens the sun of Thomas Hugens being about Eighteen Years old
as he believes take the Indians pack and taws it behind the Dore of the Hous
as he said Mitchel wors standing in the yard on which the Dore wors shut
about four Minutes then the Dore being opened and a Girl the Daughter of
Thomas Hugens being about Eleven years old came out of the hous with a
bundel under her arm Covered with an old gown or petticote which She
Carried of Som Distance to a branch The said Aughter Hugens called out to
Her obet it is now two late to wash it being then about Sunset Richerd Smith
aughter the Indians pack wors Missing come back to Hugenses and from

there to David Mitchells the Indian being with Him who owned the pack David Mitchel Informd Him that his Brother James Mitchel had seen the passage as [above related] on which Smith sent for James Mitchel to Go up to Hugenses with Him next morning which he Did but Hugens Denied He or aney of his family Had seen aney thing of the pack missing Aughter Hugens being than not at Home but Came home while they were there but wors verry unwiling to come to the hous His Mother Called out to him [. . .] you wors seen to have the Indians pack Mr. mitchel says he Saw the Indians pack opened which he took to be the same that Aughter Hugens tawsed behind the Dore and that he saw the following goods in it to wit 1 Remnant Red strouds and 1 Ditto blew 1 Remnant white Linning 1 french blanket 1 pipe Hatchet and the Chekerd shirt and farther This Examinant Saith not.

Examination of James Mitchell, February 21, 1759, Miscellaneous Records, Granville County Miscellaneous Papers, State Archives.

Longing to see battle, the Cherokees who left their towns and traveled to the Virginia backcountry in aid of the British considered themselves underutilized and underpaid as the campaigns of 1757 and 1758 ended. Some warriors vented their frustration, as they made their way home during the summer of 1758, by stealing the horses of frontier Virginians. Settlers and Indians were slain. When news of the killings reached their nation, Cherokee war parties set off in revenge. Governor William Henry Lyttelton of South Carolina urged the headmen of the Middle and Lower towns to recall their warriors and promised presents to the relatives of the victims. But he also warned that if hostilities did not cease, the Cherokees would be crushed.

To the Head-Men and Warriors of the Middle and Lower Settlements of the Cherokee Nation. The Governor of South Carolina Sends Greeting. Friends and Brothers.

The Warrior at Fort Prince George has sent me an Account of some new disturbances that have happen'd in Virginia, in which I am Sorry to hear that some of your people have been kill'd. I desire you will mark well the words I now write to you and lay them up in your hearts.

The fire that was kindled many years ago by our Fathers and your has long burnt bright between us And the Chains of Friendship which the Great King George has fixed is unsullied and free from Stain, but that it may always remain so, you may remember how often it has been concluded in publick Talks and Solemn Treaties. That whenever it shou'd happen that a Red Man was kill'd by a White, it shoud not be a Cause of War between the two Nations, but the Red people shoud Apply to The Kings Governor for Satisfaction. Notwithstanding which I am now inform'd That bad Talks have been given in some of your Towns against the people of Virginia and that some parties have taken up the Hatchet and are gon to Spill their blood, Mark again what I say to you, I have sent a Messenger to the Governor of Virginia to inform him of these things and am Confident he will give you entire Satisfaction for whatsoever Injuries have been done to you; And as a further mark of the desire I have to remove from you all Cause of complaint, I do hereby promise that If you will dispatch Runners to bring back those parties that are gone out, so that they may return without having made the path bloody, I will give presents to the Relations of your People that have been Slain. Sufficient to hide the bones of the dead Men, and wipe away the Tears from the Eyes of their friends. But if you shall refuse to make up the Matter in an Amicable way and shall Shed the blood of the Virginians, Mark again what I say to you, The Armies of the Great King are Strong and mighty. His Warriors are without number, well Arm'd, well Cloath'd, well fed, and Supplied with all the necessaries of War; but you are few, and will soon be in want of every thing when once the Trade is withdrawn from you. The English are the only Nation that can furnish you, and are willing to continue to do it, If you do not prevent them by your own faults; but if you do, you will remember my words and repent your rashness when it is too late. The Governor of Virginia has given no Orders to his People to fall upon yours, but what they have done was their own private Act.

Letter from Governor William Henry Lyttelton, Charleston, September 26, 1758, Colonial Office 5/376, British Records, State Archives, Office of Archives and History, Raleigh.

Lyttelton's promise of gifts calmed some Cherokees. Others, particularly the young warriors of the Overhills, remained dissatisfied and demanded vengeance for the deaths in Virginia. The French based nearest to them turned that anger to their advantage, sending sympathetic Creek Indians to persuade the Cherokees to strike back. The visit in March 1759 by the Mortar, leader of the pro-French Creeks, was especially effective: within a month, headmen and warriors from the Overhill town of Settico left on a purported hunting trip that resulted in the massacre of more than a dozen colonists along the Yadkin and Catawba rivers. Once again, terrified homesteaders sought refuge among the Moravians.

April 24. In the evening we heard that yesterday and the day before yesterday four persons were killed on the Yadkin, 30 miles from here, by Indians, believed to be Cherokees. [. . .]

May 6. Sunday. In the evening singstunde Br. Rogers spoke on the Text for the day: "Strong is thy dwelling place, and thou puttest thy nest in a rock," Num. XXIV, 21. It was very comforting, for shortly before the service a man had arrived in great consternation, bringing with him a little child that he had found alone in a house. He said that the people on the Yadkin were much excited about the Cherokees, who were killing every one they met; and that several families would arrive here during the night for protection,—which also came to pass.

May 7. The text for the day was again comforting and encouraging: "Peace be within thy walls, and prosperity within thy palaces." Ps. CXXII, 7. The alarming news of yesterday was much modified today, when it appeared that some distance beyond the Hollow traces of Indians had been seen, though it was not known that they had done any mischief. Nevertheless eight more families came to us and were lodged in the small cabins at the mill. [. . .]

May 9. In the afternoon Br. Jacob Loesch received a note from our sheriff, Mr. Hughes, saying that his house was surrounded by Indians, and asking that some of the refugees with us would come to the rescue of himself, his family, and the six men who were with him. Br. Loesch read the letter to the men in the evening, and a party at once rode to the home of the sheriff; the Indians fled at their approach, and the family was saved.

May 10. The three Hauser families, and many others, came to us today, so that the cabins at the mill shelter three or four families apiece, and altogether there are about 120 souls there. [. . .]

May 22. Many of the refugees are going home. It is reported that the Cherokees have made peace; and the unrest in the land has been largely the result of the blind alarm of the settlers, who believed every rumor.

May 26. Several of our German neighbors, who returned to their farms the beginning of the week, have fled to us again in great excitement, for the Indians have killed a hunter on the Terraret, twenty miles from here, and another was badly wounded.

> Bethabara Diary, 1759, in Fries, *Records of the Moravians*, 1:209, 210-211. "The Hollow" stretched northward beyond the Virginia border from what is now Mt. Airy, North Carolina. The "Terraret" is the Ararat River.

French emissaries continued to incite the Cherokees. Meanwhile Lyttelton, having been informed of the actions of the warriors from Settico, halted trade with the town and ordered the interdiction of arms intended for the nation. He also demanded that the Cherokees surrender the perpetrators, but meetings in October 1759, between the governor and a delegation led by Overhill headman Oconostota, failed to resolve the matter. In a show of force, Lyttelton led well over 1,000 troops to Fort Prince George, amid the Lower Towns. He took the Cherokee delegates with him, professing concern for their safety among the irate colonists. On his way he met another Cherokee delegation, under Round O of the Out Towns. Initially bound for

Charleston, it too was persuaded to join the march. Shortly after they reached the fort, Attakullakulla arrived: the best friend the English had among the Overhills, he was empowered to negotiate terms on behalf of the nation. The treaty signed on December 26, 1759, named as hostages twenty-two of the Indians who had accompanied the governor. They were to be detained at the fort until a like number of Indians, responsible for the deaths of the Catawba and Yadkin settlers and others, had been delivered for punishment.

Treaty of Peace and Friendship concluded by His Excellency William Henry Lyttelton Esqr. Captain General and Governor in Chief of his Majesty's Province of South Carolina with Attakulla Kulla, (or the Little Carpenter) Deputy of the Whole Cherokee Nation and other Headmen and Warriors thereof at Fort Prince George the 26th. Day of Decr. 1759.

Article I. There shall be a firm Peace and Friendship between his Majesty's Subjects of this Province and the Nation of Indians called Cherokees; and the said Cherokees shall preserve peace with all his Majesty's Subjects Whatsoever.

II. The Articles of Friendship and Commerce concluded by the Lords Commissioners for Trade and Plantations With the Deputies of the Cherokee Nation, by his Majesty's Command, at Whitehall the 7th Day of September 1730 shall be Strictly observed for the Time to come.

III. Whereas the Cherokee Indians have at Sundry Times and Places Since the 19th Day of November 1758 Slain divers of his Majesty's good Subjects of this Province, and his Excellency the Governor having demanded that Satisfaction should be given for the same according to the Tenor of the Said Articles of Friendship and Commerce abovementioned; in Consequence whereof two of those who have been guilty of perpetrating the Said Murders have already been Delivered up to be put to Death, or otherwise Disposed of, as his Excellency Shall Direct. It is hereby stipulated and agreed, that twenty two other Cherokee Indians guilty of the said Murders, shall as Soon as possible after the Conclusion of this Present Treaty in Like Manner be Delivered up to Such Persons as his Excellency the Governor or the Commander in Chief of this Province for the Time being, shall appoint to receive them, to be put to Death or otherwise disposed of, as the said Governor or Commander in Chief shall Direct.

IV. The Cherokee Indians Whose Names are herein after mentioned Vizt.; Chenshi, Ousanatah; Tallichama, Talletake, Quarrasattahi, Connasoratah, Katactoi, Otassite of Watoga, Ousanoletah of Jori, Ousanoletah of Cowatache, Chisquatalone, Skiagusta of Sticoe, Sannoiste, Whohatche, Wocyoch, Oucah, Chistanah, Nicholche, Tony, Totaiah-hoi, Shaliloske, Chistee, shall Remain as Hostages for the Due Performance of the foregoing Article in the Custody of such Persons as his Excellency the Governor shall please to Nominate for that Purpose, and when any of the Cherokee Indians, guilty of the said Murders shall have been delivered up, as is Expressed in the said Article, an equal Number of the Said Hostages shall be forthwith set at Liberty.

V. Immediately after the Conclusion of this present Treaty, the Licensed Traders from this Government, and all Persons employed by them shall have Leave from his Excellency the Governor to return to their respective Places of Abode in the Cherokee Nation, and to carry on their Trade With the Cherokee Indians in the usual Manner according to Law.

VI. During the Continuance of the present War between His Most Sacred Majesty, and the French King, if any Frenchman shall Presume to come into the Cherokee Nation, the Cherokees, shall use their utmost Endeavours to put him to Death, as one of his Majesty's Enemies; or if taken alive they shall deliver him up to his Excellency the Governor, or the Commander in Chief of this Province for the Time being, to be Disposed of, as he shall Direct, and if any Person Whatsoever, either Whiteman or Indian, shall at any Time bring any Messages from the French into the Cherokee Nation, or hold any Discourses there in Favour of the French, or tending to Set the English and Cherokees at Variance, and Interrupt the Peace and Friendship Established by this Present Treaty, the Cherokees shall use their utmost Endeavours to apprehend Such Person or Persons, and Detain him or them, Untill they Shall have Given Notice thereof to his Excellency the Governor, or the Commander in Chief of this Province for the Time being, and have received his Directions therein.

Given Under my hand and Seal at Fort Prince George in the Province of South Carolina this 26 Day of December 1759 and in the thirty third year of his Majesty's Reign.

William Henry Lyttelton (LS)

By his Excellency's Command
Wm Drayton Secretary.

We Whose Names are underwritten do agree to all and every of these Articles, and do engage for ourselves and for our Nation, that the Same shall be well and faithfully performed. In Testimony whereof We have hereunto Set our hands and Seals the Day and Year abovementioned.

Attakulla Kulla (LS.), Katagusta (LS.), Oconostota (LS), Oconeca (LS), Otassite [*illegible*] (LS), Kilcannokeh (LS)

Colonial Office 5/19, British Records, State Archives, Office of Archives and History, Raleigh. Coweetchee ("Cowatache") had stood on the west bank of the Little Tennessee River, approximately three miles northwest of Cowee, in present-day Macon County, North Carolina.

The taking of hostages soon inflamed the backcountry, igniting a sub-conflict of the French and Indian War known as the Cherokee War. Cherokees killed upwards of fifty settlers along the frontiers of Georgia and South Carolina in January and February 1760, but the primary object of their anger was the garrison of Fort Prince George, which they had besieged. On February 16, Oconostota enticed the commander from the fort and into an ambush. The officer was mortally wounded. The garrison reacted by slaying the hostages, thereby galvanizing the entire nation. Cherokees attacked Fort Dobbs on February 27 and afterward drove North Carolina colonists from the Broad, Catawba, and Yadkin river valleys.

In Return to your Excellency's News I shall give you a little nigher home, for several Days I observed That a small party of Indians were constantly about the fort, I sent out several small parties after them to no purpose, the Evening before last between 8 & 9 o'clock I found by the Dogs making an uncommon Noise there must be a party nigh a Spring which we sometimes use. As my Garrison is but small, and I was apprehensive it might be a Scheme to draw out the Garrison, I took out Capt. Bailie who with myself and party made up ten: We had not marched 300 yds. from the fort when we were attacked by at least 60 or 70 Indians. I had given my party Orders not to fire until I gave the word, which they punctually observed: We recd. the Indian's fire: When I perceived they had almost all fired, I ordered my party to fire which We did not further than 12 Steps each loaded with a Bullet and 7 Buck shot, they had nothing to cover them as they were advancing either to tomahawk or make us Prisoners. They found the fire very hot from so small a Number which a good deal confused them; I then ordered my party to retreat, as I found the Instant our skirmish began another party had attacked the fort, upon our reinforcing the Garrison the Indians were soon repulsed with I am sure a considerable Loss, from what I myself saw as well as those I can confide in they cou'd not have less than 10 or 12 killed and wounded, and I believe they have taken 6 of my horses to carry off their wounded; The next Morning we found a great deal of Blood and one dead, whom I suppose they cou'd not find in the night. On my side I had 2 Men wounded one of whom I am afraid will die as he is scalped, the other is in a way of Recovery, and one boy killed near the Fort whom they durst not advance to scalp. I expected they wou'd have paid me another visit last night, as they attack all Fortifications by Night, but find they did not like their Reception.

Extract, Major Hugh Waddell to Governor Arthur Dobbs, February 29, 1760, in Saunders, *Colonial Records*, 6:229-230.

General Jeffrey Amherst, commander in chief of the British army in America, ordered 1,200 redcoats southward to punish the Cherokee nation. Landing near Charleston in April 1760, the soldiers under Colonel Archibald Montgomery were reinforced by forty Catawba scouts, a like number of Savannah River Chickasaws, and 335 South Carolina militiamen. They torched the Lower Towns from Estatoe to Keowee, then proceeded into the Middle Towns. Five miles south of Etchoe, on June 27, the army was attacked in the Little Tennessee Valley by a combined force of Cherokees, Creeks, and Choctaws.

[June] 27th. [. . .] —The number of *Indians* that attacked us this morning, are computed at 6 or 700, and there were some *Creeks* amongst them, as our guides inform us.—How many they lost is impossible to tell; but there must be at least 40 or 50 of them killed.—They had vastly the advantage of us, with their rifle-barrel'd guns, which did execution at a much greater distance than our muskets; besides they fought us in their usual way, and we gave them our fire by platoons.—Some of the *Indians* spoke *English*, and gave us very insulting language, the *Raven of Estahtowih* was with them: The *Young Warrior* seem'd to be their commander in chief; his voice was distinctly heard the whole time, bawling loudly to his people to *fight strong*, &c.

   South-Carolina Gazette, July 19, 1760. "Estahtowih" is Estatoe.

Although Montgomery's men overcame the enemy and destroyed Etchoe, the high number of wounded soldiers, challenging terrain, lack of support from North Carolina and Virginia, and instructions to report to Canada prevented the colonel from advancing against the Overhills. The following year Amherst sent an expedition, led by Colonel James Grant, back to South Carolina to vanquish the Cherokees. Like that of Montgomery, Grant's army included contingents of Native Americans prepared for battle.

Saturday 16th May
   [Fort Ninety-Six, South Carolina.] In the Evening all our Indians, consisting of Chikasas, Catawbas, Mohaks & Stockbridge, assembled near a great Fire & danc'd the War Dance with several others peculiar to themselves.
Monday 18th May
   The Indians assembled and Danc'd again as on Saturday.

   Christopher French, "Journal of an Expedition to South Carolina," *Journal of Cherokee Studies* 2 (Summer 1977): 279. The Indians with Grant were placed under the command of Captain Quentin Kennedy, British 17th Regiment of Foot. The people "peculiar unto themselves" may have been white regulars and militiamen, dressed and painted as Indians, who had volunteered as scouts. The Chickasaw warriors ("Chikasas") with Grant came from the parent nation, in what is now western Tennessee, as well as their principal eastern settlement in the Savannah River Valley. The eastern settlement resulted from South Carolina's invitation to the Chickasaws to relocate closer to the colony to protect its frontier and its western trade route; those who accepted moved in 1723 to the vicinity of modern-day Augusta, Georgia, and became known as the Lower, or Savannah River, Chickasaws. The British referred to Iroquois Indians loyal to the crown as Mohawks ("Mohaks"). Named for a Christian mission, the Algonquian-speaking Stockbridge Indians inhabited the Housatonic River Valley in the Berkshire Mountains of western Massachusetts.

As an officer in Montgomery's expedition of 1760, Grant knew that the rugged terrain gave him little choice but to follow his former commander's northwesterly course toward the Middle Settlements. By June 10, 1761, his army had advanced to within two miles of the site of the battle Montgomery had fought near Etchoe—and was itself ambushed on the Little Tennessee ("Cowhowie") River by the Cherokees. The attack was turned back, as it had been a year earlier, and Grant quickly pushed ahead to Etchoe and two other towns in the Middle Settlements, Tasse ("Tassie") and Nikwasi ("Nuscassee").

[June] 10th[, 1761]. As the Indians had not sent Deputys to sue for Peace, It was probable that they intended to make an Attempt to save thier Country, and as we had got so near thier Towns, it was next to a Certainty that the Attack would be made that Day. Before we moved the Troops were ordered to load for the first Time since they took the Field; the advanced Guard and Piquets having only been loaded till then. [. . .]

Before the Rear had moved out of the Ground of Encampment, a few Shots were fired at the Cattle Guard from a Hill, at a considerable Distance, where One of our advanced Guards had been posted during the Night. This was immediately reported. And as their first Act of Hostility seemed to point at our Provisions, the Rear Guards were reinforced with 50 Provincials.

The Indian Corps, which has been usefull, served as Flankers to the Line, and marched in the front of the advanced Guard of Light Infantry.

About half an hour after Eight in the morning a party of them fell in with a Body of the Enemy upon our Right Flank; Their being discovered Disconcerted them, a few Shots were Exchanged, and the Cherokees tho' Numerous, gave way; But the Yelp went from front to Rear of the Line upon both Flanks, Upon a Ridge of Mountains on our Right, and on the Opposite Side of Cowhowie River, which could not be passed, on our left. This Indian Cry served as a Signal for the Attack, and they began a pretty smart Fire but at a considerable Distance. Stoping and forming in disadvantagious Ground against an invisible Enemy could answer no good End; The Line of March was therefore continued, a Platoon of Light Infantry was sent to the River

Side with orders to cover themselves in the best manner they could, and to fire from time to time at the Enemy to prevent thier drawing nearer and becoming more troublesome. [. . .]

About half a Mile from the place where the Attack begun[,] There is a Ford, and on the Opposite Side a rising Ground; As soon as the Light Infantry got over, they were posted to cover the passage of the River.

The Royal, Burtons, and the other Troops, were formed in Columns as they came up, and continued in that position 'till the Rear had passed the River. The firing was pretty Smart 'till near Twelve oClock, and Popping Shots continued till after Two; which is hardly to be believed as our loss is so very inconsiderable. [. . .]

The Cherokees were so thoroughly foiled in this Attempt, that they were neither Able to get a Prisoner or a Scalp.

Tis difficult to Judge of the Number of an Indian Enemy, but from the Disposition they had made, 'tis probable there were at least 600 of them, and they had taken possession of as strong ground as can well be imagined.

Their Loss was probably considerable as they gave us no farther trouble.

The front arrived at Etchoe at nine at Night, The Troops were Encamped as they came up, and Fires were immediately made.

Orders were given to Colonel Middleton to remain with about 1000 Men as a Guard to the Wounded and Provisions; The rest of the Troops marched at half an hour after Ten, to surprise, if possible, the Towns of Tassie and Nuscassee; But tho' the last of those places is above 18 Miles from the place we were Attacked in, not a Soul was found in either of the Towns. The Reception the Indians met with in the morning, and this movement at Night, threw them into a Pannick, which they'll not get the Better of soon. [. . .]

12th. and 13th. We halted; The Corn about the Town [Nikwasi] was destroyed, Partys were sent out to burn the scattered Houses, and to pull up Beans, Pease, and Corn, and to demolish every eatable thing in the Country.

> Journal of the March and Operations of the Troops under the Command of Lieutenant Colonel James Grant of the 40th Regiment upon an Expedition from Fort Prince George against the Cherokee, War Office 34/40, British Records, State Archives, Office of Archives and History, Raleigh. "Cowhowie River" is the Little Tennessee. Tasse stood on the Little Tennessee River, approximately one mile south of Nikwasi, in present-day Macon County, North Carolina.

Establishing a base at Nikwasi, Grant and his men continued north, destroying towns and fields in the Middle Settlements and the Out Towns before returning to Fort Prince George on July 9.

[July] 3d[, 1761]. We halted to keep the Enemy in Suspence, [. . .]

Fifteen Towns and all the Plantations in the Country, have been burnt. Above Fourteen hundred Acres of Corn, Beans, Pease, etc. Destroyed. About

15000 People including Men, Women, and Children drove into the Woods and Mountains to Starve. They have nothing left to subsist upon but a few horses which they contrived to keep out of our Way; But we found the remains of numbers of them which had been killed by themselves almost in every place we went to. Luckily nothing was left to be done on this Side. It would have been impossible for us to proceed farther.

> Journal of Lieutenant Colonel James Grant, War Office 34/40, British Records, State Archives.

Extract of a Letter from an Officer in Colonel Middletown's Regiment, dated July 10, 1761.
[. . .]
During the whole march, we found no meat in the Indian houses but horse beef; their corn mortars seemed to have had no corn beat in them for some time: They appear to have subsisted chiefly on horse flesh, and for some little time past, on the stalks of young corn boiled. They have planted a prodigious crop of corn this year, in the settlements we saw; some of the fields are new, and on the sides and tops of the hills, said to be those of the Lower Townspeople, while the former inhabitants reserve for themselves the possession of the large and fertile valleys.

> *Pennsylvania Gazette*, August 6, 1761.

The desire for war dissipated. Grant had devastated the domain of the Middle and Out-Town Cherokees, and the Lower Cherokees had not recovered from the effects of the Montgomery expedition. The Over-hills discovered that the French could not fulfill their promises of arms or assistance, and they also concluded that they were engaged in a conflict against a too-powerful enemy. Leading a delegation of Cherokee headmen, Attakullakulla (also known as Little Carpenter) entered Fort Prince George on August 28, prepared to negotiate a peace agreement. Governor William Bull of South Carolina had sent an outline of a treaty to Colonel Grant, which included a demand that one chief from each of the four major divisions of the Cherokee nation be put to death. The provision was omitted from the final version of the treaty, which was approved on December 17, 1761. Henry Timberlake wrote that the Cherokees sought an end to the war in order to resume trade with the British.

Monday 31st August [1761]
The Little Carpenter with some other Warriors return'd to Camp to give Col. Grant an Answer to his Talk, & after a very artful Speech which show'd

they were by no means inclined to kill the four People requir'd of them, (nor do I suppose we should have let them carry it to the utmost extremity if they had wished (?)) Col. Grant told them that this Article had been agreed upon between him and the Governor, but that if the latter would give up that point upon their asking it at Charles Town (where they had agreed to go) he should be satisfied that they might depend upon their Persons being safe as also all his Countrymen provided they behaved as they should and did not steal our Horses in which Case he should order them to be shot. The Carpenter acknowledged the Justice of this procedure. He seem'd much pleas'd at having so great a prospect of making Peace between his Country & his Friends the English, he further promis'd not to prevent our taking any French people that might attempt to come into this Nation.

The Man killer of Nuquasse, when he found so great a prospect of Peace say'd it did not signify to disemble any longer since his Nation & the white Men was to have Peace, That he had been in the action on the 10th that he thought it his duty to fight for his Country, & he should always be ready to do it, that they had 33 Men killed in the Action besides many others, who they suppose dyed of their Wounds. That he was one of those who fir'd upon the Waggoner at Ayoree & show'd another Indian call'd The Man of the Valley, who [he say'd] had scalp'd him.

Christopher French, "Journal of an Expedition to South Carolina," *Journal of Cherokee Studies* 2 (Summer 1977): 292.

On my arrival in the Cherokee country, I found the nation much attached to the French, who have the prudence, by familiar politeness, (which costs but little, and often does a great deal) and conforming themselves to their ways and temper, to conciliate the inclinations of almost all the Indians they are acquainted with, while the pride of our officers often disgusts them; nay, they did not scruple to own to me, that it was the trade alone that induced them to make peace with us, and not any preference to the French, whom they loved a great deal better. As however they might expect to hasten the opening of the trade by telling me this, I should have paid but little regard to it, had not my own observations confirmed me, that it was not only their general opinion, but the policy of most of their head-men; except Attakullakulla, who conserves his attachment inviolably to the English.

Henry Timberlake, *Lieutenant Henry Timberlake's Memoirs, 1756-1765* (Johnson City, Tennessee: The Watauga Press, 1927), 96-97.

For the Cherokees, peace lasted fifteen years: incensed by the effects of the Henderson land purchase and incited by the British and their Indian allies, they had begun raiding settlements in the Carolinas and Virginia by the summer of 1776. At that time, the American colonies had been engaged in armed rebellion against Great Britain for more than a year. Both sides, in the beginning, had asked the Indians to remain neutral, but before the close of 1775, British authorities ordered Superintendent John Stuart to mobilize warriors for future military operations. Although men like Willie Jones of North Carolina attempted to change their minds—the Continental Congress had chosen Jones as its superintendent of Indian affairs for the Southern Department— many Indians supported the crown because of its efforts to curb trader abuses, the Royal Proclamation of 1763, and the desire to remain supplied with British goods.

Being Just returned from the Treaties held by the Commissioners, with the lower Cherokees, and the Creek Indians, I embrace the Opportunity, by Colonel Long, of inclosing the proceedings to you. We sent an Invitation to the Overhill Cherokees also; but they not only refused to come themselves, but used all their Influence to prevent the Lower Cherokees from treating with us, sending Runner after Runner to countermand their coming down, even when they had almost reached Fort Charlotte. [*illegible*] they were sincere at the time, but as the Overhills are the ruling Division, and as we have not Goods, either to make presents, or supply the Indian Trade, it is probable that, if these last attack the White people, they will draw the former into the same measure. When we asked the Reason of the non attendance of the Overhills, the Lower Cherokees were not very explicit; they said, it might be that they expected Ammunition and other things from Stewart, and were afraid to come to us, lest he should be offended, and with hold his presents from them; and perhaps it might be that they seem unfriendly, and meant to commit Hostilities against the White people: But the Lower Cherokees said, in this last Case, that they should desire of the Overhills, that the Mountains might be the Division between them, as they were determined to remain neuter, in the present Contest between Great Britain and the Colonies. The Good Warrior, of Kewee, refused to accept of the presents destined for him, and his people; however we, at last, prevailed on him to receive them, and we have not since heard any Complaints from the Lower Cherokees. Some time after the Treaty, Mr. Wilkinson, one of the Commissioners, who lives in Kewee, and went up from Fort Charlotte, with the Indians, sent a Messenger to us at Augusta, and informed us that a party of the Overhills had brought in one White Scalp, that it was received in the Council House, and a Dance was had in Consequence of it; which is an appro[val] [*illegible*] and amounts with them to a Declar[ation of] War. [. . .] We had Authentick Intelligence of the Arrival of Stewart's Brother among the Overhills, with 30, or 40 Horse Load of Amunition. He was accompanied by Nat. Gist, and one Colbert, two men who are equally unprincipled and formidable; they are deep in the Mistery of Bush fighting, conversant in the Manners and Customs of the Indians, and quite familiar to the Frontiers of North Carolina, and Virginia. Upon the whole I am of Opinion that the Overhill Cherokees either have already commenced; or will soon commence Hostilities; but where or against which particular province, I am at a Loss to determine. I conjecture that, whenever any one of the Southern Colonies shall be attacked on the Sea Coast, they will attack that same province on the Frontiers. Mr. Wilkinson promised to obtain Intelligence of their Motions as soon as possible; it might not be amiss to direct General Rutherfurd to send some trusty person to Kewee, for Information; it is not very far from Mecklinburg, and there is no Danger in going there at this time. Having now laid before your Honourable Board all that I know respecting the Cherokees, [. . .]

> Willie Jones to "Honoured Sir," June 2, 1776, Provincial Council of Safety Records, Secretary of State Records, State Archives, Office of Archives and History, Raleigh. Fort Charlotte stood along the Savannah River near present-day Mount Carmel, McCormick County, South Carolina; it now rests beneath the waters of Thurmond Lake. "Nat. Gist" is Nathaniel Gist, Indian trader and colonial soldier; he later joined the Continental Army. Gist is the reputed father of Sequoyah, creator of the Cherokee syllabary. "One Colbert" is James Colbert, trader to the Chickasaw Indians. He commanded the contingent of Chickasaw warriors from the parent nation during Colonel Grant's 1761 Cherokee expedition. In 1779 the British appointed Colbert assistant commissary to the Chickasaws.

HONERED GENTELMEN,

This is furder to acquent you of oure Trobles; this Day I Recd an Express from Colonel Backman and it gives me account, that Last Weak there Was 40 Indens on Crooked Creek and that one Middleton is kiled there – Indins Was seen meney miles furder Down the Cuttaba River. I am applid Daley tow for Relefe; ancesly wating for youre Instructions; pray send, if Possible at Lest 1000 lbs. more Powder, besides what you first Voted, for People in the frunters will move off if not suplid with that article. I Plead for Expedition, Mr Alston the berrer is appointd Commesare for a Large Number of men and as Salt is Not to be got without youre approbetion I Hope you will Give orders to the Marchants of Cross-Creek to Let the Commessarys of Salisbery District have at Lest 300 bushels, [. . .]

> General Griffith Rutherford to Council of Safety, July 12, 1776, in Saunders, *Colonial Records*, 10:662. Crooked Creek flows through what is now Buncombe and McDowell counties, North Carolina.

The Americans counterattacked. A three-pronged force descended on the Cherokee nation in September 1776: one column from South Carolina, led by Colonel Andrew Williamson, advanced to the northwest and into the Lower Towns, Middle Settlements, and Valley Settlements; a column from North Carolina, led by Griffith Rutherford, brigadier general of militia for the Salisbury District, marched westward and ravaged the Middle Settlements and Valley Settlements; and a third column, from Virginia and led by Colonel William Christian, focused on the Overhills. Williamson's army miraculously defeated a large war party that lay in ambush in a defile known as the Black Hole, near present-day Franklin, North Carolina, on September 19. Before linking up with Rutherford at Hiwassee on the twenty-sixth, the South Carolinians destroyed Cherokee towns and fields along the Valley and Hiwassee rivers in what is now Macon and Cherokee counties.

Thursday, the nineteenth day of September, 1776, we started to the vallies, and a most difficult road it was, marching along Tinnessy River or branch, called Cowechee; the path or road we marched led us into a long valley, or rather a hollow, surrounded by mountains on all sides, only the entrance. This place goes by the name of Black Hole, and well it deserves that title. But to proceed: on our entering, our front guard, commanded by Captain [Francis] Ross, was about half through these narrows, and seeing some very fresh signs of Indians, had a mind to halt, until the two wings, that is Colonel [Thomas] Sumpter and Colonel [Le Roy] Hammon[d]'s would come up even with him; [. . .] the aforesaid Captain, being about half through these narrows, the enemy was ambuscaded all around us, and not being discovered until Captain [Edward] Hampton, who was Captain of the main guard, and marched on the front of the right wing, had ascended up the mountain, when he espied Indians behind a tree. After this discovery he instantly fired at them. This alarm opened or rather emptied our enemy's guns. To our surprise they poured down their bullets upon us beyond the standing of any common soldiers; but we being resolute, were determined not to be conquered, [. . .] we, through mercy, defeated our enemies, with the loss of thirteen gallant men. [. . .] This engagement may be spoken of as a miracle, considering the multitude of enemies, and an admirable place they had to fire on us, that we were not almost all killed; for nature never formed such an advantageous place for our enemies, [. . .] This battle continued to the space of two hours very warm. [. . .] considering the advantage they had of us, on account of the situation of the mountain they were on, and likewise the grass being so admirably long, that they always had the first shot; and also the mountain being so steep, that they could handily clear themselves, so that we had, to appearance, but little chance with them. [. . .] there was no other way to conquer them than the method we took, which was to run right upon them as hard as we could run; for it would have been next to vanity to stand and fight them. But to be short, we cleared them off their mountain, without giving them much time as to take off all their luggage; for they left baggage of about two hundred of them, that is to say blankets, moccasins, boots, some guns, matchcoats, deerskins, &c., &c. [. . .]

Saturday, the twenty-first instant, [. . .] on a sudden the front espied an Indian squaw; at her they fired two guns, which put us all in an alarm, allowing it an attack, but soon found to the contrary. Seeing no more Indians there, we sent up one Bremen, a half Indian, that was in company, to ask her some questions; for although she was wounded in the shoulder and leg, yet she could speak, and told the interpreter as follows, viz.: That all the Over-Hill Indians, and the chief of the Indians of the towns we had gone through, were at that battle that was fought the day before; and further, that they were encamped about four miles ahead, and was preparing to give us battle by the river or waters of Tinnessy. Hearing this account we started, and the informer being unable to travel, some of our men favored her so far that they killed her there, to put her out of pain. [. . .]

Sunday, the twenty-second day of September, 1776, [. . .] we marched to the waters of Highwassa, and encamped between two mountains, after a day's march of nine miles.

Monday, the twenty-third, [. . .] we set off, and always minded to take possession of all the hills and mountains we came to. We crossed a small mountain named Knotty Hill; from thence we steered to another, where we had a full view of a town called Burning-town, distant from us about one mile. So took to the right to surround it, and continued in that course about half way. By this time we espied the main body of our army marching into it. The front of the town we took, where we got peaceably, without shooting a gun, though a large town, having upwards of ninety houses, and large quantities of corn; but they had cleared themselves, and took with them the chief of all their effects, save some of their horses. A party of Colonel [John] Thomas's regiment being on the hunt of plunder, or some such thing, found an Indian squaw and took her prisoner, she being lame, was unable to go with her friends; she was so sullen, that she would, as an old saying is, neither lead nor drive, and, by their account, she died in their hands; but I suppose they helped her to her end. Here we encamped among the corn, where we had a great plenty of corn, peas, beans, potatoes and hogs. This day's march about three miles.

Tuesday, the twenty-fourth instant, we were ordered to assemble in companies to spread through the town to destroy, cut down and burn all the vegetables belonging to our heathen enemies, which was no small undertaking, they being so plentifully supplied. So after accomplishing this we were ordered to march. By this time there was an express arrived from the North army that gave us the following intelligence, viz.: That the first town they came to they surrounded it, and killed and took the number of sixteen Indian fellows and squaws, without the loss of one man, the enemy not being apprized of their coming. After this agreeable account we started, and came along a small mount, called by them Bloody Hill; and so on to another town, called Timossy, distance two miles, and encamped.

Wednesday, the twenty-fifth of September, 1776, we engaged our former labor, that is, cutting and destroying all things that might be of advantage to our enemies. Finding here curious buildings, great apple trees, and, whiteman-like, improvements, these we destroyed, and marched down said vallies to another town named Nowyouwee; this we destroyed, and all things thereunto belonging, distant two miles. From hence we started to another town called Tilicho, a brave plentiful town, abounding with the aforesaid rarities; I may call them rarities; why so? because they are hemmed in on both sides by or with such large mountains, and likewise the settlements of the soil, yielding such abundance of increase, that we could not help conjecturing there was great multitudes of them; the smallest of these valley towns by our computation, exceeded two hundred acres of corn, besides crops of potatoes, peas and beans. [. . .] I am next to inform you that we marched to another town called Cannastion, and encamped; this day's march six miles.

Thursday, the twenty-sixth, we started, and marched about two miles to another town called Canucy; here we stopped to destroy their handy work. From thence to another town named Ecochee; here we stopped, and served it as the last mentioned. From hence we steered to another, called Highwassah, where we met the North army, and encamped. This evening, we had the prayers of Mr. [James] Hall, a Presbyterian minister, being in the North army, where Brigadier General Rutherford brought us sixteen prisoners, that is to say, Nathan Hicks, Walter Scot, Matthew McMahan, Richard Rattleiff, William Thomas, Godfrey Isacks, and Alexander Vernon, Hick's old squaw, named Peg, Scot's squaw and two children, one Indian fellow, named the Barking Dog, Charles Hicks, and one old squaw; these prisoners were committed to our care to secure or commit them for punishment according to their deserts, being confederates or assistants to the Indians.

Excerpts from Captain Francis Ross's journal of the Williamson expedition against the Cherokees, September 21-26, 1776, in E.F. Rockwell, ed., "Parallel and Combined Expeditions Against the Cherokee Indians in South and in North Carolina, in 1776," *Historical Magazine and Notes and Queries*, New Series, 2 (October 1867): 217, 218-219. Knotty Hill and Bloody Hill cannot be identified. Burningtown stood on Burningtown Creek in present-day Macon County, North Carolina. Williamson's forces ravaged the Tomassees in Macon County. "Nowyouwee" is Neowee; "Tilicho" is Little Tellico; and "Cannastion" is Connostee. "Canucy" may be Clenussee, which stood near present-day Murphy. Ecochee cannot be identified.

The actions of the Carolinians dispersed the Cherokees farther into the mountains. Rutherford sent Captain William Moore and a body of troops on a mopping-up expedition along the Tuckaseegee and Oconaluftee rivers.

[. . .] Agreeable to your Orders I Enlisted my Company of Light horse men, and Entered them into Service the 19th of Oct. From thence we prepared ourselves and Marched the 29th Same Instant as far as Catheys fort, Where we joined Capt Harden, of the Tryon Troops, and Marched Over the Mountain to Swannanoa. The Next day Between Swannanoa & French Broad River we Came upon fresh Signs of five or six Indians, [. . .] we pursued our march as far as Richland Creek, where we Encamped in a Cove for the Safety of our horses; but in Spite of all our Care, the Indians Stole three from us that Night by which we perceived that the Enemy was alarmed of our Coming. We followed their Tracks the next day as far as Scots place, which appeared as if they were Pushing in to the Nation Before us Very fast & Numerous. From Scots place we took a Blind path which led us Down to the Tuckyseige river through a Very Mountainous bad way. We Continued our march Very Briskly in Expectation of Getting to the Town of Too Cowee before Night. But it lying at a Greater Distance than we Expected, we were Obliged to tie up our Horses, & Lay by till Next morning [. . .] we came upon a Very plain path, Very much used by Indians Driving in from the Middle Settlement to the Aforesaid Town. We Continued our march along sd path about two Miles, when we came in Sight of the town, which lay Very Scattered; [. . .] our small army consisting of but 97 men, we found we were not able to surround it, So we concluded and rushed into the centre of the town, in Order to surprise it. But the Enemy Being alarmed of our coming, were all fled Save two, who Trying to make their Escape Sprung into the river, and we pursued to the Bank, & as they were Rising the Bank on the Other Side, we fired upon them and Shot one of them Down & the Other Getting out of reach of our shot, & Making to the Mountain, Some of our men Crossed the river [. . .] & headed him, Killed & Scalped him with the other. Then we Returned into the town, and found that they had Moved all their Valuable effects, Save Corn, Pompions, Beans, peas, & Other Triffling things of which we found Abundance in every house. The town consisted of 25 houses, Some of them New Erections, and one Curious Town house framed & Ready for Covering. We took what Corn we stood in need of, and what Triffling Plunder was to be got, and then set fire To the Town. Then we concluded to follow the Track of the Indians [. . .] We Continued our march about a Mile, and then we perceived a Great pillar of Smoke rise out of the mountain, which we found arose from the Woods Being Set on fire with a View as we supposed to Blind their Track, that we could not pursue them; Upon which Capt Mcfadden &

Myself took a small party of men in Order to make further Discoverys, [. . .] We marched over a Large Mountain & Came upon a Very Beautiful River which we had no Knowledge of. We crossed the river & Immediately Came to Indian Camps which they had newly left; we went over a Second mountain into a large Cove upon South fork of sd river where we found [. . .] Several Camping places & the fires Burning Very Briskly. Night Coming on we were Obliged to Return to our Body A While Before day. When day appeared we made Ready and marched our men Until the place we had Been the Night Before. Our advance Guard Being forward Perceived two Squaws and a lad, who Came down the Creek as far as we had Been the Night Before, and when they Perceived our Tracks they were Retreating to the Camp from whence they Came, which was within 3 Quarters of a mile. The Signal was Given, then we pursued and took them all three Prisoners. Unfortunately our men shouted in the Chase and fired a Gun which alarm'd them at the Camp & they Made their Escape into the Mountains. The Prisoners led us to the Camp where we found abundance of plunder, of Horses and other Goods, to the amount of Seven Hundred Pounds. We took some horses Belonging to the poor Inhabitants of the frontiers which we Brought in, & Delivered to the owners. Our provisions falling short, we were Obliged to steer homeward. [. . .] we steered our course about East & So. East two days thro' Prodigious Mountains which were almost Impassable, and struck the road in Richland Creek Mountain. From thence we marched to Pidgeon River, Where we Vandued off all Our Plunder. Then there arose a Dispute Between me & the whole Body, Officers & all, Concerning Selling off the Prisoners for Slaves. I allowed that it was our Duty to Guard Them to prison, or some place of safe Custody till we got the approbation of the Congress Whether they should be sold as Slaves or not, and the Greater part Swore Bloodily that if they were not sold as Slaves upon the spot, they would Kill & Scalp them Immediately. Upon which I was obliged to give way. Then the 3 prisoners was sold for £242. The Whole plunder we got including the Prisoners Amounted Above £1,000. Our men was Very spirited & Eager for Action, and is Very Desirous that your Honnour would order them upon a second Expedition. But our Number was too Small to do as Much Execution as we would Desire. From Pidgeon river we marched home and Every Man arrived in health and safety to their Respective Habitation.

Report of Captain William Moore to General Griffith Rutherford, November 17, 1776, in Saunders, *Colonial Records*, 10: 895-897.

Spurred by the successes of the British army in the southern colonies and the prospects for increased trade, and angered by encroaching white settlement, the Cherokees in late 1780 resumed their raids. As in

1776, North Carolina mobilized its militia and attacked Cherokee towns. Governor Alexander Martin wrote to Old Tassel in the autumn of 1782, promising to have intruders removed and urging the Cherokees to resist the influences that jeopardized peace. Martin's missive also refers to the deference that state lawmakers were willing to show Congress in matters involving Native Americans. Less than ten years later, the United States concluded a peace treaty with the Cherokees in which it declared itself to be their sole protector and forbade any state or person from negotiating treaties with them.

PHILADELPHIA, February 14.

By a Gentleman just arrived from Virginia, we are informed that the Cherokees, having taken up the hatchet, were proceeding to the frontiers of Virginia and North Carolina; that Col. [Arthur] Campbell, with the Washington County[, Virginia] militia, and about 500 North Carolina militia, had marched up to the Indian settlements, killed 30 Indians, took about 30 prisoners, and destroyed 23 of their towns, together with their corn, &c. This account was from an officer on the expedition to the Governor of Virginia, which arrived just before the gentleman came away.

Pennsylvania Gazette, February 14, 1781.

TO THE OLD TASSEL AND OTHERS, THE WARRIORS OF THE CHEROKEE NATION.

Brothers:

I have received your talk by Col. Martin on behalf of yourself and all the Cherokee Nation; I am sorry that you have been uneasy and that I could not see you this last Spring as I promised you, as our beloved Men met at Hillsborough had prevented me, by agreeing and concluding among themselves that the great Council of the thirteen States at Philadelphia should transact all affairs belonging to the Red People, particularly respecting trade, peace & friendship, by which my power was suspended until the last meeting of our said beloved Men at New Bern, when they thought it was too much trouble for persons to come to Philadelphia to do the business, we could ourselves with much more ease; and accordingly I am authorized to talk to you on every subject that may concern our mutual interest and happiness.

Brothers:

It gives me great uneasiness that our people trespass on your lands, and that your young men are afraid to go a hunting on account of our People ranging in the woods & marking your trees; these things I can assure you are against the orders of your Elder Brother, and are not approved of by me and the good Men of North Carolina, but while we were consulting our Council at

Philadelphia our bad Men living near your lands thought we had laid aside all Government over them, and that they had a right to do as they pleased & not willing to obey any law, for the sake of ill gain & profit care not what mischief they do between the Red & White People if they can enrich themselves, but Brothers, I know your Complaints and will endeavor to set your minds at ease by again ordering off all these persons from your lands who have settled on them without your consent. Your friend, General Sevier, is made our first warrior for the Western Country, to whom Col. Martin carries my particular directions to have these intruders moved off. [. . .]

Brothers:

In the mean while I beg you will not listen to any bad talks which may be made by either Red or White People which may disturb our peace and good will to each other, and should mischief be done by any of our bad people be patient until you see me or hear from me, and you may be certain your Elder Brother of North Carolina will do everything in his power to give your minds satisfaction.

I am told the Northern Indians have sent you some bad talks, but do not hear them, as they wish to make variance between all the Red & American people without any provocation. But should they take up the hatchet against us, I shall be happy we can still take you by the hand in love & friendship, and let them seek their own destruction; this must certainly be the case as the people of the Thirteen United States could not be conquered by the Great King of England and his Warriors, the first and most terrible over the Big Waters, and who made all Nations before them tremble by their dreadful ships & many men; what can the power of those unfriendly Indians do when opposed to so many tried warriors as will be immediately called out against them should they persist in their evil designs?

Brothers:

Col. Martin, your friend, has told me your grievances; I wish to redress them as soon as possible. [. . .] Bad men may make you uneasy, but your elder Brother of North Carolina has you greatly in his heart, and wishes to make you sensible of it.

Governor Alexander Martin to Old Tassel, [1782], in Clark, *State Records*, 19:949-951.

Colonial Interaction

When the first Europeans arrived in what is now North Carolina, Native Americans welcomed them as they would visitors from another Indian nation: hospitably. They aided the whites' survival in the early days of exploration and settlement, acting as guides to the land and its unique flora and fauna. Later, Native Americans and colonists cooperated as trading partners and as allies in war. The Hatteras received powder and shot in exchange for ranging against enemy Indians, and North Carolina paid bounties to Native Americans who killed vermin.

North Carolina ss. To Mr. Anthony Hatch Marchent Late powder Receiver In Little River

You are hereby directed and Required for the use of the Hatteras Indyans that they may not be unprovided to serve the publick if occasion requires to deliver unto Captain John Oneale Commander on the banks and of the Indyans abovesaid twenty pound of powder and forty pounds of shott with one hundred flints [. . .] this 5th day of September 1720.

> Instructions to Anthony Hatch from Charles Eden, governor of North Carolina, September 5, 1720, Treaties, Petitions, Agreements, and Court Cases, Indians, Miscellaneous Papers, Colonial Court Records 192, State Archives, Office of Archives and History, Raleigh.

Chapter VI.
An Act for destroying Vermin in this Province.

[. . .]

II. [. . .] if it be a Servant, Slave or Indian, that shall kill any such Vermin, of which the Head or Scalp shall be produced, as aforesaid, the Master or Owner of such Servant or Slave, or he that makes claim for such Scalp or Scalps, in Behalf of an Indian, shall make Oath, before such Magistrate, that he verily believed the same was taken and killed within the Parish where the Reward is claimed: Which Oath being administered to the Person who makes the Claim, the said Magistrate is hereby directed to give the said Person a Certificate, in Words at length, for the same, which done, the said Magistrate shall immediately cause the Head or Scalp to be destroyed by burning the same.

> Laws of North Carolina, 1748, in Walter Clark, ed., *The State Records of North Carolina*, 16 vols. (11-26) (Raleigh: State of North Carolina, 1895-1906), 23: 288.

However, as described elsewhere in this volume, interaction with newcomers also brought trouble to Native Americans. For the indigenous peoples it meant the introduction of diseases for which they had no cure, resulting in their deaths by the thousands. Colonists settled the land they inhabited and hunted upon, causing resentment and in some cases precipitating open warfare. Many Indians developed a dependence upon alcohol, and some ran afoul of North Carolina law.

The Examination of John Cope a Christian Indian belonging to King Blounts Towne taken before John Lovick and Thomas Pollock Junior Esqrs. On Friday the 5th day of Augt. 1722.

The Examinant being asked what he intended by his breaking into the Presidents room the Night before did not deny the fact but [said] in his Excuse he was drunk which was all the Confession he would make.

> Examination of John Cope, August 5, 1722, Treaties, Petitions, Agreements, and Court Cases, Indians, Miscellaneous Papers, Colonial Court Records 192, State Archives, Office of Archives and History, Raleigh. King Blount's Town, or Ucohnerunt, had stood at the confluence of Town Creek and the Tar River in present-day Edgecombe County, North Carolina.

At a Speciall Court of Oyer and Terminer held at Edenton on the twenty fifth day of August Anno Domini One thousand seven hundred and twenty Six Present The Honorable Christopher Gale Esqr. Cheif Justice, Thomas Lovick, Henry Bonner Esqrs. Assistants.

[. . .]

The Jurors for Our Sovereign Lord the King on their Oath do present that George Senneka an Indian Man of Bertie precinct not having the fear of God before his eyes but mov'd by the instigation of the Devil and his own cruel feirce and Savage nature Videlicet in Bertie precinct aforesayd on or about the twenty fifth day of July One thousand seven hundred and twenty Six by force and Arms an Assault did make upon one Catherine Groom the Wife of Thomas Groom of Bertie and on two Infant Children Daughters of the Sayd Thomas and Catherine Groom with an Axe of the value of two shillings which in his hand he then hand [*sic*] he the sayd George feloniously Voluntarily and of malice forethought in Bertie precinct aforesayd Struck and barbarously wounded the Sayd Catherine on the head and also the sayd two infants with the Said Instrument then and there in like manner did wound So that of the Sayd Cruel wounds the sayd Catherine and the sayd two infants did then and there instantly dye and So the Jurors aforesayd on their Sayd Oath do say that the sayd George on the sayd Twenty fifth day of July in the sayd precinct of Bertie the aforesayd Catherine Groom and the sayd two female Children in manner aforesayd and of malice fore thought feloniously and voluntarily did kill and murder against the peace of Our Lord the King that now is his Crown and dignity and Sign'd Wm. Little pro Domino Rege Attorney General.

To which Indictment the Sayd George Senneka upon his Arraignment pleaded Guilty.

Judgment To be Hang'd.

Special Court of Oyer and Terminer, August 25, 1726, in Robert J. Cain, ed., *North Carolina Higher Court Records, 1724-1730*, vol. 6 of *The Colonial Records of North Carolina* [*Second Series*], ed. Mattie Erma Edwards Parker, William S. Price Jr., Robert J. Cain, and Jan-Michael Poff (Raleigh: State Department of Archives and History, [projected multivolume series, 1963–], 1981), 281-282.

Although Native Americans were the victims of colonization in many ways, they also adapted to and used white institutions. For example, some resorted to the courts to redress wrongs. Indian Tom Harris complained in 1703 that Matthew Winn stole his pig. The Yeopim Indians sued Daniel Civile for two years' back rent in 1715, and the Chowans sought an attachment against the estate of John Sale. Indian Thomas Duren attempted to have Indian John Robin pay an overdue promissory note in 1733. A disagreement with James Bennett, a Chowan, prompted Henry Hill to damage the Indian's corn crop; eventually the two had patched their differences sufficiently to allow each to swear for the other in regard to Bennett's alleged involvement in a burglary. The state ordered William Butler to pay damages for assault and battery to Tuscarora John Smith in 1778.

Tho. Barcock Aged 60 years or thereabuts being Deposed and sworn saith that a bout 3 a yeare ago he gave to tom Harriss an Indian a sow Shote and after he had had itt a Considerable time it Run from him and was Gott amongst Mathew Winns hoggs and the Indian Coming to me Desird me to go to Mathew Winns with him to gett the Shote being marked a Cropp Lefte Eare and 2 Slitts in the Cropp an over keel and under keell in the Right and Mathew Win Yeilded to Deliver the Shote to the Indians but never had it till Daniell Phillips Recoverd it by a Warrant from Jno. Jenins and Further saith not.

Deposition of Thomas Barcock, 1703, in William S. Price Jr., ed., *North Carolina Higher Court Records, 1702-1708*, vol. 4 of *The Colonial Records of North Carolina* [*Second Series*], ed. Mattie Erma Edwards Parker, William S. Price Jr., Robert J. Cain, and Jan-Michael Poff (Raleigh: State Department of Archives and History, [projected multivolume series, 1963–], 1974), 54.

No. Carolina Ss. Att a Court of Chancery holden at the house of Captain Richd. Sanderson on little River upon Thursday the 10th day of March 1714/15 Present the Honorable Charles Eden Esqr. Governor Captain Generall and Admirall, Thomas Pollock, N. Chevin, C. Gale, Frans. Foster, T. Knight.

Daniel Civile being brought before this Court by Vertue of a Warrant from the Honorable Nathl. Chevin Esqr. to Answer to the Yawpim Indians who likewise Appeared and Complained that the Said Civile was Indebted to them the Said Indyans in the Sum of Three pounds to be paid in Indyan Corn at Tenn Shillings per Barrel for Two Years Rent of their Town Land and the Matter being heard and debated on both Sides before this Court the said Complaint Appears to be Just[.]

Therefore it is hereby Ordered and Decreed that the Said Daniel Civile do pay unto the Said Yawpim Indyans the Said Summ of Three Pounds in Corn at the Rate of Tenn Shillings per Barrels as aforesaid with Costs Alias Execution.

> Court of Chancery, March 10, 1714/15, in William S. Price Jr., ed., *North Carolina Higher Court Records, 1709-1723*, vol. 5 of *The Colonial Records of North Carolina* [*Second Series*], ed. Mattie Erma Edwards Parker, William C. Price Jr., Robert J. Cain, and Jan-Michael Poff (Raleigh: State Department of Archives and History, [projected multivolume series, 1963–], 1977), 498.

<*Hitaw v. Sale. Attachment.*> John Hitaw King or Cheif man of the Chowan Indians comes by Edward Moseley his Attorney to prosecute an Originall Attachment granted to him by Christopher Gale Esqr. Cheif Justice against the Estate of John Sale for the sum of Eleven pounds returnable to this Court wherein the said John Complaines that Whereas the said John Sale should render unto him the sum of Eleven pounds which to the plaintiffe he oweth and from him unjustly detaineth for that to witt that whereas the said Defendante the tenth day of May One thousand Seven hundred and twenty two by his Note on Thomas Copping dated the Same day and year at Chowan aforesaid and here in Court produced did acknowledge himself indebted to the plaintiffe the Said Sum of Eleven pounds Nevertheless the said Thomas Copping the said Sum of Eleven pounds to the said plaintiffe did not pay nor this defendante hath not as yet paid but the same to pay hath denyed etc.

> General Court, Edenton, March 1723, in Price, *Higher Court Minutes, 1709-1723*, 365. John Hoyter ("Hitaw") won his suit.

North Carolina Chowan si October Court Anno Domini 1738

Thomas Duren Indian Complains of John Robin of the Precinct and province aforesaid Indian in Custody of (and so forth) for that whereas the said Defendant on the Eighth day of February in the year of our Lord one Thousand Seven hundred Thirty Three four at the precinct aforesaid made his Certain promissary Note or Script in writing Signed by him the said Defendant and here in Court produced bearing date the day and year aforesaid and by the said Note the said Defendant Did oblidge himself to pay or Cause to be paid to Thomas Du[ren] Indian the full sum of Eight Pounds Ten Shillings Currant bill Money of North Carolina for Value received By reason whereof the Defendant became and is yet liable to pay to the plaintiff the said Sum of Eight Pounds Ten Shillings as aforesaid According to the Tenour and Effect of the said note and being so liable he the said Defendant in Consideration thereof afterwards (to witt) on the day and year aforesaid at the precinct aforesaid assumed and faithfully promised to pay to the plaintiff the said Sum of Eight Pounds Ten Shillings as aforesaid according to the Tenour and Effect of the said note Nevertheless the said Defendant his promise and assumption aforesaid not regarding but Contriving and fraudulently intending the Plaintiff to Defraud and deceive the said Sum of Eight Pounds Ten Shillings as aforesaid hath not yet paid (tho often thereto required) but the same to pay hitherto hath refused and doth Yet refuse to the Plaintiffs Damage Twenty pounds as thereupon he Brings this suit (and so forth).

Duren v. Robin, October 1738, Chowan County Civil Action Papers, State Archives.

North Carolina Chowan County ss. July Quarter Sessions Anno Domini one thousand seven hundred and forty Seven.

The Jurors for our Sovereign Lord the King and the Body of the County of Chowan do present upon their Oath that Henry Hill of the Parish of St. Paul in the said County on the nineteenth Day of May in the twentieth Year of the Reign of our Sovereign Lord King George the Second, with Force and Arms at the Parish aforesaid in the County aforesaid unlawfully broke and entred the Close or Corn field of James Bennett a Chowan Indian in the Parish aforesaid in the County aforesaid and then and there cutt, dugg, houghed up and spoiled the Corn of the said James in the said Close or Cornfield then and there growing of the value of fifty Shillings lawful Money of Great Britain and other Injuries to the said James then and there did against the Peace of our Sovereign Lord the Now King [*torn*] and Dignity.

Dom. Rex v. Henry Hill, July 1747, Chowan County Criminal Action Papers, State Archives, Office of Archives and History, Raleigh.

September the 5th 1753
Timothy Walton, Marias Blanshard, Jno. Hubbard and James Gordon being in presence, with Mr. Henry Hill, Senior and the said Henry Hill Senior being then a Prisoner, taken by the above said, Jno. Hubbard Constable Very Early the same Morning, Each and Every of us heard him Say these Words, or to the Same purpose.

That on Saturday Night Last past, One James Bennet an Indian and the said Henry Hill, was together Drinking at the house of said Henry, and the said Indian, told Henry Hill, that the Store of Thos. Walton, was broke Open, and that he the said Indian was afraid they would Lay it upon him, to Which the Said Henry Answerd, You Need not be afraid, for they Can't hurt You, to which the said Indian Replyed, You and Me both here Drunk together, You Can swear for Me, and Me for You. This was Stood in to be Said on the Saturday Night, and was Repeated three or four times together, and Mr. Timothy Walton, Taking the said Henry Hill, up, in his Words (and I Likeways puting in a Word, he then Says, don't Mistake me, it was Sunday Night, and he the said Henry Hill told me Jas. Gordon particularly on the Road Coming to Justice, that the Words was Spoken on Monday Night by the said Indian, and further these deponents Saith Not.)

> Deposition of Henry Hill, September 5, 1753, Miscellaneous Records, Chowan County Miscellaneous Papers, State Archives.

North Carolina ss. The State of North Carolina. To the Sheriff of Bertie County Greeting. We command you that of the Goods and Chattels, Lands and Tenements, of William Butler late of your County (in your Bailiwick) you cause to be made the sum of Six pounds one Shilling which lately in our County Court [of] Quarter Sessions, of the trial at Windsor [our] Attorney recovered against him for the Costs and Charges of a Certain Bill of Indictment found against him by the Grand Inquest of our said County for and assault and Battery committed on the Body of one John Smith and Indian of the Tuskurorah nation whereof he the said William Butler is convicted, and liable, as to us appears of Record; and have the said Monies before our said Court, at Windsor aforesaid, on the Second munDay of August next, to render to the said Attorney his Costs, and Charges aforesaid. And have you then and there this Writ. Witness John Johnston Clerk of our said Court, at Windsor the XIV Day of Nov in the II Year of our Independence Anno Dom. 1778.

> Writ, November 14, 1778, *State of North Carolina v. Butler*, Bertie County Criminal Action Papers, State Archives, Office of Archives and History, Raleigh.

Like African Americans, slave or free, Native Americans did not enjoy legal equality with white North Carolinians. The colony banned them from casting ballots for members of the lower house in 1715. Marriage with whites was prohibited, and Indian men who sired children with white indentured women had their offspring indentured by the county court for thirty-one years. Native American slaves found guilty of mismarking livestock received harsher sentences than white male-factors. North Carolina passed laws which stated that Indians could only bear witness against African Americans and other Indians. Later,

during the Revolutionary War, the state prevented Native Americans from serving in the militia.

CHAPTER X.
(Repealed by His Majesty's Order)
Act Relating to the Biennial & Other Assemblys &
Regulating Elections & Members.

[. . .]

V. And It Is Hereby Further Enacted by the Authority aforesaid that no person whatsoever Inhabitant of this Government born out of the allegiance of His Majesty & not made free; no Negroes, Mulattoes, Mustees or Indians shall be capable of voting for Members of Assembly; & that no other person shall be allowed or admitted to vote for Members of Assembly in this Government unless he be of the Age of one & twenty years and has been one full year in the Government & has paid one year's levy preceding the Election.

Laws of North Carolina, 1715, in Clark, *State Records*, 23:12-13.

CHAPTER I.
An Act Concerning Marriages

[. . .]

XIV. And be it further Enacted, by the Authority aforesaid, That no Minister of the Church of England, or other Minister, or Justice of the Peace, or other Person whatsoever within this Government, shall hereafter presume to marry a white Man with an Indian, Negro, Mustee, or Mulatto Woman, or any Person of Mixed Blood, as aforesaid, knowing them to be so, upon Pain of Forfeiture and paying, for every such Offence, the Sum of Fifty Pounds, Proclamation Money, to be applied as aforesaid.

Laws of North Carolina, 1741, in Clark, *State Records*, 23:160.

CHAPTER VIII.
An Act to prevent stealing of Cattle and Hogs, and altering and defacing Marks and Brands, and mismarking and misbranding Horses, Cattle and Hogs, unmarked and unbranded.

[. . .]

II. [. . .] and it is Enacted [. . .] that if any free Person or Persons shall steal any Neat Cattle or Hog, or shall alter or deface the Mark or Brand of any other Person or Persons' Horse, Neat Cattle, or Hog, such Person or Persons, being thereof lawfully convicted, shall, for every Neat Cattle or Hog, he or they shall steal; or for every Horse, Mare, Colt, Neat Cattle, or Hog whose Brand or Mark he or they shall alter or deface, over and above the Value of such Neat Cattle or Hog so stole, or for every Horse, Mare, Colt, Neat Cattle, or Hog, whose Mark or Brand they shall alter or deface, forfeit and pay the Sum of Ten Pounds, Proclamation Money; [. . .] and the Offender shall, over and above the said Fine, receive Forty Lashes on his Bare Back, well laid on, and for the Second Offence, shall pay the Fine above mentioned, and stand in the Pillory Two Hours, and be branded in the left Hand, with a red hot iron, with the letter T; [. . .]

X. And be it further Enacted, by the Authority aforesaid, That if any Negroe, Indian or Mulatto Slave, shall kill any Horse, Cattle, or Hog, belonging to any Person whatsoever, without the Consent of the Owner or Owners thereof, or shall steal, misbrand, or mismark any Horse, Cattle, or Hog, such Slave or Slaves shall, for the First Offence, suffer both his Ears to be Cut off, and be publickly whipt, at the Discretion of the Justices and Freeholders before whom he shall be tried; and for the Second Offence, shall suffer Death: And the Tryal and Conviction of the said Slave or Slaves, shall be in such Manner as is prescribed by an Act of Assembly, intituled, An Act concerning Servants and Slaves.

Laws of North Carolina, 1741, in Clark, *State Records*, 23:166, 167.

CHAPTER XXIV.
An Act Concerning Servants and Slaves.

[. . .]

XVIII. [. . .] if any Woman Servant shall hereafter be delivered of a child, begotten by her Master, such Servant shall immediately after Delivery be sold by the Church Wardens of the Parish where the Offence is committed for One Year, after the Time of Service by Indenture or otherwise is expired, and the Money arising by such Sale shall be for the use of the Parish: And if any White Servant Woman shall, during the Time of her Servitude, be delivered of a Child begotten by any Negro, Mulatto or Indian, such Servant, over and above the Time she is by this Act to serve her Master or Owner for such Offence, shall be sold by the Church Wardens of the Parish, for Two Years, after the Time by Indenture or otherwise is expired: and the Money arising thereby applied to the Use of the said Parish; and such Mulatto Child or Children of such Sevant, to be bound by the County Court until he or she arrive at the age of Thirty One Years.

[. . .]

L. And to the End such Negro, Mulatto or Indian, bond or free, not being Christians, as shall hereafter be produced as an Evidence on the Tryal of any Slave or Slaves for Capital or other Crimes, may be under the greater Obligation to declare the Truth; Be it further Enacted, That where any such Negro, Mulatto or Indian, bond or free, shall, upon due Proof made, or pregnant Circumstances, appearing before any County Court within this

Government, be found to have given a False Testimony, every such Offender shall, without further Tryal, be ordered by the said Court to have one Ear nailed to the Pillory, and there stand for the Space of One Hour, and the said Ear to be cut off, a nd thereafter the other Ear nailed in like manner, and cut off, at the Expiration of one other Hour; and moreover, to order every such Offender Thirty Nine Lashes well laid on, on his or her bare Back, at the common whipping Post.

LI. And be it further Enacted, by the Authority aforesaid, That at every such Tryal of Slaves committing Capital or other Offences, the first Person in Commission setting on such Tryal shall, before the Examination of every Negro, Mulatto, or Indian, not being a Christian, charge such to declare the Truth.

Laws of North Carolina, 1741, in Clark, *State Records*, 23:195, 202-203.

CHAPTER II.
An Act to fix a Place for the Seat of Government, and for keeping Public Offices; for appointing Circuit Courts and defraying the Expence thereof; and also for establishing the Courts of Justice and regulating the Proeceedings therein.

[. . .]

L. [. . .] all Negroes, Mulattoes, bond and free, to the Third Generation, and Indian Servants or Slaves, shall be deemed and taken to be Persons incapable in Law to be Witnesses in any Cause whatsoever, except against each other.

Laws of North Carolina, 1746, in Clark, *State Records*, 23:262.

CHAPTER XXIV.
An Act to amend an Act, intituled, "An Act to regulate and establish a Militia in this State."

[. . .]

VII. And be it further enacted by the authority aforesaid, that no Frenchman, Spaniard, British deserter, Hessian deserter, Indian or slave, shall in future be received by any militia officer as a substitute for any militia soldier or officer, under any pretense whatsoever.

Laws of North Carolina, 1780, in Clark, *State Records*, 24:335-336.

The Indians who were the least free under the law were slaves. Since the inception of the colony, landowners in North Carolina had held Indians as slaves, but the practice sharply decreased with the decline in the Native American population and the transition to captive African

labor. Indian slaves were almost exclusively women and children: enslaved hundreds of miles from home, it was presumed that their lack of knowledge of the land would stifle any attempt to return to their clan. However, neither distance nor measures imposed by the colony prevented some Indian slaves from escaping.

July 5, 1716

Sir

Having this opportunity have consigned to you [*illegible*] to dispose of for my best advantage and lay out the nett produce in likely young Indian Slaves not under twelve nor Exceeding twenty years of age if you can have them or as near there unto as you can And send them in to me by the first safe opportunity.

> Letter of July 5, 1716, Thomas Pollock Papers, State Archives, Office of Archives and History, Raleigh.

To the Right Honnorable Philip Ludwell Gov[ernor] of the province of Carolina and to the Honnorable [*torn*] Humbley showeth the Humble petition of Henery Norman

That your petitioner haveing a man Servent an Indian called Georg West Who Runaway in September Last [past] Contrey to Law Feloniously Carryed away From your Honnors petetioner along With him these goods hereafter specified viz. one Conew one gunn one Linsy and wolsy Blankit one payre of Lether Briches one payre of White yoyrne Stockings one payre of mans shooes one Leather Apron one homespunn Cloth west Coate Linen with wollin two womans Shifts the one Dowlis the other Garlents one ozenbrigs shift marked with H N one blew shirt Carpenders broad Ax one Joyrne squere one payre of Joyrne Compessas one gouge one Joynter plane two Ojres one hand saw Phile one small Auger two Chisell For which Servent and goods your petitioner Humbley Craves an order From your honors if they may bee Found within this Government and as in Dutty bound shall Ever pray.

Henery Norman his mark

> Letter of Henry Norman, [1689-1694], in Mattie Erma Edwards Parker, ed., *North Carolina Higher Court Records, 1670-1696*, vol. 2 of *The Colonial Records of North Carolina* [*Second Series*], ed. Mattie Erma Edwards Parker, William C. Price Jr., Robert J. Cain, and Jan-Michael Poff (Raleigh: State Department of Archives and History, [projected multivolume series, 1963–], 1968), 326-327.

Chapter XLVI.
(Repealed by Act 4 April, 1741, ch. 24.)

[...]

VIII. And Be It Further Enacted by the Authority afors'd that no Master nor Mistress Nor Overseer shall give leave to any Negro, Mulatto or Indyan Slave (except such as wait upon their persons or wear Liverys) to go out of their Plantations without a Ticket or White servant along with them which Ticket at least the name of either the Master, Mistress or Overseer shall be subscribed & therein shall be incerted the place from whence he came & whether going under the Penalty of Five Shillings besides the charge of paying for the taking up of such slave or runaway.

Laws of North Carolina, 1715, in Clark, *State Records*, 23:63.

No. Carolina sc. At a Council held at the Council chamber in Edenton the 28th day of October Anno Domini 1724. Present The Honorable George Burrington Esqr. Governor etc. J. Lovick, E. Moseley, T. Pollock, R. West, Ths. Harvey, A. Goffe, W. Maule Esqrs. Members of the Council.
[...]
Read the Petition of John Royall concerning his Indian Slave named March being detained from him at the Tuscarora Town by King Blount.

Ordered That King Blount be Summoned to Attend this Board at the next Setting of the Council and that he bring with him the said Royalls Servant named March to answer the said Complaint.
[...]
At a Council held at the Council Chamber in Edenton the 3d day of August Anno Domini 1725.
[...]

King Blount the Chief Man of the Tuskororoes Indians appearing upon notice given him to Shew Reasons why he detained an Indian Slave named March now belonging to Mr. Francis Pugh and it being demanded why he did not bring in the said Slave He gave for Answer, that the said Slave was gone quite away from his Towne with the Senneca Indians, but assures this Board that he will Secure the said Slave named March the first time he can light on him and bring him in to answer the said Complaint and Submit to the Judgment of this Board.

Cain, *Records of the Executive Council, 1664-1734*, 147, 159. Resootska ("the Tuscarora Town") stood on Indian Creek in what is now Bertie County, North Carolina.

Indian and African slaves worked together—and occasionally committed crimes together.

North Carolina
Complaint being made that two Negroes and one Indian man belonging to James Coale have in the absence of their Master and Mistres robed the house and Caryed away severall Goods and a trunk with wearing Cloaks. [. . .] 26th of 5th month 1698.

> Warrant, Slaves, pertaining to runaways, sale, and trade, ownership, etc., Miscellaneous Papers, Colonial Court Records 192, State Archives, Office of Archives and History, Raleigh.

May the 4th. [General] Court Meet. Present: Capt. Henderson Walker Capt. Jno. Hunt Capt. Thomas Luten Mr. Jno. Hawkins Mr. Jno. Durant Justices.
Presentment is made by the Grand Jury last Generall Court against Capt. Anthony Dawson of the Precinct of Pequimons David Blake Thomas Young Henry Hamond of the precinct of Couratuck One Indian of Jacob Peterson and One Negro of the said Capt. Anthony Dawson for and that they on the fourth day of February last past in the precinct of Couratuck aforesaid in and upon one ship of War of our Soveraigne Lord the King on the Sea Shoar in the precinct of Couratuck aforesaid by force of the Wind and Sea driven and being and of all her owne men deserted with her Guns armes furniture stores Sailes Rigging and apparel habiliments of War and Ensignes of our Soveraigne Lord the King theron being remaining and standing with force and arms did enter and Maliciously advisedly and Wickedly contrive consult plot and conspire the said ship utterly to demolish and burne and destroy which to perpetrate and accomplish on the sixth day of February aforesaid the Ensignes of our Soveraigne Lord the King upon the said ship being and standing did Pull downe and remove and the Sailes Rigging and ornaments did spoil and deface and her Hul and bottom did cut and the said ship did with one great Gun shoote through etc.

> General Court, May 4, 1698, in Mattie Erma Edwards Parker, ed., *North Carolina Higher Court Records, 1697-1701*, vol. 3 of *The Colonial Records of North Carolina* [*Second Series*], ed. Mattie Erma Edwards Parker, William C. Price Jr., Robert J. Cain, and Jan-Michael Poff (Raleigh: State Department of Archives and History, [projected multivolume series, 1963–], 1971), 216-217.

Government leaders in the southern colonies became wary of any potential relationship between Native Americans and Africans, either slave or free. Fearing the two groups would unite to smite white colonists, colonial officials attempted to keep them separate.

May it please your Honour,

This House hath received Information that there are two Negro Slaves in the Cherokee Nation, which belong to one of the Indian Chiefs now in Charles Town; and as we are of Opinion it may be of dangerous Consequence to suffer those Slaves to cultivate an Acquaintance with the Cherokees; we must desire that your Honour will be pleased to purchase them from the said Indian Chief, at the Expence of the Public of this Province; and to order them to be brought down to be shipped off and sold in some of the Northern Colonies or the Islands, as the only Means to prevent their being any Ways mischievous to his Majesty's Subjects of this Province.

> The 27th day of May, 1741
> By Order of the House
> William Bull Junr. Speaker

J. H. Easterby, ed., *The Journal of the Commons House of Assembly, May 18, 1741-July 10, 1742, Series 1* (Columbia: The Historical Commission of South Carolina, 1953), 46.

Several Indian slaves sought their freedom through the colonial courts. James Manly convinced a Craven County justice that he had been born free but was forced into bondage. Ben and Limerie argued that they should be manumitted because their mothers had been free Indians. Quakers in Perquimans County petitioned to permit the manumission of Peter because he had performed "Several Meritorious Actions."

<*State of North Carolina Craven County*> To the Worshipfull the Justices of Craven County.

The Petition of James Manly an Indian humbly represents to your Honor that he was free born at Edenton and that he never has been Guilty of any Action by which his Freedom can be forfeited by any of the Laws of this or any other of the United States of America.

Your Petitioner further begs leave to inform your Worships that he has lived some Time past at Broad Creek and that on or about the [*blank*] Day of [*blank*] a Certain John Garland came to the dwelling House of the said James Manly and forcibly drove him away and sold him as a Slave to Colonel Levi Dawson for the Consideration of one hundred pounds specie.

Wherefore as your Petitioner is a Subject of this State and under the present happy Constitution humbly moves that this worshipfull Court will pass an Order for liberating or setting him free from the Service of Colonel Levi Dawson aforesaid and rastore him to his Freedom And as in Duty bound your Petioner will ever pray.

Jus. Cooke atty. for the Petitioner.

James Manleys Petition
December Term 1782.
James Gatlin and Levi Dawson
Read and Granted The Petitioner set Free
Christ. Healy C.C

Petition of James Manly, Indian, 1782, in Craven County Miscellaneous Papers, State
Archives, Office of Archives and History, Raleigh.

Sir,

In Regard to Ben a boy John Clark sold John Potter I Very well know and
his mother before him which was som talk of his Trying for his freedom and
was said that his mother Was a Indian but Regard to his Being free I know
nothing of and I Cant do him any manner of Service, But believe he has no
Manner of Chance to Get free Im Sr. your Servant.

James Clark

To Mr. John Penn
29 Octr. 1781

[Gr]anvile County Court Augt. 7th. 1782

A petition for freedom brought by Benja. Vicory against Potters eatr was
heard and tried this day and the Court was of opinion that the petitioner had a
right to his freedom from which Judgment the Defendants prayed an appeal.

On the trial James Smith in and minded as a witness who was upwards of
sixty years of age and being unable to ride as far as Hillsbgh on the motion of
the plaintiff his opposition was taken in open Court by order [of] the Court his
being duly sworn deposeth [and] saith that he acted as an overseer for [*torn*]d
Mr. Clark several years before his death and for some considerable time
afterwards for his widow that he knew the mother of the petitioner called
sarah that she was looked upon and understood to be the daughter of an
Indian free woman, that she often said she had a right to be free, and he has
frequently heard it said in the Family that she claimd his freedom that there
was some noise, that a certain person was about suing for her freedom at
which time it was observed by the old Lady or some of her [*torn*]ns that if she
did not get her cause tried before a certain old man died, whose nam[e] this
deponent forgets, who lived at a great distance from South Hampton from
whence the said woman was brought, that she would not be able to prove her
freedom, that the Family seemed very unwilling to talk publickly on this
subject, but rather inclined to keep it secret, that it was much talked of in the
neighbourhood that she ought to be free that on the death of the old woman
Mrs. Clark he was informed that the said woman Sarah and the petitioner were

allotted to John Clark, the[*torn*] the said Sarah had long hair and he believe[d] [*torn*] descended from an Indian from her [*torn*].

Augt. Court 1782 Sworn to in open Court in prese[nce] of Richd. Henderson.
Test. Reuben Searcy C.C.

John Potter one of the executors who was also present being ask'd if he wou'd consent that this Deposition Shou'd be read as evidence before the Superior Court refus'd and said he would not agree it should.
Test. Reuben Searcy C.C.

At a Court held for the County of [North]ampton the 10th. Copy of February 1757.
<*Indian Sarah plaintiff vs Sarah Clarke defendant*> In trespass Assault and Battery and Take imprisonment.

This day came the parties by their attornies and thereupon came also a Jury to wit Benjamin Williams etc. who being elected tried and sworn to by the issue joind between the said parties as aforesaid Miles Carey Gentleman attorney for the plaintiff to maintain the issue joind on the part of the said plaintiff gave in evidence to the said Jurors the deposition of Mary Hayes in these words to wit 'That about fifty Years past she knew an Indian Wench called Moll belonging to Captain Humphrey Marshall of Isle of Wight county in Virginia etc. she the said Moll had a female child called Sarah which child as she your deponent believes was afterwards the slave of Thomas Whitfield of Nansemond county in Virginia aforesaid but your deponent does not know of what tribe of indians the said wench Moll came from or of any pretension she the said Sarah hath to freedom and further saith not.' also the depositions of Cornelius Ratcliff, Rachael Norsworthy, John Sawyer and Mary Willson in the following words to wit 'Cornelius Ratcliff aged eighty two or thereabouts saith that this deponent knew that the mother of the plaintif Sarah did belong to one Captain Marshall and was always reputed to be his slave etc. he this deponent saith that he heard that the said Moll came from Cape Fear and further this deponent saith not. 'Rachael Norsworthy aged sixty nine or thereabouts saith she this deponent hath heard her mother say that her father bought the reputed mother of the plaintif and this deponent [*torn*] that she knows nothing of he[r] being free and further saith not. John Sawyer aged sixty six or thereabouts saith that he this deponent knew this Indian Moll the reputed mother of the plaintif Sarah and this deponent saith the said Moll was always a slave as far as he knew for Captain Marshall gave her away in his will as a slave and further this deponent saith. Mary Willson aged forty years or thereabouts saith that she this deponent has heard say that Moll the reputed mother of the plaintif Sarah was a Cape Fear Indian but she knows nothing of her being free and further saith not. Upon which the said Defendant by

Alexander Elmesly her attorney says the several matters and things by the said plaintif given in evidence as aforesaid are not sufficient to maintain the said issue on the part of the said plaintif nor by the Law of the Land is she bound to give any answer thereto. Wherefore for want of sufficient evidence in this behalf the said defendant prays Judgment that the jurors aforesaid may be discharged from giving their Verdict and the said action of the plaintif against her the said defendant may be quashed etc.

And at a Court held for the said County the 10th day of March 1757
This day came the parties aforesaid by their attornies aforesaid and the matters of Law reserved at the last Court to be argued being now fully debated by the council on both sides on consideration whereof it is the opinion of the Court that the demurrer is good Therefore it is considerd that the plaintif take nothing by her bill but for her false clamor be in mercy etc. And that the said defendant go hereof [*torn*] without d[el]ay and recover against the said plaintif her costs by her about her defence in this behalf espended etc.

R Kello C

Documents for Manumission of Ben, Miscellaneous Records of Slaves and Free Persons of Color, Granville County Miscellaneous Papers, State Archives, Office of Archives and History, Raleigh.

To the County Court now about to Sit in Perquimans
The Petition of the Several Subscribers Humbly Sheweth.
That whereas Samuel Smith a few Years ago Manumitted a Servant Man Named Peter (Whose Mother was an Indian and Father a Negroe) which Said Servant Man hath not been taken up nor Sold by the Court; And as he hath hitherto Always been an Orderly Servant and never that we know of bein Accused of any Villany, But on the Contrary Hath done Several Meritorious Actions in Destroying Vermin Such as Bears Wolves wild Cats and Foxes Therefore we pray that the Court may take it into Consideration and Order and Adjuje that he may remain Free and unmolested as long as he behaves himself well. And your Petitioners the Several Subscribers, as in Duty Bound shall ever pray.

April 6th. 1782. [. . .]

[*Endorsed:*]
Quaker Petition for Negro Peter
Petition to Perqs Court.

Petition for Emancipation of Peter, April 6, 1782, Slave Papers, Perquimans County, State Archives, Office of Archives and History, Raleigh.

Young Native Americans could be bound as indentured servants by their parents. Some, like Gobit, received favorable treatment from their masters. Servants who chafed at their condition, and fled, had the terms of their indentures extended after they were caught by the authorities. Jude Porrage sued for his freedom and failed, but Alexander the Indian won his case.

Ordered that Luke a Free Boy (Son of Phebe an Indian Woman) be Bound an Apprentice to Richard Ellis untill he attains the Age of Twenty One Years and that the Clerk prepare Indentures accordingly to learn the Trade of a Cooper.

Minutes of the Craven County Court of Pleas and Quarter Sessions, October 8, 1766, State Archives, Office of Archives and History, Raleigh.

The twenty fourth Day of June in the Year of our Lord one thousand seven hundred and four according to the Computation of the church of England, I Joseph Rodgers in the county of Bath in Pamlico and in the government of North Carolina being weak of body but in sound and perfect memory praised be God, do make and ordain this my last Will and Testament in manner and form following [. . .]

Item. I give to the Indian boy Gobit, two cows and calves, and one Sow and pigs, when he shall come to the age of twenty four years of age, if he shall serve honestly according to agreement.

Will of Joseph Rodgers, June 24, 1704, Beaufort County Original Wills, State Archives, Office of Archives and History, Raleigh.

Cap. Ebzr. Harker presented to this Court an Indian Man Servant of his that had been Run away from his aforesaid Master and the Courts Confering of the Costs and Damages that the aforesaid Harker had benn at Conserning the aforesaid Indian Servant man absenting him selfe from his Sarvis Ordered that the aforesaid Indian Man Named John Nead Alies Ned John Do Sarve his said Master or his assignes three years for his offence and that the Clark of the Court Draw Indenture for fore years he having one Year of his former time to be adde to the Indenture and that the said indenture be maid before Richd. Whitehurst, Esq.

Cary Godbee presented to this Court a Indian man Sarvant of his that Did Run Away with the above Said Sarvant of Capt Ebz Harkers the Court Considering of the Same Ordered that the Sad Indian Haniod Sollmon Poker Sarve his aforesaid Master three Years for his said offense and that Indenture be Made for six Years before Richd Whitehurst Esqr. there being three Years of his former time to be added.

Minutes of the Carteret County Court of Pleas and Quarter Sessions, September 2, 1730, State Archives, Office of Archives and History, Raleigh.

[3 June] Read the Petition of Jude Porridge Complaining against Majer Enoch Ward and this Court hath ordered that said Ward Appear tomorrow Morning to Answer said Petition.

[5 June] Mr. Enoch Ward was Called upon to Answer to the Petition of Jude Porridge and said Ward Appeared, and this Court hath ordered that said Jude Return into the Service of Mr. Ward and serve him after the Rate of forty five pounds per Annum until he pays the ballance of Mr. Wards Account and what said Ward hath assumed to pay for him to this day, and that said Ward pay the fees and Charge it to the Account of Jude porridge.

Minutes of the Carteret County Court of Pleas and Quarter Sessions, June 1742, State Archives. Enoch Ward purchased the indenture of Jude Porrage from James Rooks of Barnstable, Massachusetts, on November 25, 1730. Minutes of the Carteret County Court of Pleas and Quarter Sessions, December 1730, State Archives.

Alexander the Indyan by a Reference from the last Court Comes to prosecute his Suit against Juliana Lakar in a Plea of the Case and Complained That he the plaintiff Sometime in the Month of May in the year of our Lord god 1692 in and by a [retaining] writing obligatory Contracted to and with the Defendant to Serve her the Defendant the full time and terme of twelve yeares from the Date of the said Contract And the plaintiff Sayth That att the end or Expiration of the said Terme of Twelve yeares he the plaintiff was to be free and att Liberty And that the plaintiff hath Served the aforesaid terme and time according to Contract And that the Defendant hath detained the plaintiff a Servant one year over and above the time Spesifyed in the aforesaid Contract To his Damage Tenne pounds and prayes an Order for his freedom And for Plea the Defendant Cometh forth and Sayth that she never did by an writing obligation or Contract to nor with Saunders her Indyan for any turm of yeares nor never did assigne to any writing attaining to his Freedom Soe putts him to prove that She did and throws her self upon the Countey And the plaintiff likewise And the marshall was Commanded to Cause to forme twelve true and lawfull men of the [*illegible*] who neither in To whom in By whom the matter may be found And there Came mr. Isaac Wilson mr. Timothy Clare mr. William White mr. Patrick Eggerton mr. Richd. Davenport mr. pater jones mr. William Paryiter mr. Ralph Borfus [*illegible*] mr. Willm Bogue mr. John Hopkins mr. Thomas pierce and mr. Willm Moor who Impanells and Sworn Say wee of the Jury find for the plantiffe with Costs of Suit. Orderd that the plaintiffe be free from the Defendant And that the Defendant pay Costs to

Executor. And in Barr of all further proceedings the Defendant prayes an Appeall in to the next Honorable Court of Chancery which is Granted.

Minutes of the Perquimans County Court of Pleas and Quarter Sessions, October 10, 1705, State Archives, Office of Archives and History, Raleigh.

Like written laws and a system of courts, European religion was another facet of white culture that Native Americans encountered. Clergymen and some lay people attempted to lead them to Christianity, efforts that met with a degree of success. John Cope, mentioned above, was described as "a Christian Indian." Spanish explorer Juan Pardo left a Roman Catholic priest with the headmen ("caciques") whom he met in 1566, near modern-day Salisbury, and who insisted upon being catechized. Manteo was christened in 1587 by the English at Roanoke, albeit on Sir Walter Raleigh's order. Indians of the Albemarle region, among whom he traveled widely, listened attentively as Quaker missionary George Fox preached the gospel. But others plainly were reluctant to adopt a new religion. John Lawson encouraged Enoe Will to "become a Christian" after apparently misinterpreting the reason behind the Indian's fascination with a Church of England "Manual" that the former carried with him. Will politely declined the opportunity to convert, but did hope that his son could be taught to read.

The next day I arrived at Guatari, where I found more than 30 caciques and many Indians, to whom I made the customary speech. They remained under the dominion of His Holiness and of His Majesty. I was there 15 or 16 days, more or less. These caciques demanded of me that I give them someone to catechize them. Thus I left them the cleric of my company and four soldiers because there I received a letter from Estaben de las Alas that said that I should return to Santa Elena because that was suitable to His Majesty's service because there was news of Frenchmen.

"The Pardo Relation," [1566] in Charles M. Hudson, *The Juan Pardo Expeditions: Exploration of the Carolinas and Tennessee, 1566-1568* (Washington, D.C.: Smithsonian Institution Press, 1990), 312. Evidence suggests that Guatari stood near present-day Salisbury, North Carolina. The Spanish post of Santa Elena was located on present-day Parris Island, South Carolina.

The 13. of August, our Savage Manteo, by the commandement of Sir Walter Ralegh, was christened in Roanoak, and called Lord therof, and of Dasamongeuponke, in reward of his faithfull service.

"John White's Narrative of his Voyage," 1587, in David Beers Quinn, ed., *The Roanoke Voyages, 1584-1590*, 2 vols. (London: For the Hakluyt Society, 1955), 2:531. Dasemunkepeuc ("Dasamongeuponke") stood near present-day Manns Harbor, Dare County, North Carolina.

I went from this place among the Indians, and spoke unto them by an interpreter; showing them, "that God made all things in six days, and made but one woman for one man; and that God drowned the old world, because of their wickedness. Afterwards I spoke to them concerning Christ, showing them, that he died for all men, for their sins, as well as for others; and had enlightened them as well as others; and that if they did that which was evil, he would burn them, but if they did well, they should not be burned." There was among them their young king; and others of their chief men, who seemed to receive kindly what I said to them.

> Entry of November 1672, George Fox, *Journal of George Fox*, 2 vols. (London: Friends Tract Association: Edward Hicks, 1891), 2:185-186.

My Guide *Will* desiring to see the Book that I had about me, I lent it him; and as he soon found the Picture of King *David*, he asked me several Questions concerning the Book, and Picture, which I resolv'd him, and invited him to become a Christian. He made me a very sharp Reply, assuring me, That he lov'd the *English* extraordinary well, and did believe their Ways to be very good for those that had already practis'd them, and had been brought up therein; But as for himself, he was too much in Years to think of a Change, esteeming it not proper for Old People to admit of such an Alteration. However, he told me, If I would take his Son *Jack*, who was then about 14 Years of Age, and teach him to talk in that Book, and make Paper speak, which they call our Way or Writing, he would wholly resign him to my Tuition; telling me, he was of Opinion, I was very well affected to the *Indians*.

> John Lawson, *A New Voyage to Carolina*, ed. by Hugh T. Lefler (Chapel Hill: University of North Carolina Press, 1967), 57, 64-65.

The entity best organized to convert Native Americans to Christianity during the colonial period in North Carolina was the Society for the Propagation of the Gospel in Foreign Parts (SPG), the missionary wing of the Church of England. In a 1705 report, the SPG included the Tuscaroras among the North Carolina inhabitants in need of religious guidance. The agency also supported schools to educate and proselytize young Indians, especially boys. Edward Mashbourne founded a school at Sarum, near the Virginia boundary line, in the early 1700s; Chowan headman John Hoyter wished to have his son attend. The SPG endorsed Mashbourne's efforts—as well as those of "one Norris," who also proposed to establish a school for the Indians.

At a General Meeting of the Society for Propagating the Gospel in Foreign Parts, *Friday the* 16th *of* February 1705.
[. . .]
Carolina. <North with 3 Precincts Currituck, Paspitangh, Pequimimins, Chowan, Pamphlico, South>

Here are about Five Thousand Souls scatter'd l[ike] Sheep without a Shepherd, besides a great Num[ber] of *Tuskarora Indians*, who would gladly receive o[f] Missionaries.

> Annual Reports and Sermons, 1705, Sermons and Abstracts of Proceedings, Society for the Propagation of the Gospel in Foreign Parts, British Records, State Archives, Office of Archives and History, Raleigh.

<Of his Conference with a King of the Indians> I had Several conferences with one Thoms. Hoyler King of the Chowan Indians, who seems very Inclinable to embrace Christianity and proposes to send his Son to School to Sarum, to have him taught to read and write by way of foundation in order to a further proficiency for the reception of Christianity. I readily offer'd my Service to Instruct him myself he having the Opportunity of Sending him to Mr. Garats where I Lodge being but three miles distance from his Town. But he modestly declin'd it for the Present, till a General Peace was concluded between the Indians and Christians. I found he had some Notions of Noahs Flood which he came to the Knowledge of and Exprest himself After this manner—My Father told me I tell my Son. But I hope in a little time to give the Society a better acct. of him, as well as of those peaceable Indians under his Command.

> Reverend Giles Ransford to Secretary, SPG, July 25, 1712, in Robert J. Cain, ed., *The Church of England in North Carolina: Documents, 1699-1741*, vol. 10 of *The Colonial Records of North Carolina* [*Second Series*], ed. Mattie Erma Edwards Parker, William S. Price, Jr., Robert J. Cain, and Jan-Michael Poff (Raleigh: Division of Archives and History, Department of Cultural Resources, [projected multivolume series, 1963–], 1999), 143. "Sarum" was located at present-day Sarem, Gates County, North Carolina. "Mr. Garat" was Thomas Garrett Sr. The "General Peace" was a reference to the end of the Tuscarora War.

At a General Meeting of the Society for the Propagation of the Gospel in Foreign Parts, *Friday February* 20 1712/13
[. . .]

That Mr. *Mashbourne*, a School-master at *Sarum*, on the Frontiers of *Virginia*, neer *North-Carolina*, be encouraged; The Children under his Care being so well disciplin'd in the Principles of Religion, that the *Chowan* Indians, between two Towns of which he is scituate, would send theirs to him also, if they could be educated *gratis*; and for the Trouble of which, he requires no unreasonable Recompence; They have reciev'd an Offer likewise from one

Norris, towards erecting a School-house for the Children of some other Indians, his Son being expert in their Language; and whose Diligence, he hopes God will prosper with satisfactory success, in their *Instruction* and *Conversion*: [. . .]

Annual Reports and Sermons, 1712/13, Sermons and Abstracts of Proceedings, Society for the Propagation of the Gospel in Foreign Parts, British Records, State Archives.

Dr. Bray's Associates, the branch of the SPG committed to educating blacks and Indians in North America, offered financial assistance to the Reverend Alexander Stewart for a school in Mattamuskeet, Hyde County. However, the school failed after one year and attempts to establish others in eastern North Carolina were unsuccessful.

As soon as my Health would permitt, I sett out for the Benefitt of the Sea Air to a part of Hyde County call'd Atamuskeet, (this Place I formerly inform'd the Society, is seperated by an Impassable Morass from the Other parts of that County, and is only to be come at by Water, and upwards of 70 miles from Bath,) While I was there I preachd twice at the Chappel and baptized 64 White Children 1 adult White; 11 Black adults, and 11 do. Infants; and at the other Chappels in Hyde County 42 White Infants and 5 Black do.

The Remains of the Attamuskeett, Roanoke and Hatteras Indians live mostly, along that Coast mix'd with the White Inhabitants; Many of these attended at the place of public worship, while I was there, and behavd with decency, seemd desirous of Instruction and offerd themselves and their Children to me for Baptism; and after examining some of the adults I accordingly baptized, Six adult Indians; Six Boys; four Girls, and five Infants; And for their further Instruction at the Expence of a Society calld Dr. Brays Associates, who have done me the Honor of making me Superintendent of their Schools in this province have fixed a School Mistress among them to teach four Indians and two negro Boys; and four Indian Girls to read and to work, and have Supplied them with Books for that purpose, and hope that God will open the Eyes of the Whites every Where, that they may no longer keep the Ignorant in Darkness, but assist the Charitable Design of this pious society and do their best endeavours to increase the kingdom of our Lord Jesus Christ.

Rev. Alexander Stewart to Secretary, SPG, November 6, 1763, in Robert J. Cain and Jan-Michael Poff, eds., *The Church of England in North Carolina: Documents, 1742-1763*, vol. 11 of *The Colonial Records of North Carolina* [*Second Series*], ed. Mattie Erma Edwards Parker, William S. Price, Jr., Robert J. Cain, and Jan-Michael Poff (Raleigh: Office of Archives and History, Department of Cultural Resources, [projected multivolume series, 1963–], 2007), 357.

Attamaskeet, Feby. 22d, 1764

Sir

Having so good an Opportunity by Capt. Goddard, I have made bold to trouble You with this, and allso a List of what Indian Children hath been with Me to be School'd for this first Quarter just expired, As for Negroes, tho' their Masters might possibly give You some Promise to send, more, or less, and tho' some of them, made Professions of sending, both to Mr. Lockhart, and my self, Yet did they neglect the same, Neither have there been any More than Six Indians; But I assure You Sir, those People are not able to continue their Children, for if I had not fed them, three fourths of the time they did come, they must have gon with many a hungry Belly, those that are able to work must do something to prevent it, or they wou'd infallably be naked as well as starve for their friends are unable to maintain them, and those that cannot work are not Clothed sufficiently to withstand the Cold. This is realy the Case with them, As for their Capacities, there is not Objection more than Common with the White Children.

And as I have a Call to Core Sound which promises much more to my Advantage, than here I expect to move there, Early next month, I have therefore made bold, at the Bottom of the List, sent by Capt. Goddard, to request You will please to pay him forty five Shillings for this Quarter which is Due on Accountt of these Six Indians, that have been with Me; and if for it was in my Power to serve You in any Shape, at Core Sound, where I am design'd next Month, I shou'd think it, an Honor, to have yr. Commands, In the mean time, hoping You will please to favour my Request, By Capt. Goddard, I Beg leave to Remain, Sir yr., most Obedient humble servant.

Jams. Francis

[*Addressed*:]
To the Reverend Doctor
Alexr. Stewart
Aramaskeet Feby. the 20th, 1764.
Doctor Alexander Stewart, To James Francis   Dr.
£ s. d.
To the Schooling Six Indian Children Three Months, as Per 2. 5.
Agreement at 7/6 Each, Per Quarter.
A List of the above Six Indians, With their Entrance etc.
<*1763 Novr. 7th*> Then Entered for the Schooling, Two Indian Boys, Videlicet Solomon Russel, about 17 Years of Age and, John Squires about 16 Ditto. The Same Day Entered, Two Indian Girls, Videlicet, Bet Squires about 13 Years of Age and Poll. Mackey about 13 Ditto.

<Novr. 18> Then Entered Two Indian Boys Videlicet; Joshua Squires about 9 Years of Age and Bob. Mackey at 7 Ditto. All which made out their Quarter.

Jams. Francis

Sir,
Please to pay Capt. John Goddard the above Sum of Two Pounds five Shillings, and his Receipt Shall be a Discharge in full for the same from Feby. 20th, 1764. Sir, yr. very humble Servant.

Jams. Francis

[*Addressed*:]
To the Reverend Doctor Alexr. Stewart.

[*Endorsed*:]
Receiv'd Contents In full
John Goddard
Jas. Francis Rect. for
Attamuskeet School
Febr. 4th 1764
45*s*. proclamation money
33*s*. 9*d*. Sterling

> James Francis to Rev. Alexander Stewart, February 22, 1764, Papers of Dr. Bray's Associates, Society of the Propagation of the Gospel in Foreign Parts, British Records, State Archives.

Upon Shewing your letters, to some of the Inhabitants, I was fed up with Hopes of erecting three Schools in this and the neighbouring Counties in a Short time; but after I had distributed part of your Books among the School masters and encourag'd them all I could, I found at length that it was but Labour and Sorrow, owing to the mean, low Prejudices of the People of North America. I made one Short lived Effort, you may see by the Inclosed to erect a School (not altogether on the Societies plan) for the Instruction of ten Indian and negro Children at Attamuskeet in Hyde County; The master in the Letter signed Jas. Francis shews you the Objections of the people, and the Expectations we are to have.

> Rev. Alexander Stewart to Rev. John Waring, secretary to Dr. Bray's Associates, May 1, 1764, Papers of Dr. Bray's Associates, Society of the Propagation of the Gospel in Foreign Parts, British Records, State Archives. Stewart was writing from Bath, N.C., and referred to Francis's letter of February 22, 1764 ("the Inclosed"), printed above.

Governor Arthur Dobbs recommended that the SPG settle a school-master at a fort that North Carolina was constructing among the Catawbas during the French and Indian War. Dobbs even agreed to pay a portion of the salary, an offer he withdrew in 1762 after the nation, depleted by smallpox, had abandoned its towns and withdrew to South Carolina.

There is now a fort building among the Catawbees, and it is to be garrisoned, and is fix'd by the Indians consent in the midst of their Villages; he thinks this a proper opportunity to fix a Schoolmaster there to teach the Indian Children without taking them away from their Parents; if the Society would allow a Salary, and send over a proper Schoolmaster, the Governor promises to contribute £30 per annum Currency to promote so good a design, so long as he shall continue in that Government.

Whereupon it was Agreed to recommend to the Society to send over a Schoolmaster in the Holy Orders of our Church for the instruction of the Negro Children among the Catawbees, as soon as one duly qualified and willing to go over upon that Service can be procured, and they leave it to the particular consideration of the Society whether it may at present be proper to receive Mr. Read into the number of their Missionaries, and to inquire for proper persons to be sent over to Governor Dobbs to be fixed Missionaries in the Westward Parts of South [*sic*] Carolina.

Agreed [. . .] that a Schoolmaster in the Holy Orders of our Church be sent for the instruction of the Indian Catawbees Children, as soon as one duly qualified can be procured for that Service.

Journal of the SPG, April 21, 1758, in Cain and Poff, *Church of England, 1742-1763*, 179.

In my former Letter I proposed sending over a Schoolmaster with a proper Appointment to civilize and convert the Catawba Indians and that I would add to it during my Residence, that Nation consisted then of 300 Warriors in strict friendship with us, since that time by the small pox getting among them they are reduced to 60 Warriors with a proportional Number of old Men Women and Children, and have quit their Towns in this Province and have removed to So. Carolina, where they have laid them out a Township.

Gov. Arthur Dobbs to Secretary, SPG, March 30, 1762, in Cain and Poff, *Church of England, 1742-1763*, 312.

West of the Catawba nation, the Cherokees had entertained Christian missionaries. The Reverend William Richardson, a Presbyterian, preached briefly in the Valley section before he reached his destination in the Overhills. The Moravians at Salem baptized their first Cherokees in 1774 and had considered sending a missionary to the nation the following year, but their plans were thwarted by the start of the American Revolution.

Dec. 7. Passed thro the Valley where are several Towns; over one Mountain 5 Miles up & down & came to Mr. Butler's a Trader at Cheowee abt 22 Miles.

Dec. 8. At Mr. Butler's.

Sab. 10. Preached to a few white Peo: several Indians present who behaved well and after sermon Mr. Butler told them what I had said to them & talked to ym concerning God, the Author of all Mercies.

Dec. 11. Left Cheowee in ye afternoon; rode abt 7 Miles, Mr. Butler & Family in Company.

Diary of Reverend William Richardson, 1758, in Samuel Cole Williams, ed., "An Acocunt of the Presbyterian Mission to the Cherokees, 1757-1759," *Tennessee Historical Magazine*, second series, 1 (1930-1931), 131.

Jan. 11. Br. Marshall read the news from these to the Communicants, who were greatly interested. We were particularly glad to hear of the baptism of the first Cherokee Indians, Noah, and his wife Wilhlemine; and we wish for our neighboring Indian nation that the light of the Gospel may soon shine upon it.

Salem Diary, 1774, in Adelaide L. Fries et al., eds., *Records of the Moravians in North Carolina*, 13 vols. (Raleigh: Office of Archives and History, Department of Cultural Resources, 1922-2006), 2:815.

During a brief visit from a Chief of the Cherokee Nation, called Little Carpenter, who passed through Bethania on his return trip, he was asked whether, if a Brother should be sent to his Nation to teach them of their Creator, he would be kindly received; to which he replied that if Brethren came to instruct or teach their children they would be welcome.

Memorabilia of the Congregations and Societies in Wachovia, January 1775, in Fries, *Records of the Moravians*, 2:855.

Reservations

As a relative handful of whites attempted to convert Native Americans to Christianity, many more colonists wanted their lands. To preserve the fragment of territory that remained in the midst of colonial society, some nations agreed to live on reservations, hoping that the establishment of land boundaries by the colony would fend off further encroachment. North Carolina set aside acreage for the Yeopim and Machapunga (Mattamuskeet) Indians. However, the Chowans were displeased with the land allotted to them and complained to the Executive Council.

His Excellency The Right Honorable John Granville Esqr. palatin and the rest of the true and absolute Lords proprietors of all Carolina To all to whom these presents shall come Greeting in our Lord God Everlasting. Know You that we the said Lords and absolute proprietors according to our Great Deed of Grant bearing date the first day of May Anno Domini 1668 given to our County of Albemarle [unto our hands] and great Seal of our said province do hereby Give and Grant unto the King and Nation of the Yawpim Indians a Tract of Land containinge Tenne thousand two hundred and Forty Acres of Lannd [Exenge] and beinge on the North East side and south west side of North River Beginning att a pine and so North Tenne Degrees East four Miles and thence Chains there with Eighty Degrees that four miles to a Gum, then about tenne Degrees that three miles and three quarters to a Birch, Henry Cucocks line, then along the said Cucocks line south East eight poles, then south Eighty Degrees East three Miles and three quarters to the first station. The said Land being appointed Given and Granted to the said King and Nation of the Yawpim Indians. by an Order of Councill bearing date the last day of March 1703. And now in the [Title] and possession of them the King and Nation of Yawpim Indyans To Have And To Hold the said Land with all Rights and previlidges of Hunting, Hawking, Fishing Fowling [. . .] Given under the seal of the Colony the second day of October Anno Domini 1704.

Land Grant to Yeopim Indians, October 2, 1704, Book 1, p. 48 (microfilm), Camden County Deeds, State Archives, Office of Archives and History, Raleigh.

His Excellency John Lord Carteret Palatine and the rest of the true and absolute Lords proprietors of Carolina to all person to whome these presents shall come Greeting in our Lord God Everlasting Know bye that we the said Lords and absolute proprietors for and in consideration of the Sum of two Buck skins in hand paid to our Recever General by King Squires and the rest of the Indians commonly called the Mattamuskeet Indians, do hereby Give Grant sell, alien, enfeoff and confirm unto the said Squires and the rest of the

Indians commonly called the Mattamuskeet Indians a tract of Land lying and being at Mattamuskeet on Pamplycoe sound, containing by Estimation Ten Thousand two hundred and forty acres Beginning at the Mouth of old Mattamuskeet creek, runing up that creek and the Northermost branch of it to the head thereof, thence to the Lake So.West [*blank*] pole, then along the Lake Southerly to Matchapungo Bluff woods, then No. East to Pamlicoe Sound, from thence along Pamlicoe sound to the first station. To Have and to Hold the said Land with all rights and Priviledges of Hunting Hawking Fishing and Fowling with all woods, waters and rivers, with all profits and commoditys and Hereditaments to the same Belonging appertaining, Except one half of all Gold and Silver Mines unto heir the said King Squires and Mattamuskeet Indians his Heirs and assigns forever Yielding and paying unto us and our Heirs and Successors Yearly every 29th day of Septemr. The fee rent of one Shilling for every hundred acres Hereby Granted to be Holden of us our Heirs and Successors, in free and common sockage given under the Seal of the Collony, the first day of April, one Thousand seven hundred and twenty seven. Witness our Trusty and well Beloved Sir Richd. Everard Baronet Governor and the rest of our Trusty and well Beloved Councillors, who have hereuto set their Hands.

Land Grant to Mattamuskeet Indians, April 1, 1727, Book 2, pp. 149-150 (microfilm), Secretary of State Records, State Archives, Office of Archives and History, Raleigh.

North Carolina ss. To the Honorable President and Councill

The Humble Petition of Jno. Hoyter and Rest of the Chowan Indians in all Humble Maner Complaineing and shewing

That wheras upon the Humble Petition of the said Indians to this Honorable Board in the time when the Honorable Henderson walker Esqr. was President of the Councill An Order was past that the Surveyor Generall or Deputy should Lay out a tract of Land for the said Indians of six miles Square. And allso another Order in the time of the Honorable Landgrave Robt. Daniel Esqr. pursuant to the former Order.

In perseuance of the aforsaid Orders the Deputy surveyor Viz. Capt. Luten Came and undertook the said survey and by various Courses Did Lay out a tract of Land for the said Indians but wholly Contrary to the Intent and meaneing of the said Order for the Petitioners are very Confident that the Intent of the Councill was that such Land should be layd out for them as would produce Corn for theire Support and the petitioners Do say and are Ready to Averr that no part or parcel of the said Land in the said tract Layd out will produce Corn being all pines and sands and Deserts so that they have not theire Land according to the Intent and meaneing of the Honorable Board Neither for quality nor quantity it being not near six miles Square.

Wherefore Your Humble Petitioners Do Humbly Pray your Honors to take our Distressed Condition into your serious Consideration [*torn*] your Petitioners may have Releife in the Premisses Least [*torn*]erish for Bread.

And Yr. Petitioners shall Ever pray etc.

John <*his mark*> Hoyter

In Behalfe of himself and the Rest of the Nation

[1707-1708], Cain, *Records of the Executive Council, 1664-1734*, 637-638.

During the early eighteenth century the Meherrin Indians migrated southward from Virginia into the Albemarle region. Disputes between the Meherrins and North Carolina settlers prompted the colony to revise the boundaries of a reservation set aside for the nation in 1726. The new law did not eliminate friction between them and their white neighbors.

Whereas Complaint is made by the Meherrin Indians that the English people disturb them in their Settlements by coming to Inhabit and tend Corn among them and also that their Bounds allowed by order of Council Dated October the 26th 1726 and Did not Extend high Enough up from the Fork of Meherrin Neck for the remedying whereof.

Be it Enacted by his Excellency the Palatin and the rest of the true and absolute Lords proprietors of Carolina by and with the Advice and Consent of the rest of the Members of the general Assembly now met at Edenton for the North East part of said province That the Said Order of Council be Vacated and that the Indian bounds and limits shall be Extended as followeth Viz Begining at the Mouth of Meheri[n] River and so up the River to the Mouth of Horse pasture Creek formerly called Indian Creek then by the Said Creek up to the fork of it, then by the North Easterly Branch there of to the Head thereof then by a Strait Line a cross to Chowan river by the upper Line of Mulberry old Field Survey Saml. Powers Lands then along the Various Courses of the River to the first Station.

And be it also Enacted that all English people or any other living in the Said Bounds Shall move off and that no person but the Said Indians shall Inhabit or Cultivate any Lands within the Limits aforesaid while the Said Indians remain a Nation and live thereon and if any person offending against this Act, on Complaint made to Mr. John Boude who is hereby appointed Comissioner over the Said Indians to grant his Warrant to the Constable requiring him with aid if Needfull to remove such person at or before the twenty fifth of December next Ensuing and any person refusing or withstanding to remove Shall be brought before the Said Comissioner and upon his Conviction of the Same shall forfeit for the first offence Five pounds.

And if he shall still persist and refuse to go off from the Said Lands after warning from the Comissioner or his order for the Second offence shall forfeit the Sum of Ten pounds and for the third time of his so offending shall forfeit Twenty pounds and two Months Imprisonment, and give Security for his or their good Behaviour to be recovered by Bill plaint or information many Court of Record of in this Government Wherein no Essoign protection or wager of Law Shall be allowed or Admitted of.

And be it Further Enacted by the Authority aforesaid that the Said Comissioner is hereby Impowered and Ordered to reinstate and settle the said Indians in giving them Peaceable possession of the said Lands and Disposes and turns off any other person or persons Inhabiting within the said Bounds unless such Person or Persons have special leave from the Governour and Council for Continuing thereon. Provided that this Act shall not Invest the Fee Simple of the said Lands in the Indians but such persons as have patents for the same or any part thereof their Title shall be good and Valid Neither shall the said Indians have liberty or leave to Rent sell or any ways dispose of the said Lands.

Enrolled Acts, November 1729, ch. 2, Secretary of State Records, State Archives, Office of Archives and History, Raleigh.

Upon Complaint of the Maherrin Indians being disturbed in their possessions by Several persons Contrary to an Act of Assembly of this Province passed in the year 1729.

Ordered that the Attorney General do prosecute all persons who disturb the said Maherrin Indians in their Possessions.

Minutes of November 29, 1759 [*sic*], in Cain, *Records of the Executive Council, 1755-1775*, 57.

Shortly after the conclusion of the Tuscarora War, the northern Tuscaroras, led by King Blunt, occupied a tract of land between the Pamlico and Neuse rivers. But fearing retaliation from the Yemassee and their allies—which the Tuscaroras helped South Carolina defeat in 1716—they begged North Carolina to allow them to relocate northward to the Roanoke ("Morratock") River. The request was approved in 1717. White settlers fumed at the creation of the new reservation and the subsequent loss of their claims to that land. Some trespassed nonetheless. Colonial officials, having tired of repeated complaints about encroachment, finally established the boundaries of the Tuscarora reservation in 1748.

No. Carolina scilicet.

Whereas the Tuscarora Indyans by their Articles of peace with this Goverment were bounded and Limited for their Future Settlement to a Certain

Tract of Land lying between Onion quits-tah Creek on Pamptico River and
Neuse river to which Settlement they were to repaire so soon as the Warr
should be over But forasmuch as the Indyan Warr is since broken out in South
Carolina the aforsaid Tuscarore Indyans have Signified to this Goverment
that they are in Danger of being Attacked and destroyed by those Indyans and
therefore has prayed to be Allowed a Settlement on Morratock River for their
further Security Now be it known that it is hereby mutally agreed on between
the Honorable Charles Eden Governor Captain Genl. and Admiral of this
Province by and with the Advice and Consent of the Council for and on
behalfe of himselfe and the Inhabitants of this Goverment and King Blount
for and on behalfe of himselfe and the rest of the Tuscarora Indyans that
forasmuch as the said Blount and his Indyans have been very Servicable to
this Goverment and still Continues so to be And as a particular mark of
Favour from this Goverment They do hereby Give unto him the said Blount
for his further and better Support of himselfe and his Indyans all the Land
lying between Mr. Jones's Lower Line on the North side of Morratock river to
Quitmah Swamp And the said King Blount doth hereby Agree to remove all
his Indyans from off the other Lands down to Rosoossokee by Christmass
next And that they shall not molest nor disturb the Inhabitants nor their
Stocks in Hunting in any of the Adjacent Grounds but that they shall take all
the due Care therein they Can and that they Shall not nor will not Claim any
Right or property to any Other lands hereafter on Either Side of the Said
Morratock River.

In Witness whereof the said Parties have Interchangably Set their hands
and Seals this fifth day of June 1717.

Cain, *Records of the Executive Council, 1664-1734*, 486-487. "Rosoossokee" was Resootska.

CHAPTER III.

An Act for ascertaining the Bounds of a certain Tract of Land formerly laid
out by Treaty to the use of the Tuskerora Indians, so long as they, or any of
them, shall occupy and live upon the same; and to prevent any Person or
Persons taking up Lands, or settling within the said Bounds, by Pretence of
any Purchase or Purchases made, or that shall be made, from the said Indians.

I. Whereas Complaints are made by the Tuskerora Indians, of divers
Incroachments made by the English on their Lands, and it being but just that
the ancient Inhabitants of this Province shall have and enjoy a quiet and
conventient Dwelling-place in this their native County; Wherefre,

II. We pray it may be Enacted, And be it Enacted, by his Excellency
Gabriel Johnston, Esq., Governor, by and with the advice and Consent of his
Majesty's Council, and General Assembly of this Province, and it is hereby

Enacted, by the Authority of the same, That the Lands formerly allotted the Tuskerora Indians, by solemn Treaty, lying on the Morattock River, in Bertie County, being the same whereon they now dwell, butted and bounded as follows, viz., Beginning at the Mouth of Quitsnoy Swamp, running up the said Swamp Four Hundred and Thirty Poles, to a Scrubby Oak, near the Head of the said Swamp, by a Great Spring; then North Ten Degrees East, Eight Hundred and Fifty Poles, to a Persimmon Tree on the Raquis Swamp; then along the Swamp and Pocoson main Course, North Fifty Seven Degrees West, Two Thousand Six Hundred and Forty Poles to a Hickory on the East Side of the Falling Run, or Deep Creek, and down the various Courses of the said Run to Morattock River; then down the River to the first Station; shall be confirmed and assured, and by Virtue of this Act, is confirmed and assured, unto James Blount, Chief of the Tuskerora Nation, and the People under his Charge, their Heirs and Successors, forever; any Law, Usage, or Grant, to the contrary, notwithstanding.

III. Provided always, That it shall and may be lawful for any Person or Persons, that have formerly obtained any Grant or Grants, under the late Lords Proprietors, for any Tracts or Parcels of Land within the aforesaid Boundaries, upon the said Indians deserting or leaving the said Lands, to enter, occupy, and enjoy the same, according to the Tenor of their several Grants; any Thing herein to the contrary, notwithstanding.

IV. And be it further Enacted, by the Authority aforesaid, That it shall not nor may be lawful, for the Lord Granville's Receiver to ask, have, or demand, any Quit-Rents for any of the said Tracts or Parcels of Land, taken up within the said Indian Boundaries, as aforesaid, until such Time the Indians have deserted the same, and the Patentee be in Possession thereof, and then only for such Rents as shall from thence arise and become due; any Law, Usage, or Custom, to the contrary, notwithstanding.

V. And be it further Enacted, by the Authority, That no Person, for any Consideration whatsoever, shall purchase or buy any Tract or Parcel of Land, claimed, or in Possession of any Indian or Indians, but all such Bargains and Sales shall be, and are hereby declared to be null and void, and of none Effect; and the Person so purchasing or buying any Land of any Indian or Indians, shall further forfeit the Sum of Ten Pounds, Proclamation Money for every Hundred Acres by him purchased and bought; one Half to the Use of the Public, the other Half to him or them that will sue for the same; to be recovered, by Action of Debt, Bill, Plaint, or Information, in any Court or Record within this Government, wherein no Essoign, Protection, Injunction, or Wager of Law shall be allowed or admitted of.

VI. And be it further Enacted, by the Authority aforesaid, That all and every Person or Persons, other than the said Indians who are now dwelling on any of the Land within the Bounds above-mentioned, to have been allotted, laid out, and prescribed to the said Tuskerora Indians, shall, on or before the Twenty Fifth Day of March, next ensuing the Ratification of this Act, remove him or herself and Family off the said Land, under the Penalty of Twenty Pounds, Proclamation Money; And if any Person or Persons, other than the said Indians, shall neglect or refuse to move him or herself and Family off the said lands, on or before the Twenty Fifth Day of March next; and if any Person or Persons, other than the said Indians, shall hereafter presume to settle, inhabit, or occupy any of the said Lands hereby allotted and assigned for the said Tuskerora Indians, such Person or Persons shall forfeit the further Penalty of Twenty Shillings, Proclamation Money, for each and every Day he, or she, or they shall inhabit or occupy any Lands within the said Indian Bounds, after the said Twenty Fifth Day of March next; and the said Penalties to be recovered and applied in the same Manner as the Penalty in this Act first above mentioned.

VII. And whereas the said Lands belonging to the Tuskerora Indians, have been lately laid out and new Marked, by George Gould, Esq., Surveyor General, at the Request of the said Indians; Therefore be it Enacted, That the said George Gould, Esq., have and receive, for the Trouble and Expence he hath been at in laying out and marking the Indians' Land aforesaid, the Sum of Twenty Five Pounds, Proclamation Money; to be paid by the Public out of the Monies in the Public Treasury.

VIII. And whereas the Indians complain of Injuries received from People driving Stocks of Horses, Cattle, and Hogs, to range on their Lands; for Remedy whereof, Be it Enacted, That Persons driving Stocks to range, or Stocks actually ranging on the Indians' Lands, shall, and are hereby declared, to be liable and subject to the like Penalties and Forfeitures, and may be proceeded against in the same Manner, and subject to the same Recoveries, as by the Law of this Province Stocks driven or ranging upon any White People's Land are liable and subject to; and the said Indains shall and may enjoy the Benefit of the Laws in that Case made and provided, in the same Manner as the white People do or can; any Law, Usage, or Custom, to the contrary, notwithstanding.

Laws of North Carolina, 1748, in Clark, *State Records*, 23:299-301.

Indians relegated to a reservation lost their autonomy. For example, North Carolina sent Charles Worth Glover to monitor the Tuscaroras and endorsed a "king," Tom Blunt. As Tuscarora warriors grew weary of Blunt's leadership, he sought official assistance to boost his flagging support. North Carolina appointed several commissioners for Indian

affairs in 1736, and three years later the Executive Council ordered the Tuscaroras to select a king to be approved by the governor.

No. Carolina ss. Att a Councell holden at the house of Capt. Jno. Hecklefield in Little River on Wensday April the 7. 1714. Present The Honorable Thomas Pollock Esqr. President etc. [. . .]

Mr. Charles Worth Glover having reported to this board that he was Resident at King Blounts Town fowr Months by a former order of the Assembly, by which order he was to have and receive Ten pounds for the first month and £5 for every month after which amounts in the whole to £25 to be pd. At his returne but Contrary to Expectation the Treasurer refuses to pay the Same untill next year.

Robert J. Cain, ed., *Records of the Executive Council, 1664-1734*, vol. 7 of *The Colonial Records of North Carolina [Second Series]*, eds. Mattie Erma Edwards Parker, William S. Price Jr., Robert J. Cain, and Jan-Michael Poff (Raleigh: Division of Archives and History, Department of Cultural Resources [projected multivolume series, 1963-], 1984), 45.

No. Carolina sc. At a Council held at the Council Chamber in Edenton the 31st day of [July] Anno Domini 1725. Present the Honorable Sir Richard Everard Baronet Governor etc. [. . .]

King Blount Chief Man of the Tuscororoes representing to this Board that some of his People are disorderly and are throwing off their Obedience to him as their Ruler and praying the Protection of this Government and this Board being fully satisfyed of the faithfullness and Fidelity of the said Blount desired the honorable the Governor to grant a New Commission to the said Blount and to Issue a Proclamation Comanding all the Tuscororoes to render him the said Blount obedience otherwise they will be looked upon as Enemies to this Government.

Cain, *Records of the Executive Council, 1664-1734*, 158.

The 14th Day of October [1736]. Present his Excellency. [. . .]

<Comrs. for Indian Affairs, apptd.> Order'd That a Commission issue appointing Robt. West Esqr. [*blank*] Speirs Jno. Grey and Tho. Whitmel Gentlemen Commissioners for Indian Affairs.

Robert J. Cain, ed., *Records of the Executive Council, 1735-1754*, vol. 8 of *The Colonial Records of North Carolina [Second Series]*, ed. Mattie Erma Edwards Parker, William S. Price Jr., Robert J. Cain, and Jan-Michael Poff (Raleigh: Division of Archives and History, Department of Cultural Resources, [projected multivolume series, 1963-], 1988), 62.

March the 5th [1739]. [. . .]

Deputies from the Tuscarora Nation, address'd his Excellency for Leave to choose a King. Granted. And, Orderd that the Day of Election be the third

Tuesday in June next at Rehoosesky, and that the said Indians do then and there present to his Excellency for his Approbation, such Person as They shal agree upon and make choice of for their King.

Cain, *Records of the Executive Council, 1735-1754*, 87. "Rehoosesky" was Resootska.

Nations assigned to reservations were required to pay tribute to the colonial government.

[1729-1730] King *Blunt* appeared before the Governour to pay his Tribute, which he, as well as the rest, generally do once or twice every Year; and this Tribute is a quantity of Deer-Skins, dressed after the Indian manner.

John Brickell, *Natural History of North Carolina* (1737; reprint, Murfreesboro, N.C.: Johnson Publishing Company, 1968), 283.

Because the North Carolina council granted the land for reservations, the Indians who lived there were required to ask permission of the council to sell it, as the Porteskites learned. The council approved the sale to its president of 640 acres of Yeopim land in 1723; sixteen years later, it granted blanket approval to that nation to dispose of land.

North Carolina ss. Att a Council held at the honorable the Governors house at Sandy Point Sepbr. the 13th 1715. Present the Honorable Charles Eden Esqr. Governor Captain Generall and Admirall. The Honorable Nath. Chevin, Wm. Reed, Chris. Gale, T. Knight Esqrs. Lds. proprietors Deputys.
[...]
Upon Petition of the Porteskite Indians Setting forth that they had Sold some small Tracts of their Land to Mr. John Jones Isaac Jones and Captain Richard Sanderson and Also the Light Wood on their Land to Captain Sanderson and pray's that they may have Liberty To Confirm their Titles to the same Lands and Lightwood.
Ordered that the said Indians are hereby Impowred to make Good and Sufficient Titles to the aforsaid John Jones Isaac Jones and Richd. Sanderson for such Lands and light wood as they have already Sold to them provided the said Lands nor any Part thereof doe come within the Line or Boundaries of the Land formerly Sold by the said Indians to Collonell Wm. Reed And also that they on no Pretence whatsoever doe Sell or dispose of any more of their Lands nor that any person presume to Bargain Contract or Agree with the said Indians for any more Lands without Leave first had and Obteined from this Board for so doing and provided Allwayes that the said Indians have free Liberty to hunt on any of the said Lands so sold as aforsaid without any

Molestation of the Said John Jones Isaac Jones or Captain Sanderson their Heires or Assignes.

Cain, *Records of the Executive Council, 1664-1734*, 57, 58-59.

North Carolina sc. At a Council held at Edenton March the 28th Anno 1723. Present

The Honorable William Reed Esqr. President etc. Chr. Gale, Fran. Foster, Richd. Sanderson, J. Lovick, T. Pollock, M. Moore Esqrs. Lds. proprietors Deputys.

[. . .]

John Durant King, John Barber, John Hawkins, Harry Gibbs, George Durant great Men of the Yawpims came before this Board and acknowled a Sale of Land for Six hundred and Forty Acres to the Honorable William Reed Esqr. part of a great Tract laid out to them by the Government and that they were satisfyed for the same. And this Board being asked whether they consented to the said Sale gave their opinion in the Affirmative.

Cain, *Records of the Executive Council, 1664-1734*, 118.

At a Council held at Newbern the 22d February 1739. Present as before.

Read the Petition of John Durant King of the Yeopim Indians in behalf of himself and the said Nation praying an Order of Council may pass Impowering them to Sell or exchange their lands as may best suit their Conveniency and That the Sales or exchanges by them so made may be good and valid to the purchaser which was accordingly granted.

Cain, *Records of the Executive Council, 1735-1754*, 101.

James Bennet of the Chowan nation petitioned the council, in 1745, to halt the questionable sale of 640 acres of reservation land to Henry Hill, but the governor and council ultimately approved the transaction. The Tuscaroras complained in 1753 that their king had leased a portion of their land to John McCasky without their permission. The council ordered McCasky to depart.

Read the Petition of James Bennett a Chowan Indian complaining of one Henry Hills having obtained a Deed of Sale for some of the Chowan Indian Land from some Indians who had no Right to sell the same.

Ordered that Henry Hill be Summoned to Attend this Board at their next Sitting, And that Thomas Hoyster and John Robin the two Indians who sold the Land to the said Hill to Summond to Attend at the same time.

March 14, 1745/46, Cain, *Records of the Executive Council, 1735-1754*, 185, 199.

To his Excellency Gabriel Johnston Esqr. Governour and the Honourable Council.

The humble Petition of Henry Hill.

That Your Petitioner having purchased for a Valuable consideration Six hundred and forty Acres of Land lying in Chowan County of the Chowan Indians at their Special Instance and request which has Appeared to his Excellency when they appeared before him in May 1748 But by Law of this Province passed in the Year 1715 it is amongst other things Enacted that the Sale of Lands Purchased from the Indians, shall pass by Assent of Governour and Council.

Your Petitioner therefore humbly prays that he is a fair Purchaser for a Valuable Consideration your Excellency and Honours will be pleased to give Your Assent to his Purchase for said Land.

And he will pray etc.

Henry Hill

Dated Octr. 10th 1751.

Which being considered his Excellency the Governour with the Advice and Consent of Council was pleased to Approve of the said Purchase and Admit the Deed to Record and the same is hereby Ordered to be Recorded.

Cain, *Records of the Executive Council, 1735-1754*, 279.

Read the Petition of the Tuskerora Indians, setting forth that their King had in a Clandestine Manner leased to John McCasky contrary to their Inclinations and the Laws of this Province Made in their favour. Delay'd this for further consideration till to Morrow.

Minutes of March 28, 1753, in Cain, *Records of the Executive Council, 1735-1754*, 298.

The Commissioners Appointed on the 28th Day of March last to examine hear and Determine concerning the Complaint of the Tuskerora Indians made their Report in the following Words

"Pursuant to the Within Warrant the Parties Appeared and John McGasky the Defendant confessing that he held a Tract of Land by Vertue of a Lease from the Indian King Ordered and adjudged that the Defendant quit his Claim and all Pretentions to the Said Land by Virtue of the Said Lease, from which judgment the Defendant Appeals" Given under Our hands this 21st day of May 1753 signed Thomas Whitmell William Taylor Comrs.

Which Return being read and the Appellant heard it was Ordered that the Judgment of the Said Commissioners be Confirmed and that the said John

McGasky do Remove himself and his Effects off and from the Said Indians Lands Accordingly.

Minutes of September 26, 1753, in Cain, *Records of the Executive Council, 1735-1754*, 298, 301.

Indians leased or sold part or all of their reservations for a number of reasons. If game was scarce and crop lands became depleted, the only way to raise funds for food and clothing was to sell or rent the land. Having lost the vast majority of their land and people through war, disease, or alcohol; disillusioned by life on a reservation; or tired of being treated like second-class citizens by the colonial government and most of the white population, many Indians divested themselves of their homeland and left North Carolina. The Chowans sold large parcels of real property between 1733 and 1735, and a flurry of sales in 1743 and 1753-1754 shrank their holdings even further. The 1733 land deal with John Freeman included a part of their town.

Thos. Hoyter and als to John Freeman a Deed Regd. 7th. Augt 1733.

To all people to whom those presents shall come Greeting Know the that James Bennett Thos. Hiter and Jeremiah Pushing of the precinct of Chowan and County of Albemarle Indians for and in Consideration of the sum of One Hundred and twenty pounds current money of that Province to us in hand paid before the Ensealing and delivery of these presents by Jno. Freeman of the said precinct and province aforesaid Planter the rect. whereof we do hereby Acknowledge and therefore do fully acquit and Discharge the said John Freeman his Heirs Executors etc. by these presents have given granted bargained sold aliened Enfeoffd. and Confirmed and by these presents do fully and absolutely Give Grant Bargain sell alien Enfeoff convey and confirm unto the said [John] Freeman his Heirs and assigns for Ever certain parcel [*blank*] lying and being part of Chowan Town that was formerly granted [*blank*] Honorable Gentlemen of this province to them and their Heirs for Ever Beginning at the mouth of Poly Bridge Branch and do running up to the Head of it and so to a path called Aaron Blanchards Path and so along to the head of the Gum Branch and so down that to Catherine Creek and so to the first station to say Two Hundred Acres more or less To have and to hold [...].

Chowan Nation to John Freeman, August 7, 1733, Vol. W-1, 216 (microfilm), Chowan County Deeds, State Archives, Office of Archives and History, Raleigh.

Edenton, Sept. 15th. The Indians in North Carolina are in a bad way. The Chowan Indians are reduced to a few families, and their land has been taken from them.

Entry of September 15, 1752, diary of Bishop August Gottlieb Spangenberg, in Fries, *Records of the Moravians*, 1:36.

The Yeopim Indians concluded that they would rather have cash in hand instead of land they could not enjoy and chose to be free from white settlers who did not respect them. They sold several parcels of land in 1740 and 1741—including fifty acres to Edward Taylor, which he had already been leasing. All were from holdings granted to them in 1704 and 1739.

North Carolina sst, This Indenture made the twenty ninth Day of November in the year of our Lord 1740 Between John Durant of the County of Currituck in the province aforesaid King of the Yowpim Indians of the one part and Edward Taylor of the same county planter of the other parte Witnesseth that the said John Durant and in consideration of the sum of twenty two pounds ten shillings current Money of Virginia to him in hand will and truly paid at and before the Insealing and Delivery of this presents by the said Edward Taylor the Receipt whereof I doe hereby acknowledge hath Bargained Granted sold alined Enfeoffed conveyed and confirmed unto and by these presents Doth Grant Bargin sell Efieoff convey and confirm unto the said Edward Taylor his heirs and assignes all that tract or parcel of Land containing fifty acres situate Lying and Being in the county of Currituck aforesaid Begining at a black Gum at the corner of Jeremiah Stephens plantation by the Swamp Side and Runing up the main Swamp for the said fifty acres then across the Ridge to the low Ground then along the low Ground to the Indian line Joyning on the western side of Jeremiah Stevens plantation and then Back to the first Station which said fifty acres of Land is now in the possison of the said Edward Taylor by virtue of alease to him thereof made by the said John Durant Bearing Date the Day of November one thousand seven hundred and thirty one and is also parte of abiger tract of Land formerly Granted unto the King of the Yeopim Indians by patent Bearing Date the Day of October 1704 and some by order of council Dted the Day of 1739 the said John Durant is Impowered to sell and convey all or any parte of the Land Before Mentioned as by the said patent and order of counsill Relation being thereunto severly had may forever fully and absolutely appear together with all houses orchards fenses Gardens woods under woods and all other appurtenances and Improvements to the said fifty acres of Land or in any ways opportuning To have and to hold [. . .].

John Durant to Edward Taylor, November 29, 1740, Vol. 3, 27-28 (microfilm), Currituck County Deeds, State Archives, Office of Archives and History, Raleigh. The Yeopim Indians successfully petitioned the North Carolina Executive Council on March 28, 1723 and February 22, 1739/40 for permission to sell land granted to them by the colony. Cain, *Records of the Executive Council, 1664-1734*, 118; Cain, *Records of the Executive Council, 1735-1754*, 101.

Over the years, the Machapunga [Mattamuskeet] Indians sold land piecemeal that had been granted to them by the colonial council, although headman Charles Squires did purchase 200 acres on Hatteras Banks in 1740. Possibly an attempt to reconcile debts, the Machapungas sold the entire 10,240-acre tract they were granted in 1727 to a Virginia trader in 1752. Hyde County deeds found in the North Carolina State Archives also record them transferring the same land to different buyers in 1761 and again in 1792.

This Indenture made this 27 day of Septr In the year of our Lord god one thousand seven hundred and thirty one and In the third year of this Reigen of our Sovering Lord George the Second by the grace of god King of England Scotland Ireland and France defender of our Faith etc and betwen John Squirs King of the Arromuskeet Indians with the advice and consent of John Makey and Long Tom In the Precinct of Currituck and The County Arelbermerle and In the Province of North Carolina the on[e] partys and Henry Gibbs of the precinct and County and province above said of the other party Witnesseth that we the aforesaid Tom Squirs the King with John macky Long Tom for and inconsideration of the sum of Tenn pounds good Lawfull money of the province of North Carolina the Receipt where of we the said John Squires King Jno. Mackey Long tom Doth holde themselves to be fully sattisfyd Paid and contented [*blank*] error and dow by these presents acquit Exonerate and discharge him the said Henry Gibbs his heirs Executors etc. shaith given granted allinated bargained and sold enfeoffed and Confirmed and by these presents doth fully Clearly and absolutly Give Grant Bargain sell alien Enfeoff and confirmed unto the aforesaid Henr. Gibbs his heirs and assigns for Ever to a tract of Land situated Lying and being In the province of North Carolina on the South west Side of New Aromuskeet Creek commonly known by the name of [*blank*] Containing by Estimation Six hundred and forty acres be the same more or Less begining at the head of the said Creek a southerly Course to the head of [*blank*] creek between the said Henr. gibbs the said John Squirs King The Reversion and Reversions remainder and remainders of all singular of the before granted premises here by bargained and sould ment mentioned and Entended to be hear by Bargained and Sould with their and every of Rights and members and appurtenances what soever to geather with all houses orchards gardans fences woods waters high ground savaneis and marshes and others appurtainances there unto belonging or appertaining and belonging unto him the aforesaid Henr. gibbs his heirs and assigns for Ever from them the aforesaid John Squers King with Jno macky and Long Tom there heirs Executors and successors or any other person or persons Whatsoever Charming from by or under them the said Jno Squirs King with Jno Mackey Long Tom their heirs Executors or assigns or by his or theire menes etc. prescour ments and further they the said John Squirs King with Jno macky Long Tom there heirs Executers doth Covenant and agree to and with the said Henr. Gibbs his heirs Executor and assigns for Ever in the full and Just sum of one hundred and Eighty Pounds good lawfull money of north Carolina to be paid on demand on the non performance of this present Righting of Endenture that is to say they the said John Squires King with Long Tom and heirs Executers haith and Doe by these presents Enfeioffe sell and make over all their Right title and Entrest of the aforesaid Tract of land as is a Cove spacifyd and dew warrant and forever defend the same to the said Heny. Gibbs his heirs Executers from the aforesaid John Squirs King with Jno macky Long Tom there heirs Excutors Administrators forever and that he the said Henry gibbs his heirs and assigns shall and forever have Posses oquipy and Injoy the aforesaid Tract of Land without aney hindrance L[*illegible*] Trouble or molstation whatsoever from them the said Jno. Squirs King with Jno macky Long tom their heirs, Executers or any other person or persons whatsoever Claming from by or under ous In Witness where of wee the aforesaid Jno. Squiers King with Jno Mackey Long Tom haith hear unto set their hands and fixed theirs seals this Day and year as is above under Signed Sealed and delivered.

Machapunga Nation to Henry Gibbs, September 27, 1731, Vol. H, 96-98 (microfilm), Hyde County Deeds, State Archives, Office of Archives and History, Raleigh.

North Carolina sst. To all to whome these presents shall come, Know the that I Joseph Farrow for and In consideration of the sum of one hundred pounds Lawfull Money to me in hand paid by Charles Squires Indian of arrowmuskeet in the county of Currituck in the province aforesaid the Recipt whereof I Doe hereby acknowledge and my Self therewith to be fully contented and paid and have Bargained and sold and by these presents Doe Grant infeoff and confirm to the said Charles Squires his heirs Executers Administrators two hundred acres of Land lett the same be more or less Lying and Being on Hatteras Banks in the county and province aforesaid and Bounded as followeth that is to say Begining at the North side of the Cutting ridge Marsh as is by the House that Vallintine Wallis built on the said Banks so Runing to the Sound Side to a Drean called Callisis Drean so Eastward to the Sea Side and so Back to the first Station Together with all houses Edifise Improvements and all appurtenances to the said piece or parcell of Land Belonging or in any ways appertaining To have and to hold [. . .] second day April anno Domini 1740.

Jacob Farrow to Charles Squires, April 2, 1740, Vol. 3, 24 (microfilm), Currituck County Deeds, State Archives.

<*North Carolina*> This Indenture Made the twenty fourth day of November in the Year of our Lord one Thousand seven hundred and fifty two by and between Charles Squieres, George Squires Joshua Squires Timothy Squiers, chief Men of the Mattamuskeet Indians of the one part, and William Stephenson Merchant or Pedlar in the province aforesaid of the other part. Witnesseth that the said Cha[rles] Squiers, George Squires, Joshua Squieres, and Timothy Squieres, for and in consideration of the sum of eighty three pounds, current money of the Colloney of Virginia to them in hand paid and Received and they the said Indians therewith fully satisfied and Contented, Have Given Granted, Bargained, Enfeoffed and Confirmed and by these presents do absolutely Grant Sell Enfeoff, and confirm unto the said William Stephenson his Heirs and assigns forever one certain Tract of Land lying and being at Mattamuskeet on Pamlicoe Sound in the province aforesaid containing by Estimation Ten Thousand two hundred and forty acres Beginning at the Mouth of Mattamuskeet creek runing up that creek and then Northermost Branch of it to the head thereof to the Lake S.W. [*blank*] pole then along the Lake Southerty to Matchapungo Bluffwoods, then No. Et. to pamlicoe sound and from there along pamlicoe sound to the first station. Containing as aforesaid with all and singular the rights, Hereditaments, appurtenances, and appendants whatsoever to the said Land belonging or in anywise appertaining. [. . .]

Machapunga Nation to William Stephenson, November 24, 1752, Vol. 2, 148-149, no. 75 (microfilm), Land Grant Records of North Carolina, State Archives.

Following their defeat in the Tuscarora War, several thousand Tuscaroras fled North Carolina for western New York and the safety of the Iroquois Confederacy. From that haven they had begged the tribesmen who had stayed behind to join them. In 1765 a Tuscarora delegation, aided by Sir William Johnson, ventured south to persuade their brethren to settle among the Iroquois and to convince Governor William Tryon and the colonial assembly to permit the move. The next year, approximately two hundred of their Carolina kin decided to leave; to raise capital for the journey, the Tuscaroras sold a portion of their reservation. Tryon believed that the land deal would benefit the Tuscaroras and the colony. Ambushed on their way to New York by whites near Paxton, Pennsylvania, the Tuscaroras appeared relieved to be in the Six Nations—despite efforts to convert them to Christianity— and hoped to bring the remainder of their people with them.

[. . .] The Tuscaroras, who (as mentioned in a former Letter) are very desirous to bring away their People from the Southward, would no longer be put off, and are set out about a Fortnight ago for that purpose. I have furnished them with a pass, and hope they will not meet with any ill treatment from the Indiscretion of the back Settlers, who have for some time acted with great Imprudence towards all Indians, which may, if continued, produce a fresh Rupture, and overset all our proceedings.

Sir William Johnson, superintendent of Indian Affairs for the northern department, to John Stuart, September 17, 1765, in Colonial Office 5/67, British Records, State Archives, Office of Archives and History, Raleigh. Johnson had denied the Tuscarora, on August 25, 1763, their request for assistance to move their brethren in North Carolina to the Iroquois Confederacy. Sir William Johnson, *The Papers of Sir William Johnson*, 14 vols. (Albany: The University of the State of New York, 1921-1965), 10:801.

The Sachem of the Tuskerora Indians waited on me the 17th of last Month: he shewed me the Credentials You gave him and a pass obtained from Governor Fauquier of Virginia, both which together with his Talk informed me of the Intention of his Journey from Susquehanna River. He arrived at this Town very ill; I ordered a Doctor to attend on him, the best Care to be taken of him, and to be supplied from my House with every thing he wanted. This Complaint was the Mumps, of which he recovered in about a Week he dined twice at my Table which was as often as his Health would permit. I found him not only Humanized, but really Civilized As the Tract of Land the Tuskaroras hold in this Colony upon the Roanoke was granted to them by the Legislature of this Colony I acquainted the Sachem it would be necessary for his Waiting till the Meeting of the General Assembly to be held at Newbern the 30th of October next, when I would give him All the Assistance in my Power for the sale of so much of the Land as would be necessary to bear the Travelling Expences of as many of the Tuskaroras, as were willing to quit this Province, and march to join the Six Nations. The Sachem at first was very unwilling to stay himself till the above time, as he had promised his Nation, and you Sir, to return to them in seven Months from the Time of his Departure; and that that term was already expired: however upon taking further time to Consider on it, and upon my Assurance to Acquaint his Nation, thro' you, of the Necessity of his Waiting till the Meeting of Our General Assembly, he consented to go to his People settled in this Province till the above Period. The Eight Indians he brought from the Six Nations he told me he had left at the Indian Town, on the Roanoke River. He gave me Strings of Wampum during his Talk. At my Request that he would give the Governor of this Province an Indian Name, upon a days Consideration he honoured me with his own Name, Diagawekee, in Testimony of his Regard for the Care I had taken of him in his Sickness, This Name is to remain to all future Governors of North Carolina.

In a letter I have lately received from Mr. Stuart Superintendant of Indian Affairs for the Southern District, he mentions your Application for his Assistance to get the Tusks residing in this Country to remove, and join the

Six Nations; to Accomplish which End you may be assured my Assistance shall not be wanting, as also my Protection to as many of the Nation as choose to Continue in the Province. I am told their number including Men, Women and Children amounts to nearly Two Hundred and Twenty or Thirty.

I gave the Sachem a Pass under the Seal of the Province for Himself and Attendants. The Interpreter I understand is the same that came from the Six Nations with him; he seemed to be attentive to the Sachem, and behaved himself very well while at Brunswick.

Governor William Tryon of North Carolina to Sir William Johnson, June 15, 1766, in William S. Powell, ed., *The Correspondence of William Tryon and Other Selected Papers*, 2 vols. (Raleigh: Division of Archives and History, Department of Cultural Resources, 1980-1981), 1:310-311.

The Members of His Majestys Honorable Council for the said Province. And the Worshipful Speaker & Assembly thereof.

The Petition of the subscribers, the Chiefs of the Tuscarora Indians.

The Assembly sheweth

That your Petitioners Ancestors were the aborigines of the said Province & possessed of greatest part of the Lands in the same in their own right, long before it was discovered by the English.

That about the Year 1714 the said Nation of Indians concluded a solemn Treaty, with the then Lords Proprietors Deputies of North Carolina, in Writing, whereby the said Indians acknowledged the sovereignty of King George the first, of Glorious Memory, and pledged their faith to observe dutiful allegiance to him; and also surrendered to the said Lords Proprietors all the Lands in the said Province, except a small part thereof, which is described by Metes & Bounds in the said Treaty, which said parcel of Land the said Lord Proprietors Deputies, by the aforesaid Treaty, granted and confirmed to the said Tuscarora Indians, their Heirs and Assigns, in fee.

Your Petitioners further shew that from the time of concluding the said Treaty hitherto, the said Indians have most punctually, observed the same. Nevertheless several of the said Lords Proprietors Deputies, some Years after Ratification of the said Treaty, in open violation of the same obtained Patents from the rest of the Deputies for diverse parts of the Land so as afore said confirmed to the said Indians, without their Consent or Privity.

Your Petitioners further shew that the afore said Treaty being lost, the General Assembly in the Year 1748, passed an Act, whereby the said Treaty is recognized, the Bounds of your Petitioners said Land recited, and their Title thereto confirmed, but by a Clause in the said Act, persons who had obtained the said Patents are empowered to enter into & hold the Lands mentioned, therein, according to the Tenor of the said Grants from & after the time when your Petitioners should leave the same, which your Petitioners humbly hope will be considered as incompatible with the aforesaid Treaty and natural Justice, and therefore they would humbly pray that so much of the said act as tends to validate the said Patents be repealed, the said Patents rendered null & void, and your Petitioners left at Liberty to enjoy their said Land according to the original Intention of the said Treaty.

Your Petitioners further shew that about fifty years ago a considerable part of the said Nation of Tuscarora Indians removed themselves to the Northward & settled near the Mohocks where they now Live & possess, an extensive Tract of Land, in which is great plenty of Game, so that by hunting they support themselves comfortably, and have increased in Numbers greatly That Diagawehee, alias Isaac, a Sachem of the Tuscarora Indians, and several others of the said Nation living in the North, having learned the Poverty & Distress that your petitioners are reduced to, occasioned by the Destruction of Game, so that they can not any longer subsist themselves by hunting, are lately come among us your Petitioners, and have solicited us to go to the Northward, there to reside & enjoy in common with them the Blessings which their Country naturally affords, which kind Invitation about one hundred and fifty six of the Tuscarora Indians now residing in this Province have agreed to accept; but are unable to carry their Resolution into Execution unless they can raise a Sum of Money to discharge their just Debt, buy necessary Cloathing and defray the Expences of the Journey; Therefore the said Indians have unanimously agreed to sell a Part of the Land secured to them by the afore-mentioned Treaty, to wit, Beginning at the mouth of Deep Creek or Falling Run; thence up the said Creek to the head Line of our Petitioners Lands; thence by the said head Line South 57 degrees East 1280 poles; thence a Course parallel with the general Current of Deep Creek aforesaid to Roanoke River & up that to the first Station.

Your Petitioners further shew that Robert Jones, His Majesty's Attorney General, William Williams of Halifax County and Thomas Pugh of Bertie County, whose Friendship your Petitioners are well assured of, have consented to become Trustees for selling and disposing of the said Land: Your Petitioners would therefore humbly pray that an Act may pass, vesting all that part of your said Petitioners Land, lying West of the third parallel Line, in the said Robert Jones William Williams & Thomas Pugh, the Survivers or Surviver of them in fee that they may be impowered and directed to lay it out in convenient Lots, not exceeding 640 Acres each, to sell the same at publick Auction to settle and adjust all Debts due from Your Petitioners & with the Money arising from the said Sales pay the said Debts, furnish all such of the Tuscarora Indians as shall undertake to go to the Northward with their Brethren with necessary Apparel & Money to defray the Expences of the Jury [journey], and to distribute, the Surplus of the said Money, if any, equally among such of the Tuscarora Indians as shall choose to tarry behind. And that the said Trustees, for their Trouble in executing the said Trust may hold and enjoy respectively, a Lot of the said Land, to be set apart for them by your Petitioners or a Majority of them in fee

And your petitioners as in duty bound, shall ever pray &c.

Billy Taylor	Jno. Cain	Billy Hinds
mark	mark	
John Wiggins	Billy Sockey	Billy George
Billy Howard	Billy [Netops?]	Billy dennis
Captain Blunt	Captain Jo.	Captain Basket
Billy Blunt	James Blunt	John Jackit
Billy Pugh	Tom Whitmore	mark
John	John Roggers	
	Billy Owens	Isaac Miller
Billy wheeler	Billy Bennet	John Roberts
		billey Tommas
John Blunt	[loose?] Whitmell	George

Petition from Tuscarora headmen to Governor William Tryon, [before July 12], 1766, in Powell, *Correspondence of William Tryon*, 1:321-324. In a letter to Sir William Johnson, December 10, 1763, John Stuart stated that he had asked Governor Dobbs if excessive debt by the Tuscarora in his colony would hinder their move north. The Tuscarora sold the abovementioned parcel for £1500 proclamation money on July 12, 1766. An agreement between the Tuscarora headmen and Thomas Whitmell, Thomas Pugh, William Williams, and John Watson had failed upon its second reading in the lower house in 1764. The assembly and governor ratified the agreement November 10, 1766, and the Privy Council approved the act January 11, 1769. *Sir William Johnson Papers*, 10:951-952; Tuscarora Indians to Robert Jones, William Williams, and Thomas Pugh, July 12, 1766, Vol. L, 56-58 (microfilm), Bertie County Deeds, State Archives, Office of Archives and History, Raleigh; William L. Saunders, ed., *The Colonial Records of North Carolina*, 10 volumes (Raleigh: State of North Carolina, 1886-1890), 6:1284, 1294; Privy Council 5/12, British Records, Office of Archives and History, Raleigh; Privy Council 1/54, Part I, British Records, State Archives, Office of Archives and History, Raleigh; Bill for confirming a lease made by the Tuscarora Indians to Robert Jones, William Williams, and Thomas Pugh, Esquires, November 10, 1766, Session of November-December 1766, General Assembly Session Records (Oversized), State Archives, Office of Archives and History, Raleigh.

I am at present in a Hurry, having just returned from a Journey to the Frontiers of this Province; where I saw above 200 Indians, being the Body of the Tuscarora Nation, moving from Carolina to be incorporated with the 6 Nations, and to live near Sr. Wm. Johnson, I talked a good Deal with some who understood English, and I believe a School among them would be of great Use.

Philadelphia, Reverend William Smith to [Daniel Burton,] Secretary, SPG, September 22, 1766, Society for the Propagation of the Gospel in Foreign Parts, Letterbooks, Series B, 21, British Records, State Archives, Office of Archives and History, Raleigh.

Decmr. 18th.—On this day Isaac a Tuscarora Chief with another of said Nation, and Joseph Nicolaus Interpreter arrived here from North Carolina from whence they brought 160 of their Tribe to settle among the Six Nations, and several letters for Sr. Wm., by which it appeared that they with great difficulty were allowed to pass in safety thro' the Frontiers of Pennsylvania, Maryland, Virginia etc. notwithstanding they had his Pass, as also that of the Magistrates of the several Districts—that at Paxton in Pennsylvia. in their Return from North Carolina they were plundered of several things, particularly of Six Horses they had bought with Part of the money they had received for the Sale of part of their Lands in that Government.—these with many more Complaints were made known to the Six Nations, altho' Sir Wm. endeavored all he could to keep it private from them, knowing their tempers were already much sowered by such like treatment shewn to several of their People this year [*past*] as they passed thro' them Governments.—They then begged Sir Wm. would allow [*them*] some Provision, Ammunition, and Clothing to the New comers, who were now in the utmost Distress at Shamokin, not having been able to reach the Place of their Destination 'till Spring.—Sir Wm. wrote a letter by the Interpreter to Captain Graydon living at Shamokin with directions to furnish the Indians with such a quantity of Provision as they could Subsist on 'till the Spring, and to give their young men some Ammunition wherewith to kill Game,—also a letter to Governor Penn therein acquainting him with the behavior of the Paxton People, and requesting he woud have some satisfaction made to the Sufferers,—all which then made easy together with a small Present given them.

> Journal of Indian Affairs, December 18, 1766, *Sir William Johnson Papers*, 12:240. Shamokin had been a multi-ethnic Indian town located at the junction of the north and east branches of the Susquehanna River near present-day Sunbury, Pennsylania. The value of the stolen horses had been estimated at £50. Sir William Johnson expressed his displeasure to the Earl of Shelburne, secretary of state for the southern department, on December 16. He also complained to Governor John Penn of Pennsylvania on December 19, 1766 seeking satisfaction for the goods that had been stolen in Paxton. Pennsylvania finally paid the Tuscarora "Sixteen half Johanne's" for the stolen horses on October 18, 1768. E.B. O'Callaghan and Berthold Fernow, eds., *Documents Relative to the Colonial History of the State of New York*, 15 vols. (Albany, New York: Weed, Parsons and Company, printers, 1853-1887), 7:883; *Sir William Johnson Papers*, 12:231-232, 623-624.

[. . .] The Act for confirming the Lease made by the Tuscarora Indians to Robert Jones &c &c appeared to be a necessary Step to reimburse the Money that was advanced to transport One Hundred and Fifty five Indians from the Tuscarora Tribe settled on the Eastern Banks of Roanoke River to the Six Nations on the Susquehanna River: The Removal of these Indians was effected at the particular Request of Sir William Johnson, and with the Approbation of Mr. Stuart, Super Intendant of Indian Affairs. This Lease is advantageous to the Proprietor of the Soil, Earl Granville, as it lets him into the immediate Receipt of the Quit Rents which he had no Claim to while the Indians lived on that Land. The sum advanced for the Removal of these Indians and the Contingencies amounted to near Two Thousand Pounds Proclamation Money. The Remnant of this Tribe are One Hundred and four, Men, Women and Children and occupy about half the Tract of Land allotted them by Act of Assembly passed in 1748, a large Proportion of their Numbers.

> Governor William Tryon to the Earl of Shelburne, January 31, 1767, in Powell, *Correspondence of William Tryon*, 1:412.

[February] 25th. Twenty Tuscaroras arrived here with *Aucus* al *Kanigut* a Chief with them who addressed Sr. William as follows on their behalf—
Brother—
We return you many thanks in bringing our People from Carolina, where they lived but wretchedly being Surrounded by white People, and up to their Lips in Rum, so that they could not turn their heads anyway but it ran into their mouths. this made them stupid, so that they neglected Hunting, Planting etc. – We are since our arrival at Oughquago last Fall, become wiser, and see our former folly, and beg of you to prevail upon the Six Nations to allow us to remain where we now are, fearing that if we return we may fall into the same Error again, as we understand they have Liquor in plenty among them.—We also request you would give us some medicine to cure us of our fondness for that destructive liquor.
2 large Belts tied together.

Brother—
Although we have lived at a considerable Distance from you, which we have found by traveling it, yet your Name, and Words reached us, as though you was but close by, and we always paid the greatest regard to your Orders, and advice, for Instance when you desired us to leave off going to War against the Catawbas, we obeyed.—we complied also with your desire of our Joining the Army to the Westward, and lost several of our young Men in the Service.—As all is now your own, and that as Peace is spread all over the land, we have nothing now to do but to hunt, and plant for the Support of our Families, in Order to do this, we must request of you brother to help us with working Utensils, and Provisions until we can raise some of our own, otherwise we must all suffer, having nothing left us after our long Journey.—[. . .]
3 Strings

> Journal of Indian Affairs, February 1767, *Sir William Johnson Papers*, 12:273-274. The Tuscaroras settled with the Oneidas at Oquaga ("Oughquago"); the town had been located on the eastern branch of the Susquehanna River at present-day Windsor, New York. The Tuscaroras in New York maintained contact with their brethren in North Carolina and still wished for them to move north. *Sir William Johnson Papers*, 8:1093, 1094; 12:274-275, 1001.

The Tuscaroras who remained in North Carolina after the 1766 exodus made attempts to control their shrinking reservation and eke out an existence. They petitioned the colony to evict Sarah Bate from their land and, in 1773, moved on William King for his unauthorized occupancy of a portion of their land. Struggling to provide for their own needs, the Tuscaroras in 1775 leased 2,000 acres to Thomas Pugh, Willie Jones, and William Williams in exchange for a yearly distribution of blankets, shirts, boots, gunpowder, and ammunition. Eventually, settlers began to claim reservation lands to which they were not entitled. In response, the state prohibited future purchasing or leasing of Tuscarora territory and created a commission to arbitrate land disputes. The Tuscaroras later complained that whites called to testify before the commission too often failed to appear. By 1808, the pitiable fragment of the Tuscarora nation that remained in North Carolina sold what land they had left and departed, presumably for New York.

Brother,

We come to assure you of our Loyalty to the great King over the Water and to desire your Friendship and Protection; in token whereof we present you with these Deerskins: Poverty must excuse the smallness of the present, for we are mostly old men, unable to hunt, our young men having gone to the Northward with the Northern Chief, Tragaweha.

Many years ago a certain Tract of Land in Bertie County, was given by Treaty to King Blount and his Subjects, for their fidelity to the English Part of this Land we have leased to Messrs. Jones, Williams, and Pugh and we desire the lease may be confirmed, and the Penalties of the Act, of 1748, repealed, so far as relates to the Land that is leased.

We are by Education and Custom, unable to acquire a Livelihood otherwise than by Hunting, and as Ill natured Persons frequently take away and break our Guns, and even whip us for Pursuing game on their Land, We beg of your Excellency to appoint Commissioners as heretofore to hear our complaints, and redress our grievances.

One Sarah Bates has for some years rented a Tract of Land from us, but as our bounds are now become more circumscribed we choose, and if she should refuse so to do, on a friendly application, we must request you to direct the Attorney General to Eject her, and indeed to render us other services in the same manner as Mr Robert Jones was wont to do in his lifetime.

We entreat your Excelly. to dispatch our business with all convenient speed; for those Indians whom we have left at home are old men and children, incapable of providing for themselves, if cold weather should come one.

Thomas Baskett Billy Dennis
William Taylor John Caine
Whitmell Tuffdick Billy Blount
Billy Roberts James Mitchel
Lewis Tuffdick Billy Owen
Thomas Blount

Thomas Baskett and others to Governor William Tryon, November 7, 1766, Powell, *Correspondence of William Tryon*, 1:363. The land in contention may be attached to property contested in 1758 by Humphrey Bate. The Tuscarora in 1758 attempted to evict Bate from his land on the reservation citing the 1748 statute. Bate, possibly the late husband of Sarah, claimed he had purchased three hundred acres of land on the Tuscarora reservation from George Charleton. George Charleton had acquired the land from his father, William, who had been given "about six hundred Acres lying in Bertie County and known by the Name of Quitsney's Meadow joining on the Chyatuck Swamp" by the nation "for some Favours done by him for them" and could dispose of the land as he saw fit. According to Bate, the council approved William Charleton's acquisition November 7, 1723, but that approval is missing from the extant record. The colony prosecuted Sarah Bate and John Allen for trespass on Tuscarora land in 1769. Petition of Humphrey Bate, Petitions rejected or not acted on, Lower House Papers, Session of November-December 1758, General Assembly Session Records, State Archives, Office of Archives and History, Raleigh; 1769, Criminal Action Papers, Edenton District Superior Court, State Archives, Office of Archives and History, Raleigh.

Edenton October Superior Court 1770
Dominus Rex vs. Sarah Bates
Information for settling on the Indian Lands.
Reasons in Arrest of Judgment.
First. That the Penalties contained in the act of Assembly in Anno 1748 are abrogated by the act of Assembly Anno 1766.
Secondly. That in the Information there is no Averment that the Trespass was made upon that part of the Indian Lands Reserved to them by the Act in Anno 1766 and for what Appears on the Record the Trespass complained off might have been on that part of the Indian Lands Leased to Messrs. Allen Jones Willie Jones, Thomas Pugh and William Williams.
Thirdly. No Averment that Indians continue as a nation or People Residing upon these Lands.
Fourthly. No Venue laid in the Information.
5thly. miscalculation of time.
6th. not charged Contra Formam Statuti.

7thly. The Informer prayed that may forfeit [*illegible*] of a charge that she had forfeited.

For the above Reasons and many other infractions that Judgment on the Verdict of the Jury may be stayed.

Criminal Action Papers, Edenton District Superior Court, State Archives. Neither Bate nor Allen had vacated their land by October 1772 when the colony levied new fines for continuing to occupy Tuscarora land. *Dom. Rex v. Bate*, 1772, General Court Papers, Colonial Court Records 141, State Archives, Office of Archives and History, Raleigh; *Dom. Rex v. Allen*, 1772, General Court Papers, Colonial Court Records 141, State Archives.

[. . .] Upon a Complaint of the Chief of the Tuskarora Indians that one William King had entered upon and committed waste upon the Lands lying on the North side of Morattuck which lands were granted to Col. Needham Bryan by the Lords proprietors upon the failure of that nation of Indians and afterwards confirmed to him by the Legislature of this Province, it was the opinion of the Board that His Excellency should write a Letter to Willm. King to remove off the Land or to shew cause why he held possession of it.

December 18, 1773, Cain, *Records of the Executive Council, 1755-1775*, 297.

This Indenture made this second day of December in the year of our LORD one thousand Seven hundred and Seventy five Between Whitmell Tufdick Chief of the Tuskarora Indians and Wineoak Charles Sen Wineoak Charles Junior Bille Roberts Lewis Tufdick West Tufdick Bille Blunt Sen. Bille Blunt Jun. John Rodgers John Smith Bille Pugh Bille Baskit John Hicks Samuel Bridgers John Owens James Mitchell Isaac Cornelius Tom Tomas and Walter Gibsons Chieftains of the said Tuskara nation for our selves and the rest of the Tuskarora nation of the one part and Thomas Pugh Willie Jones and William Williams of the other part Witnesseth that the said Whitmell Tufdick [et al., . . .] for and in Consideration of the yearly rent or sum of Eighty Buffelo Blanketts Eighty Oznabrig Shirts Eighty pr of Boots to be made of half thicks which said Shirts and boots are to be suitable for the Indians according to their diferent sizes fifty pounds of Powder and One hundred and fifty pound of shot to be paid to the said Whitmell Tufdick [et al., . . .] their heirs and Successors, Have let Leased and farmed and by those presents so at lease and farm unto the said Thomas Pugh Willie Jones and William Williams their heirs and assigns a certain tract or parcel of land lying and being in the County of Bertie it being part of the land known by the name of the Indian Lands containing by Estimation Two thousand acres be the same more or less butted and bounded as follows Begining on the town swamp at Sam Williams line thence up the said swamp till it comes opposite to an old path that leads to Unarowick Swamp then along that to the said Swamp then up the said Swamp to the head then along a bottom till it comes to the Swamp where James Wiggins lives called Unrintaroud then along that Swamp to the mouth of Quitsna Swamp then up Quitsna Swamp being the Indian line to the head from thence along the Indian line to a persimmon tree on Rosquist then along the Indian line to the line of Jones William and Pugh then along that line to the first Station including all the lands in said bounds Except the tract of Land whereon [Wm King] now tends and being about three hundred acres. To have and to hold the said piece or parcel of land above mentioned unto the said Thomas Pugh Willie Jones and Wm Williams their heirs Executors Administrators and assigns for and during the full end and term of Ninety nine years from the Twenty fifth day of December in the year of our Lord one thousand seven hundred and seventy five yielding and laying therefore yearly and every year during the said term unto the said Whitmell Tuffdick [et al., . . .] their heirs or successors the yearly rent of Eighty Duffill blankets Eighty Ozn shirts Eighty Pair Boots to be made of half thicks which said Shirts and boots are to be suitable to the Indians according to tair different sizes fifty pound of powder and 100 Lb. of shot as aforesaid and the said Whitmell Tufdick [et al., . . .] for themselves their heirs and successors promise grant and agree to and with the said Thos Pugh Willie Jones and William Williams their Heirs Executors administrators and assigns that the said Thos Pugh Willie Jones and Wm Williams their heirs and assigns shall piaceably and quietly have hold occupy possess and Enjoy the above Granted Lands and promises with appurtenances thereunto belonging or in anywise appertertaining without the let hinderance or Molestation of us the said Whitmell Tufdick [et al., . . .] or our heirs and successors. In Witness wherof we the said Whit. Tufdick Wineoak Charles be [*illegible*] hereunto set our hands and seals the day and year above Written.

Whitmell Tufdick (Seal), John <*his mark*> Smith (Seal), Bille <*mark*> Roberts (Seal), Bille <*his mark*> Blunt Sen (Seal), West Whitmill (Seal), Wenioak <*his mark*> Charles Jun (Seal), Lewis <*his mark*> Tufdick (Seal), Thos Pugh (Seal), Willie Jones (Seal), Wm Williams (Seal), Billie <*mark*> Pugh (Seal), Wenioak <*mark*> Charles <*Sen*> (Seal), James <*mark*> Mitchell (Seal), Bille <*his mark*> Blunt Jun (Seal), Saml <*mark*> Bridgers (Seal), Tom <*mark*> Roberts Jun (Seal), Bille <*his mark*> Cain (Seal), John Hicks, John Rogers (Seal), John <*mark*> Owen (Seal), James <*his mark*> Hicks (Seal), Bille <*his mark*> Smith (Seal), Bille <*his mark*> Mitchell (Seal)

Tuscarora Nation to Thomas Pugh, Willie Jones, and William Williams, December 2, 1775, Vol. M, 316-317 (microfilm), Bertie County Deeds, State Archives, Office of Archives and History, Raleigh. For reservation land leased by Williams, Pugh, and Jones, see Bertie County Deeds, 1779, Vol. M, 400, 402, 405-407 (microfilm), State Archives. William Williams and Thomas Pugh sold their shares of the Tuscarora land to Willie Jones on March 24, 1779. Deeds-Jones, Bertie County Deeds, State Archives, Office of Archives and History, Raleigh.

North Carolina Bertie County. This Indenture made this Thirteenth day of December Anno Dominy One thousand Seven hundred and Seventy five between Whitmell Tufdick the king Indian and the rest of the Tuscororah Indians that and their Airs I William Cane William Blount Wineoak Charles Jun Wineoak Charles Sen Sam Bridges Lewis Tufdick Isaac Wheeler William Mitchell Tom Robbard Wm Pugh William Baskit John Robearts Capt. William Blount John Rodgers John Owens Tom Tommas James hix James Wiggians What Gibson West Whitmell we and our heirs and assigns for and in consideration of the yearly rents hereafter mentioned on the behalf of William King to be paid don and performed hath Granted demesed Leased let and to Let by these presents doth Grant demise Lets and to sarve let unto the said William King his heirs and assigns a parcell of Land belonging to the above said Indians begining upon the town Swamp at the mouth of the Licking Branch runing up the said branch to a line of marked trees thence the said line to a branch below blinde Johnes thence along said branch to horse peocoson thence up the said peocoson to Worley Jones line thence along his line to the town swamp thence along the said swamp to the first station. To have and to hold the said parcell of Land before mentioned the full end and term of Ninety nine years from the date above mentioned and fully to be Completed and Ended yealding and paying therefore yearly and every year during the said term unto the said Whitmill Tufdick the King Indian and the rest of the Tuscoroh Indians tha and their heirs I William Cane [et al., . . .] we and our heirs and assigns the yearly rents on Sum of fifteen pounds proclamation money and we the said Whitmill Tufdick and the rest of the Tuscororah Indians I William Cane [et al., . . .] we our heirs and assigns and for [*illegible*] them do Covenant and promise to Grant and agree to and with the said William King his heirs and assigns and to and with the every of them for and under the yearly rent herein Expired on the part and behalf of the said William King his heirs and assigns to paid and performed aforesaid shall and may peaceably have hold we occupy and Enjoy all and singular hereby demised premises and every part thereof without any let trouble Molestation Objection Interupons or denials of the said Whitmell Tufdick the King Indian the rest of the Tuscororoh Indian and there are I William Cane [et al., . . .] we our heirs and assigns or any other person or persons whatsoever Claiming or that shall or may Claim by from or under us. to which we have hereunto set our hands and fix our seats this 13th day of Dec. 1775.

Whitmell Tufdick, William Robearts *<mark>*, William Cane *<mark>*, Cap William Blunt *<mark>* (Seal), William Pugh *<mark>*, Wenioak Ch[ar]les Jun *<mark>* (Seal), John Rodges, Wenioak Charles Sen *<mark>*, John Owens *<mark>* (Seal), Tom Tommas *<mark>*, James Mitchell *<mark>*, Samuel Bridgers *<mark>*, James Hix *<mark>*, James Wiggians *<mark>*, What

Gibson <*mark*> (Seal), Isaac Wheatler <*mark*>, Tom Roberts <*mark*> (Seal), William <*his mark*> Basket (Seal), Lewis <*his mark*> Tufdick, John <*his mark*> Hicks, West Whitmill, <*Terka Re nation 1775*>

> Tuscarora Nation to William King, December 13, 1775, Vol. M, 317-318 (microfilm), Bertie County Deeds, State Archives. The Tuscaroras also leased land to Zedekiah Stone, Thomas Pugh Senior, and Titus Edwards. 1777, Vol. M, 314-315, 315-316, 318-319 (microfilm), Bertie County Deeds, State Archives.

Resolved that all persons be and they are hereby prohibited from making entries in the Tuscarora Lands in Bertie County.

Resolved, also, that William Williams, Thomas Pugh, Zedekiah Stone, Sinior Turner be and they are hereby constituted and appointed Commissioners for the Tuscaroras, being in the County aforesaid, with power to superintend and take care of their affairs, and they, or a majority of them, shall and may demand and receive any rents now due or which may become due to said Tuscaroras, and in case of default of payment, may issue warrants of distress against the persons indebted for rents, and cause the same to be delivered and applied to the proper use and behoof of the said Tuscaroras, and the said Commissioners, or a majority of them, shall take such measure as shall seem good to them to prevent ill disposed persons from bringing spirituous liquors for sale on the lands now in the possession of the said Tuscaroras.

Ordered that the above resolve be sent to the Senate for their concurrence, together with the following Message:

We herewith send for your concurrence a resolve of this House appointing certain Commissioners therein mentioned to superintend the affairs of the Tuscarora Indians in Bertie County. We also send you the petition of said Indians, etc.

> North Carolina House Minutes, December 22, 1777, in Clark, *State Records*, 12:424, 427. The Senate concurred. The resolves became law in April 1778, with the addition of Willie Jones as a commissioner. Clark, *State Records*, 24:171-173.

To the Honourable Senate and House of Commons now met at Newbern. The Petition of Whitmell Tuffdick Hedman and the rest of the Indians of the Tuskarorah Nation living in Bertie County in the State of North Carolina Humbly Sheweth.

That Whereas at a former assembly held at Newbern in the year of our lord one Thousand Seven hundred and Seventy eight you were pleased to Pass an Act of your assembly Intitled an Act for [Securing] the Tuskarorah Indians, and other [Claiming] under the Tuskarorahs, in the possession of their Lands and thereby appointed certain Commissioners who were to Determine all disputes which might happen between the white people and the said

Tuskarorahs or any of them and also where the dispute was Concerning Lands to have a jury summoned by the said Commissioners to try the Same. Notwithstanding all which your good Intentions to[wards, us.] We your unfortunate Petitioners still Labour under many of the Inconveniencies and hardships which you in your great goodness intended to remedy by the said Acts by means of the Juries not attending or not a Sufficient Number of them to [enpower] a jury according to the [Denitious] of the said Act of Assembly. As your Petitioners conceive by reason of the artfull preservation or some of his mean made use of by the Parties who contend with your Petitioners.

Your Petitioners therefore most Humbly Pray that you woud take their case under your most kindous Consideration and lay such Penalty on such Jurors who do not attend when Law fully Summoned to witt compell them to attend or by a Law for that purpose give such an allowance to be paid by the parties who fails in the dispute as well be an Incouragement to them to attend when so summoned [*illegible*].

Whitmell Tifdick, William <*his mark*> Roberts, William <*his mark*> Blunt, John <*his mark*> Randolph, Billy <*his mark*> Pugh, Lewis <*his mark*> Tufdick, West <*his mark*>Tufdick, Walter <*his mark*> Gibson, Thomas <*his mark*> Thomas, James <*his mark*> Mitchel, John <*his mark*> Roggers, Benjn. <*his mark*> Smith, John <*his mark*> Pugh

> Petition of the Tuscarora Indians in Bertie County, [1780], Joint Papers Miscellaneous, Session of April-May 1780, General Assembly Session Records, State Archives, Office of Archives and History, Raleigh. The General Assembly obliged in May 1780. Clark, *State Records*, 24:335.

At a Court of Indian Commission, held at the house of Wm. Blunt on the Indian Lands, Feby. 24, 1781, to try a matter of dispute between said Indians and Exrs. of Wm. King decd., concerning a lease said to be obtained by said King during his life time. Present: Thomas Pugh, Simon Turner and Zedekiah Stone, Commrs. appointed by the Assembly, the Indians and Executors of Wm. King also present. The Sheriff returned the following Jury: Wm. Freeman, Jno. Walston, Peter Clifton, Hugh Hyman, Sam'l Milburn, James House, Henry Averit, Elisha Rhodes, Andrew Oliver, James Bentley, William Watson and Henry Smith, Freeholders, who being sworn say that Wm. King in his life time had no right to the premises in dispute nor his Executors since his death, said lease by which he held it and under which he claimed being fraudulent and fraudulently obtained. Whereupon the Court gave judgment according to verdict, and John Bryan was appointed to execute the judgment by putting the Indians in possession.

> James Robert Bent Hathaway, *North Carolina Historical and Genealogical Register*, 3 vols. (Edenton, 1900-1903), 3:453.

Sources Cited

Adair, James. *A History of the North-American Indians, Particularly Those Nations Adjoining to the Missisippi* [sic] *East and West Florida, Georgia, South and North Carolina and Virginia*. 1775. Reprint. Ann Arbor, Michigan: UMI Books on Demand, 2002.

Albemarle County Papers, Miscellaneous Records. North Carolina State Archives, Office of Archives and History, Raleigh.

Anderson, William L., ed. "Cherokee Clay, from Duché to Wedgwood: The Journal of Thomas Griffiths, 1767-1768." *North Carolina Historical Review* 63 (October 1986): 477-510.

Archdale, John, Colonial Governors' Papers. North Carolina State Archives, Office of Archives and History, Raleigh.

Archdale, John. *A new description of that fertile and pleasant province of Carolina: with a brief account of its discovery, settling, and the government thereof to this time with several remarkable passages of divine providence during my time*. London: Printed for John Wyat, 1707.

Barlowe, Arthur. "Discourse of the First Voyage" [1584-1585]. In Quinn, *Roanoke Voyages*, 1:91-116.

Barnwell, John. "Journal of John Barnwell," Part I. *Virginia Magazine of History and Biography* 5 (April 1898): 391-402.

———. "Journal of John Barnwell," Part II. *Virginia Magazine of History and Biography* 6 (July 1898): 42-55.

Bartram, William. *Travels through North and South Carolina, Georgia, East and West Florida*. 1791. Reprint. Savannah, Georgia: Beehive Press, 1973.

Batts, Nathaniel, Papers. North Carolina State Archives, Office of Archives and History, Raleigh.

Bland, Edward. *The Discovery of New Britain*. 1651; reprint, Ann Arbor: William L. Clements Library, University of Michigan, 1954.

Bonnefoy, Antoine. "Journal of Antoine Bonnefoy, 1741/42." In Mereness, *Travels in the American Colonies*, 239-255.

Boston Gazette.

Brickell, John. *Natural History of North Carolina*. 1737. Reprint. Murfreesboro, North Carolina: Johnson Publishing Company, 1968.

Byrd, William. *History of the Dividing Line Betwixt Virginia and North Carolina*. Raleigh: North Carolina Historical Commission, 1929.

Cain, Robert J., ed. *Records of the Executive Council, 1664-1734*. Volume 7 of *The Colonial Records of North Carolina* [*Second Series*]. Raleigh: Division of Archives and History, Department of Cultural Resources, [projected multivolume series, 1963–], 1984.

————, ed. *Records of the Executive Council, 1735-1754*. Volume 8 of *The Colonial Records of North Carolina* [*Second Series*]. Raleigh: Division of Archives and History, Department of Cultural Resources, [projected multivolume series, 1963–], 1988.

————, ed. *Records of the Executive Council, 1755-1775*. Volume 9 of *The Colonial Records of North Carolina* [*Second Series*]. Raleigh: Division of Archives and History, Department of Cultural Resources, [projected multivolume series, 1963–], 1994.

————, ed. *The Church of England in North Carolina: Documents, 1699-1741*, Volume 10 of *The Colonial Records of North Carolina* [*Second Series*]. Raleigh: Division of Archives and History, Department of Cultural Resources, [projected multivolume series, 1963–], 1999.

Cain, Robert J. and Jan-Michael Poff, eds. *The Church of England in North Carolina: Documents, 1742-1763*. Volume 11 of *The Colonial Records of North Carolina* [*Second Series*]. Raleigh: Office of Archives and History, Department of Cultural Resources [projected multivolume series, 1963–], 2007.

Candler, Allen D., ed. *Colonial Records of the State of Georgia*. 32 vols. Atlanta, Georgia: The Franklin Printing and Publishing Company, 1904–.

Cape Fear Mercury (Wilmington).

Chicken, George, Colonel. "Journal of Colonel George Chicken," 1725. In Mereness, *Travels in the American Colonies*, 95-172.

Clark, Walter, ed. *The State Records of North Carolina*. 16 vols. (11-16) Raleigh: State of North Carolina, 1895-1906.

Colonial Court Records 156, General Court, Civil Papers. North Carolina State Archives, Office of Archives and History, Raleigh.

Colonial Court Records 187, Land Papers and Wills. North Carolina State Archives, Office of Archives and History, Raleigh.

Colonial Court Records 192, Miscellaneous Papers, 1677-1775. North Carolina State Archives, Office of Archives and History, Raleigh.

Colonial Office Papers, British Records. North Carolina State Archives, Office of Archives and History, Raleigh.

Cuming, Alexander, Sir. "Journal of Sir Alexander Cuming (1730)." In *Early Travels in the Tennessee Country, 1540-1800*, edited by Samuel Cole Williams, 122. Johnson City, Tennessee: The Watauga Press, 1928.

De Vorsey, Louis, Jr., ed. *De Brahm's Report of the General Survey in the Southern District of North America.* Columbia: University of South Carolina Press, 1971.

Devereux, John, Papers. North Carolina State Archives, Office of Archives and History, Raleigh.

Dictionary of Phrase and Fable.

Easterby, J. H., ed. *The Journal of the Commons House of Assembly, November 10, 1736–June 7, 1739*, in *The Colonial Records of South Carolina, Series 1.* Columbia: The Historical Commission of South Carolina, 1951.

French, Christopher. "Journal of an Expedition to South Carolina" 2 (Summer 1977): 275-301.

Fries, Adelaide L. et al., eds. *Records of the Moravians in North Carolina.* 13 vols. Raleigh: Office of Archives and History, Department of Cultural Resources, 1922-2006.

General Assembly Session Records, Session of November-December 1757. North Carolina State Archives, Office of Archives and History, Raleigh.

General Assembly Session Records (Oversized), Session of April-May 1783. North Carolina State Archives, Office of Archives and History, Raleigh.

Governors' Office Records, Council Papers, Miscellaneous Papers. North Carolina State Archives, Office of Archives and History, Raleigh.

Granville County, Miscellaneous Records, Miscellaneous Papers. North Carolina State Archives, Office of Archives and History, Raleigh.

Hariot, Thomas. "A briefe and true report of the new found land of Virginia . . . ," February 1588. In Quinn, *The Roanoke Voyages, 1584-1590*, 1:317-387.

Hazard, Samuel, ed. *Colonial Records of Pennsylvania.* 16 vols. Harrisburg, Pennsylvania: printed by T. Fenn & Company, 1851-1853.

Hazard, Samuel et al., eds. *Pennsylvania Archives.* Multiple Series. Philadelphia: Joseph Severn, 1852–.

Herbert, John, Colonel. *Journal of Colonel John Herbert, Commissioner of Indian Affairs for the Province of South Carolina, October 17, 1727 to March 1727/8.*

Edited by Alexander S. Salley. Columbia: Printed for the Historical Commission of South Carolina, 1936.

Hudson, Charles M. *The Juan Pardo Expeditions: Exploration of the Carolinas and Tennessee, 1566-1568.* With documents relating to the Pardo expeditions, transcribed, translated, and annotated by Paul E. Hoffman. Washington: Smithsonian Institution Press, 1990.

Jacobs, Wilbur R., ed. *Indians of the Southern Colonial Frontier: The Edmond Atkin Report and Plan of 1755.* Columbia: University of South Carolina Press, 1954.

Lane, Ralph. "Discourse on the First Colony," August 17, 1585–June 18, 1586. In Quinn, *The Roanoke Voyages, 1584-1590*, 1:255-294.

Lawson, John. *A New Voyage to Carolina.* Edited by Hugh T. Lefler. Chapel Hill: University of North Carolina Press, 1967.

Lederer, John. "The Discoveries of John Lederer, 1670." In *First Explorations of the Trans-Allegheny Region by the Virginians, 1650-1674*, edited by Clarence Walworth Alvord and Lee Bidgood, 169-171. Cleveland: Arthur H. Clark Company, 1912.

Longe, Alexander. "A Small Postscript on the Ways and Manners of the Indians called Cherokees." Edited by David H. Corkran. *Southern Indian Studies* 21 (October 1969): 3-49.

McDowell, William L., Jr., ed. *Documents Relating to Indian Affairs, 1750-1754*, in *The Colonial Records of South Carolina, Series 2.* Columbia: South Carolina Archives Department, 1958.

———, ed. *Documents Relating to Indian Affairs, 1754-1765*, in *The Colonial Records of South Carolina, Series 2.* Columbia: South Carolina Archives Department, 1970.

———, ed. *Journals of the Commissioners of the Indian Trade, September 20, 1710-August 29, 1718*, in *The Colonial Records of South Carolina, Series 2.* Columbia: South Carolina Archives Department, 1955.

McIlwaine, Henry Read, ed. *Official Letters of the Governors of the State of Virginia.* 3 vols. Richmond, Virginia: D. Bottom, superintendent of public printing, 1926-1929.

McIlwaine, Henry Read et al., eds. *Executive Journals of the Council of Colonial Virginia.* 6 vols. Richmond, Virginia: D. Bottom, superintendant of public printing, 1925-1966.

Mereness, Newton D., ed. *Travels in the American Colonies.* New York: Antiquarian Society, 1961.

Military Collection. North Carolina State Archives, Office of Archives and History, Raleigh.

Murray, James A. H. et al., eds. *The Oxford English Dictionary*, corrected ed. 13 vols. Oxford: Clarendon Press, 1933.

New-York Gazette, or Weekly Post-Boy (New York, New York).

New-York Mercury (New York, New York).

O'Callaghan, E. B. and Berthold Fernow, eds. *Documents Relative to the Colonial History of the State of New York.* 15 vols. Albany, New York: Weed, Parsons and Company, 1853-1887.

Palmer, William P., ed. *Calendar of Virginia State Papers and Other Manuscripts, 1652-1781.* 11 vols. 1875-1883. Reprint. New York: Kraus Reprint Company, 1968.

Parker, Mattie Erma Edwards, ed. *North Carolina Charters and Constitutions, 1578-1698.* Volume 1 of *The Colonial Records of North Carolina [Second Series].* Raleigh: Carolina Charter Tercentenary Commission [projected multivolume series, 1963–], 1963.

————, ed. *North Carolina Higher Court Records, 1697-1701.* Volume 3 of *The Colonial Records of North Carolina [Second Series].* Raleigh: State Department of Archives and History, [projected multivolume series, 1963–], 1971.

Pennsylvania Gazette (Philadelphia).

Pory, John. "Journal of John Pory," 1622. In *Records of the Virginia Company of London*, 4 vols., edited by Susan Myra Kingsbury, 3:641-642. Washington, D.C.: Government Printing Office, 1906-1935.

Powell, William S., ed. *The Correspondence of William Tryon and Other Selected Papers.* 2 vols. Raleigh: Division of Archives and History, Department of Cultural Resources, 1980-1981.

Quinn, David Beers, ed. *The Roanoke Voyages, 1584-1590.* Second Series, number 104. 2 vols. London: For the Hakluyt Society, 1955.

Rockwell, E. F., ed. "Parallel and Combined Expeditions Against the Cherokee Indians in South and in North Carolina, in 1776." *Historical Magazine and Notes and Queries*, New Series, 2 (October 1867): 212-220.

Rowan, Matthew. Colonial Governors' Papers. North Carolina State Archives, Office of Archives and History, Raleigh.

Rowan County, Minutes of the Court of Pleas and Quarter Sessions. North Carolina State Archives, Office of Archives and History, Raleigh.

Salisbury District Superior Court, Miscellaneous Land Records, Ejectments. North Carolina State Archives, Office of Archives and History, Raleigh.

Salley, Alexander S., ed. *Journal of the Grand Council of South Carolina*. 2 vols. Columbia: The Historical Commission of South Carolina, 1907.

Saunders, William L., ed. *The Colonial Records of North Carolina*. 10 vols. Raleigh: State of North Carolina, 1886-1890.

Secretary of State Records, Land Office (Colonial), Court of Claims, Entries for Warrants, 1742/43-1774. North Carolina State Archives, Office of Archives and History, Raleigh.

Secretary of State Records, Land Office (Colonial), Court of Claims, John Rice's Book of Entries for Warrants. North Carolina State Archives, Office of Archives and History, Raleigh.

Secretary of State Records, Land Office (Colonial), Proprietary and Royal Land Grants, 1712-1775, Proprietary Grants. North Carolina State Archives, Office of Archives and History, Raleigh.

Secretary of State Records, Land Office (State), Transcriptions of County Land Entry Books, Burke County Land Entries. North Carolina State Archives, Office of Archives and History, Raleigh.

Secretary of State Records, Provincial Council of Safety Records. North Carolina State Archives, Office of Archives and History, Raleigh.

Society for the Propagation of the Gospel in Foreign Parts, Letterbooks, Series A, British Records. North Carolina State Archives, Office of Archives and History, Raleigh.

Society for the Propagation of the Gospel in Foreign Parts, Letterbooks, Series C, British Records. North Carolina State Archives, Office of Archives and History, Raleigh.

South Carolina Gazette.

Stanard, William G., ed., "The Indians of Southern Virginia, 1650-1711: Depositions in the Virginia and North Carolina Boundary Case." *The Virginia Magazine of History and Biography* 7 (April 1900): 337-358.

State Treasurer, Office of, Indian Affairs and Lands. North Carolina State Archives, Office of Archives and History, Raleigh.

State Treasurer, Office of, Office of State Comptroller, Customs House Papers, Port Roanoke. North Carolina State Archives, Office of Archives and History, Raleigh.

Timberlake, Henry. *Lieutenant Henry Timberlake's Memoirs, 1756-1765*. Edited by Samuel Cole Williams. Johnson City, Tennessee: The Watauga Press, 1927.

Virginia Gazette (Williamsburg: Purdie and Dixon).

War Office Papers, British Records. North Carolina State Archives, Office of Archives and History, Raleigh.

Wright, J. Leitch, Jr., ed. "William Hilton's Voyage to Carolina in 1662." *Essex Institute Historical Collections* 105 (April 1969): 96-102.

Wroth, Lawrence C. *The Voyages of Giovanni da Verrazzano, 1524-1528*. New Haven: Published for the Pierpont Morgan Library by the Yale University Press, 1970.

Yeardley, Francis. "Journal of Francis Yeardley," 1654. In *Narratives of Early Carolina*, edited by Alexander S. Salley, 27. New York: Scribner, 1911.

Index

A

Aaron Blanchards Path, 286

Abenaki Indians, 47n

Accidents, 2, 20, 21, 70, 71, 72, 84, 122

Act of Assembly (N.C.): actions contrary to an, 178; to amend other acts, 189, 257; for ascertaining the boundaries of Indian lands, 279-281, 292; concerning marriage, 255; concerning servants and slaves, 256-257; for destroying vermin, 249; to fix a seat of government, keep public offices, appoint circuit courts, and defray their expenses, 257; for opening the Land Office (1783), 189-191; to prevent stealing of livestock and altering or defacing marks and brands, 255-256; to regulate and ascertain officers' fees (1781), 189; to regulate trade with Indians, 115-117, 134; relating to assemblies and regulating elections, 255; relating to settling on Indian lands, 298; for restraining Indians and protecting their land rights (1715), 153-155, 179, 180; and sale of Indians, 207. *See also* General Assembly (N.C.)

Act of Assembly (S.C.), 104, 105, 111, 117. *See also* General Assembly (S.C.)

Adair, James: describes agricultural practices, 24, 25, 26, 27, ball-playing, 39-40, baskets and pottery, 35-36, Cherokees, 10, 13, 15, 16, 30, 74-75, 81, 84, clans, 17-18, clothing, 7, 60, culinary practices, 27, 33-34, 58-59, 60, diplomatic protocols, 21, 44, healing methods, 62, 64, hot houses, 66-67, importance of bathing, 65, stone axes, 32, the *uktena*, 59-60; discussed warriors volunteering for combat, 192; gives details of acts of torture and scalping, 199, 202; notes diversity of Indian languages, 3, 4,

trade practices, 87; remarks on Indians' migration from Asia, 1

Adoption, 19, 202, 205, 206

Adultery, 74, 75

African Americans: belonging to James Coale accused of robbery, 260; bring smallpox to N.C., 74; children, 256, 273; do not enjoy legal equality with whites, 254; fitted out to trade with the Catawbas, 11; has hand cut off, 209; and Indian traders, 96, 97, 130, 132; owned by Mr. Benner, 226; prohibited from voting and from marrying whites, 255; punished for killing livestock, 255; as slaves, 206, 258, 259, 261; teaching of, 270, 271; warn of potential bloodshed among the Cherokee Valley towns, 96; as witnesses, 257. *See also under* Slaves

Africans. *See* African Americans

Agriculture: clans facilitated, 9; and corn, 27, 41-42, 60-61, 74, 107, 136, 149; and crops, 69, 94, 143; environment provides fertile soil for, 10; and field preparation, 23-26, 74, 135, 159; fruitfulness of, described, 138, 139; implements of, 21, 23; land used for, 144, 156, 158, 163, 166; and stockpiling food, 17. *See also individual crops by name*; Crop lands; Food; Harvesting; Plantations; Planting

Aiken County (S.C.), 78n, 219n

Alabama, 11n, 78n, 221n

Albany, N.Y., 78, 79, 153n, 214, 215, 217

Albemarle assembly, 115-116

Albemarle (Arelbermerle) County (N.C.), 85, 146n, 275, 286, 288

Albemarle region, ix, x, 142, 145, 267, 277

Albemarle Sound, 136n, 145, 147

Alcohol, alcoholic beverages: and Cherokees, 14-15, 74, 120, 127; given to Indians by Indian traders, x, 92;

Indians developed a dependence on, 250; Indians lost land and people because of, 286; leads to crime, war, 20, 21, 110, 119; prohibition from bartering or selling, 131; restricted by Indians, 121-122; sought by Cherokee attackers, 97; use of, among Indians, 49, 57, 73, 80, 118-119, among whites, 70. *See also individual types of alcohol by name*

Alexander (Indian), 265, 266

Alexander, Nathaniel (Nathl.), Col., 224, 228

Algonquian (language), ix, x, 3, 236n. *See also* Algonquian Indians

Algonquian Indians, 47n. *See also* Algonquian (language)

Allen, John, 298n

Alston, Mr. (commissary), 241

Amadas, Philip, Capt., 49

Ambassadors, 12, 45, 48

Amehetae (Amahetai) (Indian), 222

American Revolution, xii, 182, 191n, 255, 274

Amherst, Jeffrey, Gen., 235

Ammouskossittee (The Emperor), Cherokee, 77, 124, 125

Ammunition: denied to Indians, 149, 153; English made, 55; Indians supplied with, 91, 99, 127, 128, 216, 222, 224, 240, 295, 297; lack of, 125; need for, 102; purchase of, 123, 149, 220; stolen, 148. *See also* Arms; Bullets; Gunpowder; Powder and shot

Amsterdam, N.Y., 217n

Ancaster and Kesteven, Duke of (Peregrine Bertie), 155

Andrews, N.C., 141n

Animal skins: ample supply of, 116; clothing made from, 5, 6, 7, 160, 203; described, 33; dressing/tanning of, 11, 34, 131; exchanged for trade goods, 31, 86, 87, 90, 91, 92-93, 99, 112, 118, 128, 167, 171, 194; hunting for, 100, 119; as mat/bed/rug, 17, 60,

62; paid as tribute, 283, 297; as payment, 87, 88, 99; as present, 16, 50, 153; purchase of, 46, 118, 131; seizure of, 89, 126, 147; selling, 86, 92, 111, 119; used for drums, 41, 42; used in hot house construction, 66; value of, 21, 46, 89, 103, 127, 130, 147. *See also individual animal skins by name*

Animism, ix, 58, 60

Annapolis (Anopolis), Md., 89

Anson County (N.C.), 85, 157, 158, 159-160, 228

Appachancano (emperor), 194

Appalachian (Apalachian) Mountains, 66, 94, 129, 168, 169, 177, 182, 189

Appamattuck guide, 194

Appomattox River, 87

Apprentices. *See* Indenture/indentured servants

Aqua-ne-wa-rotee. *See* Brasstown Creek

Aquonatuste (Cherokee Valley town), 141n

Aramaskeet (Arromuskeet, Arrowmuskeet). *See* Mattamuskeet, N.C.

Ararat River, 231n

Archdale, John, 70, 72-73, 115, 116-117

Arch-magus, 203

Arkansas, 28n

Armor, 32

Armory, 47

Arms: bearing, 137; European-made, 32; force and, 250, 253, 260; French reneged on promise of, 238; interdiction of, 231; lack of, 155; possession of, 21, 97, 108; taking of, 212. *See also* Ammunition; Armory; Bows and arrows; Bullets; Powder and shot; Weaponry

Arrows. *See* Bows and arrows

Arson, 127, 149, 159, 209, 237

Articles of Friendship and Commerce, 232

Ashes, 23, 27, 58, 67, 138

Asia, 1, 135

Assaraquoa, Brother, Catawba, 215

Assault: attempted, by Little Carpenter, 120; failed, by Cherokees against Shawnees, 225; upon colonists by Indians, 148, 159, 250, forts, 209, 210, Indian hunters by colonists, 143, 144-145, Indian traders by Indians, 97, 118, 120, 126, Indians by Indian traders, 99-100, 101, 110, Indians is prohibited, 154-155, negro by Indians, 93. *See also* Assault and battery

Assault and battery, 251, 254, 263. *See also* Assault

Assembly (public meeting), 13, 19, 42, 106, 170

Assembly. *See* Act of Assembly (N.C.); Act of Assembly (S.C.); Albemarle assembly; General Assembly (N.C.); General Assembly (S.C.)

Atamuskeet (Attamuskeet, Attamuskeett). *See* Mattamuskeet, N.C.

Atholl, 2nd Duke of (James Murray), 155

Atkin (Atkins), Edmond: appointed superintendent for Indian affairs in the southern district, 129; Catawba reservation set by, 162, 164, 167; comments on consumption of rum by Cherokees, 118, 119, Indian traders, 106, 109, 111; concludes Treaty of Pine Tree Hill, 162-168; describes Indians' pursuit of national interests, 48, S.C. regulations on the Indian trade, 104-105, 114, 115, 128; notes importance of gift-exchanges with Indians, 49, Indians' aversion to colonial towns due to fear of contracting illnesses, 76; observes commissioners' laxity in enforcing duties, 110; states how British ignored Indian headmen while French offered them gifts, 126, 128, interaction between Indians and French officials is strictly controlled, 106; warns about excessive trade debts carried by Indians, 99, 100

Atlantic Coastal Plain (coastal region), 3, 135

Atlantic white cyprus, 38

Attakullakulla (Attakulla Kulla, Attacullahcullah, Attaculcullah, attaw kullcullah, ockulla Stotastoah): agreed to terms of treaty, 232, 233; drunken altercation of, 120-121; met to hold Council, 141; received gun and pipe hatchet, 96, Indian commission, 52; sells tract of land, 181, 182; sided with English, 239; signs peace treaty, 171. *See also* Little Carpenter

Atwood, Isaac, 93

Aucus al Kanigut, Tuscarora, 296

Augusta, Ga., 74, 78n, 119, 122, 167, 171, 236n, 240

Augusta Company, 128

Augusta Congress, 167, 168, 171, 173-174, 175

Augusta County (Va.), 137

Austinville, Va., 174n

Auston, John, 46

Avenging. *See* Revenge

Averit, Henry, 303

Axes, 32, 57, 91, 92, 160

Ayoree, 239

Ayres, Colonel, Catawba, 167-168

B

Back Bay (Va.), 146

Backman, Colonel (message bearer), 241

Bacon, Henry, Corp., 96

Bailie, Captain, 234

Baize, 6

Bald cyprus, 38

Ball. *See* Ammunition

Ball (game), 39-40, 42-43, 207

Bankruptcy, 110, 113

Baptisms, 270, 274

Barbar, Tuscarora,, 213

Barber, John, 284

Barcock, Thomas, 251

Bare Creek, 212

Bare River, 212

Bark, 200

Barking Dog, Cherokee, 244
Barlowe, Arthur, Capt., 45, 49
Barnstable, Mass., 266n
Barnwell, John, Col., 9, 117, 209, 211
Barrow, Col. (Beaufort County militia-
    man), 155
Barter, 206
Bartram, William: describes council
    house, 12-13, habitations built by
    Cherokees, 10-11, individual Chero-
    kee farm plots, 24-25, physical
    features of Cherokee headman, 4;
    makes comments about Indian
    traders, 101; notes that Cherokees
    are jealous of whites inspecting their
    land, 141; recounts Cherokee dances,
    39, 42-43, 44
Basket (Baskit), William, Capt., 294, 301,
    302
Baskets, 35
Baskett, Thomas, 298
Baskit, Bille, 299
Bate, Humphrey, 298n
Bate (Bates), Sarah, 297, 298, 298n
Bath, N.C., 208, 270, 272n
Bath County (N.C.), 70, 147, 265
Bathing, 61, 65-66, 75. *See also*
    Purification; Sweating
Batts, Nathaniel (Nath.), 142, 143
Bay trees, 138
Beads, 8, 16, 43, 45, 51, 91, 218, 220
Beamer, James, 109-110, 125, 220
Beans: Cherokees believe adulterous
    couples spoiled fields of, 74;
    cultivation of, ix, 23, 24, 25; as ingre-
    dient in bread, 27, 28, 29; as religious
    sacrifice, 57; troops destroy and
    consume crops of, 237, 243, 244, 245
Bear (Bare) River (town), 207n
Bear (Bare) River Indians, 147, 148-150,
    207n
Bearcroft, Philip, 76
Bearded Man, 226
Bear oil, 5, 27, 31, 40, 42, 83
Bear skins, 7, 17, 89

Bears, 33, 34, 131, 194, 198, 264. *See also*
    Bear oil; Bear skins
Beaufort County (N.C.), 265n
Beaufort Precinct (N.C.), 136n, 144, 145,
    155
Beaver Dam Run, 9n
Beavers, x, 6, 7, 33, 89, 91, 131, 144, 153
Bees, 138
Bell, Joseph (Jos.), Col., 80
Bell buttons, 30
Bell rackets, 43
Bells, 42
Beloved Men, 175, 195, 200, 220, 247
Belts, 6, 7, 196, 214, 296
Ben (Indian slave), 261, 262
Benn, Samuel (Samll.), 96, 97
Benner, Mr., 225, 226
Bennet, Billy, 294
Bennett (Benneett), James, 251, 253,
    284, 286
Bennett, Richard, Maj. Gen., 142
Bennett's Creek, 145, 146
Bentley, James, 303
Berkeley (Barkley), William (Wm.), Sir,
    Gov., 142
Berkeley (Berkly) County (S.C.), 88
Berkshire Mountains, 236n
Berry, Captain, 224
Bertie County (N.C.): detention of an
    Indian slave in, 259n; letter to sheriff
    of, 254; Tuscarora land in, 280, 293,
    294n, 297, 298n, 299, 301, 302, 302n
Bertie Precinct (N.C.), 145, 155, 250
Bethabara, 225
Bethania, 274
Big Bear (the great Bear), Cherokee, 141
Big Pigeon (Pidgeon) River, 190
Birds, 197
Birkenhead, Mr., 150
Bishops, 109
Black Dog of Nottely (Notoly),
    Cherokee, 93
Black Hole (defile), 242
Blacks. *See* African Americans
Blackwater River, 143

Bladen County (N.C.), 155

Blake, David, 260

Bland, Edward, 192-193

Blankets: corpses wrapped in, 81; given to Cherokees by S.C., 51, 52, by settlers, 182; land leased to Tuscarora in exchange for, 297, 299; left behind by Cherokees, 243; purchased by French-allied Indians, 93; sold to Valley Cherokees, 90; sought by Tuscaroras, 20; theft of, 258; were lost when canoe capsized, 218. *See also* Duffles

Blanshard, Marias, 253

Blinde Towne, 136

Blood, 60, 63, 193, 200

Bloody Hill, 244

Blount, Billy, 294, 298

Blount, Billy, Jun. (Blunt, Bille, Jun.), 299, 300

Blount, Billy, Senior (Blunt, Bille, Senior), 299, 300

Blount (Blunt), James, 280, 294

Blount, Sighacka, 143, 144-145

Blount, Tom, King (Blunt, Tom, King), Tuscarora: agrees to peace, 212; captures King Hancock, 211; complains of encroachment on Tuscarora land, 297-298; detains Indian slave, 259; had ties with colonists, xi; identified, 8n; leads Tuscaroras to reservation, 278, 279; N.C. endorses, as Tuscarora king, 281-282; pays tribute, 283; Sighacka tells, of broken arm, 145; wears European-style clothing, 7

Blount (Blunt), William, Capt., 294, 301, 303

Blue Ridge Mountains, 170, 183

Blunt, John, 294

Board of Trade: creates Plan for the Future Management of Indian Affairs, rescind same, 132, 133; letters to, 9, 15, 20, 21, 24, 48, 76-78, 91-92, 117-118, 126, 137, 144, 158, 161-162, 162-163, 166, 168, 170, 171-173;

promised Indian trade and future redress to Cherokee delegation, 102; provides opinion on land petition, 156

Boats, 45, 94. *See also* Canoes; Ships

Bogue, Willm., 266

Bonds: Indian traders post, 87, 88-89, 106, 129, 130, 132; paid for issuing trading license, 104; for trade goods, 90-91, 94

Bonnefoy, Antoine, 19, 202

Bonner, Henry, 250

Boone, Thomas, Gov. (S.C.), 163-166 passim

Boots, 7, 51, 87, 93, 218, 243, 297, 299

Borfus, Ralph, 266

Boude, John, 277

Bouillon (buillon), 91

Boundary lines: between Cherokees and N.C., Va., and S.C., 78, 79, 171, 173, 174-178, N.C. and S.C., 157-158, 161, 163, 165, 166, 167; disputes over, 277; establishment of, 129, 172, 187; monitoring the laying of, 133; redrawing of, 188, 189-190; of reservations, 163, 164, 278, 279-281; school founded near the Va., 268; settlers violate, 182-183, 184, 185

Bounties, 199, 249

Bowls, 86

Bows and arrows: barbed, 199; fashioned from wood and stone, 32, 160; Indians kill small game with, 31; natural remedies for curing wounds from, 64; used to hunt bears, 33, fish, 36, 38; warriors do not fear, 193; women using, 210

Boyde, Colonel, 211

Bracelets, 8, 43, 87, 91

Branding, 255

Brandy, 2

Branham (fugitive criminal), 107-108

Brass, 6, 52

Brasstown Creek, 140, 141n

Bray, Dr., 270

Bread, 195

Breaking and entering, 118, 120, 122, 123-125, 127, 253, 254
Breeches, 5, 7-8, 51
Bremen (half Indian), 243
Brewsters River, 194. *See also* Gumberry Creek
Bribes/bribery, 49, 50, 110
Brice, Captain, 208
Brickell, John, 5, 7-8
Bridgers, Samuel, 299, 300, 301
Bristol, England, 89
Britain, 221. *See also* British; British Army
British, 217n, 222, 225, 229, 238, 240. *See also* Britain; British Army
British Army, 162, 235, 246, 257
Broad Creek, 261
Broad River, 137, 167, 176, 222. *See also* Broad River Valley
Broad River Valley, 234. *See also* Broad River
Broughton, Thomas, Lt. Gov. (S.C.), 111
Brown, Samuel (Saml.), 106-107
Brunswick, 292
Bryan, John, 303
Bryan, Needham, Col., 299
Bryant, Thomas, 104
Bryson City, N.C., 26n
Buck Branch, N.C., 213n
Buck skins, 275
Buckannan, Colonel, 127
Buckles, John, 219n
Buckles, 51
Buffalo Creek, 222
Buffaloes, 6, 33, 34, 60, 167, 175, 198
Bull, William, Lt. Gov. and Gov. (S.C.): discusses relations with Catawba, 162-163, 168, Cherokee, 170, 171; discusses rum trade, 121, 122; issues Indian trade license, 105-106; letters to and from, 34, 51, 122, 162-163, 168, 170, 217n; sent outline of treaty, 238
Bull, William, Junr., 261
Bullen, Captain, 227

Bullen, James, 52
Bullets, 19, 52, 64, 72, 130, 193, 199. *See also* Ammunition; Arms; Gunpowder
Bullock, Leonard Henley, 181
Buncombe County (N.C.), 241n
Bunning, Robert (Mr. Bunyon, Mr. Bunyont), 124, 125
Burgamy pitch, 116
Burglary, 251
Burgwin, John, 89
Burials. *See* Charnel houses; Funeral customs and rites, ceremonies; Graves
Burke County (N.C.), 140n, 183, 190, 191
Burning at the stake, 219
Burning-town, 243
Burningtown Creek, 2n, 244n
Burns, John, 108
Burrington, George, 259
Burton, Daniel, 294n
Burtons (troops), 237
Butler, Mr. (trader), 95, 101, 274
Butler, William, 251, 254
Button-rattle-snake-root, 193
Buttons, 51
Byrd, William, Col. (Colonel Byrd), 87, 109-110, 196

C

Caciques, 267
Cadice, 90
Cadiz, 51
Cahnuwagaws, 217
Cain, Bille, 300
Cain, Jno., 294
Caine, John, 298
Cairn, 201
Calabash, 44, 75
Calicoes, 51
Callisis Drean, 289
Cambay, India, 138n
Camden, S.C., 3n, 162n
Camden County (N.C.), 136n, 275n
Camden Point, N.C., 136n

Cameron, Alexander (Capt. Cameron, Mr. Cameron), 52, 62, 79, 134, 141, 173, 177

Campbell, [Arthur], Colonel, 247

Camps, 194, 203, 246

Canada, 167

Cane, William, 301

Canes, 75, 81, 203

Cannastion, 244

Cannons, 47

Canoes: construction of, 16; Indians traveled in, 45, 49, 218; mentioned, 97; theft of, 258; transported goods, 19, 26; utility of, described, 38-39. *See also* Boats; Ships

Canton, N.C., 32n

Canucy, 244

Canusokehee. *See* Caunookehoe (Caunookeha)

Cape Fear Indian, 263

Cape Fear River (Cape Fair, Cape Fare), 34, 94, 117, 137, 138-139, 156, 206, 263

Cape Fear [River] valley, ix, 208

Capital offenses, 257

Capitol, the (Va.), 122

Captives, ix, xi, 206, 207. *See also* Hostages; Prisoners

Card, [Robert], Capt., 207

Carey, Miles, 263

Carolina (colony): borders of, 161; coast of, 45, 69, 94, 146; creation of, 73, 142; flora in, 31, 68; governor of, 146n, 258; Indian trade company in, 116-117; Indians in, 45-46, 73, 192, 201; inhabitants of, 224, 296; Iroquois and, 214; John Lawson explores, 1; land in, 117, 143, 147; Lords proprietors of, 85, 117, 146, 275, 277; mentioned, 81, 112, 113, 220; Piedmont, 135; and protection of the Indian slave trade, 206; and settlements in, 72, 240; traders from, 74, 127, 128; warriors from, 110; weather in, 2. *See also* North Carolina; South Carolina

Carolina Charter, 146

Carpets, 13

Carr, Wm., 124

Carter, James, 160, 223

Carteret, John, Lord, 117, 275. *See also* Earl Granville

Carteret, Robert, 180

Carteret County (N.C.), 73n, 80, 155, 266n

Cary, Thomas, 153n. *See also* Cary Rebellion

Cary Rebellion, 150, 152. *See also* Cary, Thomas

Caswell, Richard, Gov. (N.C.), 183, 184, 185-187

Catachny, 212

Catawba Confederacy, 3

Catawba headmen, 77-78, 110, 157, 158, 160-161, 164, 165, 167

Catawba Indians (Cataba, Catauba, Catawbaw, Catawbee, Cattaba, Cattaboe, Cuttaba, Katahba): alcohol use by, 118, 121-122; attacks on, 214, 217, 218; boundary of reservations of, 158, 161, 167; defend their burial grounds, 163, 165, 166; describe their culture, 160; disease and, 73, 75, 76, 77, 78-79, 135, 163; distribute and receive gifts and aid, 157, 159, 226, 227, 228; education of, 273; encroachment of, and lands of, 156, 157, 158, 160, 161, 162-163, 165, 166, 168; government of, described, 13; hunting grounds of, 162, 163, 167; Indian traders and, 9n, 85-86, 88, 106-107, 110; language of, 3; leadership within, 78n; location of, 9, 135, 137, 274; and other Indians, 46, 77-78, 161, 163, 205, 296; peace negotiations with, 45, 46, 47-48, 78-79, 167-168, 174, 215; population of, 135, 158, 161-165 passim; relations with, 216, 223; settlement of, 205, 232; and S.C., 78, 104, 156-157, 158, 161, 162, 165, 166, 167; supported English against Cherokees,

222, 223, 224, 235; and trade, 87, 88-89, 104, 126, 156-157, 158; treaties with, 156-157, 158, 160-161, 162, 163. *See also* Catawba headmen; Catawba King; Catawba Nation; Catawba towns; Charraw; Nassaw; Noostee; Sucah; Sugar Creek Town; Weyane; Weyapee
Catawba King, 157, 216
Catawba Nation, 202, 274
Catawba River (Cataba, Catabaw, Cuttaba), 9n, 85, 157, 163, 164, 168, 230, 241. *See also* Catawba River Valley
Catawba River Valley, 234. *See also* Catawba River
Catawba towns, 9, 76, 158, 161, 163, 164, 167-168
Catechna, 209
Catherine Creek, 286
Cathey, Alexr., 228
Catheys Fort, 245
Catholicism, 47n
Catostery Creek, 212
Cats, 33, 89, 264
Catterus, 90
Cattle: act to prevent killing, stealing, mismarking, and misbranding, 255-256; in Cape Fear area, 138; complaints about encroachers disturbing, 162-163; consumed by colonists and Indians, 25, 175; destroyed by Indian hunters, 143, 145, 150, 159; diet of, 69; driving stocks of, 190, 281; Indians punished for poaching, 154; killing of, 84, 184, 185, 214
Catuchee (The Tail), Cherokee, 99
Cauchi, 31-32
Cauetas, 220
Caughnawaga (Coghnawagey) Indians, 47, 217
Caunookehoe (Caunookeha), 212, 213n
Cayuga Indians, 22n
Cedar (Seder) Island, 149
Cedars, 138
Chachetcha (warrior), 220

Champion Land, 194
Charles II, King, 142, 146
Charles, King, Matchapungo, 148
Charles, Wineoak, Junior, 299, 300, 301
Charles, Wineoak, Senior, 299, 300, 301
Charleston, S.C. (Charles Town, Charlestown): British troops landed near, 235; Christopher Gale in, 208; controlled trade and diplomacy for N.C. Indians, 76; corporal dispatched to, 96; deerskin sold in, 88; disease in, 74, 76, 78; extract of letter from, 47-48; general assembly met at, 117; Indian traders in, 95, 109, 110, 111-112; Indians moved away from, 206; mentioned, 75, 157, 162, 178, 228, 261; newspaper account from, 205; port at, 126; talks with Indians held in, 76, 77, 78n, 79, 104, 221, 231-232, 239; traders licensed at, 74, 105
Charleton, George, 298n
Charleton, William, 298n
Charnel houses, 84
Charraw (Catawba town), 9n
Chatooga River, 14n
Chatooke River, 212
Chattahoochee County, Ga., 219n
Chattahoochee (Chatahootchie) River, 137, 219n, 221n
Chenshi, Cherokee, 232
Cheoah (Cheeowhee, Cheowee, Chewee) (Cherokee Valley town), 59, 60n, 99, 113, 274
Cheraw (Charraw) Indians, 75-76
Cherokee country, 239
Cherokee County (N.C.), 14n, 52n, 93n, 141n, 242
Cherokee headmen, chiefs: attend talks, 2, 76, 79, 95-96, 102-103, 124-125, 173-176, 184-186, 221, 238; and boundary lines, 79, 173-174, 176; and disease, 74, 77; hold council, 182-183; and hunting grounds, 181-182, 186; and Indian traders, 97-98, 99, 107, 108; meet King George II, 102;

offer gifts and drink to visitors, 49-50, 69; orate at Cherokee ball-play dance, 43; physical description of, 4; react to encroachment, 184, 187; receive assistance from Ga., 74; represents largest clan, 98; selected to receive Indian commissions, 52; and trade, 102-103, 124-125

Cherokee Indians (Cherekee, Cherickee, Cherrockee, Cherroekee): adoption and, 19, 202; alcohol use by, 118; attacks on, 217, 235; beliefs and opinions of, 15, 17, 182n, 229; and boundary lines with N.C., S.C., and Va., 78, 79, 171-178 passim, 187, 188; and British, 235, 236; buildings of, described, 10-11, 12-13; burial and funeral practices of, 12, 81, 83-84; colonial forces and, 183, 225; construct utilitarian implements, 30, 35; deputy agent for, 173; disease and, 73, 74-75, 77, 78, 79; distribute and receive gifts and aid, 51-52, 74, 195, 227, 230; encroachment on lands of, xii, 171, 178-179, 183, 187, 188, 190; entertainment of, 39, 44; and French, 50, 74, 140, 223, 227, 231, 233; government of, described, 13, 14-16; hunting grounds of, 95, 137, 175, 176-178, 182, 188; Indian traders and, 81, 84, 85-86, 95, 99, 105-106, 109-110, 123, 128, 134, 140-141; interact with whites, 159, 171, 182, 187; killed settlers, 231, 234; know medicinal uses of plants, 68, 69-70, 64; land deals with, 23, 25, 174, 178, 180-182, 191n; language of, ix, 3; location of, 10, 135, 137; and other Indians, 207, 216, 218, 219, 221, 222; peace negotiations with, 45, 47-48, 76-77, 141, 173-174, 185-186, 215, 231, 240; physical description of, 4, 8; practices of, 5, 8-9, 18, 58, 60-61, 66, 67, 172; preserving lands of, 172, 187, 189-191; property of, stolen, 228; prove strength in combat, 200;

raids by, 224, 226, 246; relations with, 223; religion and, 53, 55-56, 274; seek protection, 47, 174, 175, revenge, 74, 229; seize fort, 60n; and S.C., 79, 104, 114, 122, 123, 171, 172, 173, 175, 176, 232; and trade, 75, 85-86, 90, 104, 119, 123, 126, 128; and traders, 206; and visitors, 48, 77-78, 65, 126, 141, 159, 162, 274; weaponry of, 32; women among, 9, 25, 26, 47, 205. *See also* Cherokee headmen, chiefs; Cherokee Indians, Lower; Cherokee Nation; Cherokee towns, Lower, Middle, Out towns, Overhill, Valley; Cherokee War; Chickamauga Cherokee Indians

Cherokee Indians, Lower: and alcohol consumption, 120-121; and boundary agreements, 173-174, 176-178; British treaty with, 240; and governors, 124, 125; headmen of, 171-172; hold councils, 49-50, 182-183; hunting grounds of, 170, 172, 183; location of, 2n, 14n, 52n, 125n, 137; mentioned, 52, 121n; slow to recover from Col. Archibald Montgomery's expedition, 238. *See also* Estatoe; Keowee; Little Chota; Noyowe; Tomassee; Tugaloo; Ustenary

Cherokee Mountains. *See* Blue Ridge Mountains; Great Smoky Mountains

Cherokee Nation, 261

Cherokee River (Lower Cheerake). *See* Tennessee River

Cherokee towns: and adoption ceremony, 19; arranges meeting with S.C. Indian commissioner, 2; attack of, 246; Bartram explores, 24-25; colonial settlements approach, 137, 171, 173; deer killed for, 56; dispersal of, 10; governed by a war chief and a peace chief, 14, 15; harbor ambassadors, 48; independence of, 15; Indian trader collects debts in, 99; as mother towns, 14, 124; prefer to do business with honest traders, 95;

receive corn from Ga., 74, steelyards made for the Indian trade, 103; rum carried into, 122; settlers kill livestock owned by Cherokees near, 184; united behind fixing boundary line with N.C., 175. *See also individual towns by name*; Cherokee towns, Lower, Middle, Out Towns, Overhill, Valley; Mother Towns

Cherokee towns, Lower: and boundary lines, 176; communicate with The Raven, 125; corn planted in, 238; fighting in, 219-222, 229-231, 235; location of, 2n; and negotiations of, with whites, 240-241; S.C. troops attack, 242; Wolf in, 52. *See also* Estatoe; Keowee; Little Chota; Noyowe; Tomassee; Tugaloo; Ustenary

Cherokee towns, Middle: and boundary lines, 24-25, 173-174, 176-178; destruction of, 235, 237-238; encroachment of, 186; hold talks concerning validity of land purchases, 182-183; host council for commissioner of Indian affairs, 49-50, meeting with S.C. commissioner, 2; Indian trader serves arrest warrant in, 106, 107-108; killer headed toward, 220; King of Kettooah in, 14; lack of hunting ground in, 186; location of, 137; mentioned, 14n; negotiations involving headmen from, 221, 229; and relocation to Va., 109; spread of falsehoods in, 108; starvation in, 25; troops headed through, 236, 237, 242, 245; warriors from, fight and attend talks, 109-110, 173-174. *See also* Cowee; Ellijay; Etchoe; Ioree; Nikwasi; Stecoe; Whatoga

Cherokee towns, Out towns: Cherokee delegation from Round O of, 231; destruction of, 237-238; French-allied Indians to attack, 76, 77; host council for commissioner of Indian affairs, 49-50; inhabitants of, steal trader's goods, 122, 123-125; location of, 2n, 126n; messenger dispatched to, 2. *See also* Connutra; Kituwah; Stecoe; Tuckasegee

Cherokee towns, Overhill: attacked, 77, 216; and boundary lines, 173-174, 176-178; British prevented from advancing against the, 235; discuss land purchases, 182-183; encroachment on, 187; English had a best friend among the, 232; French renege on promises of arms for, 238; headmen of, 124, 173-174, 221, 231; host council for commissioner of Indian affairs, 49-50; hostile toward American troops, 241, 242, 243; Indian trader visits, 112; location of, 14n, 137; lose portion of hunting grounds, 183; medals distributed to residents of, 52; N.C. surveyors examine towns of, 186; refuse to attend proceedings for peace treaty, 240; trade goods destined for, 97, 98; young warriors of the, 230. *See also* Chota; Great Hiwassee; Great Tellico; Hiwassee; Tanasi; Tuskegee

Cherokee towns, Valley: attacks in, 96, 125; encroachment on, 186; French-allied Indians outside, 92, 93; headman of, 4, 125; host council for commissioner of Indian affairs, 49-50; location of, 14n, 125n-126n, 137; medal distributed to resident of, 52; meetings and talks in 93, 102-103, 124; and silver mine, 140; traders in, 90, 91, 93, 96-97, 105-106, 113; willing to go to war, 93. *See also* Aquonatuste; Cheoah; Connostee; Custowee; Econourste; Konahete; Little Hiwassee; Little Tellico; Neowe; Nottely; Stecoe; Tasetche; Tomotla

Cherokee War (1760-1761, 1776), 93n, 137, 162, 163, 170, 171, 183, 234

Cherokeehatchee River. *See* Broad River

Chesepian Indians, 136
Chester, John, 207
Chestowee, 207
Chestuee Creek, 207n
Cheust hartuithoo, Tuscarora, 212
Chevin, Nathl. (N., Nath.), 206, 251, 252, 283
Chickamauga (Chickamawga) Cherokee Indians, 189, 191n
Chickamauga Creek, 191n
Chickasaw Indians (Chicasahs, Chicasaws, Chikasas): appoint chargé d'affaires to serve in Cherokee nation, 48; attend Augusta Congress, 174; hunting grounds claimed by Cherokees extend to lands of, 137; and S.C., 104, 105, 114; reinforce British troops, 235, 236n; and trade, 104, 105, 219n, 241n
Chicken, George, Col., 49-50, 99, 106-107
Chickens, 127
Chief justices, 121-122, 225, 250, 252
Chiefs. See Headmen
Child rearing, 4, 5, 18, 19, 21-22, 60
Childbirth, 19
Children: and bathing, 65; Catawba, 163, 164, 167; Cherokee, 176; colonial, 148, 176; cradle-boarded, 4, 5; and creation story, 53; curbed by huskanawing, 21-22; dry scratched by priests, 58; education of, 1-2, 128; forced to flee settlements, 159; French-allied Indian, 92; headmen to seek satisfaction for, 142; as hostages, 213; mourn deceased kinsmen, 79, 81, 83; never given away in marriage by their parents, 18; noted in militia returns, 155; reared on animal skins, 60; restrained prior to green corn ceremony, 61; as slaves, 46, 206, 208, 209, 211, 258; spurn other clans, 17; and torture, 202, 203; toys of, to be sold to remote Indians,

91; and traders, 96, 97, 124, 125; utilize match coats, 6; and wampum, 47, 151. See Child rearing; Childbirth
Chinesto (Chenesto) of Sugar Town, Cherokee, 177, 178
Chinoca River. See Kentucky River
Chipanum, 136n
Chisquatalone, Cherokee, 232
Chistanah, Cherokee, 232
Chistee, Cherokee, 232;
Chiswell, John, Col., 173, 174n, 176, 177
Choctaw Indians (Chactaws, Chocktaws, Choctahs, Choctaws), 52n, 104, 105, 114, 174, 218-219, 222, 235
Cholmondeley, 3rd Earl of (George Cholmondeley), 155
Chota (Choeto, Chotee, Chottee) (Cherokee Overhill town), 93, 97-98, 175, 182-183. See also Chota, Prince of
Chota, Prince of, 195, 196. See also Chota
Chowan County (N.C.), 155, 252, 253, 285
Chowan Indians (Charah, Chawan, Choanoc, Chowanoke): attack settlers in Albemarle region, 145, 146; chief of the, 5, 7-8, 252; destruction of crops of, 253; headman of, wants son to attend Christian school, 268; inspired young men to greatness, 192; king of the, 195, 269; land of the, 146, 275, 284-285, 286; location of, 136n, 155; as member of Catawba Confederacy, 3; petition of, 276; population of, 155, 286; relegated to reservation, 145, 146; sought an attachment against an estate, 251
Chowan Precinct, 85, 269, 286
Chowan River, 136, 137, 138, 142, 145, 277
Chowan Town, 286
Chowanoc (Choanoke) (Indian town), 136, 136n
Christian, William, Colonel, 242

Christianity, 71-73, 80-81, 267-274, 290. *See also individual Christian denominations by name*; Christians; Church of England; Religion

Christians, 214, 256, 257. *See also individual Christian denominations by name*; Christianity

Chucheche (Chucheechee), Cherokee, 51, 107, 108

Chuchitchi (Indian headman), 221

Chuetheake, Cherokee, 120

Chunkey (Chungke), 39, 40

Church of England, 255, 265, 267, 268

Church wardens of the parish, 256

Churches, 47

Chyatuck Swamp, 298n

Cities. *See individual cities by name*

Civile, Daniel, 251, 252

Civility, Seneca, 151

Clans: and adoption, 19, 202, 205; benevolence of, to fellow clansmen, 17-18; Cherokee burial practices for, 84; Cherokee headmen elected out of, 14; description of duties of, 16; determined suitable marriage partners, 18; matrilineal, 16; mentioned, 9; mete out punishment, 20; placate murder of Cherokee, 98; seek compensation, 20, 107; as source of mutual aid, 16-17

Clare, Timothy, 266

Clarendon County (N.C.), 208

Clark, Mrs, 262

Clark, James, 262

Clark, John, 262, 263

Clarke, Sarah, 263

Clarksville, Va., 86n

Clay County (N.C.), 141n

Clay, china, 139, 141-142

Clay, clay pits, 44, 67, 109, 110n, 138, 194, 203. *See also* Clay, china

Clayton, Ga., 52n, 110n

Clea, Benja., 207

Clenussee, N.C., 244

Clergy, 267

Clerks, 129-130, 131, 132, 254

Clifton, Peter, 303

Climate. *See* Weather

Cloth, 7, 91, 103, 138, 205. *See also individual fabrics by name*

Clothing: Catawba, 160, 163; Cherokee, 19, 51, 90, 99; funds for, 286; huskanawing preserves precious, 22; and Indian headmen, 7-8, 45, 48, 128; Indians marveled at, worn by Verrazano's sailors, 135; Indians' sparse possessions consist of, 21; inebriated Indians cheated by traders cannot purchase, 119; made for Indian Ned, 80; of Indian dancers, mentioned, 43; theft of, 258; traditional, 5-6; Tuscarora, 20, 295; used as gambling stakes, 40; variety of, described, 5, 6, 7, 66. *See also individual articles of clothing by name*

Cloud's Creek, 189

Clubs, 32

Coale, James, 260

Coastal Indians 13, 68-69

Co-a-tee Con-na-hetta, 140, 141n

Coats, 7, 8, 20, 51

Coborn, Judith, 86

Coborn, Samuel, 86

Cock Eye Warriour, Cherokee, 98

Cockles, 38

Colane of Eurphorsee, King of the Valley, 222n

Colbert, James, 241, 241n

Collier. *See* Davies, Ambrose

Colonel Chiswell's Mines, 173, 174n, 176, 177

Commissaries, 129, 130, 131, 132, 141

Commissioners, N.C.: appointed to confirm friendship with Indians, 223; attend proceedings for Treaty of Lancaster, 215; establish boundary line with Cherokees, 176-177, 188; meet with Catawba Indians, 160-161; and Overhill Cherokee declaration of war, 240; pay for cloth for Cherokee women, 205; prevent encroachment onto Meherrin land, 277; sent to convince Cherokees to support colonial forces, 225; superintend Bertie County Tuscarora Indians, 302

Commissioners for Indian Affairs, 104-105, 114-115, 154, 186, 217, 281-282

Commissioners for the Indian Trade, 104, 106, 117

Commissions, 50, 51, 52, 109, 131, 167

Comptroller, Mr., 156

Conestoga (Conestogo), Pa., 151

Congaree (Canggaree) Indians, 3, 111

Conjurors: accompany Indian delegation, 101-102; act as record keepers, 2; advise against participation in war, 195-196; believe adulterous couples caused smallpox epidemic, 74; care for the sick, 62-63, 64, 72, 74, 75; convey religious beliefs, 53, 54; enjoy great sway among Indians, 62; guard sacred fire, 58; and inability to cure European diseases, 72; and issuance of the physic drink, 68, 70; officiate over funerals, 81-82, 84; preside over quiogozons, 55; role of, during Cherokee Green Corn Ceremony, 60-61. *See also* Disease; Doctors; Medical care; Medicine

Connasoratah, Cherokee, 232

Connostee (Cherokee Valley town), 93n, 140, 141n, 244

Connutra (Cherokee Out town), 122, 124-125, 126n

Constables, 96, 253, 277. *See also* Sheriffs

Contentnea Creek, 209, 213, 214n

Continental Congress, 240

Convenient houses. *See* Inns

Cooke, Jus., 261

Coopers (trade), 265

Coosa Indians, 3

Coosa River, 78n, 137

Cope, John, 250, 267

Copper, 140, 141, 194

Copping, Thomas, 252

Corals, 57

Core (Coranine, Coree) Indians, xi, 73, 147, 212

Core Sound, 271

Corlaer, Brother, 214

Corn: celebration of harvest of, 41, 42, 74-75; culinary preparation of, 27, 31, 42; cultivation of, ix, 23, 24, 25, 27, 136, 138; destroyed, 158, 237, 245, 247, 251, 253; and Green Corn Ceremony, 60, 61, 107; Indians share, with fellow clansmen, 17; Indians threaten to steal, from colonists, 149; lack of, 238; land could not sustain, 276; payment in, 252; purchased for the Catawbas, 224; selling of, 26, 226; troops encamp among, 243; used in tanning, 34

Cornelius, Isaac, 299

Corn-Flower, 195

Cotton (Cotten-wooll, cotton trees), 80, 138, 139

Council (N.C.): advises N.C. settlers to evacuate Cherokee territory, 178-179; claims Chowan Indians possess handwritten language, 146; concludes peace with Indians, 121; DeGraffenreid member of, 153n; and encroachment on Indian lands, 156-157, 185; Governor Dobbs cannot summon, 165-166; grants permission for private purchase of Indian land, 154; hear appeals, 154; and letter to Va. Council, 146; minutes of, 144; petitions to, 147-148, 148, 149-150; rogue traders brought before, 116; rules inhabitants cannot disturb hunters, 144

Council (Pa.), 151-152

Council (S.C.), 77, 105, 112, 114, 123, 158, 165

Council (Va.), 20, 122-123, 146, 188

Council houses: affairs of state held in, 12, 127, 128; and Cherokee smallpox epidemic, 74; chunkey fields lie near, 40; cleaned during Green Corn Ceremony, 60; of eastern N.C., described,

12-13; feasts, ceremonies, and dances held in, 19, 41, 42, 69, 192; Overhill Cherokees bring scalp to, 240; reprimand from Beloved Man in, 200; returned prisoners sequestered in, 65; sacred fire maintained in, 58; of Whatoga, described, 24-25. *See also* Town houses

Councils: about boundary lines, 79, Catawbas, 121-122, 157, 163, Cherokees, 2, 93, 95-96, 97-98, 99, 102-103, 124, 141-142, 172, 173-176, 182-183, murder, 100; at Augusta Congress, 167; between Indian headmen and whites, 120, 121; convey historical knowledge, 1-2; in Edenton, 259; governance by, ix; by Senecas, 152; war and merits of combat considered in, 192. *See also* Council (N.C.); Council (Pa.); Council (S.C.); Council (Va.)

Counsellors, 192, 197

Couratuck Precinct. *See* Currituck Precinct

Court of Chancery (N.C.), 251

Court of Claims (N.C.), 166

Courts, 251, 267. *See also individual courts by name*

Cow Branch,, 213n

Cowechee, 242

Cowee (Cherokee Middle town), 42-43, 44n, 101, 107, 110, 233n

Cowee Creek, 44n

Coweetchee ("Cowatache"), 233n

Coweta, 220

Cowhowie River. *See* Little Tennessee River

Cows, 265

Crafts. *See individual craft items by name*

Craven, James, Col., 155

Craven County (N.C.), 73n, 207n, 261, 265n

Crawford, Mr., 220

Crawford, James, 107, 120

Crawly, David, 126-127

Creek Indians: attacked the British, 235; attend Augusta Congress, 174; Caughnawagas marched against the, 217; commit hostilities on Ga. settlers, 134; diplomatic delegation of, ravaged by disease, 77; houses of, 10; location of, 11n; Lower, 221, 221n; member of, sends express to governor of Charles town, 228; and relationship with Catawbas, 47, 77-78, 221-222, Cherokees, 47, 48, 137, 219, 221-222, 240; seek change in venue for peace talks, 76-77, to undermine friendship between Cherokees and British, 52; S.C. conducts trade with, 10, 114; supported the French, 230; trade deerskin for rum, 119; Upper, 78n, 221

Crime and punishment: 20, 21, 192, 251. *See also individual crimes by name*; Crimes; Discipline and punishment; Punishment

Crimes: 154-155, 250, 253-254, 256. *See also* Crime and punishment; Punishment; Runaway slaves; Sheriff

Crooked Creek, 241

Crop lands, 286

Cross-Creek, 241

Crymble, Murray, 155-156

Crystal (christal), 91

Cuenca. *See* Joara

Culture, ix, xi

Cumberland River, 182. *See also* Cumberland River Valley

Cumberland River Valley, 9n. *See also* Cumberland River

Cuming, Alexander, 14

Currency, 88, 89, 273. *See also* Peak; Wampum

Currituck, 142

Currituck Banks, 144

Currituck County (N.C.), 287, 289

Currituck Inlet, 146

Currituck Precinct, 260, 269, 288

Cusseta (Cusita), 219, 221n

Customs, 193, 199, 203, 218, 241
Custowee (Cherokee Valley town), 140, 141n
Cutlasses, 51, 101
Cyprus trees, 138

D

Dance/dancing: and ball-playing, 39, 42-43, 44; and Cherokee physic drink, 69-70; and Cherokees' receipt of a scalp, 240; and corn harvest, 41-42; and torture, 203; war, 41, 44, 192, 206, 235. *See also* Music
Daniel (Daniell), Robert, Gov. (N.C.), 121, 147-150 passim, 276
Dannoll, Mr., 107
Dare County (N.C.), 267n
Darts, 32, 37. *See also* Fishing
Dasamongeuponke, 267
Dasemunkepeuc, 267n
Davenport, Richd., 266
David (king of Israel), 268
Davies, Ambrose (Davis, Ambrous), 107, 127
Daw, Nicholas, 148
Dawson, Anthony, Captain, 260
Dawson, John, 155
Dawson, Levi, Colonel, 261, 262
De Bonnille, Louis, Capt., 76, 78n
De Brahm, William Gerard, 65
De Graffenreid, Christopher, Baron, xi, 57, 150, 152, 153n
De Soto, Hernando, ix
De las Alas, Estaben, 267
Dean, [Anthony], 219
Death, 196, 199, 203, 250. *See also* Charnel houses; Funeral customs and rites, ceremonies; Graves
Debts, 206, 207
Deeds, 10, 286-290
Deep Creek, 85, 126n, 280, 293
Deer: in abundance in Cape Fear region, 139; consume yaupon bushes, 69; horns, bones, and hair of, used by Indians, 7, 8; hunted by Indians, 10, 31, 82, 99; Indian traders and employees prohibited from hunting, 131; meat sacrificed by Cherokee conjurer, 56; scarce in Catawba and Cherokee hunting grounds, 167, 175; sinew, 6, 7, 39, 200. *See also* Deerskin
Deerskin: acquisition of, described, 31; advice given to receive, 91; and alcohol, 119, 131; Catawba headman claims he will present, to the Indian traders, 167; and Cherokees, 95, 99, 243; decorate tobacco pipes, 30; deposited at Sugaree town by Indian trader, 126; dressed, 11, 34, 130, 131; and Indian currency, 7, 21, 46, 89; Indian girls reared on, 60; and Indian hunters in debt, 100; offered as compensation for the loss of one life, 20; prohibitions on buying, 131; paid as tribute, 283; presented to Governor Tryon, 297; raw and half-dressed, 88, 131; shipped to Philadelphia, 89; uses of, 7, 39, 42, 69, 82. *See also* Deer
Delano, Tenn., 52n
Demere, [Paul], Captain, 96-98, 195, 196
Demere, Raymond (Rayd.), Capt., 23, 25, 26, 50, 93, 93n, 120, 121n
Dennis, Billy, 294, 298
Deputy governors, 205. *See also* Governors
DeRossett (De Rosset), Lewis, Col., 155
Dewwhist, Col. (Va.), 142
Diagawehee (Diagawekee), 291, 293
Dickey, David, 183
Diet. *See* Food
Dillard, Ga., 14n
Dillon, [Garrett], 207
Dinwiddie, Robert, Gov. (Va.), 127, 223
Diplomacy: and Britain and France, 92, 106, 128-129; and Catawba Indians, 47-48, 111, 156-158, 160-161; and Charleston, S.C., 76, 77, 104; and Cherokee Indians, 47-48, 74, 76, 77, 95-96, 100, 102-103, 124-125, 185-186; between colonists and Roanoke Indians, 45; and Creek Indians, 76, 77; and explorers, 135, 138; and

illness, 74, 76, 78-79; and Indian headmen, 104, 128, 138; Indians attend funerals as sign of, 81; and N.C., 76, 121, 185-186; and peace negotiations, described, 41, 44, 152; between Saponis, Susquehannahs, and Catawbas, 46, the Tuscaroras and the Bear River Indians, 149-150; and S.C., 49-50, 51-52, 77, 95-96, 99, 102-103, 124-125, 156, 158, 219; and trade, 99, 100, 106, 117, 124-125, 131

Discipline and punishment, 58, 61, 65, 66. *See also* Crime and punishment; Punishment

Disease: and Catawba Indians, 75-76, 78, 135, 163, 164; and Cherokee Indians, 74-75, 78, 79; causes of, broached by Indians, 55, 58; Indians lose land because of, 286; Indians ravaged by, 70-72, 73, 77-78, 80; Indians repelled by colonial towns due to, 76; introduced to Native Americans, x, 249; medical care for, 62; and Pamlico Indians, 73, 147; reported tobacco helps Indians repel most, 68; seen as providential, 72; stifled Indian trade, 78. *See also individual diseases by name*; Conjurors; Doctors; Health and hygiene; Medical care; Medicine

Dismemberment, 199, 204

Disputes, 276, 277

Distemper, 196

Divorce, 18

Dobbs, Arthur, Gov. (N.C.): and Catawbas, 76, 161-162, 163, 164, 165, 166, 222, 223n, 273; and Cherokees, 223n; and land issues, 161-162, 163, 164, 165, 166; letters to, 165, 234; letters from, 22, 76, 161-162, 163-165, 165-166, 225; petitioned by white residents for protection against Indians, 159-160; and Tuscaroras, 21, 22, 294n

Doctors, 77, 97, 218. *See also* Conjurors; Disease; Medical care; Medicine

Dogs, 42, 209, 234

Dougherty, Cornelius (Daugherty, Docharty, Doharty): creditor claims property of, 95, 96; letter to, mentioned, 124; petition of, 140-141; purchases land from the Cherokees, 140-141; questions his promise to sell horses, 111-112; and suspect dealings with business partner, 110, 113; trading establishment of, patronized by French-allied Indians, 92-93

Dr. Bray's Associates, 270

Draft, military, 146

Drayton, W[ilia]m, 233

Dress, 6, 194

Drinking, 20, 253. *See also individual alcoholic drinks by name*; Alcohol

Drummond, William, Gov., 146

Drums, 1, 42, 193

Dry, William (Wm.), Col., 155

Dry scratching, 58, 61, 65, 66, 120, 121, 160

Ducks, 31

Dudca, 139, 140

Dudgeon, John, 110

Dudley, Christopher, 143, 144-145

Duffles (duffelds), 103. *See also* Blankets

Dunkard, 226

Durant, George, 284

Durant, John, King, Yeopim, 7-8, 8n, 260n, 284, 287

Duren, Thomas, 251, 252, 253

Dwellings: as cabins, 9, 12, 15, 19, 21, 22, 54, 60, 61, 62, 65, 99, 107; of Cherokees, 10-11, 75, 127; described, ix; in eastern N.C., 11; and green corn ceremony, 60, 61; in hunting camps, 31; and huskanawing, 21, 22; Indian trader refuses admittance to, 101; Indians assist in construction of, 16; and smallpox, 75; of whites', broken into by inebriated Indians, 118

Dyes, dying, 19

E

Eagles, 8, 33, 44

Ear bobs. *See* Earrings

Earl Granville, 296. *See also* Carteret, John, Lord

Earl of Shelburne, 295n

Earrings, 8, 40, 51, 87

Eastatoe Creek, 14n

Eaton, Will'm, 155

Ecochee, 244

Econourste (Cherokee Valley town), 105-106

Ecoy (Ecuy), Cherokee, 52, 177, 178

Eden, Charles, Gov. (N.C.), 144, 249, 251, 279, 283

Edenton, N.C., 136n, 250, 259, 261, 277, 282, 284, 286, 298

Edgecombe (Edgecomb) County (N.C.), 155, 250n

Education. *See* Schools

Edwards, Titus, 302n

Eggerton, Patrick, 266

Egremont, 2nd Earl of (Charles Wyndham), 167

Ela, N.C., 14n

Elderedge, John, 148-149

Elderly, 5-6, 12, 18, 26, 31, 71, 126, 151

Elizabeth I (queen), 138

Ellijay (Elejoy) (Cherokee Middle town), 49-50, 50n

Ellijay Creek, 50n

Elliott, John (the little Scotchman, Mr. Elliot), 103, 110, 111-113, 128, 219, 221

Ellis, Capt., 165

Ellis, Richard, 265

Ellis, Willis, 223

Elmesly, Alexander, 264

Emigration, 150-152, 153

Encampments, 183, 196, 237, 243

Enclosure, 163, 166

Encroachments: and attacks or war, 145, 150, 152; on Catawba land, 156-158, 161, 162-163, 165, 167, 168; on Cherokee land, 171, 173, 175, 178, 182, 185, 186-187; continued without abatement across the Piedmont, 170; endorsed by colonial governments, 172; on Indian hunting grounds, 144, 158, 167, 186-187; Indians not to be disturbed by, 169; as long source of friction between settlers and Indians, xi, 143; Meherrin Indians complain of, 146; by North Carolinians, 157-158, 165, 166, 173, 178, 184, 186-187, 188; and S.C., 157-158, 161, 162-163; and Tuscarora Indians, 150; by Virginians, 173

England: affidavits sent to, 74; agriculture in, described, 23-24; diseases in, 68; French Indians disdain, 92, 93; hosts Cherokee delegation, 102; Indian trade goods dispatched from, 87; mentioned, x, 288; North American variants of food compared to those in, 28-29, 31, 33, 37; shellfish caught in, 38; shilling in, 35n. *See also* English (people)

English (language), 235, 294

English (people), x, 194, 212, 223, 232, 239, 267, 279. *See also* England

Eno (Eenó) Indians, ix, 3

Eno River (the other side of the River), 86, 86n

Enoe Will (Will), 86

Enoree River, 159

Entertainment. *See individual types*

Epidemics, x

Equality, legal, 254

Escape, 218, 258. *See also* Runaways

Estatoe (Estahtowih, Esternorie, Estootowie) (Cherokee Lower town), 14, 124, 177, 178, 220, 235

Etchoe (Cherokee Middle town), 24, 25n, 124, 235, 236, 237

Euchees. *See* Yuchi Indians

Eufassee (Euphersee). *See* Great Hiwassee; Little Hiwassee

Eukuiknoreuit, 212

Europe, 36, 45. *See also* Europeans

Europeans, ix, 249. *See also* Europe

Evans, John, 9n, 52

Everard, Richard (Richd.), Sir, 276, 282
Executive Council, 275, 282, 287n

F

Fabrics. *See individual fabrics by name*; Cloth
Faces, painted, 192, 194, 199
Factors, 87, 125, 129-130, 131
Fair Forest, S.C., 178
Falling Run, 280, 293
Families. *See* Clans
Famine, 23, 25, 55, 58
Farming. *See* Agriculture; Harvesting; Plantations; Planting
Farrow, Joseph, 289
Fashine (fascine), 210n
Fasting, 193, 197
Fauna, x, 249. *See also individual animals by name*
Fauquier, Francis, Lt. Gov. (the Governor), 79, 291
Feast, 41-42, 202
Feathers, 5, 6, 7, 8, 30, 42, 43, 44, 194
Fences/fencing, 26, 158
Ferdinando, Simon, 49
Fire, 38, 58-59, 135, 202
Fishing, ix, 7, 10, 38, 49, 55, 138, 276. *See also* Darts; Food; Weirs
Fishing Creek, 88
Five Nations, 217. *See also* Iroquois Indians
Flannels, 90, 103
Flaps (apron), 6, 7, 93, 128
Flax, 51
Flints, 52, 63, 128
Flooding, 47
Flora, x, 249
Florida, 167, 169, 207n
Folkways, 1-52
Food: on bar tab, 70; cast by Cherokee conjurer to the four winds, 56; Cherokee require hunting grounds to acquire, 171; cultivation of crops for, 23-29; funds for, 286; and funerals, 81; in gift giving, 49; at Indian hunting camp, 31; lack of, 226; mentioned, 17; offered to Cherokee adoptees, 19; prepared by women, 94; presented to Verrazano's sailors, 135; provided to Catawbas by S.C., 163; provided to Indian delegates, 77; served during dances and feasts, 41-42; settlers provided Indians with, 227; stolen by Catawba warriors from the settlements, 157; taboos concerning, 33-34; traded, x; types of, 2, 23, 25, 26, 27-28, 29, 36-38, 138, 139; women gather, 31. *See also individual foods by name*; Agriculture; Fishing; Hunting
Fort Augusta, 74
Fort Benning, 219n
Fort Charlotte, 240
Fort Dobbs, 170, 223n, 234
Fort Granville, 170
Fort Hunter, 217n
Fort Johnson, 217n
Fort Johnston, 170
Fort Loudoun, 59, 60n, 92, 93, 97, 98, 197n
Fort Mill, S.C., 9n
Fort Moore, 76, 78n
Fort Neoheroka, xi
Fort Ninety-Six, S.C., 235
Fort Prince George: altercation at, 120, 121n; besieged, 234; Congress at, 173-174; council held at, 141, 142n; peace talk at, 238; return to, 237; signing of treaty at, 231-233; warrior at, 229
Fort Run, 214n
Fort Toulouse (Alabama), 76, 78n
Forts: built for Catawbas, 161, 163, 168; and Cherokee Indians, 98, 76-77, 120-121, 141, 195-196, 231; construction of, 159, 224; description of, 210; elderly headmen unable to visit, 128; erection of small, 223; failure to seize Hancock's, 211; French, 76, 78n, 221; near Haw River, 226; and Indian traders visit, 92, 93, 97; Indians killed in and removed from,

214; named for Lionel Reading, 213; in N.C., listed, 170; shown to Indians, 47; SPG to settle a schoolmaster at, 273; at Torhunta, 209. *See also individual forts by name*

Foster, Frans. (Fran.), 251, 284

Fowl, fowling, 127, 139, 197, 275, 276

Fox, George, 267, 268n

Foxes, 33, 89, 91, 264

France: centralized approach to diplomacy with Indians, 106, 129; and Cherokees, 19, 50, 74, 76, 77, 126, 128, 140; erect Fort Toulouse, 78n; defeat Natchez Indians, 52n; and Great Britain, 47n, 92, 109, 167, 221; hires Verrazano, 135; Indians allied with, 47n, 92, 93, 125; mentioned, ix, 176, 288; at odds with Catawbas, 161, 167; plant ambassadors in Indian nations, 48. *See also* French; French and Indian War; Stinking Linguo's

Francis I, king of France, 135

Francis, James (Jams.), 271, 272

Franklin, N.C., 2n, 242

Frazier, James, 92-93

Free blacks, 254

Freedom, 260, 261

Freeman, John, 286

Freeman, Wm., 303

French, Christopher, Capt., 93n

French, John (Coll.), 151-152

French: cannot be substituted for N.C. militia soldiers or officers, 257; capture a fort, 221; Caughnawaga Indians have strong ties to the, 217; Cherokees propose to kill, 233; conciliate themselves with the Cherokees, 223, 227, 231, 239; could not fulfill promises to Overhills, 238; foment a Creek-Cherokee war, 219; Indians who support, 218; King Hagler fears the, 216; mentioned, x, 226, 267; supported by the Shawnees, 225; turn Indian anger to their advantage, 230. *See also* France; French and Indian War

French Broad River, 189, 245

French and Indian War: and Catawba Indians, 167, 222; colonists scalp enemy Indians during, 199; conjuror prevents Cherokees from helping Va. during, 195; Great Britain in debt due to, 132; impetus for the start of the, 221; Kahnawake Indians leave Quebec for Ohio after, 47n; recruitment of Indian warrriors for, 109-110; subconflict of the, 234; trade utilized to build and maintain alliances with Indian nations during, 92; Tuscarora huskanaw their young men in readiness for, 21, 22. *See also* France; French

Frohock, John, 177, 200

Fruits, 25, 138, 139

Fugitives. *See* Runaways

Funeral customs and rites, ceremonies, 32, 40, 80, 81-84. *See also* Charnel houses; Death; Graves

Furniture, 11, 13, 67

Furs: exchanged for alcohol, 118, 131; Indian hunters in debt will not hunt for, 100; Indian traders and employees cannot buy, from white hunters, 131; made into clothing, 7, 33; needed to buy trade goods, 31, 116, 171; offered as aid, 16; wampum needed to buy, 46; worn by Catawba before European contact, 160

G

Gachadow (speaker for the Indians), 215

Galahan, Patrick, 42, 101

Gale, Christopher (Major Gale, Chris., Chr., C.), 94, 95, 149, 208, 250-251, 252, 283-284

Gale, Miles (brother to Christopher), 94

Gale, Miles, Rev. (father to Christopher), 94

Galphin, George, 219n

Game (animals), 286, 293

Games (entertainment), 39, 40-41, 70

Gar fish, 61

Garat, Mr., 269
Garden Creek, 32n
Gardia, 90
Gardiner, John, 145
Garland, John, 261
Garrett, Thomas, Sr., 269n
Garrisons, 208, 234
Gartering, 51, 90
Garters, 34
Gates County (N.C.), 145, 269n
Gatlin, James, 262
Geerick Roonee, Creek, 217
Geese, 2
General Assembly (N.C.): appointments by the, 303; boundaries of Indian lands set by the, 189-190, 277, 280; and encroachment on Indian lands, 185, 188; and land entries, 187; meetings of the, 291, 302; presents grievances of Indian hunting to governor, 145; prohibits private purchases of Indian lands, 183. *See also* Act of Assembly (N.C.)
General Assembly (S.C.), 77, 104, 105, 114-115, 117, 163. *See also* Act of Assembly (S.C.)
General Assembly (Va.), 188
George I (king of England), 292
George II (king of England) (Father King George), 102, 121, 155, 162, 288
George III (king of England), 133, 166, 167, 248
George, Tuscarora, 294
George, Billy, 294
George, Captain, 227
Georgia: Cherokees in, 2n, 14n, 126, 127, 135, 183, 191n, 234; Chickasaws move to modern-day Augusta in, 236n; Creek Indians in, 11n, 134; Cusseta located in, 219n; governor of, 167, 173-174, 175; and Indian trade, 126, 128; traders from, 75, 127, 128; trustees of, 74
Germans, 231

Gibbs, Harry, 284
Gibbs, Henry, 288, 289
Gibson, Walter (What), 299, 301-302, 303
Gift giving: to the Cherokees, 93, 127, 176, 186, 230; as defined by Indians, 49; described as bribery by Europeans, 50; given to Granganimeo, 45; Indian trader inquires as to how to dispense, 111; Indians invited to Charleston for, 76; items for, listed, 51-52; restrictions on, 104, 143; subverted by Indian traders touting favorites, 109
Girdles, 34
Gist, Nat., 241
Glen, James, Gov. (S.C.): accused of sending an army to the Cherokee nation, 124; admonishes president of N.C. council for encroachments on Catawba lands, 157-158, 161; describes illnesses that befell Indian diplomatic delegations, 76-78; Indians await answer of, regarding prohibition for Indians, 119; invites Cherokee headmen to talks, 221-222; launches a diplomatic offensive, 219; letters from, 123, 157-158, 161, 216, 221-222; letters to, 9, 76-78, 95, 95-96, 99-100, 102-103, 103, 107-108, 110-111, 111-113, 118-119, 120, 124-125, 127, 128, 157, 216, 217, 219-220, 220-221; meets with Cherokees and Catawbas, 216; orders traders to leave Cherokee nation, 123; reportedly encourages Catawbas to evict settlers, 160; trader seeks debt protection from, 95-96; urged to stop selling of rum to Indians, 118-119
Glover, Charles Worth, 281, 282
Glover, William, Sir, 10
Gobit (indentured servant), 265
Godbee, Cary, 265
Goddard, John, Captain, 271, 272

Goffe, A., 259
Gold, Cristopher, 148
Gold, ix, 140, 141
Goldsboro, N.C., 9n, 209
Good Warrior, The, Cherokee, 240
Good Warrior of Estatoe. *See* Ecoy
Gookin, Charles, Lt. Gov. (The Govr.,
    your honrs.) (Pa.), 151, 152
Gordon, James (Jas.), 253, 254
Gould, George, 281
Gourds, 1, 23, 24n, 42, 63, 204
Government. *See* Politics and govern-
    ment
Governor, the (N.C.), xi, 116, 147, 147-
    148, 149-150, 154, 224. *See also N.C.*
    governors by name
Governor, the (Pa.), 151. *See also Pa.*
    governors by name
Governor, the (S.C.), 101, 105, 114. *See*
    also S.C. governors by name
Governor, the (Va.), 123, 223. *See also*
    Va. governors by name
Governors, 131, 133. *See also* Deputy
    governors
Gowdy (Goudy), Robert, 96
Grafton, 2nd Duke of (Charles FitzRoy,
    Lord Chamberlain), 155
Graham County (N.C.), 52n, 60n
Grain, 11, 31, 139
Granganimeo, Roanoke, 45
Grant, James, Col., 93n, 235, 236, 237,
    239
Grant, Ludovick: believes Cherokees
    proceeded north to fight in Va., 127;
    confirms pledge to sell horses, 112;
    establishes complaint against Ga.
    traders, 128; informs Governor Glen
    that assistant was killed by a Chero-
    kee warrior, 99-100; letters from, 95,
    95-96, 99-100, 103, 111-113, 120,
    127, 128, 219-220, 220-221; reads
    letter, 111; reports Cherokees in
    Tuckasegee attacked trader, 120,
    peace among Indians, 220-221,
    violence among and requests for
    relief from Indians, 220-221; seeks

debt protection from Governor
    Glen, 95, 95-96; states steelyards
    intended for Indian trade were never
    delivered to the traders, 101
Granville, 3rd Earl of (Robert Carteret),
    180
Granville, Lord, 280
Granville County (N.C.), 155, 179, 228,
    262
Granville tract, 180
Graves, 195, 201, 209. *See also* Charnel
    houses; Death; Funeral customs and
    rites, ceremonies
Graydon, Captain, 295
Great Britain: assumed oversight of
    Indian nations upon France's defeat,
    167; beaver hats crafted in, 89;
    colonies engaged in armed rebellion
    against, 240; colonies of, conduct
    separate diplomatic and commercial
    interests with Indians, 128-129, grow
    hostile toward direct taxation from
    Parliament, 132; disparaged by
    French-allied Indians, 92, 93; does
    not want to provoke Catawba Indians
    over their lands, 161; and French and
    Indian War, 47n, 109, 167; and
    Indian superintendency, 129, 132;
    and Indian trade goods, 87, 132, 133,
    133-134; mentioned, 151, 176, 181;
    President Rowan complains to, 157;
    recruits Cherokee warriors to fight
    French, 109; secures Indian allies
    during American Revolution, 182;
    Timberlake emissary to the Cherokee
    for, 5; at war with France, 92. *See also*
    England; English (people); Parlia-
    ment, British
Great Canaway River. *See* Kanawha
    River
Great Hiwassee (Cherokee Overhill
    town), 52n
Great Men, 196, 212, 215
Great Prince of Chote (Chotee, Choteh).
    See Kittagusta
Great Smoky Mountains, 156

Great Tellico (Telliquo) (Cherokee Overhill town), 14n
Great Wagon Road, 155
Great Warrior. *See* Oconostota
Green, Wm., 159
Green Corn Ceremony, 60, 61, 107, 207
Green River, 177
Greene County (N.C.), 213n, 214n
Grey, Jno., 282
Griffiths, Thomas, 65, 139, 141-142
Grifton, N.C., 209
Groom, Catherine, 250
Groom, Thomas, 250
Grosgrain, 138
Guatari, 267
Guinea-Men. *See* African Americans
Gulf of Mexico (Bay of Mexico), 46
Gum Branch, 286
Gumberry Creek, 195n. *See also* Brewsters River
Gums (Gumms), 116
Gunpowder: and Cherokees, 99, 103, 180; as compensation for land, 180, murder, 20; dispensed as presents, 19, 52, 128; not used against small game, 31; restrictions on disbursement of, 91, 123, 130; and Tuscaroras, 20, 87, 297; used for tattoes by Cherokees, 8. *See also* Powder and shot
Guns: acquired by Indians, x, 32; and Cherokees, 19, 51, 97, 102, 127, 182, 243; colonists threaten to break Indians', 144; as compensation for murder, 20; coveted by Indians, 21, 91; firing, 197; and Indian funerals, 81; and Indian traders, 199-100, 107-108; Indians believe good spirit taught whites to construct, 55; Indians carrying rifle-barreled, overpower British troops, 235; Indians crawl through brush to hear sound of, 198; kill bears with, 33; lacking in Bladen County, 155; lost when canoe capsized, 218; mentioned, 199; not to be sold to Indians, 91, 123, 130, 149;

as present for Little Carpenter, 96; theft of, 258; and Tuscaroras, 20, 87; used by Indians, 208; utilized by raiding party, 148
Gutt of Toquah, Cherokee, 141

H

Hagler, King, Catawba (Haglar, Heglar, Heigler, Nopkehe): afraid of the French, 216; agrees to Treaty of Pine Tree Hill, 164; assumes leadership of Catawba nation, 78n; confers with Chief Justice Peter Henley, 224, 225; defends Catawba Indians' claim to land, 157, 160-161; given provisions by Martin Phifer, 227; informed that Pine Tree Hill cannot be confirmed, 165; killing of, 205; promises to protect N.C. from hostile Indians, 222; wants whites to stop selling alcohol to his people, 121-122
Hair, hairstyles, 6, 8, 9, 194
Hakluyt, Richard, 136n
Halifax County, 293
Hall, [James], 244
Haltem, Mr., 225, 226
Hammond, Leroy (Le Roy), Col. (S.C.), 186, 242
Hamond, Henry, 260
Hampton, [Edward], Captain, 242
Hancock, King, Tuscarora, xi, 209, 211
Haniod Sollmon Poker (Indian servant), 265
Harden, Captain, 245
Hariot, Thomas (Master Heriott): on agricultural practices of Indians in eastern N.C., 23-24; describes fruits and nuts gathered by eastern N.C. Indians, 27-28, 28-29, towns on Albemarle Sound, 9; details religious significance given by Indians to tobacco use, 67-68; discusses canoe construction, 38, Indian weapons and armor, 32, variety of animals caught and consumed by Indians, x, 33, 37; on Indian religion, 53-54; on

Indians' adeptness at fishing, 36; notes diversity of Indian languages in N.C., 3; and silk grass, 138; on spread of disease among the Indians, 70-71, 71-72; states that coastal Indians are ruled by strong chiefs, 13

Harker, Ebzr., Captain, 265

Harmon, Henry, 199, 200

Harrellsville, N.C., 136n

Harris, Captain, Catawba, 77

Harris, Colonel, 224

Harris, Tom, 251

Harrison, William, Gov. (Va.), 187, 188

Harry (runaway black), 210

Harry, Susquehannah, 46

Hart, David, 181

Hart, Nathaniel, 181

Hart, Thomas, 181

Hartwell Lake, 52n

Harvesting, 227. *See also* Agriculture; Crop lands; Planting

Harvey, Ths., 259

Hatch, Anthony, 249

Hatchets, 24, 32, 38, 51, 97, 206, 230

Hats, 7, 49, 51, 89

Hatteras Banks, 288, 289

Hatteras Indians, ix, 249, 270

Hatteras Island, N.C., 49

Hauser family, 231

Haw River, 85, 226

Hawking, 275, 276

Hawkins, John (Jno.), 260, 284

Hay, 138

Hayes, Mary, 263

Headmen: appointed by their people, 14, 15; attend conferences, 151, funerals, 82; beliefs of, 21, 216; charnel houses hold bones of, 55, 83; clothing of, 5, 7-8; and colonists, 148, 150; conduct business in Charleston, 104; Creek, 221; desire prohibition on alcohol, 119, 121-122; distraught by deface-ment of totem pole, 57; dominate governments of eastern N.C. Indians, 13; in eastern N.C., 136; exchange clothing, 45, 47-48; and families, 18, 20, 24; Governor Lyttleton addresses, 229; hold council, 128, 141-142, prominent seat during dances and feasts, 41; and illness and medical care, 62-63, 71, 135; and Indian trade, 109, 117-118, 131, 154; issued commissions, 50, 51; and Juan Pardo, 138, 139, 267; lead raiding party upon colonial settlement, 148-149; mentioned, 92, 120-121; officiate over peace ceremony, 44; and practice of religion, 54; receive presents, 49, 51; reside in townhouse, 12; seek aid for downtrodden, 16; sell land in Albemarle region, 143; sign peace treaty and alliance, 152; welcome Bartram, 25

Health and hygiene, 140; and bathing, 65-66; conjurers help maintain, 62-63; and flooding, 47; and green corn ceremony, 61; and hot houses, 66-67; Indian delegates fall sick in Charleston from poor, 77; Indians believe a bad spirit creates ill, 55; Indians believe good, led to spiritual purity, 64; Indians believe proper order of worlds needed to maintain good, 58; and physic drink, 68-70; residence along rivers and streams promotes, 10; and sequestration, 64, 65; and smallpox, 73, 74-75, 75-76; and tobacco consumption, 67-68; in war obtained through purification, 193. *See also* Disease; Doctors

Healy, Christ., 262

Hecklefeild, John, Captain (Jno. Hecklefield), 207, 282

Hemp, 7

Henderson, Richard (Richd.), 178, 179-181, 182, 263

Henderson land purchase, 240

Henley, Peter, Chief Justice (N.C.), 121-122, 222

Henrich, Christian, 225, 226-227

Henrico County (Va.), 123

Herbert, John, Col., 1, 2

Herbs, 64, 66, 69, 116
Hessians, 257
Heywood, John, Col., 155
Hick (relative of prisoner), 244
Hicks, Charles, 244
Hicks, James, 301
Hicks, John, 299, 300, 302
Hicks, Nathan, 244
Hicks, Robert, 228
Hieroglyphics, 201
Highest Skyagusta (war captain), 201
Hill, Charles, 117
Hill, Henry, 251, 253, 254, 284, 285
Hillsborough, Earl of (Wills Hill), 50, 119, 133, 134
Hillsborough, N.C., 86n, 247, 262
Hilton, William, 137-138, 138-139
Hinds, Billy, 294
Hitaw, John, 252
Hiter, Thos., 286
Hiwassee (Highwassa, Highwassah, highwassie) (Cherokee Overhill town), 62, 141n, 242, 243, 244. *See also* Great Hiwassee; Little Hiwassee
Hiwassee River, 14n, 52n, 140, 141n, 207n, 242
Hix, James, 301
Hix, Robert, 126-127
Hocomawananck Indians, 194
Hocomawananck River. *See* Roanoke River
Hoes, 23, 24, 91
Hofmann, Brother (Moravian), 225
Hogg, James, 181
Hogs: act to prevent killing, stealing, mismarking, and misbranding, 255-256; American troops eat Cherokees', 243; consumption of, 33, 175; driving stocks of, 190, 281; killing of, 147, 214; poaching of, 154; sale of, 90; stealing of, 86
Holder, Brother (Moravian), 225
Holland, 41, 90
Hollow, the, 231
Holmes, Archibald, 149

Holston River (Holstein, Holsteins), 137, 181, 182n, 189
Hominy, 27, 61
Hopkins, John, 266
Horse Pasture Creek, 277
Horse Peocoson, 301
Horse Range, the, 107, 108
Horses: act to prevent killing, mismarking, and misbranding, 255-256; carry animal skins, 50, 119; commandeered by troops, 246; dispersed from fields by women, 26; driving stocks of, 190, 281; Indian traders suffer dispute over price of, 111-112, 113; Indians deliver, to English, 212; Indians subsist on flesh of, 238; left behind by evacuating Cherokees, 243; left tired after fighting, 210; mentioned, 21, 195, 228; as part of Indian trade pack train, 97; range, 107, 108; stealing of, 108, 119, 134, 154, 157, 159, 162-163, 224, 234, 225, 229, 239, 245, 295; utilized by S.C. trade commissioners, 105
Hostages, 211, 213, 232-233. *See also* Captives; Prisoners
Hostility, 192, 194
Hot houses, 65, 66-67
Housatonic River Valley, 236n
House, James, 303
House of Commons, 302
Houses of assembly, 207
Howard, Billy, 294
Howarth, Probart, Col. (Colonel Howarth), 93, 109-110
Hoyler, Thoms., 269
Hoyster, Thomas, 284
Hoyter, John (King Highter, Jno. Hoyter), 8, 8n, 268, 276, 277
Hoyter, Thos., 286
Hubbard, Jno., 253
Hudson's Bay Company, 169
Huey, James, 155-156
Hugens family, 227
Hugens, Aughter, 228, 229
Hugens, Thomas, Senior, 228

Hughes, Mr. (sheriff), 231
Hughes, Edward, Justice, 225, 226
Hughs (Hugs), Bernard, 99-100, 122, 124
Hunger. *See* Famine
Hunt, Jno., Captain, 260
Hunter, Robert, Gov. (N.Y.), 153
Hunting: agriculture added to, 27; Catawba Indians and, 158, 166, 167; Cherokee Indians and, 10, 19, 47, 95, 171-172; on colonial land, 139, 143, 162; colonists prohibit Indians from, 144, 152-153, 247; effect of poor outcomes in, 95, 99; encroachment hinders, 171; and fire, 30, 31, 87, 145; game, 2, 8, 82; grounds, ix, 166, 197, 198, 214, 225; and Indian trade credit system, 87, 99, 100, 130; Indians are adept at, 36, 55; injuries sustained during, 64; licenses, 143-144, 145; mentioned, 8, 33, 34, 56, 96, 97; participants in, ix, 65, 108, 110, 128, 297; preparations for, 7, 22; privileges, 275, 276, 284; to recompense fellow countrymen, 21; regulations imposed for, 131, 190; Tuscarora Indians and, 86, 293, 296. *See also* Food; Hawking; Trapping
Huron Indians, 47n
Hurst, Capt. (Granville County militiaman), 155
Huskanawing, 21-22
Hyde, Edward, Gov. (N.C.), 152, 153n
Hyde County (N.C.), 270, 272, 288, 289n
Hyde Precinct (N.C.), 144
Hyman, Hugh, 303

I

Illness. *See individual diseases by name*; Conjurors; Disease; Doctors; Health and hygiene
Imprisonment, 263, 278. *See also* Prisoners; Prisons; Captives
Incest, 18
Indenture/indentured servants, 254, 256, 265, 299

India, 138n
Indian Ned, 80, 81
Indian Creek, 259n, 277
Indiana, 222n
Indians: and agriculture, 23-30; and alcohol, 118-120, 121, 122, 131; attack colonial settlements, 145-146; children of, 256; and the clans, 16-20; complain about false weights and measures, 101; conduct diplomacy, 45-52; and council houses, 12-13; and courts, 118, 257; diet of, 24, 27-29, 138-139; and disease, 70, 71; dress of, 5-8; earned reputation as being tough customers, 92; education of, 128, 270; entertainment of, 39-41; feelings of, 21, 192, 229; and fishing, 36-38; free, 261; and hunting, 17, 30-31, 100, 119, 135, 143, 144, 154, 249; and land, 21, 139, 141, 142-143, 144, 156, 168-169, 172; languages of, 1, 3-4, 94; living arrangements of, described, 9, 10-11; location of, 135, 137-139; and medical care, 62-67; physical appearance of, described, 4-5, 6, 130, 160; and politics, 15, 255; recount traditions, historical events, 1-2; restrictions on, 255; and religion, 53-61; rites and ceremonies of, 41-44; skills of, 30, 138; and slavery, 208; and tobacco use, 67-68; and trade, 69, 85, 86, 87, 90, 91-93, 95, 99-100, 113, 117, 118, 119, 122-125, 126, 130; transvestism among, 31-32; type of government practiced by, 13-16; and Verrazano, 135; and war, 100; weaponry of, described, 32. *See also individual tribes by name*
Influenza, x
Innennits, 213n
Innes, James, Col. (Coll. G. Innis), 155
Inns, 77
Interpreters: and Cherokee Indians, 97, 125, 127, 142; at court, 196, 215; fall sick, 140; and the French, 106; relay message about Overhill Indians, 243;

sought by colonists to stave off preemptive attack, 150; and trade, 94, 105, 106, 109, 125; and travel, 214, 228

Ioree I-oree (ayoree) (Cherokee Middle town), 109, 110n, 124, 141-142, 220, 221

Ioree, Prince of, 221

Iotla Creek, 110n

Ireland, 37, 176, 288. *See also* Irish

Irish, 226. *See also* Ireland

Iron, 141

Iron Mountain, 190

Iroquois Confederacy, 290. *See also* Iroquois Indians

Iroquois Indians: and Catawba Indians, 215n; and Cherokee Indians, 47, 216, 221; complain about encroachment, 166; defeat Occaneechi Indians, 86n; and Indian tributaries, 47n; languages of, ix, x, 3; location of, 22n, 153; postpone peace negotiations, 78-79; referred to as Mohawks, 236n; and Tuscarora Indians, xi, 153, 214. *See also* Cayuga Indians; Five Nations; Iroquois Confederacy; Mohawk Indians; Oneida Indians; Onondaga Indians; Seneca Indians; Tuscarora Indians

Isaac (Tuscarora chief), 293, 295

Isacks, Godfrey, 244

Isle of Wight County (Va.), 123, 142, 263

Ivey River, 183

Ivory, 51

Iwaagenst, Tuscarora, 151

Iwassee (town), 219, 220

Izard, Ralph, Esq., 117

J

Jack (Indian), 268

Jackets, 7, 80

Jackit, John, 294

Jackson, S.C., 219n

Jackson County (N.C.), 52n

Jails. *See* Prisons

Jamie, Captain, Catawba, 77

Javelin, 199

Jenins, Jno., 251

Jesuits, 47n

Jewelry. *See individual items of jewelry by name*

Jewels, 139, 141

Jo., Captain, 294

Joara, 139, 140n

John (Indian servant), 265

John, Captain, 227

Johnes, Blinde, 301

Johnny (halfbreed Johnie), Cherokee, 77

Johnson, Nathaniel, Sir, Gov. (S.C.), 126

Johnson, [William, Sir] (Col.): appointed Indian superintendent, 129; Cherokee peace treaty negotiated before, 47; and execution of "Plan of 1764," 132; reports war between Caughnawaga, Catawba, and Cherokee Indians, 217; and Tuscarora Indians, 290-292, 294, 294n, 295, 296

Johnson Hall (N.Y.), 47

Johnston, Gabriel, Gov. (N.C.), 106, 144, 145, 279, 285

Johnston, John, 254

Johnston, William, 181

Johnston County (N.C.), 155, 218

Joiner's shop, 226

Jones, Capt., 214

Jones, Mr., 279

Jones, Allen, 298

Jones, Evan, Capt., 155

Jones, Frederick, Capt., 86

Jones, Isaac, 283, 284

Jones, John, 283, 284

Jones, Pater, 266

Jones, Robert, 293, 294n, 295

Jones, Willie, 240, 297, 298, 299, 300n, 302n

Jones, Worley, 301

Jore (Joree). *See* Ioree I-oree

Juninits, 212

Justices of the peace, 144, 192, 255, 260, 261

K

Kahnawake Indians (Caughnawaga, Coghnawagey), 47, 217
Kalberlahn, Brother (Moravian), 226
Kanawha River (great Canaway), 181
Katactoi, Cherokee, 232
Katagusta, Cherokee, 233
Kearney, Thomas, 104
Kelley, Robert, 77
Kello, R, 264
Kelly, 112
Keneeteroy (Kenotoroy). *See* Connutra
Kennedy, Quentin, Captain, 235n
Kennititah (Kinettita), Cherokee, 141
Kenta (Kentah) toherooka, 212, 213
Kentucky, 9n, 178
Kentucky River (Cantucky, Chinoca, Louisa), 182
Keowee (Keewee, Keewohee, Kewee, Kewohe, Keyowee) (Cherokee Lower town): British troops torch, 235; chooses kings, 14; famine in, 23, 25; General Rutherford obtains information from, 241; The Good Warrior of, 240; Little Carpenter goes to, 120-121; mentioned, 96; messenger dispatched from, 2; "old woolf" of, 137; people of, 220; visitors to, 221; want troops dispatched, 124
Keowee River, 2n, 14n, 178n
Kettles, 27, 30, 52, 90
Kilcannokeh, Cherokee, 233
King, William (Wm.), 297, 300, 301, 303
King Blount's Town, 250, 282
Kingman, Robt., 149
Kings. *See individual kings by name*; Headmen
Kingsport, Tenn., 182n
Kirkland, Moses, 118
Kisentanewh, King (of Yansapin River), 143
Kitchen implements, 27
Kittagusta (great Prince of Chote, Chotee, Choteh), Cherokee, 52, 141, 173-174, 176-178

Kituwah (Kettewa, Kettooah, Kittawa) (Cherokee Out town), 14, 99, 100, 122, 124-125
Knight, T., 251, 283
Knives: Indians believe, to be inestimable acquisitions, 91; as presents, 51, 52, 128; as tools, 30, 34, 160; as weapons, 32, 75, 97, 107, 200. *See also* Weapons
Knotty Hill, 243
Konahete (Cherokee Valley town), 141n

L

Ladles, 86
Lakar, Juliana, 266
Lake Keowee, 2n, 121n
Lambeth, England, 136
Lambton, Richard, 108
Lame Arm, Cherokee, 98
Lampblack, 194
Lancaster, Pa., 215
Lancaster County (Pa.), 152n
Lancaster County (S.C.), 2n
Land: 224, 240, 275, 287n, 297. *See also* Boundary lines; Encroachments; Land entries; Land grants; Land Office (N.C.); Land transfers; Land warrants; Landowners; Patents, land; Surveys, land
Land entries, 85, 157, 183, 184, 185, 187, 189, 190
Land grants: for Albemarle County, 85; claimed by colonists in N.C. and S.C., 161; Crymble and Huey, 155-156; extension of, 172; to Mattamuskeet Indians, 275-276; prohibited in Indian territory, 169; for reservations, 283; and S.C., 163, 171; and Tuscarora Indians, 280; to Yeopim Indians, 275
Land Office (N.C.), 189
Landowners, 257
Land transfers: and Catawba Indians, 157, 162, 163, 165, 166; and Cherokee Indians, 140, 174, 175, 178, 181-182, 182-183, 188, 191n; between

Indians and British government, 170; Indians seek high rates for, 148; to keep settlers away from Indians, 119; location of, 142-143; and Palatines, 150, 152; to preserve peace, 174; through private purchase, 142-143, 154, 164, 169-170, 179, 183, 190; and S.C., 163, 165; and Transylvania Purchase, 178-181, 182-183; violate Indians' access to their land, 144; by the Yeopims to the Chowans, 14

Land warrants, 164, 168, 169

Lane, Ralph, 136

Languages, 17, 94, 202. *See also individual languages by name*

Laws: 193, 233, 250, 254, 267, 277. *See also* Act of Assembly

Lawson, Tuscarora, 213

Lawson, John (Surveyor): captured, xi; compiles list of Indian vocabulary, 3; on consumption of alcohol and its effects, 118, 120-121, tobacco, 29; describes "Arithmetick" game, 39, 40-41, buildings, 11, 12, 66, burial practices, 81-83, courtship and marriage, 18, dances and feasts, 41-42, forms of torture, 202, green corn ceremony, 60, healing methods, 62-63, 73, Indians' physical appearance, 5-8 passim, mats and baskets made by women, 35; discusses charity, 16-17, folkways, 4, huskanawing, 21-22, manufacture and value of wampum, 45-46, preserving tribal history, 1-2, religion, 53, 54-55, 267, traders, 86-87, yaupon bush and its use, 68-69; letter from, mentioned, 149; reported on Bear River Indians, 207n; sold and surveyed land, 152, 153n; on techniques for dressing animal skins, 34, cooking, 36, fishing, 38, hunting, 30-31

Le Sueur, Jean Paul, Capt., 76, 78n

Lead, 89, 141, 194

Lederer, John, 90, 91, 92, 94-95

Leeds, England, 86

Legislature, 291, 299

Leppar, Thomas, 147-148

Lex talionis, 20

Licking Branch, 301

Lieutenant Governor, the (S.C.), 105-106

Limerie (Indian slave), 261

Lincolnton, N.C., 140n

Linen (Linnings), 90, 103

Linguist/Linguister. *See* Interpreters

Lions (Lyon), 33

Liquor, 296. *See also* Alcohol, alcoholic beverages

Little, Thomas, 157

Little Carpenter, Cherokee, 195, 196, 238, 274. *See also* Attakullakulla

Little Chota (Cherokee Lower town), 52

Little Hiwassee (Highwassee, Higwassa) (Cherokee Valley town): creditor calls on Indian trader at, 95, 96; French Indians trade at, 92-93; Indian trader travels through, 96-97; location of, 52n; mentioned, 124, 125; talk given by headmen of, 102; trader license for, 105-106; wounded Indians from, 220n

Little River (Litle River), 89, 144, 207, 252, 282

Little Tellico (Tellicoe, Telliquo) (Cherokee Valley town), 14n, 105-106, 140, 141n, 244

Little Tennessee ("Cowhowie") River: Cherokees ambush Col. Archibald Montgomery on, 236; proximity of, to Chota, 93n, to Cowee, 44n, to Coweetchee, 233n, to Fort Loudoun, 60n, to Nikwasi, 25n, to Tanasi, 14n, to Tomassee, 2n, to Whatoga, 4n

Little Tennessee Valley, 235

Livestock, 254, 255. *See individual animals by name*; Agriculture

Lockhart, Mr. (teacher or school employee), 271

Loesch, Jacob, 225, 226, 227, 231

Logan, George, Col., 117

London, England, 25, 156
Long, Colonel (message bearer), 240
Long, Mr. (disputant against Indian), 207
Long Canes Creek, 171
Long Island, Tenn. (great island in Holston River), 181, 182n, 184, 185, 190
Long Tom, Machapunga, 289
Longe, Alexander: on Cherokee customs, 18, 53, 55-56, 60-61, 65, 83-84; corrected by Cherokee headman for improper use of sacred fire, 58; spurs customers to engage in slave raids, 206
Lords Commissioners for Trade and Plantations, 232
Lords of the Committee of Council for Plantation Affairs. See Board of Trade
Lords proprietors: ban strangers from trading with Indians, 115-116; council asserts rights of, 146; as deputies, 283, 284, 292; extend boundaries of Meherrin land, 277; and land grants, x, 85, 275, 280, 299; mentioned, 117, 147; prohibit private purchase of land from Indians, 142, 143; protect Indians, 206
Louisa River. See Kentucky River
Louisiana, 78n
Louther, King, Bear River, 148
Loves Ford, 176
Lovick, John (J.), 250, 259, 284
Lovick, Thomas (Thom's), Col., 155, 250
Lower house, 254
Lower Parts. See Cherokee Indians, Lower
Lowndes, Rawlins, President (S.C.), 183, 186-187
Ludwell, Philip, 258
Luess, Adam, 147
Luke (free Indian bound as apprentice), 265
Luten, Thomas, Captain, 260, 276

Luttrell, John, 181
Lyttelton (Lyttleton), William Henry, Gov. (S.C.): and encroachment on Catawba land, 121, 161; halted trade, 231; issued gun and pipe hatchet to Attakullakulla, 96; letters to, 25, 26, 50, 96-98, 120-121, 197n; and peace treaty with Cherokees, 232-233; and Treaty of Pine Tree Hill, 168; urges Middle and Lower towns to recall warriors, 229

M

Machapunga Indians (Matchepungo, Mattamuskeet), xi, 147, 148, 275, 288. See also Machapunga Nation
Machapunga Nation, 289n. See also Machapunga Indians
Mackey, Bob., 272
Mackey, John, 288, 289
Mackey, Poll., 271
Macon County (N.C.): Col. Andrew Williamson's troops kill Tomassees in, 244n; Cowee in, 44n; Coweetchee in, 233n; Ellijay in, 50n; Etchoe in, 25n; Little Tellico in, 14n; South Carolinians destroy Cherokee towns in, 242; Tasse in, 237n; Tomassee in, 2n; Whatoga in, 4n
Magistrates, 128, 154, 249. See also Justices of the peace
Maize. See Corn
Makey, John. See Mackey, John
Mallard duck, 6
Man of the Valley, The, Cherokee, 239
Mankiller of Nikwasi (Nuccassie), Cherokee, 52, 201
Manley (Manly), James, 261, 262
Manns Harbor, N.C., 267n
Manteo (baptized Indian), 267
Mantles, 6, 91
Manufactured goods, 206, 221
Manumission, 264
Maples, 138
March (Indian slave), 259

Nassaw (Catawba town), 9n
Natchez, Miss., 52n
Natchez Indians, 3, 51, 52n
Naval stores, 38, 138
Necklaces, 8, 45, 218
Needles, 51
Neoheroka, xi, 211, 212, 213, 214
Neowee (Cherokee Valley town), 14n
Netaske-turn-heu-rough, 212
Netops, Billy, 294
Neuroout tootsere, Tuscarora, 212
Neuse-Pamlico area, 208
Neuse River (Neuce, Neus, Nuce, Nuse),
  x, 73n, 147-148, 150, 156, 212, 278,
  279
Neuse River Indians, 147, 147-148
Nevil, Mr., 209
New Aromuskeet Creek, 288
New Begun Creek (new Begin Creeke),
  143
New Bern (Newbern), N.C.: council
  held in, 284; established, xi, 150, 152;
  excerpt from newspaper in, 218;
  Indian altar desecrated near, 57;
  interpreter serves Indians visiting,
  106; meeting of Beloved Men in, 247,
  General Assembly in, 291, Senate
  and House of Commons in, 302;
  mentioned, 181, 186
New England, 137, 139
New Hanover County (N.C.), 155
New Netherlands. *See* New York
New River. *See* Kanawha River
New York (New Netherlands) (colony),
  22n, 46, 141, 153, 166, 215, 217, 290,
  297
Newport River, 80
Niagara Falls, 217
Nicholche, Cherokee, 232
Nicholson, Francis, Lt. Gov. (His
  Excellency) (Va.), 87
Nicolaus, Joseph, 295
Nikwasi (Nequisey, "Nuscassee,"
  Nucasse, Nuccassie), 2, 4n, 24, 25n,
  236, 237
Ninety-Six, S.C., 96

Nippissing Indians, 47n
Nixson, Richard, 144-145
Noah, Cherokee, 274
No-ho-ro-co (Neoheroka) fort, 213
Nolichucky (Nollichuckei) River, 182-
  183, 189
Noostee (Catawba town), 9n
Norfolk, Va., 136n
Norman, Henery, 258
Norris, 268, 269
Norris, Thomas, 107
Norsworthy, Rachael, 263
North America: ancestors of Native
  Americans migrate from Asia to, 1;
  buffaloes in, described, 34; fish weirs
  in, described, 36-37; Great Britain
  gains vast territory in, 167-168; and
  Henderson Purchase, 181; and
  Indian ownership of land, 166;
  receives Indian trade goods, 87; and
  ronoak, 46; and Royal Proclamation
  of 1763, 179; smallpox ravages
  Indians in, 73; and tobacco, 29
North Carolina (Carolina): Coastal Plain
  of, 45, 85-86; denies guns and
  ammunition to Indians, 149; earliest
  recorded European voyage to, 135;
  eastern, 1, 8, 21, 118, 122, 153; first
  permanent English settlements in,
  142; Indian paths crisscross, 85;
  Indians as sole occupiers of, 135;
  inhabitants of, excluded from commerce with Va., 122, 123; land grants
  in, 156, 172; locations of Indian
  towns in, 136n, 141n; mentioned, 89,
  144; never vigorously pursues commerce with inland Indian nations, 85,
  126, 128; opens land office, 189;
  permits S.C. to regulate Indian trade,
  128; potential for huge profits from
  Indian trade in, 94; prohibits hunting
  and ranging on Indian lands, 190;
  private purchase of Indian lands, 143,
  190; recently ceded lands occupied
  by settlers from, 163; thirty tribes live
  in, 3; warriors told by Indian trader to

ignore talks from, 110; western, 8, 122
North Carolina Committee of Public Claims, 199
North Carolina General Court, 70, 206, 252, 260, 299n
North River, 275
Northampton County (N.C.), 155, 192-193, 195n, 263
Northward (Norrard, Norward) Indians: 118, 124, 141, 163
Nose rings, 40
Notcha (Notche) (Indian), 219
Notchee Indians. *See* Natchez Indians
Nottelly (Natalee, Notoly) (Cherokee Valley town), 93, 95, 96, 97, 98, 125. *See also* Nottely (Notley), Prince of
Nottely (Notley), Prince of, 186
Nottoway Indians, 86, 87
Nottoway (Nattoway) River, 143
Noyohee (Noyowe, Nowyouwee) (Cherokee Lower town), 14, 244
Numbers (book of the Bible), 230
Nuquasse, 239
Nuscassee, 237

O

Oaks, 138
Oath, 249
Occaneechi (Achonechy) Indians, ix, 86
Occaneechi town, 86
Occaneechi Trail, 85
Ocheese Creek, 11n
Oconaluftee River, 245
Oconeca, 233
Oconee County (S.C.), 2n, 14n, 178n
Oconostota (Oconistoto, Ouonnasto-tah), Cherokee, 52, 181, 182, 195, 196, 231, 233, 234
Ocracoke Inlet, 170n
Oglethorpe, James, Gen., 74
Ohio, 47n, 222n
Ohio River, 135, 137, 181, 182, 217, 221. *See also* Ohio River Valley
Ohio River Valley, 9n. *See also* Ohio River

Ohio Valley, 221, 225
Oil, 225
Okisco (king of Weapemeoc), 136
Old Hop, Cherokee, 97-98, 195, 196, 221
Old Tassel, Cherokee, 187, 247
Old Warrior (Warier), Cherokee, 141
Old Wolf (old woolf of Keowee), Cherokee, 141
Oliver, Andrew, 303
Olives, 139
Omens, 196
Onandine Indians, 214
Oneale, John, Captain, 249
Oneida Indians (Annonida, Onandine), 22n, 78-79, 214n, 296n
Onion quits-tah Creek, 279
Onondaga Indians, 22n
Onslow County (N.C.), 155
Ooanoke (town), 136
Opessa, Shawnee, 151, 152n
Opossums, 33
Oquaga (town), 296n
Oranges, 139
Oration: to beseech charity for needy, 16; Cherokees refrain from inter-rupting during, 14; conducted in townhouse, 12; at diplomatic con-ference, 45; during funerals, 81-82; given by elderly headmen, 128, as opening address at Cherokee ball-play dance, 43; at peace ceremonies, 44, 47; in public shaming, 21; to Va. commissioners, 215
Osburn, Alexander (Alexdr.), 160
Ossa (mountain in fable), 201
Ossomocomuck (region), 45n
Ostenaco (Jud Friend, Jud's Friend, Juds Friend, Judge's Friend, Otassatch, Ottassatie, Ustenecah), 52, 98 173, 174-178
Otassite of Watoga, Cherokee, 232, 233
Otters, 7, 91, 139, 194
Otto, N.C., 25n
Oucah, Cherokee, 232
Oughquago (town), 296

Ousanatah, Cherokee, 232
Ousanoletah of Cowatache, Cherokee, 232
Ousanoletah of Jori, Cherokee, 232
Outer Banks, ix, 170n
Outside Towns. See Cherokee towns, Out
Overseers, 259, 262
Owens (Owen), Billy, 294, 298
Owens, John, 299, 301
Oyeocker (guide), 194, 195
Oznabrigs (Ozenbrigs, Oznaburgs) (fabric), 80, 90

P

Packhorse men, 111, 117, 129-130, 131, 132
Pacolet River (Packlet Creek), 177
Pagett, John, 213
Paint: ball-players wear, 43; as currency used by remote Indians, 91; on faces, 192, 194, 199; peace delegates bedecked in, 44; as a present, 128; on scalps, 30; sold to Valley Cherokees, 90; used to judge creditworthiness of Indians, 87; on war-poles, 203; worn by Cherokees, 8. See also Vermillion
Palatines (Pallatines), 115-116, 117, 154, 156
Palisade, 227
Palmer, Robert, 176-177
Palmettoes, 139
Pamlico (Pamplico), 211, 212, 265
Pamlico (Pampticough, Panticough) Indians, ix, 3, 70, 73, 147, 149
Pamlico (Pamphlico) Precinct, 269
Pamlico (Pamplico, Pamptico) River, x, 73, 136n, 149-150, 212, 213n, 278, 279
Pamlico (Pamlicoe, Pamplycoe) Sound, 276, 290
Panther Swamp Creek, 213n
Panthers, 7, 33, 60
Pardo, Juan, 31-32, 139-140, 140n, 267
Parers (tools), 23
Parks, George (Geo.), 90, 91, 106

Parliament, British, 132
Parridge, Tuscarora, 20
Parris Island, S.C., 267
Partridg, 207
Paryiter, William, 266
Pasqeunoc (Pysshokonnok, Woman's Towne), 136, 216
Pasquotank County (N.C.), 155
Pasquotank Indians, ix
Pasquotank (Paspitangh) Precinct, 269
Pasquotank (Pascotanck) River, 143
Pate, Jeremiah, 122-123
Patents, land, 147, 158, 164, 169
Pawhatan, King of, 195
Pawhatan (town), 195
Paxton, Pa., 290, 295
Peace: articles of, 278; between Catawbas and Iroquois, 215, Catawbas and Shawnees, 202, Cherokees and the English, 239, Indians and Christians, 269, northern Tuscarora and N.C. government, 212; dress during, 194; lasts fifteen years for the Cherokees, 240; talks between Cherokees and Northward Indians, 141, between Creeks and Cherokees, 76, 77, postponed due to disease, 78, 78-79; tokens of, 220; treaties between Cherokees, Catawbas, and Creeks, 47-48, Cherokees and Caughnawagas, 47, colony of Va. and Indians in the Albemarle region, 142, Indians and Robert Daniel, 121, Palatines and the Indians residing in the Neuse/Trent river areas, 152, Saponi, Susquehanna, and Catawba Indians, 46, U.S. and Cherokees, 247; treaties sought by Tuscaroras with the colony of Pa., 151; of victims' spirits, 192
Peaches, 42, 81
Peachtree Creek, 52n
Peak (peack, Peake), 16, 20, 45-46, 91, 194. See also Currency; Wampum
Pearl, 91
Peas, 23, 28, 29, 63, 140, 237, 242, 245

Peckers (tool), 23
Pee Dee River, 118, 156, 167
Peg (squaw), 244
Pelion (mountain in fable), 201
Pellitory bark, 22
Penn, John, Gov. (Pa.), 262, 295, 295n
Pennsylvania, 47n, 150, 151-152, 155, 221, 295
Pequea Creek, 152n
Perquimans, 264
Perquimans County (N.C.), 155, 261, 267n
Perquimans (Pequimimins, Pequimons) Precinct, 260, 269
Perquimans River, 136n
Peter (manumitted servant), 264
Peter (slave), 261
Peter, Captain, Catawba, 77
Petersburg, Va., 85
Peterson, Jacob, 260
Petitions, 261, 262, 264, 266, 284, 285, 292-294, 302
Petticoats, 6
Phebe (Indian woman), 265
Phenix City, Alabama, 221n
Phifar (Phifer), Martin, 227, 228
Philadelphia (Philadia.), Pa., 89, 151-152, 247-248
Phillips, Daniell, 251
Physic (fisicke; Cassena, *Ilex cassena*, Yaupon) drink: 44, 61, 64, 65, 68-70, 193
Physicians. *See* Doctors
Pickens County (S.C.), 14n
Piedmont, the: and boundary between N.C. and S.C., 161, 163, 167; Catawba Indians occupy, 135; Crymble and Huey grant in, 161; Indian alcohol use in, 118; Indian language groups in, ix, 3; and Occaneechi Trail, 85; panic in the western, 225; settlements established in, 155; white encroachment in, 170
Pierce, Thomas, 266
Pigeon, the, Cherokee, 93
Pigeon (Pidgeon) River, 32n, 190, 246

Pigs, 26, 251, 265
Pinckney, William, 219n
Pine Tree Creek, 162
Pine Tree Hill, 162n
Pineapples, 139
Pines, 138, 202
Piney (pyny) barren, 194
Pipe hatchet, 96, 107
Pipes, 220, 225, 226
Pipes, tobacco: construction and decoration of, described, 29; given to Indians as presents, 52, 226; as markers of peace, 44, 220, 225; mentioned, 46; tomahawks serve as, 32; trader forced to extinguish his, 58; used for purification, 67-68; utilized by Cherokees, 29-30
Pistols, 97, 98
Pitch, 138, 203
Pittsburgh, Pa., 221
Plaid (fabric), 6
Plains (fabric), 6, 20
Plan for the Future Management of Indian Affairs, 132, 133
Plantains, 139
Plantations, 194
Planting, 296. *See also* Plants
Plants, 116. *See also* Planting
Plate (currency), 91
Plumpton, Henry, 142, 142-143
Plunder, 243, 245, 246
Poaching, 127, 147, 148, 150, 178, 184, 185
Poker, Haniod Sollmon, 265
Politics and government: and allotment of farmland, 24; and Catawbas, 47-48, 160-161; and Cherokees, 14-15, 47-48, 102-103; conducted in townhouses, 12; and England, 102-103; and France, 106; Indian nations forced to act due to, 100; Indians deliberate issues before committing to an answer or action concerning, 16; issuance of Indian commissions subverts, 50-51; lack coercive power, 15, penal laws, 20; and making peace,

44; and Proclamation of 1763, 129; strong chiefs dominate, in eastern N.C., 13; and tobacco, 29; and trade, 106, 109, 110, 122, 132, 133; and Tuscaroras, 122-123, 150-152; types of, practiced by Indians, 13-16

Polk County (N.C.), 178n

Polk County (Tenn.), 52n, 207n

Pollock, T. (Thomas), 259, 282, 284

Pollock, Thomas, 251

Pollock, Thomas, Junior, 250

Pollock, Thos., Col., 213

Pollock, Thos., Esqr. (president of council), 212

Poly Bridge Branch, 286

Pompions, 245

Poplars, 138

Population, ix, x, 153

Porcelain (Porcelan), 36, 46

Porrage (Porridge), Jude, 265, 266

Porter, Joshua, 144

Porteskite Indians, 283

Portugal, 35n

Pory, John (Master Porey), 137, 138

Pot ashes, 138

Potatoes, 243, 244

Poteskite (Porteskite, Porteskyte) Indians, 144

Pots, 52

Potter, John (archbishop of Canterbury), 155, 262, 263

Pottery, 35-36, 42, 69, 75

Poverty, 297

Pow, King, Catawba, 50

Powder and shot, 249, 299. *See also* Gunpowder

Powell, William, 148-149

Powell (Powels) Mountain, 182

Powers, Saml., 277

Poyntz, Stephen, 156

Prenche hura (Indian), 227

Presbyterians, 244, 274

President, the (Va.), 123

Price, Aaron, 107, 108

Price, George (Mr. Price), Ensign, 173

Priests, Christian, 267

Priests, Native American. *See* Conjurors

Prisoners: Capt. Francis Ross receives sixteen, 244; Capt. William Moore takes two squaws and a boy as, 246; fate of war, foreshadowed in dance, 41; Henry Hill Senior taken as, 253; Indian, rebel in garrison, 208; Indian squaw taken by Col. John Thomas as, 243; required to bathe after being with the enemy, 65; secured to war-poles, 203; taken by Catawbas, 205; Cherokees, 234, 237, warriors, 202; torture of, described, 204; war, adopted by Cherokees, 19. *See also* Captives; Hostages; Prisons

Prisons, 96, 112, 116, 121-122. *See also* Prisoners

Prithard, J., 91

Privy Council, 129, 155-156, 169, 170, 179, 294n

Proclamation of 1763, 129, 133, 168, 169, 170. *See also* Royal Proclamation of 1763

Promissory notes, 251, 252

Provisions, 210, 211, 216, 225, 227, 237, 246, 295, 296

Prukets, 89

Psalms (book of the Bible), 231

Pugh, Billy (Bille), 294, 299, 300

Pugh, Francis, 104, 259

Pugh, Lewis, 303

Pugh, Thomas, 293, 294n, 297, 298, 299, 300, 302, 303

Pugh, Thomas, Senior, 302n

Pugh, William (Wm.), 301

Punch, 70

Punch bowls, 142

Pungo River (Machapungo River), 10, 148

Punishment, 192, 200, 202, 203, 232, 255, 257, 278. *See also individual forms of punishment by name*; Crime and punishment; Discipline and punishment

Purification, 192, 193, 197. *See also* Bathing; Sweating

Pushing, Jeremiah, 286

Q

Quakers, 261, 264, 267
Quarrasattahi, Cherokee, 232
Quebec, 47n, 169, 217
Quiogozons (royal tombs), 55, 82-83
Quitmah Swamp, 279
Quitrents, 162
Quitsna Swamp, 300
Quitsney's Meadow, 298n
Quitsnoy Swamp, 280

R

Rabbits, hares (conies), 6, 33
Rabun County (Ga.), 14n, 52n, 110n
Raccoons, 6, 33, 91
Raids, 197, 206, 208, 225, 240, 246
Raleigh, Walter, Sir, x, 13, 45n, 49, 267
Randolph, John, 303
Ranging, 190
Ransford, Giles, 269n
Raquis Swamp, 280
Rarookakeo (Indian town), 212
Ratcliff, Cornelius, 263
Rattleiff, Richard, 244
Rattles, 63
Rattlesnakes, 59-60, 63, 138
Raudauqua-quank (town), 207n
Raurooka (town), 213
Raven (war name), 201
Raven of Estahtowih, 235
Raven of Hiwassee (Mankiller of Hiwas-
    see, the Raven), Cherokee, 51, 52n,
    93, 124, 125, 220
Raven of Tanasi (Tunesee), 112
Raymond, Tho., master, 89
Read, Robert, 80, 273
Reading, Lyonell (Lionel), 150, 213
Reading, 267, 269, 270
Receiver-general, 208
Red Creek, 127
Reed, William (Wm.), Colonel, 206, 283,
    284
Reeds, 35, 36, 66
Reedy River, 79, 173, 177
Religion: altar complex for, described,
    57; and bathing, 65-66; and burials,
81-82; creatures possessing features
of multiple worlds respected, 59-60;
description of Indian, 53-54, 55-56;
and diseases, 70, 71-72, 75; as a facet
of white culture, 267; and good
health, 64; and green corn ceremony,
60-61; and Indian mounds, 12;
Indians reticent to share tenets of,
with whites, 54-55; Native Americans encounter European, 193; and
physic drink, 68, 69-70; sacred fire
respected, 58; and tobacco use, 67-
68; Upper World, Terrestrial World,
and Lower World, described, 58; war
had a place in practice of, 192. *See also
individual denominations by name;*
Christianity; Clergy; Conjurors
Relocations, 77-78
Reservations, Indian: for Catawba
    Indians, 158, 161-162, 163-164, 165,
    166, 167-168; Chowan Indians
    relegated to, 145-146, 276-277;
    Governor Dobbs on, 161, 163, 164,
    166; Indians and whites dispute over,
    158, 297-303; for Meherrin Indians,
    277-278; N.C. assigns eastern Indians
    to, after Tuscarora War, xi, 153; and
    S.C. governor, 161; tribes sell and/or
    lease land from, 286-290; for Tus-
    carora Indians, 161, 164, 278-283; for
    Yeopim, Mattamuskeet, and Chowan
    Indians, 275-277
Resootska (Rehoosesky, Rosoossokee)
    (town), 259n, 279, 283n
Reuiroota (Reuroota) (town), 212, 213n
Revenge, 192, 193, 194, 199, 204, 216,
    229, 230
Revolutionary War. *See* American
    Revolution
Rhodes, Elisha, 303
Ribbons (ribbands), 43, 51, 90
Richardson, William, 274
Richland Creek, 245
Richland Creek Mountain, 246
Rieussett (Riusset), John, Col., 155
Rings, 40, 87, 194

Rising faun. *See* Kennititah

Rites and ceremonies: for Cherokee adoption, 19; conducted in town-houses, 12; for greeting of strangers, 45; for making peace, 44, 47-48; physic drink dance as, 69-70; presentation of gifts in, 49-50; to remember historical events, 1-2; smoking of tobacco in, 29-30; torture was a notable, 202. *See also* Corn; Dance/dancing; Funeral customs and rites, ceremonies; Green Corn Ceremony; Purification

Roanoke (roanoack, Roanoak, Ronoak). *See* Peak

Roanoke (Roanoak, Ronoak) (decorative shell beads), 8, 45, 46

Roanoke Indians, 270

Roanoke (Roanoak) Island, 13, 85, 135, 136, 142, 267

Roanoke (Morattuck, "Morratock") River, 47n, 142, 143, 150, 194, 278, 291, 293, 295

Robbard, Tom, 301

Robbery, 254, 260

Robearts, John, 301

Robearts, William, 301

Roberts, Billy (Bille), 298, 299, 300

Roberts, John, 294

Roberts, Tom, 302

Roberts, Tom, Jun, 300

Roberts, William, 303

Robertson, James, Capt., 184, 185, 186

Robin, John, 251, 252, 284

Robinson, J., 106

Robinson, Thomas, 223n

Rodgers (Rodges, Roggers), John, 294, 299, 300, 301

Rodgers, Joseph, 265

Rogers, Brother (clergyman), 230

Roman Catholics, 267

Rooks, James, 266n

Roonee, Geerick, Creek, 217

Roots, 116, 194

Ropes, 26

Rosemary, 209

Rosquist, 300

Ross, Captain [Francis], 242

Round O, Cherokee, 221, 231

Rowan, Matthew, President (N.C.), 157-158, 161

Rowan County (N.C.), 160, 170, 217, 218, 222, 223

Royal Proclamation of 1763, 173-174, 178, 179, 180, 181, 240. *See also* Proclamation of 1763

Royal Troops, 237

Royall, John, 259

Rufin, Guillermo, 31

Rum: and Cherokees, 14, 15, 90, 97, 127, 182; consumed to excess by Little Carpenter, 120, 121; disturbances by Indians inflamed by, 122; eradicates large swathes of Indian population, 73; headmen desire, not be sold to their people, 121; Indian king given, 57; Indian Ned given, 80; and Indian traders, 87, 131; Indians purchase, 118; sold for horses, 119; and Tuscaroras, 87, 296

Runaways, 210, 258, 259, 265. *See also* Escape

Rushes, 35, 81

Russel, Solomon, 271

Russell, Charles, 88

Russetts, Mrs., 216

Rutherford, Griffith, Col. (Brigadier General), 155, 241, 242, 244, 245

Rutherford (Rutherfurd), John, 176, 177

Rutherford County (N.C.), 187, 190, 191

Rye, 28

S

Sachem, Tuscarora, 291, 292, 293

Saddles, 51, 52

Sale, John, 251

Salem, N.C., 274

Salem, S.C., 178n

Salisbury, N.C., 121-122, 176, 226, 267

Salisbury (Salisbery) District, 241, 242

Sallowee (Saluy, Young Warrior of Estatoe), 177
Salt, 64, 98, 241
Sanderson, Richard (Richd.), Capt., 144, 251, 283, 284
Sandy Point, 283
Sannoiste, Cherokee, 232
Santa Elena (location), 267
Santee River, 137
Saponi (Saponia, Sapora) Indians, ix, 46-47n, 155
Sarah (free Indian), 262, 263
Sarem, N.C., 269
Saroonka Heust he noh neh, Tuscarora, 212
Sarum (town), 268, 269
Sashes, 34
Sasle, John, 252
Sassafras tree, 63
Saunderson, Richard, 145-146
Savages, 194, 197
Savannah Indians, 91n. *See also* Shawnee Indians
Savannah River, 2n, 78n, 137, 219n, 235, 241n. *See also* Savannah River Valley
Savannah River Valley, 207n, 236n. *See also* Savannah River
Savanukah (Coronoh, Raven of Chota, Savonocko, Savanooko, Savanuca), Cherokee, 181, 182, 183, 184, 185-186
Sawyer, John, 263
Scalping (Sculping), 32, 41, 199-200, 204, 234, 239, 245, 246. *See also* Scalps
Scalps, 30, 199, 203, 213, 218, 237, 240. *See also* Scalping
Schoharie Creek, 217n
Schools, 268, 269, 270, 272, 273, 294
Scissors (Sizars), 51, 90, 91
Scot, Walter, 244
Scotland, 6n, 288
Scots place, 245
Scouts, 159, 235-236n
Searcy, Reuben, 263
Secotan (location), 136
Secretary (N.C.), 147

Secretary of State (southern department), 167
Self-defense, 20
Selkirk, 2nd Earl of (Charles Douglas), 156
Senate (N.C.), 302
Seneca (Seneques, Sennaca, Sinakers) Indians, 22n, 151-152, 159, 160n, 217, 259
Senneka, George, 250
Sequoyah, Cherokee, 1
Serges (fabric), 51
Servants, 256-257
Settico (Overhill town), 230, 231
Settlements: alcohol in, 121, 122; and Catawba Indians, 156, 157-158, 160, 161, 162-163, 165; and Cherokee Indians, 137, 171, 178-179, 182-183, 184, 186-187, 188; and Chowan Indians, 146; and Creek Indians, 134; effect of, on Indians' hunting, 86, 144-145, 158, 171, 186-187; and Indian land, 138, 148, 150, 156, 158, 160, 162-163, 165, 169, 171, 178-179, 182-183, 184, 186-187, 188; Indians attacked or harassed, 145-146, 147-150, 182, stole from, 119, 134, 159; inhabitants of, harass and steal from Indians, 144-145, 153-155, 157-158; mentioned, 34, 134, 173, 179, 180; Roanoke, 85; and S.C., 137, 157-158, 160, 162-163, 171; spread of, 72-73, 129, 137, 139, 142, 147, 155, 161, 163, 165, 168, 169, 170, 171, 172, 183; and Tuscarora Indians, 86, 149-150, 152
Seven Confederate Nations of Canada, 47
Sevier, General (first warrior for western country), 248
Shakori (Schoccores) Indians, 86
Shaliloske, Cherokee, 232
Shamokin (location), 295
Sharp, John, 99, 101
Sharpe, Wm., 183

Shawnee (Shanaws, Shawanois, "Shaw-noise," Shawnese) Indians, 9, 151-152, 159-160, 202, 205, 225. *See also* Opessa; Savannah Indians
Sheep, 69
Sheld, G., 207
Shells, 91. *See also* Peak; Roanoke (currency); Roanoke (beads); Wampum
Sheriffs, 123, 231, 254. *See also* Constables
Shipping, 89
Ships, 49, 206, 260. *See also* Boats; Shipping; Sloops
Shirts: abusive French-allied Indian demands, 92; given for land transfers, 176, 297, 299, to Cherokees by S.C. as presents, 51, to Indian Ned, 80; and Indian headmen, 7, 128; made of deerskin, 7; sold to Valley Cherokees, 90; used to judge creditworthiness of Indians, 87
Shoes, 7, 51, 80, 203, 226
Shot, 20, 31, 87, 91, 123. *See also* Swan shot
Shute, Gyles, 144
Silk grass, 6, 138
Silk worms, 138
Silver, 8, 40, 43, 66, 141, 224. *See also* Silversmiths
Silver Bluff, 219
Silversmiths, 139
Singing, 1, 19, 43, 44, 66, 75, 193, 204. *See also under* War
Siouan languages, ix, 3
Six Nations, 215, 290, 291, 295, 296. *See also* Iroquois Indians
Skeona (Cherokee place of spirits), 58
Skiagusta of Sticoe, Cherokee, 232
Skienah, Cherokee, 124
Slave Catcher of Connutra (Slave Ketcher of Kenntory), Cherokee, 124
Slave catcher, The (war name), 201
Slaves: act concerning, 256-257; African American, 260-261; Core Indians as, 147; dress and tan raw animal skins, 34; given by Indians in exchange for alcohol, 118; Indian women and children as, xi, 46, 208, 258; kill vermin, 249; offered as compensation for the loss of one life, 20; orators enumerate, 81; prisoners as, 65, 205-206, 246; punishment of, 19, 218, 254, 255; social status of Indian, 257; traders and, 206, 207; Tuscarora, 35, 150, 151. *See also* African Americans; Manumission
Slocumb, John, 106
Sloops, 149
Smallpox, x; devastates the Pamlico Indians, 147; Indian treatment for, described, 73; among Indians seen as providential, 72; outbreak stifles Indian trade, 78; ravages the Catawbas, 73, 75-76, 161, 163, 164, 273, the Cherokees, 73, 74, 79
Smith, Mr. (letter bearer) , 165
Smith, Benjn. , 303
Smith, Bille, 300
Smith, George, Colonel, 223
Smith, Henry, 303
Smith, James, 262
Smith, John, 251, 254, 299, 300
Smith, Richard, 227, 228
Smith, Samuel, 264
Smith, William, 294n
Smithing, 45
Snakes, 59-60, 138-139
Snow Hill, 213n
Snowden, James (Jams.), 70
Soap ashes (Soe-ashes), 138
Society for the Propagation of the Gospel in Foreign Parts (SPG), 268, 269, 270, 273
Sockey, Billy, 294
South Carolina: baskets made in, 35; boundary of, 78, 166, 171, 173, 175, 176, 177, 187, 188; Catawbas and, 88-89, 156-158, 160-163, 165, 166, 167, 272, 273; Cherokees and, 35, 74, 122, 123, 127, 135, 137, 140, 183, 234, 235; commissioner of Indian

affairs in, 114; competes with Va., 126; constructs forts, 60n, 121n, 161, 163; currency, 88; governors, 95, 126, 167, 168, 173-175, 216, 219, 229, 232, 233, 238; grants lands, 171; hunting grounds in, 183; and Indians, 68, 91n, 188, 134, 236n; inhabitants barter rum, 119, 122; merchants, 84; migration to, 91; military aid from, xi, 208, 209, 211, 242; militia, 183, 235; northwestern, 2n; reservation approved by, 167; residents of, 140; seat of government in, 76; settlements in, 240; trade with, 74, 78, 85, 86, 95, 104-106, 110, 112, 113, 122, 123, 126, 127, 128, 156-157, 158; troops, 210; Tuscarora and, 150, 152-153, 209, 214, 278, 290; war in, 279
South Hampton, 262
Southern Indians, 142
Southport, N.C., 170n
Sowing, 23
Spain, 67, 72, 74, 140n. *See also* Spaniards
Spangenberg, August Gottlieb, 109, 286n
Spaniards, x, 200, 257, 267. *See also* Spain
Speedwell (sloop), 89
Speir, John, 104
Speirs, _____ (commissioner of Indian affairs), 282
Spies, 211
Sports, 39, 151
Spruill, Godfrey (Godfr), 10
Squiers, Timothy, 290
Squires, Bet, 271
Squires (Squieres), Charles, 288, 289, 290
Squires, George, 290
Squires, John, 271, 288, 289
Squires, Joshua, 272, 290
Squires, King, Mattamuskeet, 275, 276
Squirrels, 6, 33
Squirs, John. *See* Squires, John
Squirs, Tom, 288
St. James's Palace, 129, 155, 179
St. John's Parish, 80

St. Lawrence River, 34, 47n
St. Paul Parish, 253
Standing Turkey, 196
Starky, John, Col., 155
Starling, George, 126
Starvation, 238
Statesville, N.C., 170n
Stecoah, N.C., 52n
Stecoah (Stekoa) Creek, 52n, 110n
Stecoe (Cherokee town, Stekoe, Sticoe, Stecowee Old Town), 51, 52, 109, 110n, 122, 124-125
Stecoe River, 221
Steel, Captain, 209
Steel (Steill), Robert, 110, 157
Steelyards (Iron Yards), 101, 103
Stephens, Col., 74
Stephens, Jeremiah. *See* Stevens, Jeremiah
Stephens County (Ga.), 14n
Stephenson, William, 290
Stevens, Aaron, 78
Stevens, Jeremiah, 287
Stewart, 240, 241
Stewart, Alexander (Alexr.), 270, 271, 272
Stinking Linguo's, 92-93
Stockbridge, 235
Stockings, 7, 51
Stone, Zedekiah, 302, 302n, 303
Stones, 160
Strouds, 51, 59, 90, 97, 103, 205, 229
Stuart, Henry, 182
Stuart, John (Captain Stewart, Father in Charles Town, John Stewart, King's Superintendent of Indian Affairs, Mr. Stuart): and Catawbas, 135, 137, 164; and Cherokees, 13, 14, 15, 79, 137, 178; describes agricultural practices of Indians, 24, 34; and discussions concerning boundary lines, 79, 171, 172, 173, 176; explains Indians' feelings, 144, 192, forms of punishment, 21-21, need for luxuries, 90, 91-92; on Indian trade, 115, 117-118, 119, 129-132, 133, 134; and Indians' relationship with the British, 51, 240;

letters from, 20-21, 24, 34, 48, 51, 52, 62, 91-92, 117-118, 119, 126, 134, 137, 144, 171-173; letters to, 122, 182-183, 290, 291n; meets with governors and headmen, 48, 167, 175; and Tuscaroras, 290-291, 294n, 295
Sturgeons, 36, 37, 138
Suarez, Andres, 139
Sucah (Catawba town), 9n
Sugar, 90, 139
Sugar Creek, 9n, 164, 165
Sugar Creek Town (Catawba), 164
Sugar Town, 177, 178
Sugaree (Shutterees) Indians, 126, 127n
Suicide, 75
Sumpter, Colonel [Thomas], 242
Sunbury, Pa., 295n
Superintendent of Indian Affairs, 240, 291. *See also* Superintendents, Indian
Superintendents, Indian: and Augusta Congress, 167; and boundary lines, 171, 172, 173, 174, 175, 176, 177; and Catawba Indians, 162, 164, 168; and Cherokee Indians, 171, 172, 173, 175, 178, 180-181 182; deputy for, 134, 141; duties of, 129, 133; and Henderson Purchase, 178, 181; and Indian town, 201, 209; plotted with Indians during American Revolution, 183, 186; and Proclamation of 1763, 180-181; and regulations for the southern district, 129-132; and S.C. governor, 165, 172; and trade, 131, 132, 133; and Treaty of Pine Tree Hill, 162, 163, 164, 165, 168. *See also* Superintendent of Indian Affairs
Superior Court and Court of Claims, the (N.C.), 166. *See also* Courts
Surry County (Va.), 123
Surveyor generals, 152, 281. *See also* Surveyors
Surveyors (N.C.), 158, 162-164, 166. *See also* Surveyor generals
Surveys, land: of Catawba, 163, 164, 166, 167, 168; in Cherokee territory to be

voided, 190; and Chowan Indians, 276; mentioned, 88-89, 156; prohibited in Indian territory, 169; for the Tuscarora reservation, 161-162. *See also* Surveyor generals; Surveyors (N.C.)
Susquehanna River, 291, 295, 296n
Susquehanna River Valley, 47n
Susquehannah (susquhanah) Indians, 46, 47n
Suttellitchee (Suttallitchee, Suttelletchee, Warrior of Tasetche [Tecethece]), 102
Swamp cane, 35
Swamps, 138, 197, 198, 210. *See also* Swamp cane
Swan shot, 130. *See also* Shot
Swann, Samuel (Saml.), Maj., 147
Swannanoa, N.C., 245
Swans, 44, 69
Sweating, 64, 66, 75. *See also* Bathing; Purification
Sweetwater Creek, 60n
Swepsonville, N.C., 85
Swiss (Swists), 156
Swords, 42, 210
Sycamore Shoals, 178

T

Tacite of Hiwassee (Hyowassie), Cherokee, 221, 222n
Tadirighrones, Catawba, 214
Taherooka (Toherooka). *See* Neoheroka
Tallapoosa River, 78n
Talletake, Cherokee, 232
Tallichama, Cherokee, 232
Tamassee, S.C., 2n
Tanasi (Tanassee, Tanissee, Tannassie, Tannissee) (Cherokee Overhill town), 14, 96, 97-98
Tannessie, Prince of, Cherokee, 77
Tanning, 7, 11, 34, 131
Tar, 138
Tar River, 250n
Tarhunta (Tarhuntah), 212, 213

Tasetche (Tecethece) (Cherokee Valley town), 102, 103n
Tasse ("Tassie"), 236, 237
Tassetee of Stekoe, Cherokee, 52
Tasttuith, 212
Tattoos, 8
Tawasaws (French-allied Indians), 222
Taylor, Captain, Catawba, 77
Taylor, Billy, 294
Taylor, Edward, 287
Taylor, William, 285, 298
Tea, 90
Teague, Captain, 200
Teatontaloga, 217n
Tellico (Telliquo), 14, 26, 62, 97, 98. *See also* Great Tellico; Little Tellico
Tellico Creek, 14n
Tellico Lake, 60n, 93n
Tellico River, 14n
Templeton, David, 157
Tennessee, 9n, 14n, 48n, 135, 178, 207n
Tennessee River (Tenasee, Tenesee), 14n, 59, 60n, 137, 181, 189
Teonnottein, Tuscarora, 151
Terraret, 231
Terrutawanaren, Tuscarora, 151
Thames River, 136
Theft: by Cherokees upon Indian traders, 97, 98, 120, 122, 123-125, 127; Indians shamed for, 21; S.C. traders', of deerskin, 126-127; upon settlers by Indians, 147, 148-149, 157, 159
Thickety Creek, 159
Thomas, [John], Colonel, 243
Thomas, William, 244
Thos, Catawba, 46
Thread, 51, 80, 90
Thurmond Lake, 241n
Tidewater region, 3
Tifdick, Whitmell. *See* Tufdick, Whitmell
Tiftoe (Tifftoe, Tufftoe, the Warrior Keowee), 52, 177
Tiger River, 174
Tilicho, 244
Timber, 141, 168, 175

Timberlake, Henry, Lt.: comments on pipe smoking with the Cherokees, 29-30; describes canoe construction, 38-39, Cherokee dress, 5-6, climate in Cherokee nation, 25-26, consumption of yaupon tea among the Cherokees, 68, 69-70, Indians' fishing, 36-37, physical appearance of Cherokees, 8-9, variety of weaponry utilized by Cherokees, 32; says Cherokees wanted to end war to resume trade with British, 238
Tin, 141
Tinnessy River, 242, 243
Tobacco: can be grown in Cape Fear, 139; as currency to pay fines for trading without permission, 116; given as presents, 52, 226, as token of peace, 44, 220, 225; mentioned, 46; prohibition from smoking, lit with temple fire, 58; sharing pipes to smoke, as sign of amity, 29-30; smoking, as form of purification, 67-68; sprinkling powdered, to appease Indian gods, 67, 68; varieties of, 29, 30, 32. *See also* Pipes, tobacco
Toccoa, Ga., 52n
Toisnot (Tostehant, Tostohant), 122, 212, 213
Toisnot Swamp, 213n
Tokens, 192
Tomahawks, 26, 30, 32, 199, 203, 218, 234
Tomassee (Timossy, Tomausey) (Cherokee town), 2
Tomassee Indians, 244
Tommas, Billey, 294
Tommas [Tomas], Tom, 299, 301
Tomotla (Timothly, Timotly, Tomatla, Tomatly, Tommothy) (Cherokee Valley town), 102, 103n, 111, 113, 124, 125n-126n
Tony, Cherokee, 232
Too Cowee, 245
Toole (Tool), Matthew, 87, 88-89, 110-111, 118-119, 160

Tools, x, 258
Torhunta (Narhantes), 9
Torture, 41, 202, 204
Tossetee (Man Killer, Tosetee, Tossitee, Tossittee), Natchez, 51, 52n, 108
Totaiah-hoi, Cherokee, 232
Totem poles, 57
Town Creek, 250n
Town houses, 192, 200. *See also* Council houses
Towns: activity in, 35; description and list of, in eastern N.C., 9, 136; eradicated by smallpox, 73; European and colonial, 139; and funeral rites, 81; hunting and, 31, 65, 119, 131; independent of one another, 15-16; land surrounding, 23, 24, 26; location of, 10; mentioned, 128, 135; trade and, 87, 104, 105, 111, 116, 119, 128, 131, 132. *See also individual towns by name*
Towns, the. *See* Cherokee towns, Overhill
Toys, 91
Trade: and abuse/violence, xi, 92-93, 101, 102-103, 118; alcohol sold to Indians in, 118-119, 121, 122, 131; of animal skins and furs, x, 31, 34, 89, 131, 167, 171; and Britain, 7, 102, 128-129, 13; and Catawba Indians, 9n, 121-122, 160, 167; and Cherokees, 15, 35, 74, 96-98, 100, 102, 105-106, 107-108, 127, 128, 171, 216; of cloth and clothing, x, 5, 6, 7; commissioners, 78, 154; competition over, 126-127, 128; control of, 132, 133; credit, 87, 99, 100, 130; debt, 99, 100, 113, 130, 157; and disease, 74, 78; embargo on, 122-125, 149, 231; and financial problems, 95; and the French, 92-93, 128; and Ga., 127, 128; goods and their prices, 90-91, 130; and hunting, 15, 17, 100, 131; and Indian burial practices, 81, 84; and Iroquois Indians, 216; licenses, 104, 105-107, 110-115; mutual

convenience of, x, 90-92, 249; network, ix; and Nottoway Indians, 87; potential for substantial profits from, 94, 221; proposals for, 12, 115, 116-117; prospects of, increased, 246; protection of routes for, 236n; provides weaponry to Indians, 32, 149; and public monopoly, 115, 117; regulations, 100, 103, 104-105, 111, 126, 128-132, 134; resumption of, 238; slave, x, 206, 208; and S.C., 76, 78, 101, 104-105, 115, 117, 127; and superintendency, 129-132; of tools, 34, 38; and Tuscarora Indians, 86, 87, 122-123, 152; and Va., 85, 86, 127; whites lack goods for Indian, 45, 240. *See also* Factors; Trade commissioners; Trade goods; Traders
Trade commissioners, 101, 104-105, 106-107, 110, 114-115, 117. *See also under* Trade
Trade goods: and Catawba Indians, 162; and Cherokees, 90-91, 97-98, 120, 178, 186; and the French, 92-128; and Ga., 128; and hunting, 128, 162; and Indian headmen, 128, 120; and Indian traders, 87, 90-91, 108, 109, 111, 132, 119, 154; Indians boycott, when in debt, 100; Indians cannot live without, x, 117; Indians receive, despite transfer of supervision, 133; Indians sell land to acquire, 178; interred with the dead, 81; mentioned, 106, 110; not to be sold to inhabitants of N.C., 123; require protection, 94, 95; stopped by trade embargoes, 122-125; and Tuscarora Indians, 87. *See also under* Trade
Traders: abuse by, 98, 99-100, 101-102, 110, 117-118, 131, 132-133, 225, 240, of, 77, 92-93, 97, 98, 120; and African Americans 130, 132; and alcohol, 74, 92, 118-119, 122, 131; and animal skins, furs, or peltry, x, 119, 131; appointed for public Indian trade, 78; as bearers/sources of information, 2,

106, 131; and Catawba Indians, 167; cheat Indians, 101, 103, 111, 113, 150; and Cherokee Indians, 2, 42, 50, 53, 74, 93, 95-96, 97, 98, 99-100, 103, 105-106, 108, 112, 120, 123, 124, 125, 127, 134, 140-141, 186, 206, 233; and commissaries, 130-131, 132; competition between, 104, 110, 111, 126; and credit and creditors, 87, 95-96, 99, 100; and Creek Indians, 134; exert influence with Indian clients, 100, 109-110; and Ga., 127, 134, 128, 74; goods sold by, listed, 90-91, 194; and hunting, 131, 186; Indians require purification of, 193; and land sales, 88-89, 140-141, 274, 288; licensed, 74, 104, 105-106, 107-108, 119, 122, 129-130, 132; mentioned, 59; paid bond for trade goods, 87, 88-89; precarious business partnership between, 111-113; and religion, 53, 58; and S.C., 50, 74, 77, 107, 127; and superintendencies, 132, 133; and theft, 98, 124-125, 126, 127, 134; and trade regulations, 103, 104, 113, 126; and Tuscarora Indians, 150, 152; unlicensed, 74, 107, 108, 110, 119, 122; and Va., 85, 86, 126-127, 274, 30; women and, 94, 206; and the Yamasee War, 117. *See also* Trade

Trading licenses: dispensed in Ga., 128; Indian traders exceed the limits of, 111, must note employees on back of, 129-130, 132; issuance of, 74, 104-105, 129, 132; mentioned, 114, 119, 126. *See also under* Trade; Traders

Tragaweha, Tuscarora, 297

Trails, Indian, 24, 25, 85

Transylvania Company, 178-179, 179-181, 182-183. *See also* Henderson, Richard

Trapping, 131. *See also* Hunting

Treaties: between Catawbas and the Indian superintendency, 162, Cherokees and N.C., 176-178, Edmond Atkin and the Catawbas, 164, the English and Cherokee Indians, 233, the English and Tuscarora Indians, 292; commissioners for N.C., 184; concluded by Barnwell, 211, in Charleston, 104; demand death of Cherokee chiefs, 238; lands allotted to the Tuscaroras by, 280; stipulations of, 229. *See also individual treaties by name*

Treaty of DeWitt's Corner, 183

Treaty of Long Island of Holston, 183, 184, 185, 187, 188

Treaty of Paris (1763), 168

Treaty of peace, 232

Treaty of Pine Tree Hill, 162, 163-164, 165, 167, 168

Trent River, 150

Trespass, 263, 298, 298n

Tribute, 213, 283

Trousers, 80

Troy, Patrick, 107-108

Trumpets, 199

Truncheons. *See* Clubs

Trunks, 51, 90

Tryon, William, Gov. (N.C.): establishes boundary between N.C. and the Cherokees, 79, 173, 174-176; and lease of Tuscarora land, 297-298; letters from, 291-292, 295-296; letters to, 133, 298n; states N.C. settlements have advanced beyond Fort Dobbs, 170; and Tuscarora Indians' move to N.Y., 291-292, 292-294

Tryon, N.C., 178n

Tryon Peak (Mountain), 177, 178n

Tryon Troops, 245

Tuccaseegey parts. *See* Cherokee towns, Out towns

Tuckaleechee (Tucherechee), 124, 126n

Tuckasegee (Tuccaseagia, Tuckasega) (Cherokee Out town), 51, 52n. 120, 220

Tuckasegee (Tukesege) Path, 85

Tuckasegee River (Kettewa, Tuckaseegee, Tuckasehchee, Tuckasejah,

Tuckyseige), 14n, 52n, 59, 99, 100n, 126n, 190, 221n, 245. *See also* Tuckasegee River Valley

Tuckasegee River Valley, 2n

Tufdick (Tuffdick), Lewis, 298, 299, 300, 302, 303

Tufdick, West, 299, 303

Tufdick (Tuffdick), Whitmell (Whit., Whitmill), 299, 300, 301, 303

Tugaloo (Toogoloo, Tooguloo, Tuegelo) (Cherokee Lower town), 52, 52n, 99, 122, 219

Tugaloo River, 14n

Tuke, Thomas, 142-143

Tulip tree, 38

Tuotee, 97, 98n

Turkeys, 7, 31, 86, 175

Turner, George, 195, 197n

Turner, Simon, 303

Turner, Sinior, 302

Turpentine, 116

Turrepine, Cherokee, 171-172

Tuscarora (Tuscarara, Tuscarore, Tuscaroroe, Tuscarouda, Tuscororah, Tuscorodo, Tuskarora, Tuskaroro, Tuskerora, Tuskeruro, Tuskorora, Tuskororo) Indians: attack settlers, xi, 145, 146, 149-150, 208, 279; complaints of, 20, 284; fighting of and against, 9, 21, 22, 194, 278; headmen of, 5, 7-8, 78-79, 147, 150-152, 211, 209n; hunting tactics of, described, 30-31; invited to exchange prisoners, 211; and Iroquois Indians, 22n, 153, 214; and lease of land, 300-303; monitoring of the, 281; N.C. seeks restitution from, 147; ordered to select a king, 282; and plans for a move northward, xi, 150, 151-152, 293; population and reservation size of, 155, 158, 161, 164; refuse to surrender three murder suspects, 122-123; and religion, 268, 269; repulsion of, 209, 290; runaway slave flees to, 210; skills of, 35, 140;

speak Iroquoian language, ix, x, 3; subsistence of, 297; and trading, 86, 87, 109. *See also* Torhunta; Tuscarora Nation; Tuscarora Indians, Northern; Tuscarora Indians, Southern; Tuscarora towns; Tuscarora War

Tuscarora Indians, Northern, 150, 211, 278

Tuscarora Indians, Southern, 153, 214

Tuscarora (Tuskurorah) Nation, 254, 280, 294

Tuscarora towns, 161, 212, 259

Tuscarora War (1711-1715), xi, 101, 150, 152, 154, 208, 269n, 278, 290

Tuskegee (Cherokee Overhill town), 60n

Tusquitee Bald (Tuskequa Mount Mountain), 140, 141n

Tusquitee Mountains, 141n

Twelve Mile Creek, 163, 164

Tyler, Young, 213

Typhus, x

Tyrrell County (N.C.), 155

U

Ucohnerunt (King Blount's Town), 250n, 282

Uktena, 59-60

Unarowick Swamp, 299

Union County (N.C.), 2n

Unrintaroud, 300

Upper Cherokee. *See* Cherokee towns, Overhill

Upper Creek. *See under* Creek

Upper Norfolk County (Va.), 142

Upper Towns. *See* Cherokee towns, Overhill

Ushery, 91

Ustenary (Cherokee Lower town), 14, 14n

Usteneue, Cherokee, 99

V

Valley River (River Tellicoe), 14n, 93n, 97, 141n, 140, 141n, 242

Valley River Valley, 103n

Valley settlements (Valley towns), 90, 242, 244
Valley towns, 244
Van Corlaer, Arent, Gov. (New Netherlands), 153n
Vance, D., 183
Vann, John (Jno.), 90-91, 105-106
Vaudreuil-Cavagnal, Marquis de (Pierre François De Rigaud) ("Governor of Moville"), 76, 78n
Verelst, Harman, 74
Vermillion (vermilion), 52, 90, 91, 194. *See also* Paint
Vermin, 249
Vernon, Alexander, 244
Verrazzano, Giovanni da, ix, 135
Vestry, 80
Vicory, Benja., 262
Virginia: and Augusta Congress, 167, 173-174; and boundary lines, 79, 171, 173, 174, 187, 188; and Cherokee Indians, 79, 109-110, 127, 171, 172, 173, 174, 180, 183, 187, 188, 225, 229; and commerce, 85, 86, 122-123; commissioners, 184, 195, 225; competes for control of Indian trade, 126; first permanent English settlements established in, 142; governor of, 167, 173-174, 175, 214, 230; and Henderson Purchase, 180, 181; and Indians, 86n, 136n, 146, 202; mentioned, x, 91n, 137, 189; as name given to land claimed by Roanoke colonists, 45; provisions for travelers headed to and from, 227; raiding of settlements in, 145, 240; residents of, construct a fort, 221, move to N.C., 155; runaway slave sold into, 210; and treaty, 184; troops, 183, 196-197, 223; and Tuscarora Indians, 122-123, 153, 295
Vizards. *See* Masks
Volunteers, 192, 193
Vonore, Tenn., 14n, 60n, 93n
Voting, 254, 255

Voyages, 135, 137-139
Vultures, 209

W

Wabash River, 216
Waccamaws, ix
Waddell, Major Hugh, 234
Waistcoat, 7, 8, 51
Wake County (N.C.), 189
Walker, Henderson, Capt., 147, 260, 276
Wallis, Vallintine, 289
Walston, Jno., 303
Walton, Thos., 254
Walton, Timothy, 253, 254
Wampum (Wampons): and boundary line, 174, 175, 176; described, 46; given to governor of N.C., 184, 186, 291, to Iroquois, 153; Indians sacrifice, at altar, 57; King Hagler requests silver arm and breast plates with, 224; Little Carpenter claims that George Turner has not brought, 196; presented by Cherokees to Six Nations, 47, by Tuscaroras to Pa. and to the Iroquois, 151, 152, to the Catawbas, 46; used to solemnize wishes and promises, 45; wearing of, as belt, 214, by dancers, 43, in ears, 194, in hair, 8. *See also* Currency; Peak
War: allies in, 249; between Indians and whites, xi, 128, 148, 159, 172, 250; and bone gathering, 84; and Catawba Indians, 163; and Cherokee Indians, 14, 47, 102, 124, 163, 171, 172, 178, 182, 183; cry, song, and whoop, 193, 199, 204; declaration of, 48, 198, 241; depicted on tobacco pipes, 30; dress in, 194; Indian traders as factor in, 101, 103, 104, 109, 110, 119; Indians believe European diseases mimic, 71, 72; and Indians' debts, 99, 100, 157; Indians lose land and people in, 286; justification for, 20, 100, 118, 192; names, 200, 201; and Northward Indians, 163; participants in, 31-32,

81, 82; parties, 202, 205, 206, 217; Proclamation of 1763 reduces chances of, 168; tactics described, 197; towns offered protection during, 9; weapons used during, 32; women's grief during, 47. *See also names of individual wars*; War captains; Warriors

War captains, 2, 16, 41, 65, 82, 131, 192, 201

War dances. *See under* Dance/dancing

Ward, Major Enoch, 266

Waring, John, 272n

Warrior of Tomatla (Tommothy) 102-103, 113

Warriors: assist inebriated headman, 120; Catawba, 76, 122, 157, 158, 160-161, 162, 163, 164; Cherokee, 77, 137, 173-174, 175, 182; Choanoke controls 700, 136; customs of, 199; dance, 44; deterred from battle, 195; effects of cowardice in, 21, 82; Europeans dispense few presents to, 49; fight and hunt, 31, 65; and the French 19, 109-110, 161; graves of, 201; head, often poorest residents, 15; kill whites, 124; killed as retribution, 192; and land boundaries and sales, 173-174, 175, 182; mentioned, 59; number of, 13, 137, 158, 193, 197; present wampum to Pa., 151; and prisoners, 202, 205, 206, 208; seek war to cancel debts, 100; and S.C. governor, 102; suffering by, 204; of Tuckasegee, 220; Tuscarora, 281. *See also individual names of warriors*; War; War captains

Warriour of Keowee, 125

Warriour of Nottely (Nottally), 125

Washington, N.C., 213n

Washington County (Va.), 247

Watauga Creek, 4n

Watauga (Wataugah) River, 178, 182-183, 184

Wateree Creek, 118

Wateree Indians, 3, 3n, 75-76

Wateree River, 3n, 162

Watson, John, 294n

Watson, William, 303

Waxhaw Indians (flat heads), 1-2, 2n, 4, 5, 41-42

Waxhaws (town), 205

Wealth, 221

Weapemeoc (Weopomiok), ix, 136, 136n

Weaponry, 42, 45, 65, 71, 99-100, 101. *See also individual weapons by name*; Ammunition; Armory; Bullets; Gunpowder; Powder and shot

Weather, 222

Webster, N.C., 52n

Weights and measures, 95, 101, 103, 111, 131

Weirs (dams), 36-37, 68. *See also* Fishing

Weiser, Conrad, 215

West, Georg, 258

West, Robert (Robt.), Col., 104, 155, 259, 282

West Indies, xi, 67

Western Indians, 126

Westminster, England, 136

Westo Indians (Oestacks), x, 91

Wests Mill, 44n

Westward Indians, 86

Wetumpka, Ala., 78n

Weyane (Catawba Kings Town), 9n

Weyanoake Creek, 142, 143

Weyapee (Catawba town), 9n

Whatoga (Cherokee Middle town), 4, 4n, 44n, 24-25, 110n

Whatoga, Prince of, Cherokee, 4, 25

Wheat, 23-24, 28, 29, 89

Wheatler, Isaac, 302

Wheeler, Billy, 294

Wheeler, Isaac, 301

Whipping, 99-100, 218. *See also* Punishments

Whistles, 199

White, John, x

White, William, 266

White County (Ga.), 52n

White earth. *See* Clay, china

White Oak Creek, 177
Whitehall, 133, 232
Whitehurst, Richd, 265, 266
Whitfield, Thomas, 263
Whitmell, Tuscarora, 294
Whitmell (Whitmel, Whitemeal), Thomas (Tho.), 109, 282, 285
Whitmell (Whitmill), West, 300, 302
Whitmore, Tom, 294
Whittier, N.C., 52n
Whohatche, Cherokee, 232
Whooping, 197
Wiggan (Wiggen), Eleazer, 2, 206, 207
Wiggins (Wiggians), James, 300, 301
Wiggins, John, 294
Wildcats, 91
Wilhlemine, Cherokee, 274
Wilkinson, Edward (Edwd.), 91, 106
Wilkinson, Mr. (Indian commissioner), 240, 241
Will (guide), 268
Will, Enoe, 267
Willenawah (Willinnawah), Cherokee, 52
Willes, Sir John, 156
William, Lord Craven (Earl of Craven), 86
William (brig), 89
Williams, Benjamin, 263
Williams, John, 127, 181
Williams, Sam, 299
Williams, William, 293, 294n, 297, 298, 299, 300, 302
Williamson, Andrew, Colonel, 242
Williamson, Dove, 210
Willoughby, Mr., 143
Willows, 138
Wills, Sir Charles, 156
Willson, Mary, 263
Wilmington, 1st Earl of (Spencer Compton) (Lord President), 155
Wilson, Isaac, 266
Wilson County (N.C.), 213n
Windsor, N.Y., 254, 296n
Wine, 49

Wingandacoa, 45
Wingina, Roanoke, 45
Wings, 61, 194
Winn, Matthew, 251
Winter-house, 193
Wire, 8-9, 52
Wiroances. *See* Headmen
Woccon Indians, 3
Wocyoch, Cherokee, 232
Wolf of Keowee, Cherokee, 177
Wolves, 17, 33, 138, 198, 209, 264
Women: activities of, 34, 35, 67, 194; beloved, 69; as captives, 141, 142, 206, 208, 213, 216, 219; Catawba, 163, 216; Cherokee, 43, 47, 69, 124, 205, 219; and child-rearing, 5, 18, 60, 61, 65, 256; colonial, 148, 159; Creek, 219; dance, 42, 43; and husbands, 18, 83, 94; and huskanawing, 21, 22; Indian beliefs about, 53, 72, 82; killed, 100, 219; Kituwah, 100; men work with, 31-32; mentioned, 4; and mourning the dead, 79, 81, 83; noted in militia returns, 155; participate in and accompany men to war, 205-206, 210, 211; physical appearance of, 5, 6, 7, 8-9; prepare food, 27, 56, 94; present belts as signs of peace, 47, 151; receive presents, 51; sexual relations with, prohibited, 64; as slaves, 209, 211, 258; take part in torture, 202, 203, 204; tend and distribute crops, ix, 25-26, 94; and tobacco, 30, 68; and traders, 59, 94, 96, 97, 124, 125; Tuscarora, 151, 211; used as term of insult, 101, 215
Wool, 80
Worley, Henry, 151-152
Wounded, the, 199
Wragg (Wrags) and Lambton, 127
Wrist plates, 40
Writing, 269
Wyley, Samuel (Mr. Wyley), 163, 164
Wythe County (Va.), 174n

Y

Yadkin River, 47n, 230, 231. *See also* Yadkin River Valley

Yadkin River Valley, 232, 234

Yamasee (Yemassee) Indians, xi, 3, 205, 252, 278. *See also* Yamasee War

Yamasee War (1715), 101, 104, 117, 158

Yeardley, Francis, 140

Yellow Bird, Cherokee, 77

Yeopim (Yawpin, Yowpim) Indians, 7-8, 146, 251-252, 275, 284, 287

Yeopim (Yansapin) River, 143

Yonge, Sir William, 156

York County (S.C.), 127n

Yorkshire County, England, 86

Young, Thomas, 260

Young Warrior (Warier), Cherokee, 141, 142, 235

Younger fry. *See* Children

Yssa, 139, 140n

Yuchi Indians, 207n

Yw-facee River. *See* Hiwassee River